The Institute on Statelessness and Inclusion (ISI) is an independent non-profit organisation dedicated to promoting inclusive societies by realising and protecting the right to a nationality for all. Established in August 2014, ISI is the first and only human rights NGO dedicated to working on statelessness at the global level. ISI is incorporated in the Netherlands, where it has Public Benefit Organisation (PBO) status.

TABLE OF CONTENTS

PRINCIPLES ON DEPRIVATION OF NATIONALITY AS A NATIONAL SECURITY MEASURE

ACKNOWLEDGEMENTS

This publication is a product of the generosity, goodwill and creativity of a multitude of people from around the world and all walks of life, who have contributed their time, expertise, skills, resources, stories, outputs and intellectual property towards it. Over two years ago, when we first started thinking about this report, the choice of thematic focus was an obvious one − both because of the urgency and importance of shining a spotlight on the practice of deprivation of nationality, and the wonderful partnership we had already developed with a few close allies in exploring this phenomenon, and ultimately, drafting the **Principles on Deprivation of Nationality as a National Security Measure.** We remain deeply indebted to Laura Bingham and her colleagues at Open Society Justice Initiative, Christophe Paulussen and his colleagues at the Asser Institute, and Claire Fourel and her colleagues at Ashurst LLP, for their extensive collaboration and contributions to the research, thinking and analysis that underlines much that is in this report. Indeed, a number of the chapters in Part Two, on global trends, international standards and the effectiveness of citizenship stripping, borrow directly from the research conducted in collaboration with these partners.

We are also extremely grateful to the over 60 experts − leading academics, public prosecutors, UN officials, independent experts, NGO advocates, litigators and affected persons - from various fields including human rights, statelessness, security and counter-terrorism, refugee protection, child rights and migration, who advised us, reviewed draft text and guided us along a 30 month journey, which led to both the development of the Principles as well as the conceptualisation and delivery of this World's Stateless Report.

This report also casts a critical eye on situations of mass deprivation of nationality, targeting minority communities such as the Rohingya of Myanmar, Dominicans of Haitian origin and communities of Muslim and migrant heritage in Assam, India. Our own work on these (and many other similar contexts) has been informed and enriched by the courageous and tenacious activism and advocacy of human rights defenders, grass roots groups and NGOs operating in these countries. Through the report, we honour the work of these groups, including the many Rohingya activists who we collaborate with, such as those who joined our advocacy efforts before the Dutch parliament; groups working to counter discriminatory bureaucracies in Assam as well as our 125 NGO partners from around the world who showed solidarity with them in a joint statement; and groups such as *Reconocido* who continue to offer energy, creativity and commitment in the face of ever shrinking space in the Dominican Republic (and who contributed an essay to this report).

A special thank you to all our external contributors who have made this a richer, more diverse and insightful publication: Amanda Weston, Andrew Hales, Alfredo Oguisten, Anna Belique, Bronwen Manby, Christophe Paulussen, Christopher Bertram, Cóman Kenny, Elena Lorac, Fateh Azzam, Jawad Fairooz, Jose Arraiza, Kipling Williams, Laetitia van den Assum, Laura Bingham, Laura Robson, Marina Arraiza Shakirova, Martin Scheinin, Matthew Gibney, Melanie Khanna, Paola Quiñones, Phyu Zin Aye, Rene de Groot and Tendayi Achiume.

Our thanks also to our NGO partners who reviewed and/or contributed to some of the regional chapters – Chris Nash and Nina Murray (Europe), Christoph Sperfeldt, Davina Wadley and Ravi Hemadri, (Asia and the Pacific), Azizbek Ashurov (Central Asia), Florencia Reggiardo (the Americas), Bronwen Manby and Liesl Muller (Africa), and Drewery Dyke and Thomas McGee (MENA).

The report's **editorial team** was made up of ISI staff, interns and volunteers. Laura van Waas and Amal de Chickera served as co-editors, conceptualising the report and its content, reviewing and editing both external and internal contributions and drafting the various introductory texts. Georgia Field served as assistant editor, with specific oversight of Part Two, for which she edited and reviewed draft essays and coordinated with all contributors. Special thanks to former colleagues Michiel Hoornick and Ileen Verbeek, for their contributions to the regional updates and general coordination of Part One, and to Michiel for drafting the chapter on addressing statelessness through UN human rights frameworks. Alena Jascanka was responsible for design and layout of the report, and our special thanks to our friend Hanna Kim for her design concept and art direction for the cover.

We are particularly grateful to our interns and volunteers: Ottoline Spearman for her help in reviewing first drafts of external contributions, putting together regional updates for Part One and for drafting the essay titled 'International Law Standards Pertaining to the Arbitrarily Deprivation of Nationality' in Part Two; Rán Þórisdóttir for her help in also putting together regional updates in Part One and drafting of the essay titled 'Expanding Deprivation of Nationality Powers in the Security Context: Global Trends' in Part Two; Nannie Skold and Vera Karanika for drafting a number of the country overviews in Part One; Anne Brekoo and Amanda Brown for contributing to the country overviews and for research and drafting related to the development of the Principles on Deprivation of Nationality and Amanda for also conducting the interview with the UN Special Rapporteur on contemporary forms of racism. The report was proofread by Ottoline Spearman and Vera Karanika.

As an NGO dependant on funding, we would not have been able to publish this report without the generous backing of our donors. We are particularly grateful to the Sigrid Rausing Trust, for its support of ISI and the issue, and to Open Society

Justice Initiative for supporting our work on deprivation of nationality and this report.

Any undertaking of this nature has a way of taking over and demanding more time, including time that would otherwise be spent with family and loved ones. We all thank our families for their patience, encouragement and support throughout this process. We would also like to thank all members of our Board and Advisory Council, for their ongoing counsel, support and trust in us.

This report – like so many other tools and resources – ultimately exists for one primary reason: to enable us to collectively do better at protecting the right to a nationality, combatting statelessness and enhancing the quality of life and inclusion of stateless persons. This report is for the stateless of the world and to all persons who can, have and will continue to work on their behalf. As this report shows, our strength is in our collaboration.

Finally, this is our first major publication after Stefanie Grant – ISI's founding Chair – has stepped down from her duties. Stefanie's quiet encouragement, reassurance and wisdom has guided all our work. On the issue of deprivation of nationality, she played an integral role chairing the expert meetings, reviewing drafts and recommending other experts to involve. We dedicate this report to Stefanie, as a token of our unending gratitude to her, for believing in the idea of ISI and the people behind it.

PART I

STATELESSNESS
AROUND THE WORLD

THE STATE OF STATELESSNESS IN THE WORLD IN 2020

INTRODUCTION

Every three years, we publish our flagship "World's Stateless" report, reflecting on the state of statelessness and the right to nationality from the helicopter view of our global engagement on the issue. This edition coincides with the start of a new decade and follows closely on the heels of the mid-way point of the UNHCR-led #IBelong campaign to end statelessness by 2024, which was marked with a high-level event in Geneva in October 2019. This makes the question of where we stand today and what we can expect from tomorrow more salient. Here we offer some overall observations on the state of statelessness in the world in 2020.

> **Othering is on the rise around the world.
> Linked to the rise of nationalism, it is among the
> most pressing problems of the 21st century."**
>
> Laetitia van den Assum
> Former ambassador of the Netherlands
> and former member of the Rakhine Advisory Commission

CITIZENSHIP UNDER THREAT

Where once the phenomenon of statelessness may have felt like a finite issue for which the trajectory would be one of (stop-and-start) progress, ultimately heading towards the reduction of cases, this world view has been distinctly disrupted by developments that have unfurled even since our last World's Stateless report was published in January 2017. The past three years have been dominated by 'crisis' and the uncomfortable dawning realisation that citizenship is under threat in ways not seen for generations – prompting the thematic focus of this World's Stateless report on deprivation of nationality, to which Part 2 is entirely dedicated.

At the centre of this picture is the deep deterioration of the situation of the Rohingya community in Myanmar, who endured large-scale atrocity crimes in August 2017, leading to well-founded allegations of crimes against humanity and genocide being levelled against Myanmar; and the mass disenfranchisement of 1.9 million people in Assam, India, in August 2019. Beyond the headlines, other stateless communities that are fighting for recognition and rights have also experienced regression of their position in society, such as in the Dominican Republic, or felt the consequences of shrinking democratic space, with harsh crackdowns on protest in Kuwait and elsewhere. Meanwhile, people whose belonging was not previously questioned have had their citizenship status challenged – including under the United States' 'denationalisation taskforce' and as came to light in the UK's 'Windrush scandal'.

The securitisation and instrumentalisation of citizenship policy has led to a wider resurgence of denationalisation, with national security or counter-terrorism arguments offered as justification for its use against so-called 'foreign fighters' by several countries including the UK, Australia, the Netherlands, Belgium and Denmark. The political use of individual denationalisation has also made a worrying comeback, with human rights defenders, journalists and political opponents being silenced or side-lined through (the threat of) deprivation of nationality across numerous countries including Bahrain, Azerbaijan, Turkey and Tanzania. We also stand at the beginning of a new era of 'digital identity', in which sophisticated biometric technology is increasingly being embraced as the go-to tool for authenticating identity and promoting inclusion. But the first cracks are already starting to appear in places like Kenya where for some parts of the population the new system only brings a new form of exclusion. This is not to mention the continuing need to address the long-standing root causes of statelessness and ensure that appropriate remedies and reparations are achieved for protracted cases around the world.

All of these challenges, and more, were the subject of scrutiny and debate during ISI's World Conference on Statelessness in June 2019, which brought together 300 advocates, activists, academics, artists and other stakeholders from over 60 countries, for three days of debate, information sharing and networking. Taken together, five of the key takeaways from this global, interdisciplinary gathering capture the global picture well in this regard, offering a synopsis of where further action is needed:[1]

- **Key takeaway 1:** *"Discrimination and the intersection of multiple discrimination are the real drivers of state policies, legislation and practices that cause and perpetuate statelessness. Racism, xenophobia, patriarchy and the other underlying causes of discrimination therefore lie at the root of most statelessness, and the enduring exclusion and disadvantage of stateless people and communities. Collectively, these are the biggest obstacles to tackling statelessness and can only be overcome through a joined-up and multi-sectoral response that takes its lead from stateless people."*

---

[1] The full report of ISI's World Conference on Statelessness (2019) is available at https://files.institutesi.org/World_Conference_on_Statelessness_Report_2019.pdf. Note that this report includes six further "key takeaways" from the conference that relate to what type of action is needed to provide an appropriate and effective response to statelessness.

- **Key takeaway 2:** *"The arbitrary deprivation of nationality of the Rohingya, their statelessness, denial of legal status and protection, and the exclusion and marginalisation they have endured for decades are all contributing factors towards the persecution and genocide of this community. There is no sustainable way forward from this crisis that does not include the protection of the right to nationality and ending the statelessness of the Rohingya."*

- **Key takeaway 3:** *"The unfolding crisis in Assam, which has led to almost two million people being deprived of their Indian nationality, the displacement caused by the Syria conflict and Venezuela crisis, the continued disenfranchisement of Dominicans of Haitian origin, the endurance of gender discriminatory nationality laws in a quarter of the world's countries, are all demonstrative of the persistence and indeed escalation of statelessness and its impacts around the world. These big issues require bold, innovative and committed responses."*

- **Key takeaway 4:** *"The recognition and promotion of every child's right to a nationality is crucial and must be prioritised by both the human rights and development sectors. Special emphasis and greater urgency must be placed on addressing intergenerational statelessness and protecting the right to a nationality of the children of stateless parents, to break the cycle of exclusion."*

- **Key takeaway 5:** *"Nationality deprivation is a discriminatory and arbitrary practice violating international norms. The increasing use of this measure by States in the name of (inter)national security, in spite of the mounting evidence that it does not advance security and may even be counterproductive, undermines citizenship as a core democratic institution and is negatively impacting any advances made internationally to address statelessness."*

THE NUMBERS QUESTION

A central question that is raised time and again, but still eludes an easy or fully satisfying answer is: *how many people are actually stateless in the world today?* Measuring statelessness is methodologically complicated and in some contexts also politically charged,[2] which means that this is simply not a straight-forward matter. For many years, UNHCR estimated the number of stateless persons worldwide to be "at least 10 million",[3] but the most recent *Global Trends* report (published in June 2019) does not give a more specific estimate for the total global stateless population other than

---

[2] See Institute on Statelessness and Inclusion, 'Counting the world's stateless: reflections on statistical reporting on statelessness' in *UNHCR Statistical Yearbook 2013* (2014) available at: http://www.unhcr.org/54cf99f29.pdf
[3] See UNHCR's annual "Global Trends" reports published from 2013-2018, available at https://www.unhcr.org/search?comid=56b079c44&&cid=49aea93aba&tags=globaltrends.

that it is "in the millions".[4] This report collates data covering 78 countries, accounting for 3.9 million stateless people, but acknowledges that the "true global figure" is significantly higher, given the enduring gaps in statistical reporting.[5]

We explored the challenges involved in capturing, collating and reporting global statelessness data in detail in the first edition of our World's Stateless report, published in 2014.[6] We concluded this study, with the estimate that the total figure for the number of people living without a nationality in the world to be at least 15 million.[7] Since then, the number of cases of statelessness globally that were reported annually as solved, has been matched or outpaced by the estimated number of children who are born without a nationality each year due to inherited statelessness.[8] As such, in ISI's latest statistical analysis update (July 2019), we observed that "there have, to date, been no developments on such a scale to suggest that there has since been any major global shift in these aggregate numbers and ISI continues to use the estimate of at least 15 million to indicate how many people it understands to be stateless globally, drawing on existing statistical information".[9] This was prior to the publication of the final version of the Assam National Register of Citizens (NRC) in Assam, India, on 31 August 2019. A total of 1,906,657 residents – approximately 6% of the population of Assam – were excluded from this list, pushing them to the brink of statelessness.[10] At the time of writing however, the full and lasting ramifications of this situation were not clear, including because appeals processes were ongoing. This means that it is too early to judge the exact impact in statistical terms of the situation in Assam and therefore too early to readjust the overall global estimate. What is unmistakable is that in the current global climate in which citizenship is increasingly under threat, there is an acute risk that the number of people affected by statelessness will grow further.

---

[4] UNHCR, *Global Trends: Forced displacement in 2018* (2019) available at
https://www.unhcr.org/globaltrends2018/. Complete country-by-country data on persons under UNHCR's statelessness mandate is found in "Table 7", available at https://www.unhcr.org/statistics/18-WRD-table-7.xls.
[5] Ibid. Note that "improve quantitative and qualitative data on stateless populations" is Action 10 of the *UNHCR Global Action Plan to End Statelessness 2014-2024* (2014) available at
https://www.refworld.org/docid/545b47d64.html.
[6] Institute on Statelessness and Inclusion, *The World's Stateless* (2014) available at
https://files.institutesi.org/worldsstateless.pdf.
[7] Ibid. This figure was based on a review of UNHCR's statistical reporting, supplementary and alternative data sources. It attempts to account also for stateless people who are displaced (refugees and IDPs) – generally included in UNHCR data on displaced populations – as well as Palestinian refugees who are affected by statelessness.
[8] See Institute on Statelessness and Inclusion, *Statelessness in numbers: 2017* and *2018*, available at
https://files.institutesi.org/ISI_Statistics_Analysis_2017.pdf and
https://files.institutesi.org/ISI_statistics_analysis_2018.pdf.
[9] Institute on Statelessness and Inclusion, *Statelessness in numbers: 2019. An overview and analysis of global statistics* (July 2019) available at https://files.institutesi.org/ISI_statistics_analysis_2019.pdf.
[10] See for a synopsis of the background to and publication of the NRC in Assam, *Joint Statement: 125 Civil Society Organisations condemn the exclusion of 1.9 million people from the Assam NRC and call for urgent action to protect everyone's right to a nationality* (September 2019) available at https://files.institutesi.org/cso-joint-statement-on-assam-nrc.pdf. A further discussion of the situation in Assam can also be found in Part 2 of this report.

In spite of the evidently global scope and far-reaching ramifications of the issue, as set out above, the absence of more comprehensive and reliable data can cause difficulties. It may lead to situations in which key decision-makers or influencers disengage with the issue because, without an estimate for the number of people affected, they are unpersuaded by its urgency or lack confidence that they fully grasp what the situation is. Monitoring and showing progress, or regression, is also hampered when statistical information is unavailable, incomplete or unreliable. Moreover, a detailed internal review of the sources and methods used to produce UNHCR's annual population statistics on statelessness, published in October 2019, commented on the "disjointed and inconsistent" nature of this data reporting, which relies on records that "can be inaccurate, contradictory or disorganised".[11] This evaluation concludes that "the joint effort of member states, international community and technical experts will be needed to obtain valid and reliable estimates for the global number of stateless persons *for the very first time".*[12]

A sub-group on 'data' that can coordinate such efforts to improve global and county-level estimates of the number of stateless persons has now been established under the auspices of the UN's Inter-Agency Working Group on Statelessness, as well as a Technical Advisory Group to offer methodological guidance. However, even as these initiatives advance, the numbers question is likely to remain complex and contested. Exploring alternative ways of thinking and communicating about the scale of statelessness and innovating the use of numbers could therefore be warranted. What figures do we have? How do we use the *absence* of data as data? What numbers actually *matter* to stateless individuals and communities themselves and why? By reflecting more freely on the numbers question, we may reach new insights about the global phenomenon of statelessness and how to tackle it. If we understand statelessness as fundamentally a human rights issue – the most extreme violation of the right to a nationality – then even if the scale of the problem is a relevant consideration, the issue at its core is about the depravation of individual rights. It can therefore be a mistake to place too much emphasis on numbers, and instead, pursuing a more qualitative approach is equally, if not more, important.

"I feel a sense of more belonging"

Parsu Sharma-Luital,
formerly stateless activist from Bhutan
at the ISI World Conference on Statelessness in 2019

---

[11] L. Chen, P. Nahmias, S. Steinmuller, 'UNHCR Statistical Reporting on Statelessness', *UNHCR Statistical Technical Series: 2019/1* (October 2019) p.11-12, available at
https://www.unhcr.org/statistics/unhcrstats/5d9e182e7/unhcr-statistical-reporting-statelessness.html.
[12] Emphasis added. Ibid, p. 13.

TURNING MOMENTUM INTO MOVEMENT

While statelessness remains hard to measure in 2020 and the challenges that confront us seem only to be mounting, there is also greater recognition of the importance of strengthening our capacities, resources and collaboration, to respond in more strategic, effective and sustainable ways. Statelessness is not the 'forgotten'[13] issue that it once was, it is no longer absent from the international agenda, nor is it a cause that lacks champions. We have already come to take for granted that UN and regional human rights bodies pay regular attention to the right to a nationality and the rights of stateless people – and the next section of this report explores what this engagement looks like in respect of the Universal Periodic Review, UN Treaty Bodies, Special Mandate Holders and other frameworks under the Human Rights Council, with a particular focus on new developments over the last three years. A global framework for galvanising action by states to resolve existing cases and prevent new ones is also now available by way of UNHCR's #IBelong Campaign to End Statelessness – and the essay in this section by Chief of UNHCR's Statelessness Section, Melanie Khanna, takes stock of the state of this campaign as it enters the second half of its lifespan.

Importantly, stateless activists from around the world are more connected, mobilised and heard than ever before and there is a vibrant community of civil society actors, many of which have also joined forces to amplify their impact by convening in regional and thematic networks. For the first time in its illustrious history, the Nansen Refugee Award honoured the work of Azizbek Ashurov, an advocate who has dedicated his life to addressing statelessness.[14] He said of this recognition: "This year's award focuses on statelessness and this means recognition to all people, organisations and networks in the world who contributed and continue to make efforts to resolve one of the most pressing problems of our time. This award is a testament that the stateless people of the world are being heard and it is a symbol of hope that their problems can be resolved".[15]

Inter-disciplinary scholarship on statelessness is also rapidly developing to fill the knowledge-gaps that we still contend with and new teaching and capacity building initiatives on statelessness are sprouting up in different academic hubs. This means that statelessness literacy is greatly enhanced across a new generation of researchers, lawyers and policymakers. The scope and diversity of artistic work around statelessness has also begun to emerge. The CANCELLED Arts Programme, devised by *Empathy and Risk* and hosted by ISI's World Conference on Statelessness in June 2019, featured or archived the work of over 50 artists and cultural agents. It

---

[13] António Guterres, then U.N. High Commissioner for Refugees, in a Q&A for *Time* (2011) available at http://content.time.com/time/world/article/0,8599,2090561,00.html.

[14] See further the section on Asia and the Pacific, and the country profile on Kyrgyzstan in this report.

[15] From an interview with Azizbek Ashurov in Institute on Statelessness and Inclusion, *Monthly Bulletin: November 2019* (2019) available at https://mailchi.mp/786624d82c4a/monthly-bulletin-november-2019.

also showcased a number of new works that were produced especially for the Conference through a process of co-creation by artists who were 'matched' by ISI with activists, advocates and academics working in different countries and contexts – demonstrating once more the value of interdisciplinary collaboration.

As will come to light in the regional sections of this report, over the three years since we published the last edition of the World's Stateless, the courts have revealed themselves to be a particularly important actor within the wider ecosystem of stakeholders that can influence the outcomes on statelessness. Domestic as well as regional courts have, in some cases, become the last stalwart of the institution of citizenship: protecting it against abuse of power, discrimination and eroding rule of law.[16] Courts have also helped to ensure that children's best interests are given due consideration in citizenship decisions affecting children and to enforce safeguards against statelessness;[17] and asserted the need for identifying stateless persons in order to ensure due protection of their rights.[18] This fast-gathering body of jurisprudence has served to further demarcate how states' discretion is limited by international law and to affirm that individuals can 'win' their claim to nationality. In some cases, however, courts have failed to enforce human rights standards in the context of disputes relating to citizenship – in particular situations of individualised denationalisation – so there is still more work to be done.[19] At the time of writing, a watchful eye is being kept especially on both the International Court of Justice and the International Criminal Court in the Hague, where procedures have been initiated in response to the grave abuses inflicted upon the Rohingya.

Also highlighted across the regional sections and country profiles in this report – as well as in the essay by Melanie Khanna – is the potential for further progress to be achieved in the coming 4-5 years in accordance with pledges made during UNHCR's High Level Segment on Statelessness in October 2019. An impressive 360 pledges were made in total: 252 by States, 70 by civil society organizations, and 38 by international and regional organisations. It is nevertheless important to note that not all of these pledges contained concrete actions or specified a timeframe for implementation – many were more generally descriptive. There was also an evident

---

[16] For example, in domestic proceedings in Kenya lodged against the roll-out of the National Integrated Identity Management System (NIIMS), as discussed in the Africa section of this report; and in regional proceedings, in cases such as African Court on Human and Peoples' Rights, *Anudo Ochieng Anudo v. United Republic of Tanzania*, App. No. 012/2015 (2018); African Committee of Experts on the Rights and Welfare of the Child, *African Centre of Justice and Peace Studies (ACJPS) and People's Legal Aid Centre (PLACE) v the Republic of Sudan*, no. 002/2018 (2018); and ECtHR, *Alpeyeva and Dzhalagoniya v. Russia* (2018), Applications nos. 7549/09 and 33330/11.

[17] For example, in domestic proceedings in Australia and South Africa in 2018-2019.

[18] For example, in the European Court of Human Rights case of *Hoti v. Croatia* (2018), Application no. 63311/14.

[19] For example, in a remarkable and concerning judgement in early 2020, the UK's Special Immigration Appeals Commission turned down the appeal against revocation of citizenship in the high-profile case of Shamima Begum, even while considering that the circumstances of the case were such that "the appeal will not be fair and effective" and acknowledging that leaving Begum stranded in al-Roj camp in Syria exposed her to conditions that would breach the prohibition of torture, inhuman or degrading treatment under the European Convention on Human Rights.

divergence in the level of engagement with this process by states from different regions of the world. While 34 countries in Africa made 146 pledges, far fewer states participated from Europe (13), the Americas (10) and Asia and the Pacific (8, of which 5 were from Central Asia). Only one country in the Middle East and North Africa (Mauritania) made a pledge. Still, if all 14 pledges of law reform, 34 pledges relating to accession to the UN statelessness conventions, 34 pledges addressing data collection or mapping studies and other pledges on capacity building, awareness raising and international cooperation are implemented, this would mean important steps forward. This is especially the case for specific issues, such as addressing gender discrimination in nationality laws, protecting the child's right to a nationality (and birth registration) and implementing statelessness determination procedures, which featured strongly in the pledges made. Disappointingly, other contexts, including situations in which citizenship has come under new or increased strain in recent years, were not addressed in this pledging process.

Much hard work lies ahead, if we are to successfully promote the adoption, preservation and implementation of citizenship policies that respect everyone's right to a nationality, combat discrimination and support inclusive societies, democracy and the rule of law. The decade now passed has also shown us how high the stakes are and reinforced the urgency of turning the momentum that the issue has gathered into genuine, inclusive and effective movement. In the second half of the #IBelong campaign and even after the decade of action it has championed comes to a close in 2024, we must find ways to accelerate meaningful progress. This means taking a stronger stance against situations where citizenship is under threat and holding States accountable for the implementation of not only fresh pledges made in 2019 but the full spectrum of international obligations they already hold in terms of the right to a nationality. We must also work to further strengthen solidarity among actors working across the field of statelessness and take steps to ensure that global and national advocacy on statelessness is rooted in the experiences and demands of those directly impacted. This was also expressed in two of the further key takeaways from ISI's World Conference on Statelessness in 2019 that we would like to close with here:

- **Key takeaway 6:** *"All actors must prioritise listening to and learning from the lived experiences of those directly affected by statelessness, including stateless children, in order to imagine and implement useful and sustainable actions to address statelessness and protect the human rights of stateless persons."*

- **Key takeaway 7:** *"If a global movement is to flourish, it must provide a safe and equal space for all types of actors to come together and collectively drive the issue forward. Such a space will only begin to take shape when individuals and institutions reflect on and make concerted efforts to address power imbalances, recognise and deal with privilege and combat barriers to equal participation. Resources, language, freedom of movement and safety are all very real barriers which must be recognised and confronted."*

ADDRESSING STATELESSNESS THROUGH UN HUMAN RIGHTS FRAMEWORKS

The right to a nationality is a fundamental human right, and human rights are to be enjoyed by all persons, including the stateless. Article 15 of the Universal Declaration of Human Rights (UDHR) states that everyone has the right to a nationality and that no one shall be arbitrarily deprived of their nationality nor denied the right to change their nationality. The right to a nationality is also explicitly protected under six of the core UN Human Rights Treaties:

- Article 24 (3) of the International Covenant on Civil and Political Rights (ICCPR) states that every child has the right to acquire a nationality;
- Article 7 of the Convention on the Rights of the Child (CRC) contains the same right, and emphasises that States Parties must ensure that no child is stateless;
- Article 5(d)(iii) of the Convention on the Elimination of All Forms of Racial Discrimination (CERD) guarantees the right to a nationality to everyone, regardless of race, colour, or national or ethnic origin;
- Article 9 of the Convention on the Elimination of All Forms of Discrimination against Women grants women equal rights with men to acquire, change or retain their nationality, as well as with respect to the nationality of their children;
- Article 18 of the Convention on the Rights of Persons with Disabilities (CRPD); and
- Article 29 of the International Convention on the Protection of the Rights of All Migrant Workers and Members of their Families (CMW) affirm the right to a nationality for persons with disabilities and children of migrant workers respectively.

In the fight against statelessness, the international human rights framework therefore serves as an important platform upon which to place - and keep - the issue on the agenda. This contribution looks at how the Universal Periodic Review, UN Treaty Bodies, Special Mandate Holders and other frameworks under the Human Rights Council have been promoting and monitoring the implementation of the right to a nationality and the rights of stateless persons, with a particular focus on new developments over the last three years (i.e. since the publication of ISI's last World's Stateless Report).[1]

UNIVERSAL PERIODIC REVIEW

The Universal Periodic Review (UPR) is a mechanism of the UN Human Rights Council through which the human rights situation of each UN Member State is periodically reviewed. There are three 'sessions' per year at which 14 States are reviewed and a full 'cycle' of reviews (all UN Member States) takes 4-5 years to complete. The UPR held its first session in April 2008. Over the first two cycles, attention for the right to a nationality and statelessness grew. From 187 relevant recommendations out of a total of 21,355 recommendations in the First Cycle, this number rose to 586 out of 36,331 in the Second Cycle, with the percentage of relevant recommendations going from 0.9% to 1.6%. Over these two cycles, 162 countries out of the 192 reviewed received at least one relevant recommendation (84% of all States reviewed).[2]

The Third Cycle of the UPR started on 1 May 2017 and as of 1 January 2020, 112 countries have been reviewed in this Cycle. Together, these countries received 372 relevant recommendations out of the roughly 25,570 given thus far.[3] Although it is not possible to present a full overview of the Third Cycle until all States have been reviewed, the percentage thus far has dropped from 1.6% to 1.45%. A total of 89 out of the 112 countries reviewed at the time of writing received at least one relevant recommendation, which still equates to four out of every five States reviewed.

Overall, the considerable volume of relevant recommendations shows that the right to a nationality remains on the agenda for the countries where the enjoyment of this right is not always self-evident. Since 2017, nine countries (out of the 112) received ten relevant recommendations or more. The Dominican Republic received most, with a total of 23.[4] This is followed by Qatar (17), South Africa (14), the Bahamas (13), Bahrain (12), Cyprus (12), Slovenia (11), Serbia (11) and Jordan (10).[5] There

---

[1] For an introduction to the various Human Rights Bodies, see:
https://www.ohchr.org/EN/HRBodies/Pages/HumanRightsBodies.aspx.
[2] Institute on Statelessness and Inclusion, 'Statelessness & Human Rights: The Universal Periodic Review' (2017), available at http://www.institutesi.org/Statelessness-and-UPR.pdf.
[3] Not all Working Group reports containing the recommendations made have been adopted by the Human Rights Council at the time of writing, so this number might slightly alter after adoption.
[4] Ibid. Since the 23rd Session in November 2015, ISI has published analyses of the relevant recommendations made during each session, which are accessible at https://www.institutesi.org/core-activities/human-rights-advocacy.
[5] Argentina, Barbados, Benin, Botswana, Bhutan, Brunei Darussalam, Cameroon, Canada, Cape Verde, the Comoros, Côte d'Ivoire, the DRC, Italy, Rep. of Korea, Madagascar, Malaysia, Malta, Mauritius, Monaco, the Russian Federation, San Marino, Switzerland and the UAE – 23 countries – received over five recommendations.

remain, however, countries that are under-recommended: India, Saudi Arabia and Iran received only two, and Sri Lanka and Iraq received a mere one.

In terms of topics, the most recommendations made (100 in total) have been those regarding signing or ratifying the Statelessness Conventions. This is followed by recommendations on civil and birth registration (77), gender discrimination in nationality laws (64) and other forms of discrimination (52). Also mentioned, but less frequent, are recommendations specifically on preventing, reducing or ending statelessness (29), on children (15), on rights of stateless persons (12), and on statelessness determination procedures (11). Notably absent in this period are recommendations on arbitrary deprivation of nationality, of which there were only six. Five of those were given to Bahrain in May 2017, and one to Qatar in May 2019.[6]

The focus of the Third Cycle of the UPR is on implementation and follow-up.[7] While there does not seem to be an increase in the number of recommendations on statelessness so far, relevant recommendations have been repeated almost verbatim in this cycle, showing commitment to ensure follow through on these issues where the implementation of previous recommendations has not progressed.[8] For example, during the review of Brunei Darussalam in the 2nd Cycle in 2014, France recommended to:

"Respect the fundamental principle of equality between men and women, in particular by allowing women from Brunei Darussalam to transmit their nationality to their children and by raising the age of marriage for women" and to *"withdraw reservations to CEDAW"*.

In 2019, in the 3rd Cycle review, France recommended Brunei Darussalam to:

"Respect the fundamental principle of equality between women and men, in particular by allowing Brunei women to transmit their nationality to their children and by removing reservations to Article 9 of CEDAW".[9]

In total, 98 Members States and UN non-member observer State Palestine made at least one recommendation relevant to statelessness. Of these countries, Argentina was the most active with 18 relevant recommendations in the sessions 27-34. Mexico (17), Kenya (15), Côte d'Ivoire (14) and Slovakia (14) follow suit. The top 16

---

[6] Institute on Statelessness and Inclusion, 'Universal Period Review – 33rd Session', available at https://files.institutesi.org/UPR27_stateless.pdf; https://www.institutesi.org/UPR33_Analysis.pdf.
[7] UPR-Info, 'OHCHR takes steps to focus on implementation' (2017), available at https://www.upr-info.org/en/news/ohchr-takes-steps-to-focus-on-implementation.
[8] In some cases, the Third Cycle recommendations were more concrete and specific than in the Second Cycle. Further analysis should show whether these are individual cases, or if this is a general trend.
[9] Since the 23rd Session in November 2015, ISI has published analyses of the relevant recommendations made during each session, which are available at https://www.institutesi.org/core-activities/human-rights-advocacy.

countries were together responsible for over half of the total given recommendations.[10]

UN TREATY BODIES

As mentioned previously, six of the core UN human rights treaties cover the right to a nationality directly under a specific Article.[11] Moreover, all of the UN human rights treaties affirm rights which are to be enjoyed by everyone within a State's jurisdiction, including stateless people. This means that the right to a nationality and the rights of stateless persons are issues that fall squarely within the mandates of the UN Treaty Bodies – the committees of experts created to monitor implementation of the treaty norms.

The right to a nationality has been a particularly well-grounded theme in the work of the Committee on the Rights of the Child (CRC). In the years 2017 to 2019, the Committee held nine sessions (74-82),[12] with recommendations on birth registration and legal identity - often combined with access to citizenship - being particularly consistent.[13] Other reoccurring recommendations are to ratify the two Statelessness Conventions,[14] to establish a statelessness determination procedure and to provide safeguards for children who would otherwise be stateless.[15] It has also made recommendations to address gender discrimination in nationality laws where that

---

[10] Apart from the countries mentioned above, Brazil (13 recommendations), Honduras (12), Uruguay (12), Spain (10), Germany (9), Sierra Leone (9), Iceland (8), the Philippines (8), Portugal (8), France (7) and Peru (7).

[11] Article 24(3) ICCPR; Article 7 CRC; Article 5(d)(iii) CERD; Article 9 CEDAW; Article 18 CRPD; Article 29 CMW. In 2018, ISI prepared Statelessness Essentials focussed on the CRC and the CEDAW: https://www.institutesi.org/resources/statelessness--human-rights-the-convention-on-the; https://www.institutesi.org/resources/statelessness-and-cedaw.

[12] Since the 75th Session in May 2017, ISI has published analyses of the relevant recommendations made during each session, which are accessible at https://www.institutesi.org/core-activities/human-rights-advocacy-crc.

[13] For example, it recommended Serbia to "ensure full implementation of the new regulations that enable immediate birth registration of children whose parents do not have personal documents and initiate procedures to establish the nationality of children born to stateless parents or those whose nationality is unknown." Serbia (7 March 2017) CRC/C/SRB/CO/2-3.

[14] Bahrain (07 February 2019) CRC/C/BHR/CO/4-6; Norway (06 June 2018) CRC/C/NOR/CO/5-6; Spain (09 February 2018) CRC/C/ESP/CO/5-6; Marshall Islands (09 February 2018) CRC/C/MHL/CO/3-4; Palau (02 February 2018) CRC/C/PLW/CO/2; Vanuatu (04 October 2017) CRC/C/VUT/CO/2; Denmark (04 October 2017) CRC/C/DNK/CO/5; Qatar (02 June 2017) CRC/C/QAT/CO/3-4; Cameroon (02 June 2017) CRC/C/CMR/CO/3-5; Antigua and Barbuda (02 June 2017) CRC/C/ATG/CO/2-4.

[15] Angola (06 June 2018) CRC/C/AGO/CO/5-7; Italy (28 February 2019) CRC/C/ITA/CO/5-6; Bahrain (07 February 2019) CRC/C/BHR/CO/4-6; Malta (31 May 2019) CRC/C/MLT/CO/3-6; Japan (28 February 2019) CRC/C/JPN/CO/4-5; Palau (02 February 2018) CRC/C/PLW/CO/2; Estonia (03 February 2017) CRC/C/EST/CO/2-4; Côte d'Ivoire (31 May 2019) CRC/C/CIV/CO/2; Denmark (04 October 2017) CRC/C/DNK/CO/5; Norway (06 June 2018) CRC/C/NOR/CO/5-6; Mongolia (02 June 2017) CRC/C/MNG/CO/5; Lebanon (02 June 2017) CRC/C/LBN/CO/4-5; Seychelles (09 February 2018) CRC/C/SYC/CO/5-6; Tajikistan (04 October 2017) CRC/TJK/CO/3-5; Democratic People's Republic of Korea (04 October 2017) CRC/C/PRK/CO/5.

leads to a risk of statelessness for children,[16] and to improve data collection on statelessness.[17]

Some of the Committees have started to directly raise aspects from other mandates, as well as from other human rights mechanisms and the Sustainable Development Goals. For example, the Committee on the Rights of Migrant Workers (CMW) recommended Madagascar in October 2018 to:

"(a) Guarantee that all children of Malagasy migrant workers abroad and of migrant workers in Madagascar are registered at birth", in which it made direct reference to *"target 16.9 of the Sustainable Development Goals and the commitments made as part of the universal periodic review process (A/HRC/28/13, para. 108.62)".*[18]

This is important as it shows that Committees such as the CMW and the CRC are taking a more holistic approach towards their mandate and are looking beyond their respective Conventions to fulfil implementation of its articles. For civil society, this could offer an opportunity to target multiple human rights mechanisms, instead of a single Committee whose mandate covers the situation best.[19]

A recent development is the cooperation of different Committees in General Comments or General Recommendations. In 2017, the CMW and the CRC adopted two Joint General Comments, which include useful language clarifying treaty norms relating to childhood statelessness. The first includes explicit references to statelessness as a basis of protection for children in such a context;[20] the other

---

[16] Mauritania (05 October 2019) CRC/C/MRT/CO/3-5; Côte d'Ivoire (31 May 2019) CRC/C/CIV/CO/2; Syrian Arab Republic (28 February 2019) CRC/C/SYR/CO/5; Bahrain (07 February 2019) CRC/C/BHR/CO/4-6; Lebanon (02 June 2017) CRC/C/LBN/CO/4-5; Qatar (02 June 2017) CRC/C/QAT/CO/3-4; Bhutan (02 June 2017) CRC/C/BTN/CO/3-5.

[17] Lao People's Democratic Republic (05 October 2019) CRC/C/LAO/CO/3-6; Guinea (28 February 2019) CRC/C/GIN/CO/3-6; Argentina (06 June 2018) CRC/C/ARG/CO/5-6; Cameroon (02 June 2017) CRC/C/CMR/CO/3-5.

[18] Madagascar (15 October 2018) CMW/C/MDG/CO/1. Also the CRC has increasingly referenced SDG16.9, e.g. in: Malta (31 May 2019) CRC/C/MLT/CO/3-6; Côte d'Ivoire (31 May 2019) CRC/C/CIV/CO/2; Japan (28 February 2019) CRC/C/JPN/CO/4-5.

[19] For example, the Statelessness Network Asia Pacific (SNAP) and ISI made a joint submission to the 22nd session of the Committee of the Rights of Persons with Disabilities with respect to Myanmar's obligations under Article 18 of the Convention of the Rights of Persons with Disabilities (CRPD), specifically the right to a nationality. The Committee recommended in October 2019 to: "Take the legal and other measures necessary to guarantee the right to a nationality without discrimination, and take effective policy measures to remove all barriers for persons with disabilities, including those from ethnic minority groups, to the enjoyment of their rights to a nationality, birth registration and civil documentation, to enable them to exercise all the rights enshrined in the Convention." Myanmar (22 October 2019) CRPD/C/MMR/CO/1, available at https://undocs.org/en/CRPD/C/MMR/CO/1. The joint submission by SNAP and ISI can be found at https://www.institutesi.org/resources/the-statelessness-network-asia-pacific-snap-and-isi.

[20] 'Joint general comment No. 3 (2017) of the Committee on the Protection of the Rights of All Migrant Workers and Members of Their Families and No. 22 (2017) of the Committee on the Rights of the Child on the general principles regarding the human rights of children in the context of international migration' (16 November 2017) CMW/C/GC/3-CRC/C/GC/22, available at https://undocs.org/en/CMW/C/GC/3-CRC/C/GC/22.

goes into detail on the right to nationality.[21] A key paragraph in the second Joint General Comment, following Article 7 CRC and Article 29 CMW, describes the following:

"While States are not obliged to grant their nationality to every child born in their territory, they are required to adopt every appropriate measure, both internally and in cooperation with other States, to ensure that every child has a nationality when he or she is born. A key measure is the conferral of nationality to a child born on the territory of the State, at birth or as early as possible after birth, if the child would otherwise be stateless."[22]

It also calls for the repeal of nationality laws that discriminate with regard to the transmission or acquisition of nationality in relation to not only the child and/or their parents' race, ethnicity, religion, gender, disability, but also regarding migration status and gender.[23]

In addition to the periodic reviews, UN Treaty Bodies have another tool to monitor the implementation of the obligations deriving from each respective Convention: Individual Complaints. Article 5 of the Optional Protocol to the International Covenant on Civil and Political Rights (OP-ICCPR) offers such a tool.[24] In an Individual Communication in May 2019, the Human Rights Committee found that by denying child benefits to a stateless mother and her child, the Dutch State violated the child's right to state protection as formulated in Article 24(1) of the ICCPR.[25] Another Individual Communication against the Netherlands on childhood statelessness is still pending before the Human Rights Committee,[26] while

---

[21] 'Joint general comment No. 4 (2017) of the Committee on the Protection of the Rights of All Migrant Workers and Members of Their Families and No. 23 (2017) of the Committee on the Rights of the Child on State obligations regarding the human rights of children in the context of international migration in countries of origin, transit, destination and return' (16 November 2017) CMW/C/GC/4-CRC/C/GC/23, available at https://undocs.org/en/CMW/C/GC/4-CRC/C/GC/23.

[22] Ibid, para 24.

[23] Ibid, paras 25 and 26.

[24] Article 5, Optional Protocol to the ICCPR.
   1. The Committee shall consider communications received under the present Protocol in the light of all written information made available to it by the individual and by the State Party concerned.
   2. The Committee shall not consider any communication from an individual unless it has ascertained that:
   (a) The same matter is not being examined under another procedure of international investigation or settlement;
   (b) The individual has exhausted all available domestic remedies. This shall not be the rule where the application of the remedies is unreasonably prolonged.
   3. The Committee shall hold closed meetings when examining communications under the present Protocol.
   4. The Committee shall forward its views to the State Party concerned and to the individual.

[25] HRC-CCPR, 'Views adopted by the Committee under article 5 (4) of the Optional Protocol, concerning communication' No. 2498/2014 (24 May 2019), available at https://undocs.org/en/CCPR/C/125/D/2498/2014.

[26] Open Society Justice Initiative, *Litigation: Zhao v. Netherlands*, available at https://www.justiceinitiative.org/litigation/zhao-v-netherlands. During the periodic review of the Netherlands in July 2019, the UN Human Rights Committee also called upon the State ensure that stateless persons in the country are adequately identified and protected, as well as to fulfil the right to a nationality for stateless children born in the country (The Netherlands (25 July 2019) CCPR/C/NLD/CO/5, available at https://undocs.org/en/CCPR/C/NLD/CO/5).

under the CRC, there is a case pending against Switzerland regarding the deportation of a stateless child as well as three complaints pending (against France and Finland) concerning the repatriation of children whose parents are allegedly associated with Islamic State where the right to a nationality may also be at issue.[27] It will therefore be interesting to watch the further development of jurisprudence on the right to a nationality from the UN Treaty Bodies on the basis of Individual Communications in the coming years.

UN SPECIAL MANDATE HOLDERS

Since 2017, statelessness and the right to a nationality have been picked up by a number of Special Mandate Holders. Most notably, when the new Special Rapporteur (SR) on minority issues Fernand de Varennes took up his mandate in August 2017, he selected statelessness as the theme of the first year of his tenure, presenting a report on global statelessness as a minority issue to the UN General Assembly in July 2018.[28] In the report, the SR identifies the main causes and underlying patterns that result in the loss or deprivation of citizenship for minority groups. According to the report, it is not a coincidence that more than three-quarters of those who are stateless belong to minorities; rather, it is the result of systematic targeting of minorities, or disproportionate impact of policies and practices.[29] The United Nations' annually convened forum to address minority issues in November 2017 focused on the theme "Statelessness: A Minority Issue" and raised the importance of citizenship for minority rights. The forum resulted in a set of concrete recommendations under the auspices of the Human Rights Council.[30] The SR on minority issues is now working to "develop a practical guide on how to address the growing challenge of the statelessness of minorities".[31]

Tendayi Achiume, UN Special Rapporteur on contemporary forms of racism, racial discrimination, xenophobia and related intolerance, dedicated her first thematic report in 2018 to the topic of racial discrimination in the context of laws, policies and practices concerning citizenship, nationality and immigration. In the report, she reiterates that while statelessness has a number of causes, "it is often the result of longstanding discrimination against racial and ethnic minorities, indigenous peoples and religious groups" and is often "the foreseeable product of discriminatory laws,

---

[27] See 'Table of pending cases before the Committee on the Rights of the Child', available at https://www.ohchr.org/Documents/HRBodies/CRC/TablePendingCases.pdf.
[28] 'Report of the Special Rapporteur on minority issues Statelessness: a minority issue' (20 July 2018) A/73/205, available at https://undocs.org/en/A/73/205.
[29] UNHCR, 'This is our Home: Stateless Minorities and their Search for Citizenship' (November 2017), available at http://www.unhcr.org/59f747404.pdf.
[30] 'Recommendations of the Forum on Minority Issues at its eleventh session on the theme "Statelessness: a minority issue"'(28 January 2019) A/HRC/40/71, available at https://undocs.org/en/A/HRC/40/71.
[31] 'Report of the Special Rapporteur on minority issues' (15 July 2019) A/74/160, available at https://undocs.org/en/A/74/160.

policies and practices that aim to exclude or have the effect of excluding people who are considered as foreign, often on the basis of their race, colour, descent, ethnicity, national origin or religion".[32]

In December 2018 and July 2019, the SR on minority issues, the SR on contemporary forms of racism, racial discrimination, xenophobia and related intolerance, the SR on freedom of religion or belief, and the Chair-Rapporteur of the Working Group on Arbitrary Detention issued two statements expressing their concern on the National Register of Citizens (NRC) in the Indian state of Assam, which could render 1.9 million people stateless.[33] The SR on Minority Issues also raised this in a July 2019 report to the General Assembly.[34]

Other Special Mandate Holders have also raised the right to a nationality. For example, in late 2017, the Working Group on Arbitrary Detention issued a decision on the case of Said Imasi, a stateless man kept in an Australian detention centre for nearly 8 years.[35] The decision holds that the ongoing detention of Imasi - like with many other complex migration cases - is unlawful, indefinite and arbitrary, and denies Imasi his right to challenge his incarceration before a court.[36] In February 2018, the UN Working Group on Arbitrary Detention issued its Revised Deliberation No. 5 on deprivation of liberty of migrants, which mainstreamed statelessness as part of the considerations.[37]

Nationality and statelessness issues have also been an area of interest in the country visits carried out by Special Procedures. In both of the State visits conducted by Tendayi Achiume in 2019 – to Qatar and the Netherlands – she addressed statelessness directly. On the Netherlands, she recommended the establishment of a statelessness determination procedure that comports with international human rights standards, stating her concern that the revocation of citizenship

---

[32] 'Report of the Special Rapporteur on contemporary forms of racism, racial discrimination, xenophobia and related intolerance' (25 April 2018) A/HRC/38/52, available at https://undocs.org/en/A/HRC/38/52.

[33] Statement by: Mr. Ahmed Shaheed, Special Rapporteur on freedom of religion or belief; Mr. Fernand de Varennes, Special Rapporteur on minority issues; Mr. Seong-Phil Hong, Chair-Rapporteur of the Working Group on Arbitrary Detention: OHCHR, 'Assam's National Register of Citizens risks stirring tensions and potential humanitarian crisis, UN experts warn' (27 December 2018), available at https://www.ohchr.org/EN/NewsEvents/Pages/DisplayNews.aspx?NewsID=24048&LangID=E; OHCHR, 'UN experts: Risk of statelessness for millions and instability in Assam, India' (3 July 2019), available at https://www.ohchr.org/EN/NewsEvents/Pages/DisplayNews.aspx?NewsID=24781&LangID=E.

[34] 'Effective promotion of the Declaration on the Rights of Persons Belonging to National or Ethnic, Religious and Linguistic Minorities' (15 July 2019) A/74/160, available at https://undocs.org/A/74/160.

[35] 'Every day I am crushed': the stateless man held without trial by Australia for eight years' *The Guardian* (14 January 2018), available at https://www.theguardian.com/australia-news/2018/jan/15/every-day-i-am-crushed-the-stateless-man-held-without-trial-by-australia-for-eight-years.

[36] 'Opinion No. 71/2017 concerning Said Imasi' (21 December 2017), available at http://www.ohchr.org/Documents/Issues/Detention/Opinions/Session80/A_HRC_WGAD_2017_71_EN.docx.

[37] Working Group on Arbitrary Detention, 'Revised Deliberation No. 5 on deprivation of liberty of migrants' (7 February 2018), available at http://www.ohchr.org/Documents/Issues/Detention/RevisedDeliberation_AdvanceEditedVersion.pdf.

disproportionately affects Dutch people of Moroccan and Turkish descent. [38] On Qatar, she raised the position of the Al Ghufran clan and the Bidoon, who remain stateless. She also recommended "to amend the 2005 Citizenship Law to prevent arbitrary deprivation of nationality, to ensure redress and the right of appeal for all persons who have been deprived of their nationality [and to] prohibit the deprivation of nationality that results in statelessness".[39] In July 2019, Achiume published her Legal Opinion on India's obligations under International Law to not deport Rohingyas in a case before the Supreme Court of India, where she addressed India's international commitments to satisfy the principles of racial equality in the context of citizenship.[40]

The UN Special Rapporteur on the rights of persons with disabilities, Catalina Devandas-Aguilar, visited Kuwait in early December 2018 and spoke with stateless Bidoon with disabilities. In her statement, she remarked that "Many of them are unable to register and obtain an ID card issued by the Central Agency for Remedying Illegal Residents' Status, which is a prerequisite to access any services.[41] Special Rapporteur on the situation of human rights in Myanmar, Yanghee Lee has also called on Myanmar a number of times to ensure the right to citizenship for the Rohingya.[42]

UN HUMAN RIGHTS COUNCIL

Starting in 2008, the HRC regularly adopted resolutions on 'Human Rights and Arbitrary Deprivation of Nationality', with the UN Secretary General releasing several reports on the same issue between 2009 to 2015.[43] However, since 2016, there have been no further resolutions or reports dedicated specifically to this issue. Instead, the focus of the HRC has shifted to discussions about the Rohingya. The UN Fact-Finding Mission on Myanmar, established by HRC resolution 34/22, paid

---

[38] 'End of Mission Statement of the Special Rapporteur on Contemporary Forms of Racism, Racial Discrimination, Xenophobia and Related Intolerance at the Conclusion of Her Mission to the Kingdom of the Netherlands, The Hague'(7 October 2019), available at https://www.ohchr.org/EN/NewsEvents/Pages/DisplayNews.aspx?NewsID=25100&LangID=E.

[39] 'End of Mission Statement of the Special Rapporteur on Contemporary Forms of Racism, Racial Discrimination, Xenophobia and Related Intolerance, Prof. E. Tendayi Achiume, at the Conclusion of Her Mission to Qatar Doha, Qatar' (1 December 2019), available at https://www.ohchr.org/EN/NewsEvents/Pages/DisplayNews.aspx?NewsID=25374&LangID=E.

[40] SR Racism, 'Legal Opinion on India's obligations under International Law to not deport Rohingyas' (12 July 2019), available at https://www.ohchr.org/EN/Issues/Racism/SRRacism/Pages/AmicusBriefs.aspx, paras. 5, 42, 43 and 48.

[41] 'End of Mission Statement by the United Nations Special Rapporteur on the rights of persons with disabilities, Ms. Catalina Devandas-Aguilar, on her visit to Kuwait' (5 December 2015), available at https://www.ohchr.org/EN/NewsEvents/Pages/DisplayNews.aspx?NewsID=23974&LangID=E.

[42] Most recently: 'Situation of human rights in Myanmar (30 August 2019) A/74/342: https://undocs.org/A/74/342.

[43] See https://www.ohchr.org/EN/Issues/Pages/Nationality.aspx for a list of all the HRC resolutions related to the right to a nationality.

particular attention to the lack of legal status as the cornerstone of decades-long oppression.44 The annual HRC resolution on the "Situation of human rights of Rohingya Muslims and other minorities in Myanmar" also paid considerable attention to it. Led jointly by the Organisation of Islamic Cooperation (OIC) and the European Union (EU), the most recent resolution in September 2019 emphasised the importance of citizenship multiple times.[45] The emerging statelessness situation in Assam also received attention within the Human Rights Council when the High Commissioner on Human Rights, Michelle Bachelet, raised the issue in her opening statement of the 42nd session of the Human Rights Council on 9 September 2019.[46]

Statelessness outside of particular situations has not often been included in Human Rights Council resolutions since 2017. For example, the exercise of full citizenship rights is mentioned in the preamble of the September 2017 and 2019 texts of the bi-annual resolution "From rhetoric to reality: a global call for concrete action against racism, racial discrimination, xenophobia and related intolerance",[47] and in the March 2017 resolution on birth registration, States are urged to identify and remove barriers relating to nationality and statelessness.[48] However, these unfortunately remain exceptions. Addressing statelessness and promoting the right to a nationality are absent in the resolutions relating to, among others, elimination of discrimination against women, the human rights of migrants, freedom of religion and belief, human rights defenders and terrorism and human rights – demonstrating that there is more work to be done to fully mainstream the issue across related subject areas.[49]

---

[44] 'Report of the independent international fact-finding mission on Myanmar' (12 September 2018) A/HRC/39/64, available at https://undocs.org/A/HRC/39/64, paras 20 and 21.

[45] Adopted by a recorded vote (37 to 2, with 7 abstentions): 'Situation of human rights of Rohingya Muslims and other minorities in Myanmar' (26 September 2019) A/HRC/RES/42/3, available at https://undocs.org/A/HRC/RES/42/3, preamble and paras. 10, 16 and 17.

[46] 'Opening statement by UN High Commissioner for Human Rights Michelle Bachelet' (9 September 2019), available at https://www.ohchr.org/EN/NewsEvents/Pages/DisplayNews.aspx?NewsID=24956&LangID=E.

[47] 'From rhetoric to reality: a global call for concrete action against racism, racial discrimination, xenophobia and related intolerance' (9 October 2017) A/HRC/RES/36/24, available at https://undocs.org/A/HRC/RES/36/24; 'From rhetoric to reality: a global call for concrete action against racism, racial discrimination, xenophobia and related intolerance' (27 September 2019) A/HRC/42/29, available at https://undocs.org/A/HRC/RES/42/29.

[48] 'Birth registration and the right of everyone to recognition everywhere as a person before the law' (24 March 2017) A/HRC/RES/34/15, available at https://undocs.org/A/HRC/RES/34/15.

[49] 'Terrorism and human rights' (26 September 2019) A/HRC/RES/34/15, available at https://undocs.org/A/HRC/RES/42/18; Elimination of all forms of discrimination against women and girls (11 July 2019) A/HRC/RES/41/6, available at https://undocs.org/A/HRC/RES/41/6; 'The human rights of migrants' (11 July 2019) A/HRC/RES/41/7, available at https://undocs.org/A/HRC/RES/41/7; 'Recognizing the contribution of environmental human rights defenders to the enjoyment of human rights, environmental protection and sustainable development' (21 March 2019) A/HRC/RES/40/11, available at https://undocs.org/A/HRC/RES/40/11; 'Freedom of religion or belief' (21 March 2019) A/HRC/RES/40/10, available at https://undocs.org/A/HRC/RES/40/10.

ARBITRARY DEPRIVATION OF NATIONALITY

The theme of this World's Stateless Report – arbitrary deprivation of nationality – was once a relatively pertinent issue for the HRC and the subject of several UN Secretary General reports. In the past few years, however, it has become less visible under the UN human rights mechanisms due to the discontinuance of the regular resolution on this theme after 2016. This development is remarkable given that it comes at a time when citizenship stripping is increasingly frequent and such HRC resolutions are needed more than ever.

There have also been very few recommendations on deprivation of nationality in the Universal Periodic Review over the same period, with the exception of Bahrain and Qatar, which received four and one recommendations respectively in the Third Cycle.[50] It is noteworthy, for example, that while the Dominican Republic received 23 recommendations related to the stateless population of Haitian descent, none were worded as recognising the situation in the country as arbitrary deprivation of nationality, and the State was urged instead to amend the Citizenship Law and/or ensure that it is implemented without discrimination.[51]

The problem of arbitrary deprivation of nationality has nevertheless featured in the work of a number of Special Mandate Holders. As laid out above, three Special Procedures and the Chair of the Working Group on Arbitrary Detention in December 2018 and July 2019 expressed their concern on the National Register of Citizens (NRC) in the Indian state of Assam.[52] Tendayi Achiume paid particular attention to deprivation of nationality as a counter-terrorism measure in her State visits to the Netherlands and Qatar, as well as in her amicus brief to the Dutch Immigration and Naturalisation Service in October 2018.[53] In the same year, citizenship stripping and national security were also prominent in her report to the

---

[50] 'Report of the Working Group on the Universal Periodic Review: Bahrain' (10 July 2017) A/HRC/36/3, available at https://undocs.org/A/HRC/36/3. See also ISI, 'Universal Periodic Review: 37th Session' (May 2017), available at https://files.institutesi.org/UPR27_stateless.pdf; 'Report of the Working Group on the Universal Periodic Review: Qatar' (11 July 2019) A/HRC/42/15, available at https://undocs.org/A/HRC/42/15. See also ISI, 'Universal Periodic Review: 33rd Session' (May 2019), available at https://www.institutesi.org/UPR33_Analysis.pdf.
[51] 'Report of the Working Group on the Universal Periodic Review: Dominican Republic' (18 April 2019) A/HRC/41/16, available at https://undocs.org/A/HRC/41/16; ISI, 'Universal Periodic Review: 32nd Session', available at https://www.institutesi.org/UPR32_stateless.pdf.
[52] Statement by: Mr. Ahmed Shaheed, Special Rapporteur on freedom of religion or belief; Mr. Fernand de Varennes, Special Rapporteur on minority issues; Mr. Seong-Phil Hong, Chair-Rapporteur of the Working Group on Arbitrary Detention: OHCHR, 'Assam's National Register of Citizens risks stirring tensions and potential humanitarian crisis, UN experts warn' (27 December 2018), available at https://www.ohchr.org/EN/NewsEvents/Pages/DisplayNews.aspx?NewsID=24048&LangID=E; Statement by: Mr. Ahmed Shaheed, Special Rapporteur on freedom of religion or belief; Mr. Fernand de Varennes, Special Rapporteur on minority issues; Ms. E. Tendayi Achiume, Special Rapporteur on contemporary forms of racism, racial discrimination, xenophobia and related intolerance: OHCHR, 'UN experts: Risk of statelessness for millions and instability in Assam, India' (3 July 2019), available at https://www.ohchr.org/EN/NewsEvents/Pages/DisplayNews.aspx?NewsID=24781&LangID=E.
[53] Amicus Brief to the Dutch Immigration and Naturalisation Service (23 October 2018), available at https://www.ohchr.org/EN/Issues/Racism/SRRacism/Pages/AmicusBriefs.aspx.

Human Rights Council on "racial discrimination in the context of laws, policies and practices concerning citizenship, nationality and immigration",[54] focussing particularly on its impact on racial (in)equality. This builds partially on the work of her predecessor, Mutuma Ruteere, who touched upon the issue in his final report in 2017.[55]

Overall, the picture on this issue is therefore mixed. The Human Rights Council has not (yet) commented explicitly on (the evolving use of) withdrawal of nationality in related resolutions such as those on human rights and terrorism, or on human rights defenders – and nor has this topic been the subject of its own resolution since 2016. On the other hand, the relevant human rights norms and the existing body of work of the human rights mechanisms has started to have important ripple effects beyond the human rights field. For example, in September 2019, the UN Counter Terrorism Centre published a "Handbook on Children Affected by the Foreign-fighter Phenomenon" that devoted significant attention to the CRC and the recommendations issued by its Committee. In particular, it took language from its 2017 Joint General Comment with the CMW when talking about serving the child's best interests on a case-by-case basis, in the context of security interests.[56] In sum, there is scope for more to be done to renew and expand attention to arbitrary deprivation of nationality within the UN human rights system, as well as significant potential for the further cross-fertilisation of these human rights norms into related fields.

---

[54] 'Report of the Special Rapporteur on contemporary forms of racism, racial discrimination, xenophobia and related intolerance' (25 April 2018) A/HRC/38/52, available at https://undocs.org/en/A/HRC/38/52.
[55] 'Report of the Special Rapporteur on contemporary forms of racism, racial discrimination, xenophobia and related intolerance' (9 May 2017) A/HRC/35/41, available at https://undocs.org/en/A/HRC/35/41.
[56] 'Joint general comment No. 3 (2017) of the Committee on the Protection of the Rights of All Migrant Workers and Members of Their Families and No. 22 (2017) of the Committee on the Rights of the Child on the general principles regarding the human rights of children in the context of international migration' (16 November 2017) CMW/C/GC/3-CRC/C/GC/22, available at https://undocs.org/en/CMW/C/GC/3-CRC/C/GC/22; UNCCT, 'Handbook Children affected by the foreign-fighter phenomenon: Ensuring a child rights-based approach' (September 2019), available at https://www.un.org/counterterrorism/ctitf/sites/www.un.org.counterterrorism.ctitf/files/ftf_handbook_web_reduced.pdf.

THE #IBELONG CAMPAIGN REACHES ITS MIDPOINT

BY MELANIE J. KHANNA[*]

So much has taken place since UNHCR launched the ten-year Campaign to End Statelessness (known as the #IBelong Campaign) in 2014 that it can be difficult to keep track. This edition of the World's Stateless thus provides a welcome opportunity to recall some of the highlights and take stock of the state of the #IBelong Campaign as it enters the second half of its lifespan. The High-Level Segment on Statelessness (HLS) that took place on October 7, 2019 in Geneva helps with this exercise and enables States and others to speak about their achievements and make concrete, time-bound commitments to accelerate progress. Thanks to information provided by States at the HLS and a separate analysis undertaken by UNHCR, the international community now has a good understanding of the key accomplishments as of the time of writing this essay (January 2020). These are set out below in relation to the Actions in the Global Action Plan to End Statelessness:[1]

Action 1:

Resolve existing major situations of statelessness

Achievements:

- Kyrgyzstan has become the first country to resolve all known cases of statelessness on its territory.
- Partial achievements in Côte d'Ivoire, Iraq, Kenya, Malaysia, the Russian Federation, Thailand, Turkmenistan and Vietnam.

Action 2:

Ensure that no child is born stateless

Achievements:

- Six States have introduced provisions in their nationality laws to grant nationality to children born in their territory who would otherwise be stateless (Armenia, Cuba, Estonia, Iceland, Luxembourg and Tajikistan).

---

[*] **Melanie Khanna** is Chief of the Statelessness Section at the Office of the United Nations High Commissioner in Geneva. *The views in this essay are the author's and do not necessarily represent the views of UNHCR or of the United Nations.*
[1] UN High Commissioner for Refugees, 'Global Action Plan to End Statelessness: 2014-2024' (November 2014), available at https://www.unhcr.org/statelesscampaign2014/Global-Action-Plan-eng.pdf.

- Two States have introduced provisions in their nationality law to grant nationality to children born to nationals abroad who would otherwise be stateless (Cuba and Paraguay).

Action 3:
Remove gender discrimination from nationality laws

Achievements:

- Two States have reformed their nationality laws to allow women to confer nationality to their children on an equal basis with men (Madagascar and Sierra Leone). Two States have withdrawn reservations to CEDAW Art. 9(2) (Democratic People's Republic of Korea and Iraq).
- One State has introduced reforms to its nationality law to grant women and men an equal ability to confer nationality on spouses (Lesotho). One State has withdrawn reservations to CEDAW Art. 9(1) (Iraq).

Action 4:
Prevent denial, loss or deprivation of nationality on discriminatory grounds

- No State has reformed its nationality laws to remove provisions which permit denial, loss or deprivation of nationality on discriminatory grounds.

Action 5:
Prevent statelessness in cases of state succession

- There have been no cases of state succession since 2014.

Action 6:
Grant protection status to stateless migrants and facilitate their naturalisation

Achievements:

- 11 States have established statelessness determination procedures (Argentina, Brazil, Bulgaria, Costa Rica, Ecuador, Kosovo, Montenegro, Panama, Paraguay, Uruguay and Turkey). Two States have improved their statelessness determination procedure (Hungary and Italy).
- Nine States have introduced procedures for facilitated naturalisation for stateless migrants (Argentina, Bolivia, Brazil, Ecuador, Estonia, Iceland, Luxembourg, Paraguay and Uruguay).

Action 7:
Ensure birth registration for the prevention of statelessness

- As noted in the Global Action Plan to End Statelessness, UNHCR does not have baseline data on how many children are left stateless as a result of not having their births registered that would enable it to track progress against this Action.[2]

Action 8:
Issue nationality documentation to those with entitlement to it

Achievements:

- One State has issued nationality documentation to all those with entitlement to it (Kyrgyzstan).
- Partial achievements in 11 States (Côte d'Ivoire, Dominican Republic, Iraq, Kenya, Latvia, Malaysia, Niger, Philippines, Tajikistan, Thailand and Yemen).

Action 9:
Accede to the UN Statelessness Conventions

Achievements:

- 11 States have acceded to the 1954 Convention (Angola, Colombia, Chile, El Salvador, Guinea-Bissau, Haiti, Mali, Malta, Niger, Sierra Leone and Turkey).
- 14 States have acceded to the 1961 Convention (Angola, Argentina, Belize, Burkina Faso, Chile, Guinea-Bissau, Haiti, Italy, Luxembourg, Mali, North Macedonia, Sierra Leone, Peru and Spain).

Action 10:
Improve quantitative and qualitative data on stateless populations

Achievements:

- Quantitative population data on stateless populations is publicly available for three more States compared with 2014.
- Qualitative studies on stateless populations have been conducted in 25 additional States.

Many of the achievements above are significant. It is notable, for example, that there have been 25 new accessions to the UN Statelessness Conventions since the Campaign was launched, bringing the total numbers of Parties to the 1954 Convention on the Status of Stateless Persons and the 1961 Convention on the

---

[2] Notably, global birth registration rates have risen significantly in the last two decades. According to UNICEF, about 3 out of 4 children under 5 have their births registered as compared with about 6 out of 10 in 2000. Rates remain lowest in Africa. See https://www.unicef.org/media/62981/file/Birth-registration-for-every-child-by-2030.pdf.

Reduction of Statelessness to 94 and 75, respectively. While there is still a great margin for improvement, these treaties are both now on solid footing as compared to five years ago. The political will to resolve existing situations of statelessness is clearly stronger in certain countries and progress has been made accordingly, including across Central Asia. Law reforms that will help prevent statelessness at birth have been made in nine States. The number of States that have dedicated statelessness determination mechanisms has more than doubled since the Campaign was launched, up from a modest ten to 21.

Having noted these achievements, it's important to acknowledge up front that reductions in the number of stateless persons globally are not taking place fast enough to the meet the Campaign's 2024 deadline. Data concerning statelessness remains weak, so it's difficult to know exactly how many cases of statelessness are resolved and how many new cases are created each year. However, the data that is available is not encouraging with respect to achieving an end to statelessness by 2024.[3] Many governments continue to have a poor understanding of the issue and thus a long distance to travel before taking the steps necessary to fully resolve their statelessness situations. At the same time, some governments maintain deliberate forms of discrimination or exclusion that leave certain groups stateless. In order to accelerate reductions, the international community should prioritise improving global data and establishing clear linkages between statelessness situations and the 2030 Development Agenda. If there were clear evidence demonstrating that statelessness negatively affects States' ability to achieve certain Sustainable Development Goals (SDGs), the case for reform would be more persuasive. This is a critical area for endeavour over the next five years, as advocates now require stronger arguments in support of inclusive societies and citizenship policies to use in places where these policies have not found favour or are in peril.

Still, developments to date are remarkable, including a huge rise in public awareness and political engagement evidenced by the many new regional declarations and national action plans on statelessness. While there were no regional declarations fully dedicated to the subject five years ago, there are now four: the Abidjan Declaration on the Eradication of Statelessness covering West Africa, the Declaration of the International Conference of the Great Lakes Region on the Eradication of Statelessness, the N'Djamena Initiative on the Eradication of Statelessness covering Central Africa, and the Arab Declaration on Legal Identity and Belonging covering members of the League of Arab States (not counting the Brazil Declaration, which has a dedicated chapter on statelessness and covers the Americas). Regional organisations, most notably the Economic Community of West African States (ECOWAS), have helped spur action, which has led to the adoption of many new action plans at the national level.

---

[3] The most comprehensive global statistics available on statelessness can be found in UNHCR's annual *Global Trends* report, the most recent version of which is available here: https://www.unhcr.org/globaltrends2018/.

Activism by civil society has also been a key catalyst. At the grassroots level, NGOs worked closely with UNHCR and government authorities to achieve an end to statelessness in Kyrgyzstan, nationality for the Makonde minority in Kenya, and the resolution of thousands of cases of statelessness in Thailand, to name just a few examples. The remarkable milestone in Kyrgyzstan and the key role of the NGO Ferghana Valley Lawyers Without Borders received wonderful global attention at the 2019 Nansen Award Ceremony, where the head of that organisation, Azizbek Ashurov, became the first person ever working solely on statelessness to win the prestigious prize. Ashurov has also helped to found a new civil society network in Central Asia to apply lessons learned in Kyrgyzstan elsewhere. Moreover, new civil society networks have also been established in the Americas, South East Asia, and Africa to complement the only one that existed prior to 2014, the European Network on Statelessness (ENS). The first-ever global NGO focused on statelessness, the Institute on Statelessness and Inclusion (ISI), was founded around the same time the #IBelong Campaign was launched. Advocacy by ISI has increased the attention paid to statelessness by the human rights mechanisms of the United Nations, including the Universal Periodic Review.

Compared with the landscape pre-2014, there is now clear recognition by many who work on women's rights, children's rights, and minorities' rights that statelessness is an important, cross-cutting issue. The publication in 2015 by UNHCR of the special report "I am Here, I Belong: The Urgent Need to End Childhood Statelessness"[4] was instrumental in giving rise to the Coalition now led by UNHCR and UNICEF on Every Child's Right to a Nationality,[5] which is active in 20 States and growing. The 2017 report "This is Our Home: Stateless Minorities and their search for citizenship"[6] likewise generated increased interest from certain actors including Minority Rights Group and the UN Special Rapporteur on Minority Issues. In 2018, for the first time, statelessness was the focus of the UN Forum on Minority Issues. The World Conference on Statelessness hosted by ISI in June 2019 highlighted the range of new actors in this space and the energy they bring to the issue. The Conference also underscored the importance of the adoption of the SDGs to advocacy efforts, particularly SDG 16.9's focus on legal identity for all, including birth registration, by 2030. This target, and the overall aspiration to leave no one behind, have together allowed UNHCR and others to begin to frame statelessness appropriately as a development issue and not just a human rights one. The Secretary-General's updated Guidance Note on Statelessness[7] and new UN

---

[4] UN High Commissioner for Refugees, 'I Am Here, I Belong: The Urgent Need to End Childhood Statelessness' (3 November 2015), available at: https://www.refworld.org/docid/563368b34.html.

[5] UNHCR and UNICEF, 'IBELONG: Coalition on Every Child's Right to a Nationality', available at https://www.unhcr.org/ibelong/unicef-unhcr-coalition-child-right-nationality/.

[6] UN High Commissioner for Refugees, '"This is Our Home" Stateless Minorities and their Search for Citizenship' (3 November 2017), available at https://www.refworld.org/docid/59e4a6534.html.

[7] UN Secretary-General, 'Guidance Note of the Secretary General: The United Nations and Statelessness', (November 2018), available at: https://www.refworld.org/docid/5c580e507.html.

Key Messages on statelessness[8] published in 2018 show the evolution in the UN's approach and collaborative work on the issue. A number of Member States have begun to act as champions individually and collectively. Over a dozen such States now meet regularly in Geneva as a "Group of Friends of the Campaign to End Statelessness" to discuss ways in which they can help advance the Campaign's objectives.

Knowledge on statelessness is being disseminated with new dedicated annual statelessness courses at the International Institute of Humanitarian Law and the University of Melbourne complementing the summer course at Tilburg University. The first academic institute fully devoted to statelessness, the Peter McMullin Centre on Statelessness, was launched in Melbourne in 2018 and is contributing much-needed research and teaching resources in the Asia Pacific region and beyond. There is a growing trend towards the inclusion of questions on nationality and statelessness in official population censuses, which should help to improve the significant global underestimate that currently prevails.

It would be impossible to scan the horizon without taking dispiriting note of the fact that the situation of the world's largest known stateless population, the Rohingya, has dramatically worsened in recent years, with severe persecution and violence leading to new large-scale displacement in 2017. Apart from the constructive final report submitted by the Advisory Commission on Rakhine State in 2017,[9] there has been excruciatingly little progress made. However, on 23 January 2020, the International Court of Justice ruled that Myanmar must take measures to protect the Rohingya from genocide and prevent the military from committing acts of genocide,[10] which is the first step in the right direction.

The rise of xenophobia and ethno-nationalism in many parts of the world threatens the project of full belonging and citizenship for all. The National Register of Citizens published in August 2019 in Assam, India is a particularly concerning case in point. The exclusion of some 1.9 million residents who sought recognition as Indian citizens leaves an extraordinary number of people at risk of statelessness and sets a worrying precedent. The situation in the Middle East also continues to put displaced Syrians and their offspring at risk of statelessness due to a combination of risk factors including gender discrimination in nationality laws, family separation, loss of civil documentation, sexual and gender-based violence and difficulty accessing birth registration. Those affected by or affiliated with ISIS fighters face many of the same

---

[8] UN Secretary-General, 'Key Messages on statelessness' (November 2018), available at:
https://www.refworld.org/docid/5c87a6a44.html.
[9] Advisory Commission on Rakhine State, 'Towards a Peaceful, Fair and Prosperous Future for the People of Rakhine: Final Report of the Advisory Commission on Rakhine State' (August 2017), available at
http://www.rakhinecommission.org/app/uploads/2017/08/FinalReport_Eng.pdf.
[10] See https://www.icj-cij.org/files/case-related/178/178-20200123-ORD-01-00-EN.pdf?mc_cid=d585a02416&mc_eid=%5BUNIQID%5D.

risk factors as well as possible deprivation of nationality. The rise in interest by States in deprivation of nationality as a counter-terrorism measure is another general area of concern as compared with 2014.

Fortunately, the commitments that States and others made at the HLS in October 2019 will help ensure additional progress soon. Some 358 pledges were made by Governments (which accounted for the vast majority of these), international organisations, and civil society.[11] These include new pledges to resolve statelessness, to reform nationality laws, to accede to the UN Statelessness Conventions, and to improve data on statelessness, among other topics. Some pledges, such as those by Kenya, Rwanda, Sierra Leone and Turkmenistan, are extremely significant as each of these States committed to completely resolving all cases of statelessness before 2024. Liberia and Eswatini also each made an important commitment to pursuing reforms to allow mothers to confer nationality to their children on the same basis as fathers. Additionally, over 20 States pledged to establish dedicated statelessness determination procedures, and more than 30 States committed to collect better qualitative and quantitative data. Many of the pledges made by international organisations such as the Inter-Parliamentary Union, UNICEF, and OHCHR will provide an important hook for strengthened partnerships and concrete follow up on workshops and events, as will many of the regional organisation and civil society pledges, such as those by the World Council of Churches and the Global Campaign on Equal Nationality Rights.

The HLS itself was ground-breaking, as it was the first global high-level event convened by UNHCR focused solely on statelessness. The event was framed by a very moving and personal conversation between UNHCR Goodwill Ambassador, Cate Blanchett, and statelessness activist, Maha Mamo, who spoke about her own decades-long struggle to obtain citizenship. This was befitting, as personal testimonies by people who have acquired citizenship since the #IBelong Campaign was launched have become one of the defining features and strongest assets of the Campaign.[12] The participation of Cate Blanchett, Maha Mamo, the UN Deputy Secretary-General, Amina Mohammed, the High Commissioner for Refugees, Filippo Grandi, and others helped attract record levels of media attention to the cause[13] and ensured that a broader audience understands the difference that having citizenship makes. UNHCR and others will now need to step up efforts to support implementation of the pledges made at the HLS so as not to lose the momentum.

---

[11] The full list of results may be found here: https://www.unhcr.org/ibelong/results-of-the-high-level-segment-on-statelessness/.

[12] You can watch the stories of Artee and Jirair here: '#IBelong: Solving statelessness in Thailand' *YouTube*, (31 March 2017), available at https://www.youtube.com/watch?v=fgkqqppvwsY; 'Citizenship opens new world for stateless man from Georgia' *YouTube*, (15 February 2018), available at https://www.youtube.com/watch?v=WBdvCsw1Syc&t=12s.

[13] E. Batha, 'Film star Cate Blanchett backs drive to end plight of 10 mln stateless' *Thomas Reuters Foundation* (7 October 2019), available at http://news.trust.org/item/20191006223443-j46mb.

However, even that won't be enough for the international community to succeed in ending statelessness by 2024, as implementation of all pledges received alone cannot achieve that result. Almost no pledges were made to remove forms of discrimination from nationality laws other than gender discrimination, for example. Therefore, it is essential that the coming years see momentous breakthroughs and unprecedented levels of investment in order to take the Campaign across the finish line.

STATELESSNESS IN AFRICA

OVERVIEW OF STATELESSNESS IN THE REGION

Statelessness is a significant but poorly documented problem in Africa. Of the 48 countries in Sub-Saharan Africa,[1] just four reported data on the number of stateless persons in the country in the global statistical reporting published by UNHCR in June 2019.[2] A further seven countries were marked with an asterisk, denoting that UNHCR has information about stateless persons but no reliable data.[3] Notwithstanding the common challenges in ascertaining an accurate picture of the scale of statelessness anywhere in the world, it is especially difficult to quantify in Africa because the stateless population overlaps with a larger undocumented population whose nationality status may be unclear until put to the test through efforts to acquire documentation.[4]

The main root causes of statelessness in Africa are nonetheless known,[5] offering an insight into the reach of the phenomenon and the diversity of people affected. Of the 25 States that still discriminate against women in their ability to transmit nationality to their children, seven are in sub-Saharan Africa – although it is also important to note that the two countries to reform their laws most recently to address this inequality were both in Africa (Madagascar and Sierra Leone in 2017).[6] Racial, religious, and ethnic discrimination are present in the nationality laws of several African States[7] and result in individuals being unable to acquire nationality. Many African States do not have safeguards guaranteeing nationality to children born in their territory who would otherwise be stateless,[8] with the result that children

---

[1] North African countries are included in the Middle East and North Africa regional chapter of this report.

[2] These countries are: Burundi, Cabo Verde, Côte d'Ivoire and Kenya, which together reported a total stateless population of 711,589 (the majority of which are accounted for by the tally of 692,000 in Côte d'Ivoire). UN High Commissioner for Refugees, '2018 Global Trends: Table 7. Persons under UNHCR's statelessness mandate' (2019) available at: https://www.unhcr.org/statistics/18-WRD-table-7.xls.

[3] Ibid.

[4] The challenge of statistical reporting in Africa is discussed in B. Manby, "How will the UNHCR's statelessness campaign affect Africa?" in *African Arguments* (2014) available at: https://africanarguments.org/2014/11/12/how-will-the-unhcrs-statelessness-campaign-affect-africa-by-bronwen-manby/.

[5] See in particular the extensive research conducted by Bronwen Manby, as published by Open Society Foundations, UNHCR and in the comprehensive monograph *Citizenship in Africa. The Law of Belonging*', Hart Publishing 2018.

[6] Burundi, Liberia, Mauritania, Somalia, Sudan, eSwatini and Togo. See, UNHCR 'Background Note on Gender Equality, Nationality Laws and Statelessness 2019' (2019) available at: https://www.refworld.org/docid/5c8120847.html.

[7] B Manby, *Citizenship Law in Africa: A Comparative Study* (Open Society Foundations, 2016) 60-62, available at: https://www.refworld.org/docid/56a77ffe4.html.

[8] Ibid, 49-52.

continue to be born stateless across Africa – whether in the context of discriminatory laws, conflicts of law situations or the intergenerational perpetuation of statelessness.

State succession, both the legacy of decolonisation and more recent succession situations, leading to the resulting (re)drawing of borders and (re)definition of national belonging are another a cause of statelessness in Africa – especially for minority groups and historic migrants who arrived pre-independence.[9] Nomadic and cross-border populations have been among those affected in this context and continue to face practical and political challenges to acquisition or recognition of nationality today because relevant laws and procedures are not designed to accommodate them.[10] Migrants, especially migrants without a regular immigration status, can also struggle to maintain their connection with their country of origin, especially because of difficulties acquiring documentation; can often cannot obtain nationality in the country of residence. Refugees and especially former refugees, from countries where it has been declared that the circumstances justifying refugee status no longer apply and a refugee document no longer provides a valid immigration status, face similar difficulties. These challenges generate statelessness, particularly in subsequent generations born outside the parents' country.[11]

Statelessness has also resulted in Africa from the lack of due process and the broad discretion granted to State officials responsible for the issuing of birth certificates and identity cards, which in practice determine an individual's access to proof of nationality.[12] The introduction of new biometric technologies and digital identity systems in Africa has been heralded as a solution to the documentation 'gap', but if the underlying legislative and policy structures that determine access to citizenship are not addressed, this change may increase rather than decrease the incidence of statelessness.[13] A final source of statelessness that is of note in Africa and which is another area in which developments should be closely followed is the targeted denial or deprivation of nationality as a political tool. While this practice is not new and indeed a number of high-profile cases were reported in the region in the 1990s, it has been back in the headlines in several countries in the region as the measure has again been imposed on political opponents and journalists.[14]

---

[9] Ibid, 2

[10] See for instance on East Africa, B. Manby, 'Statelessness and Citizenship in the East African Community' (2018) available at: https://www.refworld.org/docid/5bee966d4.html.

[11] This is related to limited access to naturalisation as well as problems maintaining contact with the country of origin. L Hovil, 'Ensuring that today's refugees are not tomorrow's stateless: solutions in a refugee context' in L van Waas and M Khanna (eds), *Solving Statelessness* (Wolf Legal Publishers, 2016).

[12] B Manby, *Citizenship Law in Africa: A Comparative Study* (Open Society Foundations, 2016), 116.

[13] B. Manby, *"Legal Identity" and Biometric Identification in Africa*, in Newsletter of the American Political Science Association's Organized Section on Migration and Citizenship, Summer 2018, Vol. 6, No. 2, available at: http://connect.apsanet.org/s43/wp-content/uploads/sites/13/2018/08/APSA-Migration-Citizenship-Newsletter-6-2-Summer-2018-.pdf.

[14] See for analysis and news stories on this issue: http://citizenshiprightsafrica.org/theme/loss-and-deprivation-of-nationality/

Digital identity and citizenship in Africa

As digital identity systems are introduced in more countries, including as part of the push to implement Sustainable Development Goal 16.9 and provide 'legal identity' to all by 2030, the fault lines of in/exclusion are increasingly being laid bare. The experience with the National Integrated Identity Management System (NIIMS) in Kenya has brought to light. NIIMS is intended to become a Single Source of Truth about Kenyan citizens and NIIMS registration will be required to access universal healthcare, get a passport, register as a voter, apply for a driving licence, register a mobile phone number, pay taxes, open a bank account and more. However, those who have historically struggled to secure identity documents and be recognised as citizens may remain shut out and there is even a risk that people who were previously recognised in day-to-day practice as citizens will be registered as foreigners if they cannot produce the required documentation to demonstrate citizenship.[15] The Nubian Rights Forum, Kenya Human Rights Commission and Kenya National Commission on Human Rights filed constitutional petitions against the roll out of the system. On 30 January 2020, Kenya's High Court handed down its judgment, recognising the risk of disenfranchisement and exclusion and ruling that the implementation of NIIMS must be suspended until the government puts a comprehensive legal framework to address the discriminatory nature of the system.[16] As this example shows, while the shift towards digital identity management in Kenya and elsewhere could help to generate a better picture of the scale and spread of nationality problems in the region in the coming years, it may also exacerbate them.[17]

---

[15] Open Society Justice Initiative, Kenya's National Integrated Identity Management System - Briefing Paper (2019) available at:
https://www.justiceinitiative.org/publications/kenyas-national-integrated-identity-management-scheme-niims.
[16] See for an analysis of the case and the Kenyan experience: Privacy International, *Why the Huduma Namba ruling matters for the future of digital ID, and not just in Kenya*, 30 January 2020, available at:
https://privacyinternational.org/news-analysis/3350/why-huduma-namba-ruling-matters-future-digital-id-and-not-just-kenya; Vivek Maru, Laura Goodwin, Aisha Khagai, and Mustafa Mahmoud, *Digital IDs Make Systemic Bias Worse*, 5 February 2020, available at: https://www.wired.com/story/opinion-digital-ids-make-systemic-bias-worse/.
[17] See further Institute on Statelessness and Inclusion, *Making SDG16.9 work for the wider Sustainable Development Agenda: Lessons from the citizenship, statelessness and legal identity community - Policy brief* (2019) available at:
https://files.institutesi.org/legal_identity_policy_brief.pdf

REGIONAL STANDARDS AND INTERGOVERNMENTAL COMMITMENTS

The right to a nationality has received significant attention within the African Human Rights system, where a succession of court rulings in 2018 – 2019 have built on earlier jurisprudence[18] and helped to further crystallise the understanding of this norm in the African regional context.[19] The African Charter on Human and Peoples' Rights does not contain a right to a nationality. However the African Commission on Human and Peoples Rights which oversees the implementation of the Charter has found that Article 5 (which provides that "[e]very individual shall have the right to the respect of the dignity inherent in a human being and to the recognition of his legal status") includes the right to a nationality.[20] In 2013, a resolution of the African Commission on Human and Peoples' Rights (ACommHPR) reaffirmed this position (originally established in the ACommHPR's case law) in general terms.[21] In 2018 and 2019, the African Court on Human and Peoples' Rights built on these decisions in two cases brought against Tanzania. It referred directly to Article 15 of the UDHR, which prohibits arbitrary deprivation of nationality, asserting this to be customary international law,[22] while also affirming that the right to a nationality is implied within the concept of "legal status" in Article 5 of the Charter.[23]

Article 6(3) of the African Charter on the Rights and Welfare of the Child provides that "Every child has the right to acquire a nationality" and 6(4) requires States Parties to grant nationality to an otherwise stateless child born in their territory.[24] These rights are explored in detail in a General Comment of the African Committee

---

[18] Including African Commission on Human and Peoples' Rights, *Amnesty International v. Zambia*, no. 212/98 (1999); *John K. Modise v. Botswana*, no. 97/93 (2000), *Malawi Africa Association and others v. Mauritania* nos. 54/91, 61/91, 98/93, 164/97 à 196/97 and 210/98 (2000); *Legal Resources Foundation v. Zambia*, no. 211/98 (2001); and *Open Society Justice Initiative v. Côte d'Ivoire*, no. 318/06 (2015); African Committee of Experts on the Rights and Welfare of the Child, *IHRDA & OSJI v. Kenya* (Kenyan Nubian Minors Decision), no. 002/09 (2011).

[19] African Court on Human and Peoples' Rights, *Anudo Ochieng Anudo v. United Republic of Tanzania*, App. No. 012/2015 (2018) and *Kennedy Gihana & Others v. Republic of Rwanda*, App. No. 017/2015 (2019); African Committee of Experts on the Rights and Welfare of the Child, *African Centre of Justice and Peace Studies (ACJPS) and People's Legal Aid Centre (PLACE) v the Republic of Sudan*, no. 002/2018 (2018).

[20] Including in African Commission on Human and Peoples' Rights, *John K. Modise v. Botswana*, no. 97/93 (2000).

[21] African Commission on Human and Peoples' Rights (ACommHPR), Resolution 234 on the Right to Nationality, 23 April 2013. This position had already been taken in, *Modise v Botswana*, Communication 97/93, ACommHPR (6 November 2000), para 91 and *Amnesty International v Zambia*, Communication No. 212/98, ACommHPR (5 May 1999), para 58.

[22] *Anudo Ochieng Anudo v. United Republic of Tanzania*, App. No. 012/2015, African Court of Human and Peoples' Rights, Judgment of 22 March 2018. See for a discussion of the case B. Manby, 'Case note on Anudo Ochieng Anudo v Tanzania (Judgment) (African Court on Human and Peoples' Rights, App No 012/2015, 22 March 2018)' in *Statelessness and Citizenship Review* (volume 1:1, 2019) available at: https://statelessnessandcitizenshipreview.com/index.php/journal/article/view/75/25.

[23] *Robert John Penessis v. United Republic of Tanzania*, App. No. 013/2015, African Court on Human and Peoples' Rights, Judgment of 28 November 2019

[24] African Charter on the Rights and Welfare of the Child (adopted 11 July 1990, entered into force 29 November 1999) CAB/LEG/24.9/49, arts 6(3) and 6(4).

of Experts on the Rights and Welfare of the child, adopted in April 2014.[25] The General Comment recognises the "profoundly negative impact on respect for and fulfilment of other human rights" of statelessness and the need for not only nationality, but also proof of nationality, in order to be able to access rights. Following its jurisprudence in *The Institute for Human Rights and Development in Africa and the Open Society Justice Initiative (on behalf of children of Nubian Descent in Kenya) v. Kenya*, the ACERWC adopts a purposive reading of Article 6(3) stressing that the best interests of the child requires that children should acquire a nationality from birth and must not be made to wait until they turn 18.[26] In its 2018 decision on the case of *African Centre of Justice and Peace Studies (ACJPS) and People's Legal Aid Centre (PLACE) v the Republic of Sudan*, the ACERWC further elucidated the relationship between the right to a nationality as protected in Article 6 and Article 3 of the children's Charter on non-discrimination, concluding that the applicant had been arbitrarily deprived of her Sudanese nationality.[27]

The Protocol to the African Charter on Human and Peoples' Rights on the Rights of Women in Africa is more limited in its promotion of women's equal right to acquire, retain and transmit nationality than the international standards, providing only that "a woman shall have the right to retain her nationality or to acquire the nationality of her husband" and "a woman and a man shall have equal rights with respect to the nationality of their children *except where this is contrary to a provision in national legislation or is contrary to national security interests*".[28] This clause permitting national law to override the principle of gender equality runs counter to the general provisions on gender equality in the protocol as well as the African Charter on the Rights and Welfare of the Child as interpreted in the aforementioned General Comment and jurisprudence. In the 2018 case against Sudan, the ACERWC explicitly outlined that "unlike children born to a Sudanese father, children born to a Sudanese mother have to go through an administrative process to be considered as Sudanese nationals by birth" leading it to conclude that "the law treats differently these groups of children on the basis of the gender of their parents […] a prohibited ground of discrimination".[29]

---

[25] African Committee of Experts on the Rights and Welfare of the Child, 'General Comment No. 2 on Article 6 of the ACRWC: "The Right to a Name, Registration at Birth, and to Acquire a Nationality"' (2014), ACERWC/GC/02.

[26] See also Safeguards against childhood statelessness under the African human rights system by Ayalew Getachew Assefa in Chapter 11.

[27] African Committee of Experts on the Rights and Welfare of the Child, *African Centre of Justice and Peace Studies (ACJPS) and People's Legal Aid Centre (PLACE) v the Republic of Sudan*, no. 002/2018 (2018).

[28] Protocol to the African Charter on Human and People's Rights on the Rights of Women in Africa (adopted 7 November 2003, entered into force 25 November 2003), art 6 (emphasis added).

[29] African Committee of Experts on the Rights and Welfare of the Child, *African Centre of Justice and Peace Studies (ACJPS) and People's Legal Aid Centre (PLACE) v the Republic of Sudan*, no. 002/2018 (2018) para 40.

Following the publication of a study on The Right to Nationality in Africa in 2014,[30] the African Commission on Human and Peoples' Rights adopted the text of a draft Protocol to the African Charter on the Specific Aspects of the Right to a Nationality and the Eradication of Statelessness in Africa in 2015.[31] The draft text was transmitted to the political organs of the African Union (AU), considered and amended by state experts in three meetings during 2017 and 2018, and finally approved at ministerial level by a meeting of the Specialised Technical Committee (STC) on Migration, Refugees and IDPs in November 2018. In February 2019, the Executive Council of the AU approved the progress of the draft Protocol to the STC on Justice and Legal Affairs, the final stage before adoption.[32] In October 2019, on the occasion of UNHCR's High Level Segment on Statelessness, the African Union Commission pledged the following: "No later than by the end of 2020 the African Union Commission commits to submit the draft Protocol to the African Charter on Human and Peoples' Rights on Specific Aspects of the Right to Nationality and Eradication of Statelessness in Africa for adoption by the AU Assembly". If adopted substantially in the form approved by the African Commission on Human and Peoples' Rights, the text would provide significant advances on international law in relation to provisions on the acquisition of nationality at birth and access to naturalisation, as well as an article dedicated to the situation of nomadic populations.

This evolving regional human rights framework is complemented at the sub-regional level by several intergovernmental initiatives around the issue of statelessness. The first of these was the Abidjan declaration by the Heads of State of the Economic Community of West African States (ECOWAS), adopted in 2015[33] – later given more detailed content in the Banjul Plan of Action of ECOWAS on the Eradication of Statelessness. In 2016, the SADC Parliamentary Forum adopted a Resolution on the Prevention of Statelessness and the Protection of Stateless Persons in the Southern Africa Development Community (SADC) Region.[34] It called on governments to take a series of actions including the adoption of a SADC Ministerial Declaration and Action Plan on Statelessness, but work to achieve this is still underway. Meanwhile, the International Conference on the Great Lakes Region adopted their own sub-regional Declaration on the Eradication of Statelessness at a

---

[30] ACommHPR, 'The Right to Nationality in Africa' (2014) available at:
https://www.refworld.org/pdfid/54cb3c8f4.pdf.
[31] Final Communiqué of the 18th Extraordinary Session of the African Commission on Human and Peoples' Rights, 7 August 2015.
[32] Decision on the Reports of the Specialised Technical Committees (STCs), 34th Ordinary Session of the Executive Council, 7-8 February 2019, Addis Ababa, Ethiopia, Executive Council of the African Union, 8 February 2019, EX.CL/Dec.1032(XXXIV).
[33] Abidjan Declaration of Ministers of ECOWAS Member States on the Eradication of Statelessness (2015) available at https://www.unhcr.org/ecowas2015/ENG-Declaration.pdf.
[34] Resolution on the Prevention of Statelessness and the Protection of Stateless Persons in the SADC Region (2016) http://citizenshiprightsafrica.org/wp-content/uploads/2017/01/Resolution-Statelessness_SADCPF-40th-Plenary-Assembly_2016.pdf.

Heads of State Summit in 2017.[35] The ICGLR secretariat has now committed "to support and submit at the next ICGLR Regional Inter-Ministerial committee the consolidated draft action plan of ICGLR on the eradication of statelessness in the Great Lakes Region (2017-2024) for its final adoption by March 2020".[36] In December 2018, a group of experts from member states of the Economic Community of Central African States (ECCAS) adopted a resolution on the N'Djamena Initiative on the Eradication of Statelessness in Central Africa.[37] ECCAS has since pledged to adopt a Regional Action Plan, guided by the N'Djamena Initiative, in 2020.[38] West African States made more pledges at UNHCR's 'High Level Segment' (HLS) on Statelessness in 2019 than any other region in the world, followed by Southern Africa.[39]

Overall, the collective significance of these initiatives is to establish political recognition of the problem of statelessness on the African continent, as well as legal guidance on the steps to be taken to eradicate it. While implementation is always a challenge, the commitments made are based on an understanding of the citizenship issues created by Africa's colonial past, and the need to resolve the status of the many millions of Africans whose nationality is currently undetermined. This recognition is all the more important in the context of rapid roll-out of new identification systems, often undertaken without the necessary reforms to nationality laws and procedures that would ensure that they operate to include (as argued) or to exclude.

Pledges by African States at
UNHCR High Level Segment on Statelessness

The significant progress achieved over the past few years in putting statelessness on the agenda of states in the African region was evidenced by the impressive rate of participation in UNHCR's High Level Segment on Statelessness convened as part of its Executive Committee meeting in October 2019. 34 of the 48 countries in the region (equivalent to 70%) made a 'Pledge' on the occasion of this event, together accounting for more than half of the total tally of pledges made by states. Importantly, many of these pledges were for concrete action, including 17 countries promising to enact reforms to their

---

[35] Declaration of International Conference on the Great Lakes Region (ICGLR) Member States on the Eradication of Statelessness (2017) available at: https://www.refworld.org/docid/59e9cb8c4.html.

[36] UNHCR, Results of the High-Level Segment on Statelessness (2019) available at: https://www.unhcr.org/ibelong/results-of-the-high-level-segment-on-statelessness/.

[37] N'Djamena Initiative on the Eradication of Statelessness in Central Africa (2018) available at: https://data2.unhcr.org/en/documents/download/67429.

[38] UNHCR, Results of the High-Level Segment on Statelessness (2019) available at: https://www.unhcr.org/ibelong/results-of-the-high-level-segment-on-statelessness/.

nationality laws to address the drivers of statelessness. Six countries pledged to amend gender discriminatory provisions, such as eSwatini that committed "to undertake national consultations on gender equality in nationality laws and initiate the necessary reforms to uphold citizens' equal ability to confer nationality on spouses and children by end of 2024". Others pledged to address gaps in the legislation, for instance to fulfil every child's right to a nationality, such as the Central African Republic pledge, by the end of 2021, to insert a provision providing for grant of nationality at birth to children born on the territory who would otherwise be stateless. There were also pledges to address the exclusion of minority groups from citizenship, for instance by Kenya ("By 2020, recognize and register Kenyan citizens members of the Shona community, who qualify for citizenship under the law") and Uganda ("By 2024, ensure that the Maragoli, Benet, Ugandan-Asian and other unrecognised communities present in Uganda since before 1926 are recognised as citizens of Uganda"). Other forms of action were also pledged, including data collection (21 countries, three of which pledged to include a relevant question in the next national population census); accession to the statelessness conventions (11 to the 1954 Convention and 15 to the 1961 Convention); the adoption or implementation of National Action Plans (17 countries) and the introduction of Statelessness Determination Procedures (11 countries). If such progress is achieved in the coming 3-5 years, this would mean considerable change to the picture of statelessness in Africa.

CIVIL SOCIETY ENGAGEMENT

Civil society networks and organisations in Africa have made significant contributions through advocacy towards the eradication of statelessness in Africa, at continental, regional and national levels. Organisations supporting the Citizenship Rights in Africa Initiative (CRAI),[40] an informal continental network of NGOs working on issues related to nationality and statelessness, have engaged with the African Union (AU) and its regional intergovernmental bodies, especially in relation to the draft protocol. At the 2019 HLS, African NGOs and networks made 35 pledges aimed at the eradication of statelessness in Africa through advocacy; data

---

[40] See list of organisations working on the right to a nationality at http://citizenshiprightsafrica.org/network.

collection; awareness-raising; capacity building and legal assistance. In Southern Africa, local CSOs have collaborated to form the Southern African Nationality Network (SANN),[41] and work is underway to establish an East African network.

Kenyan civil society has led campaigns that have resulted in the decision of the Kenyan government to recognise some formerly stateless groups as Kenyan; while in South Africa, NGOs have mobilised to litigate children's rights to birth registration and nationality. African NGOs also played an important role in the development of African jurisprudence on the right to nationality, most notably the African Court's first decision on nationality, *Anudo v United Republic of Tanzania*.[42] Civil society advocacy also contributed greatly, alongside UNHCR, to the decision of the Pan African Parliament to add the right to nationality to its agenda and support efforts to eradicate statelessness in Africa.[43] In November 2019, the Fourth African Judicial Dialogue, convened by the African Court on Human and Peoples' Rights to discuss contemporary human rights issues, highlighted the issue of statelessness, the importance of the draft protocol, and the role of the judiciary.[44]

The Citizenship Rights in Africa website, (re-)launched in the second half of 2016, offers an impressive database of news articles, reports, legislation and jurisprudence about nationality law, identification and statelessness in Africa. It is searchable by country, theme, and type of media, serving as a key resource for all those engaged in efforts towards the realisation of the right to a nationality in Africa.[45]

YASAH KIMEI

"It is important that work on "legal identity for all" emphasises "for all" — those who could be left behind."

Yasah has been personally affected by lack of documentation and discriminatory application systems. He now works as 'Programme Administrator" with the Nubian Human Rights Forum in Kenya. He is an activist and human rights defender working in Kibera on citizenship and nationality as well as

---

[41] http://sann.africa/

[42] 'Africa's Human Rights Court Strengthens Protections for the Right to Nationality' Open Society Foundations, 28 March 2018 http://citizenshiprightsafrica.org/africas-human-rights-court-strengthens-protections-for-the-right-to-nationality/

[43] 'Report on the Workshop on the Right to Nationality in Africa', Pan-African Parliament, 9 August 2017 http://citizenshiprightsafrica.org/pan-african-parliament-report-on-the-workshop-on-the-right-to-nationality-in-africa/

[44] Final Communique Fourth African Judicial Dialogue, 30 October – 1 November 2019, Kampala, Uganda, African Court on Human and Peoples' Rights, 7 November 2019 http://citizenshiprightsafrica.org/final-communique-fourth-african-judicial-dialogue-30-october-1-november-2019-kampala-uganda/

[45] See http://citizenshiprightsafrica.org/.

gender-based violence, assisting a team of paralegals to help others overcome discrimination and obtain documentation of citizenship.

COUNTRY PROFILES

To complement the regional overview of the state of statelessness in Africa, the following sections explore the situation at national level in greater detail, in four countries where there are significant challenges and interesting recent developments, in fulfilling the right to a nationality for all: Côte d'Ivoire, Kenya, South Africa and Zimbabwe.

Cote d'Ivoire

The Ivorian Nationality Code is highly restrictive. In order to acquire Ivorian nationality at birth, at least one parent of the individual must be an Ivorian citizen. Despite the state's ratification of the 1961 Convention in 2013, the law does not offer protection to otherwise stateless children born on the territory and the provisions that provide for the possibility of deprivation of nationality fail to include a safeguard against statelessness. The law is also discriminatory on the basis of gender and disability: a woman who has acquired Ivorian nationality through naturalisation cannot confer nationality upon her children unless her spouse has died, and naturalisation is only available to persons without mental or physical handicaps.[46] However, in the October 2019 High-Level Segment, Côte D'Ivoire pledged to grant nationality to otherwise stateless children born on the territory, as well as reforming the nationality law to make it more gender-equal.

At the end of 2017, Côte d'Ivoire estimated the stateless population to be around 700,000.[47] Statelessness (and risk thereof) is particularly problematic among descendants of pre-independence migrants - such as the Fula people - who were brought into the country during colonial times to work on plantations and did not receive nationality when the country gained independence.[48] Despite having been

---

[46] Institute on Statelessness and Inclusion and la Coalition de la société civile de lutte contre l'apatridie, 'Joint Submission to the Human Rights Council at the 33rd Session of the Universal Periodic Review: Côte D'Ivoire' (4 October 2018), available at https://files.institutesi.org/UPR33_Cote_dIvoire.pdf.

[47] UNHCR, 'The Lost Children of Côte D'Ivoire', available at https://www.unhcr.org/ibelong/the-lost-children-of-cote-divoire/.

[48] UNHCR, 'Cattle herders face a life of limbo in Côte D'Ivoire', available at https://www.unhcr.org/news/stories/2019/5/5cd2e5a44/cattle-herders-face-life-limbo-cote-divoire.html.

in the country for generations, historical migrants and their descendants still have no nationality.[49]

Another group at risk of statelessness are foundlings (abandoned children), who are not entitled nationality by law and must comply with the normal birth registration procedures, which can add an additional barrier to acquisition of nationality.[50] UNHCR estimates that there are as many as 300,000 stateless people living in Côte d'Ivoire because of this phenomenon.[51] In 2018, a landmark court decision granted nationality to five children, and a judge in Soubre subsequently followed that decision and issued nationality certificates to an additional six children.[52] However, granting nationality to foundlings *ad hoc* through court decisions does not offer a holistic and appropriate solution to the issue.

Birth registration is a prerequisite for Ivorian nationality, but all births must be registered within three months, and late registrations fall under local courts, with attendant higher expenses. Public servants lack proper training on how to register new-born babies and are often accused of corruption and extortion, while the general public is ill-informed about birth registration procedures.[53] As a result, only 65% of children under the age of five have been registered at birth.[54]

In August 2018, UNHCR, the Government of Côte d'Ivoire and the National Institute of Statistics launched a project to map and improve data on statelessness in the country. This nation-wide mapping is aligned to the Banjul Plan of Action of the Economic Community of West African States (ECOWAS) on the eradication of statelessness 2017 − 2024.[55] The results were yet to be published at the time of writing.

Kenya

According to UNHCR, by the end of 2018 there were 18,500 stateless people in Kenya.[56] Today, a significant number of Kenyans transition into adulthood without

---

[49] Institute on Statelessness and Inclusion and la Coalition de la société civile de lutte contre l'apatridie, 'Joint Submission to the Human Rights Council at the 33rd Session of the Universal Periodic Review: Côte D'Ivoire' (4 October 2018), available at https://files.institutesi.org/UPR33_Cote_dIvoire.pdf.

[50] Ibid.

[51] UNHCR, 'The Lost Children of Côte D'Ivoire', available at https://www.unhcr.org/ibelong/the-lost-children-of-cote-divoire/.

[52] UNHCR, 'Campaign Update, January - March 2019' (March 2019), available at https://www.refworld.org/docid/5ca5bfc77.html [accessed 8 November 2019].

[53] Institute on Statelessness and Inclusion and la Coalition de la société civile de lutte contre l'apatridie, 'Joint Submission to the Human Rights Council at the 33rd Session of the Universal Periodic Review: Côte D'Ivoire' (4 October 2018), available at https://files.institutesi.org/UPR33_Cote_dIvoire.pdf.

[54] UNICEF, 'Country Profiles: Cote d'Ivoire', available at https://data.unicef.org/country/civ/#.

[55] UNHCR, 'UNHCR launch mapping of statelessness in Côte d'Ivoire' (Sep 2018), available https://www.unhcr.org/blogs/mapping-statelessness-cote-divoire/.

[56] UNHCR, 'UNHCR Statistics – The World in Numbers', available at http://popstats.unhcr.org/en/overview.

identification documents due to gaps in registration, identification problems, and citizenship procedures.[57] Kenya's law specifies that stateless persons who have lived in Kenya continuously since its independence (1963), and their descendants, can acquire Kenyan citizenship by registration. Foreigners who arrived after independence, but who lived legally in Kenya continuously for seven years, are also eligible under certain conditions.[58] In 2016, the Kenyan Government recognised the Makonde, an ethnic group native to the region, as Kenyan citizens, also extending the deadline for stateless persons present in Kenya since independence and their descendants to register for nationality from 2016 to 2019.[59] While these developments signal that the issue of statelessness has gained governmental attention, a significant number of people in Kenya remain stateless – for example, the Shona community, who arrived in Kenya 70 years ago, remain unregistered, as well as members of the Pemba, Barundi, Nubian and Nyarwanda communities.[60] Encouragingly, in the UNHCR October 2019 High-Level Segment, Kenya pledged to recognise and registers members of the Shona community as Kenyan citizens.

At a conference in April 2019 which discussed the eradication of statelessness in the Great Lakes region,[61] the key outcomes for Kenya included the re-establishment of a task force on statelessness; the validation and implementation of the National Action Plan to eradicate statelessness (that was drafted already in 2017); recognition of the Shona community as Kenyan citizens; a new birth and death registration act that provides safeguards to prevent statelessness; and accession to the statelessness conventions.

Meanwhile, in early 2019, Kenya introduced a new digital identification system, called the National Integrated Identity Management System (NIIMS). There are worries that unregistered individuals might be left out and that this could lead to further *disenfranchisement* of Kenyan citizens and aggravate the exclusion of stateless people in Kenya because those left without a *Huduma Namba* would be unable to access public services.[62] Responding to litigation raising concerns over data privacy,

---

[57] Kenya Human Rights Commission, 'A Call to Action to End Statelessness in Kenya' (24 January 2019), available at https://www.khrc.or.ke/2015-03-04-10-37-01/blog/675-a-call-to-action-to-end-statelessness-in-kenya.html.

[58] UNHCR, '"This is our Home": Stateless Minorities and their search for citizenship' (2017), available at https://www.unhcr.org/ibelong/wp-content/uploads/UNHCR_EN2_2017IBELONG_Report_ePub.pdf.

[59] Ibid.

[60] Kenya Human Rights Commission, 'A Call to Action to End Statelessness in Kenya' (24 January 2019), available at https://www.khrc.or.ke/2015-03-04-10-37-01/blog/675-a-call-to-action-to-end-statelessness-in-kenya.html; B. Manby, 'Statelessness and Citizenship in the East African Community', *UNHCR* (September 2018), available at http://citizenshiprightsafrica.org/wp-content/uploads/2018/11/Statelessness-and-citizenship-in-the-East-African-Community.pdf.

[61] UNHCR, 'Ministerial Conference on the Eradication of Statelessness in the Great Lakes Region', available at https://www.unhcr.org/ibelong/wp-content/uploads/Great-Lakes-Region-Outcome-Document-of-the-Ministerial-Conference-on-the-Eradication-of-Statelessness-April-2019.docx

[62] Kenya Gazette Supplement No. 16 / (Acts No. 18) (4 January 2019), available at http://kenyalaw.org/kl/fileadmin/pdfdownloads/AmendmentActs/2018/StatuteLawMischellaneousNo18of2018.pdf.

registration in NIIMS as a precondition to access all public services and further discrimination of marginalised groups, the High Court of Kenya decided in April 2019 that the government could proceed with data collection, but that registration should be voluntary and access to services should not depend on enrolment.[63] Between April and May 2019, about 35 million Kenyans were registered.[64] However, in summer 2019, the Kenyan government drafted a new law governing NIIMS – the Huduma Bill - which disregards the High Court ruling. According to the proposed legislation, the Huduma Namba will be required to access public services such as universal healthcare, financial services, public schooling, application for a passport and more.[65] Criticisms of the bill include the monetary penalties and prison sentences for late birth and death registration, transacting without NIIMS and tampering with the number. On 30 January 2020, Kenya's High Court ruled that the implementation of NIIMS must be suspended until an appropriate legislative framework is put in place to deal with both data privacy issues and to ensure that the roll out is not discriminatory.[66] This ruling opens a new chapter for issues of documentation, digital ID and citizenship in Kenya and it remains to be seen what the impact is on statelessness and the right to a nationality in the country.

South Africa

South Africa is understood to have a substantial stateless population, although the country has no dedicated mechanism for identifying statelessness and no official statistics for statelessness exist.[67] South Africa has not ratified either statelessness convention, despite having pledged to do so.[68] The South African NGO Lawyers for Human Rights outlines groups at risk of statelessness, including the children of foreigners (predominantly from Zimbabwe), the children of South African nationals born abroad, orphans, abandoned children, unaccompanied foreign minors, victims of ID theft or duplication, children of undocumented parents, and communities in border areas, among others.[69] South Africa has been criticised for its restrictive and discriminatory nationality acquisition processes – perhaps most notably by 12 states in the 27th session of the Universal Period Review in 2017,[70] where criticism focussed

---

[63] Namati, 'Stopping the Digital ID Register in Kenya – A Stand Against Discrimination', available at https://namati.org/news-stories/stopping-the-digital-id-register-in-kenya-a-stand-against-discrimination/.

[64] V. Matinde, 'Kenya looks to enforce NIIMS registration' *Web Africa* (17 July 2019), available at http://www.itwebafrica.com/ict-and-governance/256-kenya/246159-kenya-looks-to-enforce-niims-registration.

[65] The Huduma Bill (2019), available at https://www.ict.go.ke/wp-content/uploads/2019/07/12-07-2019-The-Huduma-Bill-2019-2.pdf?mc_cid=ab69d4b274&mc_eid=%5BUNIQID%5D.

66 New York Times, *Kenya's High Court Delays National Biometric ID Program*, 31 January 2020, available at: https://www.nytimes.com/2020/01/31/world/africa/kenya-biometric-ID-registry.html.

[67] Lawyers for Human Rights and Institute on Statelessness and Inclusion, 'Joint Submission to the Human Rights Council at the 27th Session of the Universal Periodic Review: The Republic of South Africa' (22 September 2016), available at http://www.institutesi.org/SouthAfricaUPR2016.pdf.

[68] J. P. George, 'Statelessness and Nationality in South Africa' (2013), available at http://www.lhr.org.za/publications/statelessness-and-nationality-south-africa.

[69] Ibid.

[70] Lawyers for Human Rights, 'Press Statement: States ask South Africa to Give Rights to the Stateless', available at http://www.lhr.org.za/news/2017/press-statement-states-ask-south-africa-give-rights-stateless.

upon South Africa's Citizenship Act, which only grants citizenship to children if their birth has been registered. Therefore, although the right to nationality is enshrined in the South African Constitution, there are many children at risk of statelessness, including those whose parents are undocumented or without valid immigration status, foundlings, and unaccompanied foreign minors,[71] as well as children born abroad to South African parents.[72]

There were a number of positive high-profile court cases in 2018 regarding children and statelessness – for example, in *Naki v Director General Home Affairs*, the high court ruled that children born in South Africa have the right to access birth registration, regardless of their parents' legal status.[73] However, human rights groups, as well as refugee and children's rights organisations, expressed concern about an October 2018 government proposal to discontinue issuing birth certificates to foreign children, which would violate the South African Constitution and international law. In addition to difficulties relating to access to birth registration, South Africa prohibits dual citizenship and requires individuals to relinquish their non-South African citizenship in order to apply for South African citizenship. For Zimbabweans as well as for other foreign-born individuals, this creates a risk of statelessness both during the application process, as well as after, in the case of those whose applications have been rejected.[74] It is partly due to discrimination of non-nationals on the labour market that it is considered necessary to apply for South African citizenship, even when the applicant has the right to residency.

Stateless people in South Africa are at risk of long-term arbitrary detention, largely as a consequence of the country not recognising stateless individuals who do not qualify for refugee status.[75] Furthermore, around 700,000 persons have had their identity blocked following the issuance of multiple or duplicate identity numbers due to administrative mistakes, corruption and fraud.[76] Blocked identity occurs when a person's legal status is blocked on the Home Affairs system, meaning that they are not afforded basic rights such as voting, travelling or access to their bank account.

---

[71] Lawyers for Human Rights and Institute on Statelessness and Inclusion, 'Joint Submission to the Human Rights Council at the 27th Session of the Universal Periodic Review: The Republic of South Africa' (22 September 2016), available at http://www.institutesi.org/SouthAfricaUPR2016.pdf.

[72] J. P. George, 'Statelessness and Nationality in South Africa' (2013), available at http://www.lhr.org.za/publications/statelessness-and-nationality-south-africa.

[73] K. Mpofu, 'High Court rules children born in South Africa can be registered, regardless of their parents' legal status' *Ground Up* (28 August 2018), available at https://www.groundup.org.za/article/high-court-rules-all-children-born-south-africa-regardless-their-parents-legal-status-can-be-registered/.

[74] D. Brotman, 'The faces behind SA's citizenship nightmare', *Mail and Guardian* (5 July 2018), available at http://mg.co.za/article/2018-07-05-00-the-faces-behind-sas-citizenship-nightmare.

[75] Lawyers for Human Rights and Institute on Statelessness and Inclusion, 'Joint Submission to the Human Rights Council at the 27th Session of the Universal Periodic Review: The Republic of South Africa' (22 September 2016), available at http://www.institutesi.org/SouthAfricaUPR2016.pdf.

[76] Parliamentary Monitoring Group, 'Duplicate IDs, Uncollected IDs, Residence Permit backlog, Initial Permit Transformation Plan: progress report by Home Affairs' (13 August 2012), available at https://pmg.org.za/committee-meeting/14682/.

A plethora of documents is required to unblock identity, which many people do not possess, and this has left a considerable number stateless.[77]

Zimbabwe

In 2016, UNHCR estimated that Zimbabwe had a stateless population of 300,000,[78] which placed it as the country with the second largest reported population of stateless people in Africa. This number has not been updated since then, as "a study is being pursued to provide a revised estimate of statelessness figures".[79] Zimbabwe's high number of stateless persons is in part due to the key gap in the Zimbabwean nationality law, which lacks a safeguard to grant citizenship to children born stateless in the territory. The government also has yet to ratify the 1961 UN Convention on the Reduction of Statelessness and the Convention of the Rights of Migrant Workers and their Families, which provides some protection to migrant workers in terms of nationality.

Studies have shown that birth registration remains a significant problem, particularly in areas such as Matabeleland where almost 50% of children go unregistered, which poses a major risk of statelessness. In this regard, in 2019 the Zimbabwean Human Rights Commission has launched a national enquiry into the level of access to documentation for Zimbabweans.[80] However, this may still be a problem given that granting and revocation of citizenship is extremely politicised, and cases of refusal of passports and revocation of citizenship of political figures and commentators continue to surface.

In February 2019, the Cabinet approved the repeal of the Citizenship of Zimbabwe Act, replacing it with the Zimbabwe Citizenship Act as part of an ongoing process to align the bill with the provisions of the 2013 Constitution.[81] This new act allows dual nationality for Zimbabwean citizens by birth, and also establishes a Citizenship and Immigration Board which is authorised to administer the granting and revocation of citizenship by descent or registration, extending this power from one (the Registrar-General) to three administrators, but retaining a high degree of executive discretion.[82] Notably, the Bill increases the required 5 years of residence before naturalisation to 10 years, further restricting access to naturalisation.

---

[77] Lawyers for Human Rights, 'ID Blocking: A Growing Threat to Nationality', available at http://www.lhr.org.za/blog/2013/9/id-blocking-growing-threat-nationality.

[78] UNHCR, 'Global Trends: Forced Displacement in 2015'.

[79] UNHCR, 'Global Trends: Forced Displacement in 2018', p. 69.

[80] 'Zimbabwe Human Rights Commission launch national inquiry into issues around access to national documentation in Zimbabwe' *Kubatana* (20 March 2019), available at http://kubatana.net/2019/03/20/zimbabwe-human-rights-commission-launch-national-inquiry-into-issues-around-access-to-national-documentation-in-zimbabwe/.

[81] 'Zimbabwe: Cabinet Okays Citizenship Law Amendments to Bring Dual Citizenship' *All Africa* (27 February 2019), available at https://allafrica.com/stories/201902270121.html.

[82] Zimbabwe Citizenship Bill (2018), available at http://www.justice.gov.zw/imt/wp-content/uploads/2018/06/Zimbabwean-Citizenship-Bill.pdf.

STATELESSNESS IN THE AMERICAS

OVERVIEW OF STATELESSNESS IN THE REGION

The Americas has been heralded as the region which promises to lead the way in the eradication of statelessness.[1] This is based on the understanding that the number of stateless people in the region is relatively low and that nationality law frameworks in the region already provide a combination of *jus soli* and *jus sanguinis* provisions. *Jus soli*, in particular, helps to ensure that any case of statelessness lasts, at most, no more than one generation because it provides access to nationality to all persons born on a State's territory regardless of the nationality - or statelessness - of their parents.[2] The Americas is also a region in which the right to a nationality enjoys a strong position in domestic legal frameworks,[3] and legislative reforms are helping to improve the identification and protection of stateless persons as well as reduce the risk of new cases of statelessness from emerging.[4]

Nevertheless, statelessness remains a significant phenomenon in the Americas – more so than the current statistical picture would suggest. At the end of 2018, a total of only 6,892 stateless persons were reported in the region, according to data

---

[1] UN High Commissioner for Refugees (UNHCR), Remarks by Commissioner António Guterres, 'Out of the Shadows: Ending Statelessness in the Americas Event' (18 November 2014), available at http://unhcrwashington.org/resources/video-gallery/out-shadows-ending-statelessness-americas-event

[2] Americas Network on Nationality and Statelessness, 'Annual Report' (2015), available at http://static1.squarespace.com/static/55eb3459e4b021abebfec2bd/t/570dc6aa04426215739ab87c/146052063710//Red+ANA+Annual+Report+2015.

[3] For example, there are constitutional protections against deprivation of nationality in many countries in the region. In Canada, legal provisions that were previously introduced to give the government greater power to revoke citizenship from people convicted of crimes such as terrorism were repealed in 2017 (Government of Canada, 'Changes to the Citizenship Act as a result of Bill C-6' (22 August 2018), available at https://www.canada.ca/en/immigration-refugees-citizenship/news/2017/10/changes_to_the_citizenshipactasaresultofbillc-6.html). Moreover, in the case of *Maslenjak v. United States*, the US Supreme Court found that the government cannot revoke a person's U.S. citizenship for lying to immigration authorities, unless the withheld facts would have resulted in denial of citizenship (B. Chappel, 'Supreme Court overturns Lower Court on grounds for stripping U.S. Citizenship' *NPR* (22 June 2017), available at https://choice.npr.org/index.html?origin=https://www.npr.org/sections/thetwo-way/2017/06/22/533954802/supreme-court-overturns-ruling-on-stripping-u-s-citizenship).

[4] For example, Brazil's draft legislation to grant nationality to people not considered nationals of any other state, in compliance with the 1954 Convention and Suriname's 2014 amendment of Law 1975 on Nationality and Residence removing gender inequality and giving equal rights to women to pass on nationality to their children and spouses. See also, UN High Commissioner for Refugees (UNHCR), 'Submission by the United Nations High Commissioner for Refugees for the Office of the High Commissioner for Human Rights' Compilation Report - Universal Periodic Review: Brazil' (November 2011), p. 2. available at http://www.refworld.org/docid/4ed361722.html; UN High Commissioner for Refugees (UNHCR), 'UNHCR applauds Suriname for ensuring gender equality in nationality laws' (2014), available at www.unhcr.org/53d20b756.html.

compiled by UNHCR.[5] Yet, numbers are incomplete and lack precision, as a result of factors such as the absence of stateless determination procedures in many countries, the lack of accurate data due to countries not including statelessness within their statistics, and non-standardised birth registration processes in remote areas.[6]

Moreover, since 2015, UNHCR stopped reporting on the number of stateless persons in the Dominican Republic (DR), which is the country that previously reported the highest stateless population in the Americas. In 2015, UNHCR reported a total stateless population of 136,585 in the Americas, of which 133,770 were living in the Dominican Republic.[7] As discussed below, the situation in the Dominican Republic remains unresolved, however update figures have not been released and in the meantime this population is not captured in the official statistics. In early 2020, a new report on statelessness in the United States estimated the number of people affected by or at risk of statelessness to be around 218,000, which is far larger than was previously assumed.[8] This population is also unaccounted for in the overall regional (and global) data on statelessness. Elsewhere in the region, in countries where figures are reported, there has been a slight *increase* in the count for the number of stateless persons, from 2,815 in 2015 to 3,100 in 2018. This increase likely responds to awareness raising efforts and the establishment of statelessness determination procedures having an impact on the identification of stateless persons and thereby state reporting.

As such identification and mapping efforts continue, the official tally for the number of stateless persons in the Americas can be expected to rise significantly as it is clear from these examples that statelessness remains unreported or underreported in most countries in the region. Factors such as discriminatory nationality laws,[9] gaps in *jus soli* regimes and in the registration and documentation of populations,[10] and mass migration, also combine to generate new cases of statelessness in the region. As discussed below, documentation and citizenship issues that have come to light in the context of the humanitarian crisis in Venezuela – which has led to over three million

---

[5] UN High Commissioner for Refugees (UNHCR), 'Global Trends: Forced Displacement in 2018' (2018), available at https://www.unhcr.org/5d08d7ee7.pdf.

[6] For a detailed analysis and critique of the challenges and gaps in statistical reporting on statelessness, see Institute on Statelessness and Inclusion, *The World's Stateless Report* (2014), available at http://www.institutesi.org/worldsstateless.pdf.

[7] UN High Commissioner for Refugees (UNHCR), 'Global Trends: Forced Displacement in 2015' (2015), available at http://www.unhcr.org/576408cd7.pdf.

[8] Centre for Migration Studies, 'Statelessness in the United States: A Study to Estimate and Profile the US Stateless Population' (January 2020), available at https://cmsny.org/wp-content/uploads/2020/01/StatelessnessReportFinal.pdf.

[9] Barbados and the Bahamas, for example, restrict the right of women to transmit their citizenship to a child born abroad. See further: https://equalnationalityrights.org/countries/americas.

[10] Juliana Vengoechea Barrios, 'Do jus soli regimes always protect children from statelessness? Some reflection from the Americas', in Institute on Statelessness and Inclusion, *World's Stateless Report* (2014), available at: http://children.worldsstateless.org/3/safeguarding-against-childhood-statelessness/do-jus-soli-regimes-always-protect-children-from-statelessness-some-reflection-from-the-americas.html.

people fleeing to Colombia (1.4 million), Peru (over half a million), Ecuador (over 220,000), Argentina (130,000), Chile (over 100,000) and Brazil (85,000) – make it a case in point that eradicating statelessness in the Americas remains a challenging goal to achieve.[11]

Preventing childhood statelessness in the Americas

In a region where *jus soli* is the predominant means to acquire citizenship at birth – a doctrine widely understood to be effective in preventing statelessness among children – it is interesting to discover that childhood statelessness is nonetheless a phenomenon that requires ongoing attention in the Americas. As exposed, for example, in a study of Brazil, Chile and Colombia published in 2017, "even facially generous *jus soli* provisions are only as effective as their implementation, and do not guarantee nationality to everyone".[12] The study concluded that where there are exceptions to or conditions for the enjoyment of jus soli citizenship, or where other policy shortcomings, administrative deficiencies or obstacles to birth registration come into play, children face significant barriers in accessing nationality and may end up stateless. Legal counselling and strategic litigation have proven to be important techniques to breaking down these barriers and asserting the right of every child to a nationality – as shown by the experience in Chile, for instance, where such work eventually led to a government commitment to ensure that children were not missing out on citizenship.[13] However, the issue of childhood statelessness became of renewed and urgent concern in the context of the humanitarian crisis in Venezuela, which has caused more than three million people to flee to other countries in the region. Almost half have been taken in by neighbouring Colombia: over 1.4 million people have arrived from Venezuela since 2015 and an estimated 25,000 children have been born to Venezuelan

---

[11] UNHCR, 'Number of refugees and migrants from Venezuela reaches 3 million' (8 November 2018), available at https://www.unhcr.org/news/press/2018/11/5be4192b4/number-refugees-migrants-venezuela-reaches-3-million.html.

[12] Juliana Vengoechea Barrios, "Born in the Americas. The Promise and Practice of Nationality Laws in Brazil, Chile, and Colombia" Open Society Foundations (2017) available at https://www.justiceinitiative.org/uploads/8c4136e4-c25d-4255-9afd-d66d20e71da1/born-in-the-americas-20170323.pdf.

[13] Delfina Lawson and Macarena Rodriguez, 'The role of Legal Clinics and local communities in securing the right to a nationality in Chile', in Institute on Statelessness and Inclusion, *World's Stateless Report* (2014), available at: http://children.worldsstateless.org/3/litigating-against-childhood-statelessness/the-role-of-legal-clinics-and-local-communities-in-securing-the-right-to-a-nationality-in-chile.html.

parents on Colombian soil.[14] Given the reported challenges Venezuelan citizens have faced as a result of the crisis in acquiring documentation and accessing (functioning) consular assistance abroad, the alarm was raised that children born outside Venezuela may struggle to have their nationality recognised or documented. This factor, combined with a restriction in the Colombian jus soli rules that would discount many of these children from birth-right citizenship in Colombia, prompted concern of a risk of a major new situation of childhood statelessness. Responding to this concern, raised in both domestic and international advocacy efforts, in August 2019, Colombian President Ivan Duque announced that Colombia would amend its nationality law to allow children born to Venezuelan refugees between August 2015 and August 2021 to receive Colombian nationality if they are born stateless or at risk of becoming stateless.[15] Colombia's constitution, however, remains fundamentally unchanged and so further efforts are needed to put in place a full and lasting safeguard to prevent cases of childhood statelessness occurring on Colombian territory. Encouragingly, there were further commitments made towards fulfilling every child's right to a nationality at UNHCR's 2019 High-Level Segment on Statelessness, with six countries from the Americas making pledges on improving birth registration procedures, and three countries making pledges on reducing childhood statelessness.

REGIONAL STANDARDS AND INTERGOVERNMENTAL COMMITMENTS

In the Americas, the established regional human rights system (the Inter-American system) is composed of two bodies: the Inter-American Commission on Human Rights (IACommHR) and the Inter-American Court of Human Rights (IACtHR), created under the auspices of the Organisation of American States (OAS). Article 20 of the American Convention on Human Rights (ACHR) protects the right to a

---

[14] S. Held, 'Venezuelan Crisis: Stateless Children facing limbo in Colombia' *Al Jazeera* (21 August 2019), available at https://www.aljazeera.com/ajimpact/venezuelan-crisis-stateless-children-facing-limbo-colombia-190821140410615.html.

[15] M. Janetsky, 'No country to call home: some babies born in Colombia to Venezuelan parents lack birthright citizenship' *USA Today* (August 12 2019), available at https://eu.usatoday.com/story/news/world/2019/08/11/birthright-citizenship-babies-venezuela-migrants-colombia/1887388001/.

nationality.[16] This provision, the accompanying case law of the Inter-American Court and the work of the Inter-American Commission provide a robust legal framework for the protection of the right to a nationality.

Cases brought before the IACtHR, even if few in number,[17] have reinforced guarantees against statelessness which establish limits to State discretion in this regard.[18] For example, in the case of *Ivcher Bronstein v. Peru,* the IACtHR ruled that the deprivation of nationality of Mr Bronstein, which rendered him stateless, was a violation of articles 20(1) and 20(3) of the ACHR, which set out the right to a nationality and the prohibition of arbitrary deprivation of nationality.[19] In two other landmark cases, *Yean and Bosico v. Dominican Republic* and *Expelled Haitians and Dominicans v. Dominican Republic*, the court fleshed out the obligations held by States in respect of the right to a nationality. In *Yean and Bosico v. Dominican Republic,*[20] the court ruled that the denial of birth certificates to two girls born to Haitian migrant fathers and Dominican national mothers was arbitrary and discriminatory, concluding that the denial of birth certificates amounted to a breach of Article 20 of the ACHR. Importantly, the court also concluded that denying the girls nationality and leaving them stateless placed them in a "situation of extreme vulnerability" which led to other rights violations.[21] In *Expelled Haitians and Dominicans v. Dominican Republic,*[22] the court affirmed that the failure of the DR to grant citizenship to otherwise stateless children born on the territory was an arbitrary denial of the right to nationality. The court also found that the 2013 Constitutional Court decision and the promulgation of Law 169-14 violated equal protection under the law and right to nationality.[23] In 2019, the IACtHR issued a resolution of compliance on *Girls Yean*

---

[16] Article 20 ACHR reads: "1. Every person has the right to a nationality. 2. Every person has the right to the nationality of the state in whose territory he was born if he does not have the right to any other nationality. 3. No one shall be arbitrarily deprived of his nationality or of the right to change it. See also F. Lapova, 'Comentario al Artículo 20 de la Convención Americana' in E. Alonso Regueira (ed), *La Convención Americana de Derechos Humanos y su proyección en el Derecho Argentino* (2013), p. 333-353 available at: http://www.derecho.uba.ar/publicaciones/libros/pdf/la-cadh-y-su-proyeccion-en-el-derecho-argentino/020-lavopa-nacionalidad-la-cadh-y-su-proyeccion-en-el-da.pdf and M.J. Recalde Vela, 'How far has the protection of the right to nationality under international human rights law progressed from 1923 until the present day? An analysis of this progress against the backdrop of the 5 elements of Article 20 of the American Convention on Human Rights' (2014) LLM thesis, Tilburg University, available at http://arno.uvt.nl/show.cgi?fid=136225.

[17] Inter-American Court of Human Rights, 'Cuadernillo de Jurisprudencia de la Corte Interamericana de Derechos Humanos N° 2: Migrantes' (2015) pp 12-14, available at https://www.scribd.com/document/270035590/N-2-MIGRANTES-Cuadernillo-de-Jurisprudencia-de-la-CIDH.

[18] See also *The perpetuation of childhood statelessness in the Dominican Republic* by David Baluarte in Chapter 12.

[19] Inter-American Court of Human Rights, *Ivcher Bronstein v. Peru* (2001), available at https://static1.squarespace.com/static/55eb3459e4b021abebfec2bd/t/57b1dfe21b631ba919057b70/14712749 79362/Inter-American+Court%2C+Case+Ivcher+Bronstein+vs.+Peru.pdf.

[20] Inter-American Court of Human Rights, *Girls Yean and Bosico v. Dominican Republic* (2005), no. 12,189.

[21] Ibid, para. 175.

[22] Inter-American Court of Human Rights, *Expelled Haitians and Dominicans v. Dominican Republic* (2014).

[23] For a more detailed analysis of this case, see D. Baluarte, ' The perpetuation of childhood statelessness in the Dominican Republic' *World's Stateless Children*, available at http://children.worldsstateless.org/3/litigating-against-childhood-statelessness/the-perpetuation-of-childhood-statelessness-in-the-dominican-republic.html.

and Bosico v. Dominican Republic, and *Case of the Expelled Haitians v. Dominican Republic,*[24] declaring that the Dominican Republic failed to comply with its obligations to execute pending reparations measures, and ordering the State to adopt necessary measures such as, *inter alia,* adopting domestic legislation allowing the facilitation of the process of acquiring nationality through late declaration of birth, and granting necessary documentation to certify identity and nationality.

The IACommHR has also played an active part in promoting action to address statelessness in the Dominican Republic and elsewhere. A Working Group on Implementation of Human Rights Policies in the Dominican Republic,[25] in operation for a year between March 2018 and March 2019, had the task of monitoring recommendations and commitments related to the acquisition of nationality, among other issues. It did not however deliver any concrete outcomes in relation to the implementation of these rulings. In a 2016 report by the IACommHR – issued under the auspices of the Special Rapporteurship on the Rights of Migrants – a detailed overview of regional standards for the protection of vulnerable groups in the Americas is elaborated, including stateless persons.[26] The IACommHR has also welcomed legal action taken by Colombia (child's right to nationality), Panama (protection granted to stateless persons; opportunity for naturalisation), Paraguay (new law for protection and naturalisation of stateless people) and Uruguay (statelessness determination procedure) to prevent statelessness, calling on states to keep adopting measures to ensure an effective enjoyment of right to nationality and to prevent and eradicate statelessness in the Americas.[27]

Several resolutions of the OAS General Assembly have also urged states to take action against statelessness, including calling for the review national legislation to prevent and reduce statelessness, accessions to the statelessness conventions, and cooperation with UNHCR.[28] In 2014, the Brazil Declaration and Plan of Action was adopted by 28 countries and three territories in Latin America and the

---

[24] IACtHR, 'Caso de las niñas yean y bosico y caso de personas dominicanas y haitianas expulsadas vs. república dominicana' [Spanish] (12 March 2019), available at
http://www.corteidh.or.cr/docs/supervisiones/yean_12_03_19.pdf.
[25] 'IACHR Installs Working Group on Implementation of Human Rights Policies in the Dominican Republic' *Relief Web* (3 April 2018), available at https://reliefweb.int/report/dominican-republic/iachr-installs-working-group-implementation-human-rights-policies.
[26] See Inter-American Commission on Human Rights' Special Rapporteurship on the Rights of Migrants, 'Human Rights of Migrants, Refugees, Stateless Persons, Victims of Human Trafficking and Internally Displaced Persons: Norms and Standards of the Inter-American Human Rights System (Human Mobility, Norms and Standards)' (2016) OEA/Ser.L/V/II Doc. 46/15, available at
http://www.oas.org/en/iachr/reports/pdfs/HumanMobility.pdf.
[27] OAS, 'IACHR Welcomes Actions to Protect the Right to a Nationality and to Prevent Statelessness in the Region' (February 25 2019), available at
https://www.oas.org/en/iachr/media_center/PReleases/2019/042.asp.
[28] Organisation of American States, General Assembly (RES. 2826) (June 4 2014), available at
https://static1.squarespace.com/static/55eb3459e4b021abebfec2bd/t/57b1e04e1b631ba919058080/14712750 86862/OAS%2C+General+Assembly%2CRES.+2826.pdf.

Caribbean.[29] Within this, Chapter six is dedicated to statelessness and sets our several recommendations for action as part of an 'eradicating statelessness program', including (a) accession to the statelessness conventions, (b) the harmonisation of internal legislation and practice on nationality with international standards, (c) the establishment of effective statelessness status determination procedures and (d) the adoption of legal protection frameworks that guarantee the rights of stateless persons.[30] In 2018, Argentina became first country in the Americas to join the "Towards Zero Statelessness" program created by UNHCR,[31] which measures progress that States make towards ending statelessness, including those under the "Eradicating Statelessness" program in the Brazil Plan of Action. Costa Rica and Brazil also made progress in 2018 by granting citizenship to formerly stateless people.[32] Further progress also looks set to be made following UNHCR's High-Level Segment on Statelessness in October 2019, where 10 countries made pledges[33] on issues concerning birth registration, statelessness determination procedures, awareness raising, conducting of studies, reduction of childhood statelessness, capacity building, and one pledge to amend the nationality law (Haiti).

Finally, the level of accession to the 1954 and 1961 Conventions on statelessness is high in the Americas, with the majority of countries in Latin America being States parties to both conventions. Accessions to the conventions over the past three years include Colombia (1954 Convention, 2019) Haiti (1954 and 1961 Conventions, 2018) and Chile (1954 and 1961 Conventions, 2018). Yet, it is important to note that the countries that are known to have significant problems of statelessness – such as the Dominican Republic, Venezuela, and the United States – are not States parties to either convention.

---

[29] These were Antigua and Barbuda, Argentina, Bahamas, Barbados, Belize, Bolivia, Brazil, Cayman Islands, Chile, Colombia, Costa Rica, Cuba, Curacao, El Salvador, Ecuador, Guatemala, Guyana, Haiti, Honduras, Jamaica, Mexico, Nicaragua, Panama, Paraguay, Peru, Saint Lucia, Suriname, Trinidad and Tobago, Turks and Caicos, Uruguay and Venezuela. 'Brazil Plan of Action', available at
https://www.acnur.org/fileadmin/Documentos/BDL/2014/9865.pdf?file=t3/fileadmin/Documentos/BDL/20 14/9865.
[30] Brazil Declaration (3 December 2014), available at
https://www.acnur.org/fileadmin/Documentos/BDL/2014/9865.pdf?file=t3/fileadmin/Documentos/BDL/20 14/9865.
[31] UNHCR, 'Programa "Erradicación de la Apatridia" Mecanismo de Evaluación y Seguimiento "Hacia Cero Apatridia"', [Spanish] (September 2018), available at https://www.refworld.org.es/docid/5bacf9914.html.
[32] Americas Network on Nationality and Statelessness, 'Annual Report: 2018', available at
https://static1.squarespace.com/static/55eb3459e4b021abebfec2bd/t/5ccae1b9e6a9f30001b6f1bb/155679993 7700/FINAL+30+04++English+version.pdf.
[33] Argentina, Belize, Bolivia, Colombia, Costa Rica, Guyana, Haiti, Panama, USA, and Uruguay.

United Stateless:
An NGO of stateless people, for stateless people

United Stateless is a grassroots organisation both formed and run by stateless people in the U.S., with the mission to build and inspire community among those affected by statelessness, and to advocate for their human rights. The U.S. lacks a legal framework to identify and address statelessness, rendering the issue largely invisible. United Stateless came to be as a result, initially, of "a simple conversation between several stateless persons who found each other through social media or by tracking a few and far-between newspaper articles about individual cases".[34] This quickly led to a desire by those who understand the situation first hand to build a community and advocate jointly to improve the situation of those affected. Established in 2018, United Stateless' goals now include empowering the stateless, raising awareness both nationally and globally, and advocating for legislative changes – including changes in domestic nationality law, accession to statelessness conventions, and the creation of a statelessness determination procedure. Their work includes networking with international and national NGOs, governments, the media, immigration law practitioners, and others.[35] One such example is the ground-breaking collaboration with Columbia University's School of International and Public Affairs in November 2019, where United Stateless organised an event that raised awareness of legal, political, and academic issues regarding statelessness.[36]

CIVIL SOCIETY ENGAGEMENT

The Americas Network on Nationality and Statelessness (or Red ANA, the network's acronym in Spanish which has become its shorthand name) was launched in November 2014 together with UNHCR's #IBelong Campaign. It is a network of civil society organisations, academic initiatives and individual experts working on

---

[34] See further https://www.unitedstateless.org/about-us. See also this early interview with Nikolai Levasov, one of the founders of United Stateless, in the August 2017 monthly bulletin of the Institute on Statelessness and Inclusion, available at: https://files.institutesi.org/stateless_bulletin_2017-08.pdf.

[35] United Stateless, 'About Us', available at https://www.unitedstateless.org/about-us.

[36] '2019 Migration Symposium – Statelessness & Belonging in a Globalized World', available at https://www.eventbrite.com/e/2019-migration-symposium-statelessness-belonging-in-a-globalized-world-tickets-79474409097.

resolving statelessness in the Americas. Starting its activities in earnest in 2015, Red ANA has helped to unite civil society efforts in the Americas towards the prevention of statelessness in the region and the promotion of the #IBelong Campaign's goals.

Civil society in the region has continued to work towards the establishment of formal statelessness determination and naturalisation. Since 2017 - in addition to Ecuador and Brazil, which were the only States that had such procedures - Costa Rica, Mexico, Uruguay, Argentina, Paraguay, and Panama have all established formal statelessness determination mechanisms. Meanwhile, in the Dominican Republic, civil society continued to focus on ensuring the right to nationality for those affected by the 2013 court decision arbitrarily depriving tens of thousands of their citizenship. This included the publication of an Advocacy Guide about the right to nationality without discrimination and the fight against statelessness in the Dominican Republic by Dominicanos por Derecho, Red ANA, the Institute on Statelessness and Inclusion CEJIL and RFK,[37] as well as organising screenings of the documentary "Down to the Root". In the United States, *United Stateless*, a new statelessness network, has helped to put the right to nationality and statelessness on the public agenda.

Finally, throughout 2018 and 2019, civil society in the Americas focused on the emerging risk of statelessness for children born to Venezuelan parents outside of Venezuela. Civil society has monitored these issues in Colombia, Chile, Peru, and other countries that have limitations to acquire a nationality by *jus soli*, promoting the right to nationality for stateless children and litigating cases. For instance, following discussions, during the ISI World Conference on Statelessness in the Hague in June 2019, leading civil society and academic experts on statelessness issued recommendations to States in the Americas regarding the guarantee of the right to nationality and the eradication of statelessness in relation to mixed migratory flows from Venezuela.[38]

MAHA MAMO

"For most people a passport is a travel document, but for me it means everything. It means I exist. It's finally a sign I belong somewhere"

Maha was born in Lebanon to Syrian parents of different faiths – her mother, Muslim, her father, Christian. This made it

---

[37] Available at:
https://static1.squarespace.com/static/55eb3459e4b021abebfec2bd/t/5bb26ffdc83025ec9aa4a1a8/153842073 4962/RD+Manual+de+Incidencia+SP+4.pdf.
[38] Joint statement available at: https://files.institutesi.org/Expert-statement-statelessness-Americas2019.pdf.

impossible to register either their marriage or her birth, obtain Syrian identity documents or acquire Lebanese citizenship. In 2015, Maha was resettled in Brazil and in 2016 was given refugee status and an ID card for the first time. In 2018, Maha was awarded Brazilian citizenship – ending 30 years of statelessness. Maha is a prominent spokesperson for stateless people in Brazil and around the world; and in partnership with UNHCR is part of the international effort to change legislation and practices around the world in the #IBelong Campaign.[39]

COUNTRY PROFILES

To complement the regional overview of the state of statelessness in the Americas, the following sections explore the situation at national level in greater detail, in four countries where there are significant challenges and interesting recent developments, in fulfilling the right to a nationality for all: Colombia, Venezuela, the Dominican Republic and the United States of America.

Colombia

Although UNHCR has consistently reported Colombia to have only around a dozen recorded stateless persons, the actual number of people who are stateless or at risk of statelessness is believed to be much higher. As one of few Latin American countries in which citizenship is not automatically acquired upon birth on its territory,[40] several groups in Colombia continue to be at risk of statelessness.

Due to the country's geographic location, Colombia is a host and transit country for many migrants including approximately 1.4 million Venezuelans.[41] Whereas children born to Venezuelan migrants in Colombia previously constituted the largest group of stateless (or at risk) persons, the implementation of *Resolución 8470* on 20 August 2019 has made it possible for more than 24,500 children in this

---

[39] Listen to Maha Mamo talk about her experience of statelessness and of advocacy for the right to a nationality in TEDx Place Des Nations Women (2019) available at: https://www.youtube.com/watch?v=RzffChmXKyA.
[40] Juliana Vengoechea Barrios, "Born in the Americas. The Promise and Practice of Nationality Laws in Brazil, Chile, and Colombia" Open Society Foundations (2017) available at https://www.justiceinitiative.org/uploads/8c4136e4-c25d-4255-9afd-d66d20e71da1/born-in-the-americas-20170323.pdf.
[41] S. Held, 'Venezuelan Crisis: Stateless Children facing limbo in Colombia' *Al Jazeera* (21 August 2019), available at https://www.aljazeera.com/ajimpact/venezuelan-crisis-stateless-children-facing-limbo-colombia-190821140410615.html.

category to be recognised as Colombian citizens.[42] Children born in Colombia to Venezuelan parents after 19 August 2015 up until 20 August 2021 are now eligible for citizenship under the resolution. However, children born in Colombia to non-Venezuelan parents continue to be at risk of statelessness in cases where the parents are not residents, and children are not eligible for citizenship from a parent's country of origin.[43] In early 2020, the Constitutional Court of Colombia issued an important ruling in a case against the *Registraduría Nacional del Estado Civil* (National Civil Registry) brought by the Venezuelan parents of two children born in Colombia.[44] Both children had been denied Colombian nationality and, unable to obtain Venezuelan nationality either, were left at severe risk of statelessness. The Court concluded that the National Civil Registry violated the rights to a nationality and legal personhood of the children of the claimants by not taking into consideration the risk of statelessness that the children were in at their time of birth. The court stressed provisions in the CRC (article 7) and ACHR (article 20.2) and cited the 1954 and 1961 Conventions in stressing the duty of the state to prevent statelessness. This ruling may help to pave the way for more systemic policy reform with regard to lifting the limitations on *jus soli* citizenship for children born stateless in Colombia.

Other groups at risk of statelessness include members of Colombia's indigenous population as well as people who have been forcibly displaced. Although figures are unavailable, forcibly displaced people – especially in border regions – are at risk of not being able to assert their nationality and are thereby at risk of statelessness.[45] Furthermore, indigenous and afro-descendent communities face additional barriers to register births and a heightened risk of having their nationality questioned.[46] However, mobile registration units have been in operation for over a decade and have led to an increase in rates of birth registration.[47]

The Dominican Republic

The Dominican Republic is one of very few countries in the Americas with a large stateless population, a situation that has resulted from the denial and deprivation of

---

[42] Registraduría Nacional del Estado Civil, 'Colombia concede nacionalidad a hijos de migrantes venezolanos nacidos en el territorio nacional', 5 August 2019, available at
https://wsr.registraduria.gov.co/Colombia-concede-nacionalidad-a-hijos-de-migrantes-venezolanos-nacidos-en-el.html. See also the interview with Ana María Moreno Sáchica from the Colombian Ministry of Foreign Affairs about her working experiences and the Venezuelan crisis in the Institute on Statelessness and Inclusion, *Monthly Bulletin - September 2019*, available at: https://www.institutesi.org/resources/monthly-bulletin---september-2019.
[43] Institute on Statelessness and Inclusion, 'The World's Stateless: Children' (2017).
[44] Sentencia T-006/20, 17 January 2020, available at:
https://www.corteconstitucional.gov.co/Relatoria/2020/T-006-20.htm.
[45] J. Martínez, A. Rincón & M. Amorocho, 'Focos de apatridia en Colombia: escenarios, retos y déficit de garantías' (2019), 49 Revista de la Facultad de Derecho y Ciencias Politicas 131.
[46] Institute on Statelessness and Inclusion, 'The World's Stateless: Children' (2017).
[47] PLAN, 'Birth registration in emergencies: a review of best practices in humanitarian action' (2014), available at https://www.ohchr.org/Documents/Issues/Children/BirthRegistrationMarginalized/PlanInternationalGeneva_5.pdf.

nationality to Dominicans of Haitian descent. What began as a "practice of registry officials in refusing to register the birth of children of Haitian migrants born in the Dominican Republic [has] gradually expanded through the adoption of various measures, laws, and judicial decisions of other branches of the Dominican State".[48] The September 2013 ruling of the Constitutional Court known as '*La Sentencia*', was a watershed moment, excluding citizens of Haitian descent from the country's *jus soli* system, with retroactive effect.

After this judgment, the number of stateless persons in the Dominican Republic was reported as being 210,000 in 2014 and 133,770 in 2015[49] (out of a total of 136,835 in the Americas as a region, at that time).[50] The reduction in the figure can in part be attributed to the introduction of Law 169-14 in 2014, which aimed to rectify some of the injustices caused by *La Sentencia* and introduced naturalisation procedures for many of those affected. However, UNHCR's subsequent statistical reporting does not include any numbers for the Dominican Republic; stating instead that "UNHCR is currently working with the authorities and other actors to determine the size of the population that found an effective nationality solution under Law 169-14".[51] Progress to remedy this situation of arbitrary deprivation of nationality is therefore difficult to track. According to Dominican authorities, 20,872 birth certificates have been issued to these individuals and 19,521 identification cards are eligible to be requested.[52] However, civil society groups working in the country remain deeply concerned by the scale of the problem, and the impact that the lack of statistical information has on their work.[53]

Law 169-14 has received much criticism, and has been rejected by the Inter-American Commission of Human Rights (IACHR) on the grounds of that it treats Dominican citizens as foreigners, thus violating their right to a nationality.[54] There have also been concerns from civil society actors that this conflates a human rights issue – the right to a nationality – with one of migration and naturalisation, which has the potential to be "politically contentious, logistically challenging and xenophobic".[55] This law is yet another consequence of a long legacy of systematic

---

[48] IACommHR, *Denationalisation and statelessness in the Dominican Republic* (2016), available at:
http://www.oas.org/en/iachr/multimedia/2016/DominicanRepublic/dominican-republic.html
[49] UNHCR Statistics, 'The World in Numbers', available at http://popstats.unhcr.org/en/overview.
[50] UNHCR, 'Populations: 2015', available at http://reporting.unhcr.org/population.
[51] UNHCR, 'Global Trends: Forced Displacement in 2018', available at https://www.unhcr.org/5d08d7ee7.pdf.
[52] Inter-American Commission on Human Rights, 'Chapter V: Follow-Up on Recommendations Issued by the IACHR in its Country or Thematic Reports', 2017 Annual Report, available at
http://www.oas.org/en/iachr/docs/annual/2017/docs/IA2017cap.5RD-en.pdf, p. 774.
[53] Institute on Statelessness and Inclusion, 'Statelessness in Numbers: 2019: An Overview and Analysis of Global Statistics' (July 2019).
[54] Inter-American Commission on Human Rights, 'Situation of Human Rights in the Dominican Republic' (2015), available at http://www.oas.org/en/iachr/reports/pdfs/DominicanRepublic-2015.pdf.
[55] Dominicanos por Derechos, The Institute on Statelessness and Inclusion and The Center for Justice and International Law, 'Joint Submission to the Human Rights Council at the 32nd Session of the Universal Periodic Review: The Dominican Republic' (12 July 2018), available at
https://files.institutesi.org/UPR32_DominicanRepublic.pdf.

discrimination towards Dominicans of Haitian descent, and has contributed towards a growing racist and xenophobic rhetoric directed towards those who have spoken out against this law, who have been branded as 'traitors'.[56]

The Dominican Republic has received a lot of international scrutiny and pressure regarding its exclusionary laws, including during the 32nd Session of the Universal Periodic Review (UPR) in January 2019.[57] The country received 23 recommendations, including recommendations to resolve the existing situations of statelessness, ratify and implement the UN Statelessness Conventions, improve the system of birth registration, and combat discrimination in access to nationality.[58] The issue also continues to be the subject of efforts within the Inter-American human rights system to ensure an effective remedy, including through a resolution issued by the IACtHR in 2019 declaring that the Dominican Republic had failed to comply with its obligations to execute reparations following the decisions in *Girls Yean and Bosico v. Dominican Republic* in 2005, and *Case of the Expelled Haitians v. Dominican Republic* in 2014, and ordering it to adopt necessary measures.[59]

Venezuela

Venezuela is not a signatory to either statelessness convention, although the country has signed up to the Brazil Declaration and Plan of Action which aims to eradicate statelessness in the region by 2024.[60] The groups most at risk of statelessness are indigenous communities as well as families affected by the humanitarian crisis in Venezuela – especially those without any documentation and children born in exile who are unable to access Venezuelan consular services or acquire nationality in the State of birth.[61] This situation is aggravated by the fact that, already in 2016, 570,000 children in Venezuela were reported to lack birth registration documents.[62] Most affected are children in remote areas of the country and/or who belong to an

---

[56] Inter-American Commission on Human Rights, 'Denationalization and Statelessness in the Dominican Republic', IACHR: *Dominican Republic* (2016) available at
http://www.oas.org/en/iachr/multimedia/2016/DominicanRepublic/dominican-republic.html.
[57] The joint civil society submission on the right to a nationality in the Dominican Republic by Dominicanos por Derechos, The Institute on Statelessness and Inclusion and The Center for Justice and International Law, made ahead of this UPR session is available at https://files.institutesi.org/UPR32_DominicanRepublic.pdf.
[58] Institute on Statelessness and Inclusion, 'Universal Periodic Review – 32nd Session Overview and analysis of recommendations made on nationality and statelessness' (January 2019), available at
https://files.institutesi.org/UPR32_stateless.pdf.
[59] IACtHR, 'Caso de las niñas yean y bosico y caso de personas dominicanas y haitianas expulsadas vs. república dominicana' [Spanish] (12 March 2019), available at
http://www.corteidh.or.cr/docs/supervisiones/yean_12_03_19.pdf.
[60] UNHCR, 'Brazil Declaration and Plan of Action', available at https://www.acnur.org/cartagena30/en/brazil-declaration-and-plan-of-action/.
[61] UNICEF, 'Venezuela: Resumen Actividades' (2016), available at
https://www.unicef.org/venezuela/media/166/file/UNICEF%20Venezuela.%20Resumen%20de%20actividades%20Final%20Digital%202016.pdf; C. Armario, 'Venezuela exodus raises worries of babies being stateless' *AP News* (14 May 2019), available at https://apnews.com/9f9ad4c92ef84d41a8e5077ecf18403d.
[62] UNICEF, 'Derecho a la Identidad: La cobertura del registro de nacimiento en México' (2018), available at
https://www.refworld.org.es/pdfid/5c48b7f34.pdf.

indigenous group. The Venezuelan government and UNICEF have developed projects to overcome the geographic and economic barriers to birth registration, however the crisis may have also impacted these efforts.[63] According to Worldbank data, the birth registration coverage rate in Venezuela in 2017 was 81%.[64]

Since 2015, more than 1.4 million Venezuelans have fled to neighbouring Colombia,[65] where children born to Venezuelan parents were at risk of statelessness. As discussed above, prior to August 2019, children born in Colombia to Venezuelan parents were effectively unable to access citizenship from either country. Venezuelan authorities required children to be registered within Venezuela or at one of its consulates – all of which closed in Colombia in February 2019 following severed diplomatic ties.[66] Meanwhile, Colombia is one of the only countries in the region to not automatically grant birth-right citizenship but rather requires at least of the child's parents to be domiciled.[67] However, in August 2019, and after pressure from the UN, human rights experts and civil society, Colombia introduced a decree which recognises children born in Colombia to Venezuelan parents since 19 August 2015 and up until 20 August 2021 as Colombian citizens.[68] This decree is estimated to have granted citizenship to more than 24,500 children who would otherwise have been at risk of statelessness.[69] There is little analysis available as to what extent Venezuelans who have fled to other countries and children born to Venezuelan parents elsewhere in the region also face a risk of statelessness.

The United States of America

The United States is a country with a citizenship tradition based on *jus soli* under which the conferral of citizenship by birth in the territory is enshrined in the Constitution. However, actions by the Trump Administration have suggested that this birthright is under strain. Various news outlets reported in 2018 that,

---

[63] UNICEF, 'Venezuela: Resumen de actividades' (2016).

[64] See https://data.worldbank.org/indicator/SP.REG.BRTH.ZS?locations=VE&view=chart.

[65] UNHCR, 'Refugees and migrants from Venezuela top 4 million: UNHCR and IOM' (7 June 2019), available at https://www.unhcr.org/news/press/2019/6/5cfa2a4a4/refugees-migrants-venezuela-top-4-million-unhcr-iom.html.

[66] C. Armario, 'Venezuela exodus raises worries of babies being stateless' *AP News* (14 May 2019), available at https://apnews.com/9f9ad4c92ef84d41a8e5077ecf18403d.

[67] European Network on Statelessness, 'Colombia acts to ensure children born to Venezuelan parents are not left stateless - but there's still room for improvement' (5 September 2019), available at https://www.statelessness.eu/blog/colombia-acts-ensure-children-born-venezuelan-parents-are-not-left-stateless-there-s-still-room.

[68] Registraduría Nacional del Estado Civil, 'Colombia concede nacionalidad a hijos de migrantes venezolanos nacidos en el territorio nacional', available at https://wsr.registraduria.gov.co/Colombia-concede-nacionalidad-a-hijos-de-migrantes-venezolanos-nacidos-en-el.html.

[69] European Network on Statelessness, 'Colombia acts to ensure children born to Venezuelan parents are not left stateless - but there's still room for improvement' (5 September 2019), available at https://www.statelessness.eu/blog/colombia-acts-ensure-children-born-venezuelan-parents-are-not-left-stateless-there-s-still-room.

increasingly, the U.S. State Department is denying issuing passports to Americans born near the U.S.-Mexico border, throwing their birth certificates and citizenship into question.[70] Indeed, an in depth study into U.S. policy, practice and rhetoric around citizenship., published in late 2019 under the title "Unmaking Americans", found that the regime was under threat in three key ways: 1) denaturalisation by way of revocation of U.S. citizenship acquired through naturalization; 2) denial and revocation of U.S. passports among both naturalized citizens and citizens by birth alike; and 3) Political attacks on citizenship by birth in the form of "policy proposals and surrounding rhetoric regarding the status of children born in the United States to non-citizens".[71] The study uncovered a budget reallocation of $207.6 million from naturalisation processing to immigration enforcement, including denaturalisation and deportation and that a dedicated team had been formed with the intension of referring approximately 1,600 people for prosecution (i.e. to effect denaturalisation) after reviewing an estimated 700,000 immigration files for evidence of fraud.[72] The report also concluded that this operation selectively targeting people on the basis of national origin, laying bare a pattern of discrimination against minorities.

U.S. law makes no provision for the protection of stateless persons and there is no procedure for identifying stateless people. However, a recent report by the Centre for Migration Studies estimates that the number of people affected by or at risk of statelessness in the U.S. is as many as 218,000 – a figure far higher than was previously thought.[73] Stateless persons are often unable to obtain identification and travel documents, and many lack work authorization. Recent actions taken by the Trump Administration, such as removing work authorisation for persons in the process of claiming asylum, may also impede access to work for stateless persons.[74] Stateless persons also face the risk of deportation to countries to which they have no meaningful links, as well as prolonged or indefinite immigrant detention.

Finally, discriminatory practices undermining the equal right to citizenship of children are still at place in U.S legislation – including gender-based distinctions in the right to transmit nationality by *jus sanguinis* if a child is born abroad. Remarkably, the U.S. Supreme Court in the case of *Sessions v. Morales-Santana* (2017) 'resolved' the

---

[70] This process started under the Bush administration, and has continued under Trump. K. Sieff, 'US is denying passports to Americans along the border, throwing their citizenship into question' *The Washington Post* (13 September 2018), available at https://www.washingtonpost.com/world/the_americas/us-is-denying-passports-to-americans-along-the-border-throwing-their-citizenship-into-question/2018/08/29/1d630e84-a0da-11e8-a3dd-2a1991f075d5_story.html.

[71] Open Society Foundations, 'Unmaking Americans: Insecure Citizenship in the United States' (2019), available at https://www.justiceinitiative.org/publications/unmaking-americans

[72] Ibid.

[73] Centre for Migration Studies, 'Statelessness in the United States: A study to estimate and profile the US Stateless population' (January 2020), available at: https://cmsny.org/publications/stateless-in-the-united-states/.

[74] N. Narea, 'A new Trump administration proposal could put asylum seekers out of a job' *Vox* (11 September 2018), available at https://www.vox.com/policy-and-politics/2019/9/11/20853362/trump-work-permit-asylum.

problem of discrimination by mandating an extension of the residency requirement for unwed U.S. citizen mothers to pass on their nationality to children born abroad, choosing to apply a more burdensome standard on mothers, as opposed to easing the burden on fathers. This has increased the risk of statelessness for children born abroad. Moreover, if a child does not have a *biological* connection to a U.S. citizen parent, the child will not be a U.S. citizen at birth, a loophole that increases the risk of statelessness with regards to children born through assisted reproductive technology and surrogacy abroad. The U.S. State Department has reportedly rejected citizenship applications of children of same-sex couples, who were born abroad through a surrogate parent, on the false account that they are born out of wedlock even if the parents are legally married in the U.S.[75] In February 2019, news outlets also reported that tens of thousands of adoptees may never have received U.S. citizenship due to the complexity of international adoption procedures.[76] The Adoptee Citizenship Act that would have addressed the issue is still pending.[77]

---

[75] 'Fathers Sue State Dept., Pompeo Over Denial of Child's Citizenship' *Advocate* (12 September 2019), available at https://www.advocate.com/family/2019/9/12/fathers-sue-state-dept-pompeo-over-denial-childs-citizenship.
[76] 'Tens of Thousands of Adoptees Learn They Aren't US Citizens, Even After Decades Living Here' *NBC Washington* (1 February 2019), available at https://www.nbcwashington.com/news/local/tens-of-thousands-of-adoptees-learn-they-arent-us-citizens-even-after-decades-living-here/3297/.
[77] Adoptee Citizenship Act, H.R.2731 (2019), available at https://www.congress.gov/bill/116th-congress/house-bill/2731.

STATELESSNESS IN ASIA AND THE PACIFIC

OVERVIEW OF STATELESSNESS IN THE REGION

According to UNHCR statistics, Asia and the Pacific region is home to an estimated 2.1 million stateless people.[1] This means that the region is home to over 50% of the world's stateless population that is accounted for within the global statelessness data compiled and reported by UNHCR. As in other parts of the world, this figure is likely to be a significant underrepresentation of the scale of statelessness and nationality problems in the region. One reason for this is that several Asian countries that have very large populations are marked with an asterisk (*) in global statistics, indicating that UNHCR has information about stateless persons but no reliable data to report. Among these countries are China, India and Indonesia. Moreover, in Asia and the Pacific, there is a strong interaction between statelessness and displacement, such that some displaced stateless populations may not be 'visible' within the statelessness data, because they are reported by UNHCR in other statistical categories (i.e. as refugees or IDPs).[2] Finally, the issue continues to evolve in the region – as it does elsewhere – and developments such as the fall-out emerging from the introduction in India of the National Register of Citizens and the Citizenship Amendment Act that entered into force on 1 January 2020 further complicate efforts to get a grip on the scale of the phenomenon.

The root causes of statelessness across the region are diverse, with some being particular to certain sub-regions. In South East Asia and South Asia, discriminatory laws, policies and practices on the basis of gender, race and religion have significantly contributed to statelessness. The Rohingya continue to serve as the most extreme example of this type of deliberate and targeted exclusion, which in their case has been coupled with and served as a catalyst for persecution and forced displacement. Some 1,000 km north in Assam, India, 1.9 million people have been pushed to the brink of statelessness after the Indian government excluded them from a national register published in 2019 because they could not prove ancestry or birth

---

[1] UNHCR, '2018 Global Trends report' and accompanying Table 7 statistical overview (2019) available at: https://www.unhcr.org/globaltrends2018/.

[2] Note that UNHCR exceptionally reports Rohingya IDPs in Myanmar and Rohingya refugees in Bangladesh in both statistical categories, meaning that they are (also) accounted for in the global statelessness data. However, the same is not the case for Rohingya refugees in other countries in the region, who are 'counted' only as refugees in the data compiled. See further Institute on Statelessness and Inclusion, 'Statelessness in numbers: 2019. An overview and analysis of global statistics' (July 2019) available at https://files.institutesi.org/ISI_statistics_analysis_2019.pdf.

in the country pre-dating 1971. Here too, this process has had a particular impact on minority groups.

Gender discrimination in nationality laws also causes statelessness in the region. While many countries have reformed their gender discriminatory nationality laws in the past 15 years, Nepal, Brunei Darussalam, Malaysia and Kiribati continue to discriminate against women in their ability to confer nationality on their children or spouses. These are three of the 25 countries worldwide where mothers are unable to confer their nationality on equal grounds with men.[3] Moreover, around 15% of countries with other forms of gender discrimination in their nationality laws are located in the region.[4]

Migration and displacement are also a cause of statelessness in the region and can exacerbate the effects of discriminatory citizenship laws and practices. For instance, after being forcibly displaced during the Khmer Rouge regime in the 1970s, many Cambodians who were in exile in Vietnam have lost their documentation or any proof of having lived in Cambodia. This has resulted in problems with recognition of nationality. While some have since regained Cambodian citizenship, others remained stateless – in Vietnam[5] and/or following return to Cambodia.[6] Groups whose traditional lifestyles are based on travel across the contemporary borders of states are also vulnerable to statelessness. The Sama Dilaut, a mobile or nomadic maritime people of Southeast Asia, are one such group who face acute discrimination and risk of statelessness.[7]

Across Central Asia, statelessness is mainly a consequence of ethnic-based discrimination in the aftermath of state succession. After the dissolution of the Soviet Union in 1991, large numbers of people were left stateless in successor states across Central Asia (and Europe). A total of 280 million people had lost their citizenship, including a total of 60 million in Kazakhstan, Turkmenistan, Uzbekistan, Tajikistan and Kyrgyzstan.[8] Since then, the vast majority of these people have received a nationality, but statelessness is still a significant problem, with Uzbekistan and Tajikistan reportedly having large stateless populations. As with other the wider region, the issue of statelessness in Central Asia is not comprehensively mapped.

---

[3] UNHCR, 'Background Note on Gender Equality, Nationality Laws and Statelessness 2016' (8 March 2016). See also *Campaigning for gender equality in nationality laws* by Catherine Harrington in Chapter 13.
[4] Global Campaign for Equal Nationality Rights, 'Asia Pacific', available at https://equalnationalityrights.org/countries/asia-pacific.
[5] UN, 'UN hails Viet Nam's moves to end statelessness of Cambodian refugees' (20 July 2010) available at: https://news.un.org/en/story/2010/07/345232.
[6] Reuters, 'No room on water, no home on land for Cambodia's ethnic Vietnamese' (27 June 2019) available at: https://www.reuters.com/article/us-cambodia-landrights-refugees/no-room-on-water-no-home-on-land-for-cambodias-ethnic-vietnamese-idUSKCN1TS03L.
[7] See also *Stateless at sea* by Helen Brunt in Chapter 10.
[8] M. Farquharson, 'Statelessness in Central Asia', UNHCR (2011), available at http://www.unhcr.org/4dfb592e9.pdf.

However, in recent years, more accurate baseline figures of stateless persons have been obtained through mapping studies (e.g. in Tajikistan and parts of Malaysia). According to the Central Asian Network on Statelessness (CANS), as of January 2020, some 116,000 are awaiting a solution to their stateless situation (8,400 in Kazakhstan, 7,800 in Tajikistan, 3,700 in Turkmenistan and 95,860 in Uzbekistan). Central Asia is the sub-region that has shown the most substantial progress in addressing statelessness over the past few years – with notable developments in the second half of 2019. Following Kyrgyzstan, which was the first country in the world to resolve all known cases (more than 13,000) of statelessness on its territory,[9] Tajikistan endorsed an amnesty law that will positively impact some 20,000 stateless people and will greatly facilitate their access to naturalisation.[10] Kazakhstan amended its Code on Marriage and Family to allow universal birth registration for all children regardless of the legal status of their parents, helping to prevent statelessness among children born to parents who are undocumented and people with undetermined nationality. Finally, Uzbekistan (where the largest number of stateless persons reside compared to all other Central Asian countries in the region) initiated a Bill on citizenship, according to which stateless persons who arrived in the republic before 1995 and have since been residing in the country automatically become citizens of Uzbekistan. The Bill has already been approved by the lower house of Parliament and at the time of writing was under consideration by the upper house with plans for formal adoption before 1 May 2020. If adopted, the Bill would create a pathway to citizenship for some 50,000 stateless persons.

The Rohingya 'crisis' and the regional response

In 2017, hundreds of thousands of stateless Rohingya were targeted in a brutal 'clearance operation' by the Myanmar military and civilian groups, which perpetrated crimes against humanity and acts of genocide against them. Between 25 August and 31 December 2017, an estimated 655,000 Rohingya fled to Bangladesh. The Rohingya 'crisis' spans the region and far beyond, with refugees now totalling over one million in Bangladesh. Moreover, hundreds of thousands have, over the years, fled into other countries in the region including Malaysia, Pakistan, Saudi Arabia and Thailand.

The events of 2017 and thereafter in Myanmar occurred amidst an information blackout with significant restrictions placed on

---

[9] UNHCR, 'Kyrgyzstan ends statelessness in historic first' (4 July 2019) available at https://www.unhcr.org/news/press/2019/7/5d1da90d4/kyrgyzstan-ends-statelessness-historic-first.html.

[10] Radio Free Europe, 'Tajik Lawmakers Approve Bill Legalizing 20,000 Stateless Residents From Former Soviet Republics' (11 December 2019) available at https://www.rferl.org/a/tajik-lawmakers-approve-bill-legalizing-20-000-stateless-residents-soviet-republics/30320097.html.

aid workers and the media. The Myanmar government received condemnation from a range of international actors. However, the international community response was largely ineffective in protecting Rohingya against the extensive atrocities committed against them, in bringing relief to the hundreds of thousands of refugees living in precarious conditions in Bangladesh, and in compelling Myanmar to address the structural root causes of the crisis. The year 2018 saw failed attempts to implement back-door repatriation deals, despite it being unsafe for Rohingya to return, a UN Security Council stalemate resulting in inaction at the highest level, the crack down on information and intimidation of journalists, the side-lining of Rohingya voices and a general overall failure of leadership. However, through the concerted efforts of Rohingya activists, journalists, NGOs and UN actors, the body of evidence and documentation on the crimes against humanity and genocide perpetrated by the Myanmar forces continued to grow over 2018.

In 2019, Rohingya still in Rakhine state continued to be restricted in their freedom of movement and their access to food, health care and education was severely limited. Restrictions on the media and aid workers in Rakhine curbed the ability to monitor the situation, report on the crisis and deliver essential humanitarian aid. Those in the camps live in squalor with severe overcrowding and limited access to essential services including health and education. Bangladesh also imposed significant restrictions on fundamental rights relating to the registration of births, access to education, possession of SIM cards and freedom of movement. However, in 2019, the international community finally made some significant solution-orientated progress. The final report of the Independent International Fact Finding Mission, as well as the extensive reporting of the UN Special Rapporteur on the situation of human rights in Myanmar, maintained a spotlight on the crisis. Further, on 11 November 2019, The Gambia submitted its Application Instituting Proceedings and Requesting Provisional Measures before the International Court of Justice, condemning Myanmar for violating its obligations under the 1948 Genocide Convention and requesting the institution of provisional measures to prevent ongoing acts of genocide. On 23 January 2020, the ICJ ruled that Myanmar must enact these provisional measures to protect the Rohingya and prevent the military from committing further acts of genocide. This ruling is legally binding, and Myanmar's compliance will be monitored by the UN Security Council.

Three days after The Gambia filed its case, on 14 November 2019, a case was also filed in Argentina under the principle of 'universal jurisdiction', which allows the prosecution of international crimes committed anywhere in the world. This case marked the first time that legal action has been taken directly against Myanmar's de facto leader Aung Sang Suu Kyi.[11] On the same day, the International Criminal Court (ICC), launched an investigation into "crimes against humanity of deportation across the Myanmar-Bangladesh border and persecution on grounds of ethnicity and/or religion against the Rohingya population".[12]

REGIONAL STANDARDS AND INTERGOVERNMENTAL COMMITMENTS

Unlike Africa, the Americas and Europe, the Asia and Pacific region does not have a regional human rights framework, with its own treaty, court and commission (or equivalent bodies). This lacuna means that there is a dearth of regional norms and jurisprudence relating to protecting the human rights of stateless persons and ensuring the right to a nationality. In the absence of such a regional framework, the importance of the international UN framework is greater.

Yet, the level of accession to the 1961 and the 1954 statelessness Conventions in the region is very low, with two countries States parties to the 1954 Convention (Philippines and the Republic of Korea), one country party to the 1961 Convention (New Zealand), and three country parties to the both conventions (Australia, Turkmenistan and Azerbaijan). Only two States made pledges relating to accessions to the statelessness conventions at UNHCR's High Level Segment on statelessness in October 2019, so while in some other parts of the world these treaties are moving closer to universal acceptance, that is not the case in Asia and the Pacific.

At sub-regional level, the Association of South East Asian Nations (ASEAN) adopted its own non-binding Human Rights Declaration in 2012, which largely mirrors the

---

[11] 'Aung Sang Suu Kyi faces first legal action over 'existential threat' to Rohingya' *The Telegraph* (14 November 2019), available at https://www.telegraph.co.uk/news/2019/11/14/aung-san-suu-kyi-faces-first-legal-action-existential-threat/.

[12] International Criminal Court, Press Release (14 November 2019), available at https://www.icc-cpi.int/Pages/item.aspx?name=pr1495.

Universal Declaration of Human Rights. Article 18 of the ASEAN Human Rights Declaration affirms that "Every person has the right to a nationality as prescribed by law. No person shall be arbitrarily deprived of such nationality nor denied the right to change that nationality."[13] Although there is no entity within ASEAN that specifically looks into nationality and statelessness issues, the mandates of two of its Commissions are relevant to statelessness. The ASEAN Intergovernmental Commission on Human Rights (AICHR) and ASEAN Commission on the Promotion and Protection of the Rights of Women and Children (ACWC) focus their work on developing strategies for the promotion and protection of human rights. The ACWC is, for example, mandated to propose and support appropriate measures relating to the elimination of all forms of violation of the rights of women and children. The ACWC can propose a wide variety of measures to end childhood statelessness, including through resolving gender discrimination in nationality legislation, and permitting all otherwise stateless children to have the right to a nationality and identity documents. It has taken an interest in these issues, for instance co-hosting (with UNHCR) a 2-day regional consultation workshop in Vietnam in November 2018 on ensuring the recognition of legal identity for all women and children in ASEAN. The workshop "resulted in an agreement that Member States need to prioritize the issues of universal birth registration, access to nationality for foundlings, gender equality in nationality laws and improved data collection".[14] The AICHR has reportedly also discussed the Rohingya 'crisis' in private[15] and individual AICHR representatives have publicly called on ASEAN member countries to take more effective measures to protect the human rights of the Rohingya.[16] However, with small budgets and non-binding force, there are significant limitations as to what these Commissions can achieve. More generally, commentators have criticised ASEAN's response to the situation of the Rohingya and suggested that a clearer and stronger agenda is needed.[17]

---

[13] ASEAN, 'ASEAN Human Rights Declaration' (2012), available at http://www.asean.org/storage/images/ASEAN_RTK_2014/6_AHRD_Booklet.pdf.

[14] UNHCR, 'The Campaign to End Statelessness: October – December 2018 Update' (2018) available at https://www.refworld.org/docid/5c1783737.html.

[15] Hui Ying Lee, 'ASEAN's Limited Role in Solving the Rohingya Crisis' in *The Diplomat* (12 October 2018) available at https://thediplomat.com/2018/10/aseans-limited-role-in-solving-the-rohingya-crisis/.

[16] The Jakarta Post, 'AICHR reps call for regional approach to Rohingya crisis' (23 April 2018) available at https://www.thejakartapost.com/seasia/2018/04/23/aichr-reps-call-for-regional-approach-to-rohingya-crisis.html.

[17] See for instance Champa Patel, 'Root Causes of Rohingya Crisis Must Not be Ignored' *Chatham House* (28 September 2017) available at https://www.chathamhouse.org/expert/comment/root-causes-rohingya-crisis-must-not-be-ignored?gclid=CjwKCAiAhJTyBRAvEiwAln2qB-I9p3hSco5QHoHeZo_KvjXvLz92k4YP9mfRKBlyJrpBwM5dugRa-RoCs64QAvD_BwE; Human Rights Watch, 'ASEAN: Don't Whitewash Atrocities Against Rohingya' (19 June 2019) available at https://www.hrw.org/news/2019/06/19/asean-dont-whitewash-atrocities-against-rohingya; Tan Sri Syed Hamid Albar, Laetitia van den Assum, Kobsak Chutikul, 'Time to step up for the Rohingya' *Bangkok Post* (16 September 2019) available at https://www.bangkokpost.com/opinion/opinion/1750879/time-to-step-up-for-the-rohingya.

Next to ASEAN, the 'Bali Process on People Smuggling, Trafficking in Persons and Related Transnational Crime' is a forum for states and international organisations to interact in policy dialogue, information sharing and practical cooperation to address challenges in the region.[18] A total of 48 members – a combination of states and international organisations such as IOM and UNHCR - work together to address a variety of related issues. The nexus between (irregular) migration and the risk of statelessness is gaining more recognition in the region and beyond. In March 2016 during the Sixth Bali Process Ministerial Conference, ministers and delegates of member states and organisations endorsed the 'Bali Process Declaration on People Smuggling, Trafficking in Persons and Related Transnational Crime'. This declaration confirms the core objectives and priorities of the Bali Process, including "measures to prevent and reduce statelessness, consistent with relevant international instruments" in the context of complex irregular migration.[19] In 2018, the 'Bali Process Civil Registration Assessment Toolkit' was published, which recognises the link between birth registration and protecting the right to a nationality, as well as articulating the importance of and methodologies for ensuring civil registration reaches stateless persons.[20] Also in 2018, the Bali Process co-Chairs (Australia and Indonesia) undertook a 'good offices' visit to Bangladesh and Myanmar, and there have been calls for the Bali Process to bring its resources and expertise to bear in the context of the mass displacement of the Rohingya and address the related risk of human trafficking, migrant smuggling and exploitation.[21]

In June 2018, as part of the UNHCR-UNICEF coalition on Every Child's Right to a Nationality, a regional conference on the Right to Legal Identity and Prevention of Statelessness in Central Asia took place. Five Central Asian States exchanged positive developments in addressing childhood statelessness and reflected on how to overcome legislative and administrative gaps. They expressed their intention to continue efforts to ensuring no child is born stateless and ensure birth registration for all, and reaffirmed their partnerships with UNHCR, UNICEF and ESCAP.[22]

---

[18] For more information on the Bali Process, see http://www.baliprocess.net/
[19] 'Bali Declaration on People Smuggling, Trafficking in Persons and Related Transnational Crime, The Sixth Ministerial Conference of the Bali Process on People Smuggling' (23 March 2016).
[20] 'Bali Process Civil Registration Assessment Toolkit' (January 2018) available at https://www.baliprocess.net/UserFiles/baliprocess/File/Bali%20Process%20Civil%20Registration%20Assessment%20Toolkit%20FINAL.pdf.
[21] Filippo Grandi, United Nations High Commissioner for Refugees, 'Statement to the Seventh Ministerial Conference of the Bali Process' (7 August 2018) available at https://www.unhcr.org/admin/hcspeeches/5b69a6e47/statement-seventh-ministerial-conference-bali-process.html; Asia Dialogue on Forced Migration, 'Avoiding a crisis within a crisis: The risk of human trafficking, migrant smuggling and related exploitation arising from the displacement in Cox's Bazar' (March 2019) available at https://cpd.org.au/wp-content/uploads/2019/03/Avoiding-A-Crisis-Within-A-Crisis.pdf.
[22] See further the 'Joint conclusions to prevent statelessness by birth registration of all children born in the countries of Central Asia' (7-8 June 2018) available at https://www.unhcr.org/ibelong/wp-content/uploads/Central-Asia-Joint-Conclusions-of-the-Regional-Conference-on-the-Right-to-Legal-Identity-and-Prevention-of-Statelessness-June-2018-1.pdf.

In October 2019, during UNHCR's High-Level Segment marking the half-way point of their #IBelong Campaign to end Statelessness by 2024, only eight countries in Asia and the Pacific made 'pledges' on action to address statelessness (Azerbaijan, Indonesia, Kazakhstan, Kyrgyz Republic, Philippines, Tajikistan, Thailand and Turkmenistan). Seven of these pledges related to birth registration, four were on data collection, two related to accession to the statelessness conventions and there was one pledge each on reform of the nationality law and statelessness determination procedures. If these pledges are implemented, we could see an increase in statelessness data for the region, which would help to determine the magnitude of the problem and pave the way for reform and more commitment to implementing law and policy change to help tackle the issue. Lastly, a pledge by Turkmenistan to resolve all existing cases of citizenship is especially promising, and following the example of Kyrgyzstan, could set a precedent for other states to follow suit.

Law Clinics and Paralegals
Fight Discriminatory Nationality Practice

On 31 August 2019, in Assam, India, the deadline to register with the National Register of Citizens (NRC) closed. This process had been introduced to verify citizenship and identify any foreigners, with a view to enabling their subsequent expulsion. A total of 1.9 million people – equivalent to 6% of the population of Assam – were excluded from the final list and left at serious risk of statelessness.[23] Under the NRC, applicants were required to prove that they or their family lived in India prior to 24 March 1971, the year Bangladesh was formed. The process was oppressively bureaucratic, imposing a burden of proof which was impossible for many individuals to fulfil. It also placed immense pressure on individuals and their families due to the cost of applying and appealing, the loss of work, the strain on family life, the emotional and psychological impact, the loss of livelihood through detention and the rise in hate-crimes and hate-speech. It has been suggested that those deemed non-citizens should be 'returned' to Bangladesh – however, as these individuals have not resided in Bangladesh for decades and do not hold Bangladeshi citizenship, it is not clear that Bangladesh would even accept them and meanwhile several large detention

---

[23] See for a concise overview of the background 'The biggest mass-disenfranchisement of the 21st Century: 125 Civil Society Organisations condemn the exclusion of 1.9 million people from the Assam NRC and call for urgent action to protect everyone's right to a nationality' *Joint Statement* (September 2019) available at https://files.institutesi.org/cso-joint-statement-on-assam-nrc.pdf.

camps are under construction in India. This situation has created enormous uncertainty for those left off the register, and has galvanised a movement of people to provide those in need with crucial legal advice to help them navigate the highly criticised appeals process that is foreseen in the form of 'Foreigner Tribunals'.[24] One such example is the organisation 'Parichay',[25] which was created on 1 October 2019. Made up of various law schools, the organisation works with lawyers and paralegals on the ground to assist those excluded from the NRC. They assist lawyers in drafting appeals to the decisions taken to exclude persons, undertake research on associated legislation, train other lawyers and paralegals, and are also documenting the way the Foreigner Tribunals are working. According to founding member, Darshana Mitra, "We want to be able to make sure that nobody is deprived of this identity and at least you have access to all necessary legal aid for you to be able to effectively contest and appeal against your exclusion from this identity".[26]

These types of services are not unique to India and the situation in Assam. Similar extraordinary efforts by lawyers and paralegals can be seen in other countries in the region too and these activities have proven to be a very effective means of fighting discriminatory nationality practice. Namati's paralegal programme provides training in various different legal issues including citizenship. The Urdu-speaking or 'Bihari' community in Bangladesh are one group who have benefited from this programme. In 2008, the Biharis finally gained recognition as Bangladeshi citizens thanks to legal proceedings, combined with advocacy. Having entered the country already in 1947, or before, following the split of India and Pakistan, after the 1971 war for independence of Bangladesh, the Biharis found themselves housed in camps, where many remain to this day. Due to discrimination, a large portion have not been able to fully realise their rights and access the citizenship they are entitled to. Following the landmark 2008 legal victory, trained Bihari paralegals now give legal advice to help others pursue

---

[24] Amnesty International, 'Designed to Exclude: How India's courts are allowing Foreigners Tribunals to render people stateless in Assam' (November 2019) available at https://amnesty.org.in/wp-content/uploads/2019/11/Assam-Foreigners-Tribunals-Report-1.pdf.

[25] Parichay, available at https://www.parichay.org.in/.

[26] A. Singh, '"Citizenship Isn't Just A Status" - Lawyers Step In To Help NRC Excluded' (7 October 2019) available at https://www.thecitizen.in/index.php/en/NewsDetail/index/9/17668/Citizenship-Isnt-Just-A-Status---Lawyers-Step-In-To-Help-NRC-Excluded.

citizenship.[27] In Malaysia, the Development of Human Resources for Rural Areas (DHRRA) has been providing legal assistance to stateless communities in West Malaysia since 2006 through an initiative known as Projek Mendaftar Anak Malaysia, stepping up this work from 2014 onwards.[28] Under a wider statelessness mapping project, it has offered in excess of 12,000 stateless persons legal support to acquire or confirm citizenship of Malaysia,[29] while also collecting valuable data to reveal patterns of injustice, including discrimination, that allow for evidence-based policy advocacy.[30]

CIVIL SOCIETY ENGAGEMENT

Addressing situations of statelessness – including most notably the Rohingya – and promoting the right to a nationality have long been areas of engagement of civil society organisations in different countries across Asia and the Pacific. This work has been spurred on by a number of key successes in which statelessness has been resolved to a large extent for certain populations following collaboration between civil society, UN agencies and governments – such as through the passing of the Grant of Citizenship to Persons of Indian Origin Act in Sri Lanka in 2003 that created a pathway to citizenship for the Hill Country Tamils and the Bangladesh High Court ruling in 2008 that recognised the citizenship of the Urdu-speaking 'Bihari' community. An impressive array of local and national civil society initiatives have carved out a space to work on nationality and statelessness issues, from Kyrgyzstan to Thailand and from Nepal to Malaysia. Over the past decade, there has been growing coordination among these civil society actors, as well as new actors emerging.

Launched in November 2016, the Statelessness Network Asia Pacific (SNAP) is a civil society organisation whose goal is to promote collaboration on addressing statelessness in the region.[31] Tackling statelessness requires a combination of both

---

[27] Namati, 'Citizenship – Bangladesh', available at https://namati.org/ourwork/citizenship/bangladesh/.
[28] DHRRA, 'Legal action to address childhood statelessness in Malaysia' in Institute on Statelessness and Inclusion, *World's Stateless: Children* (2017) available at http://children.worldsstateless.org/3/litigating-against-childhood-statelessness/legal-action-to-address-childhood-statelessness-in-malaysia.html.
[29] UNHCR, 'Ending statelessness in Malaysia' (2018) available at https://www.unhcr.org/en-my/ending-statelessness-in-malaysia.html.
[30] For instance, Development of Human Resources in Rural Areas Malaysia, Voice of the Children, Yayasan Chow Kit, Global Campaign for Equal Nationality Rights, Statelessness Network Asia Pacific and Institute on Statelessness and Inclusion, 'Joint Submission to the Human Rights Council at the 31st Session of the Universal Periodic Review: Malaysia' (March 2018) available at https://files.institutesi.org/UPR31_Malaysia.pdf.
[31] See further https://www.statelessnessnetworkasiapacific.org/.

targeted advocacy and technical work, and as such SNAP also functions as an NGO specialist on the issue. SNAP's work both directly assists affected populations and provides tools and frameworks for governments, UN and civil society actors that address statelessness, such as policy and legislative reform models, and legal and paralegal assistance and training. To date, SNAP's work has included developing evidenced-based research, tools and training to support members and leaders of affected communities in their national work and identifying and disseminating good practices relevant for the region through utilising international and regional mechanisms, supporting direct assistance through paralegal projects and strategic litigation and government engagement.

Peacebuilding to address root causes of statelessness and campaign work to raise public awareness and ensuring the voices of stateless people are heard have been critical to seeing change in the region. SNAP has identified considerable opportunities for short-to-medium term outcomes for stateless populations in Asia and the Pacific. As such, together with its 100 members across more than 20 countries, SNAP has developed an advocacy strategy that draws from effective change processes to date and identifies key tactics that can be employed to address statelessness in the region. These successful approaches need to be expanded and targeted strategically to address the gravity of the context in the region and SNAP aims to build member capacity and develop a robust Secretariat to further develop the strategies, tools and interventions needed in targeted countries.

Civil society has also played an important catalytic role in addressing statelessness in Central Asia, where organisations have come together to form the Central Asia Network on Statelessness (CANS) – launched in June 2016. In the last five years (2015-2019) more than 194,000 persons under UNHCR's statelessness mandate were identified in Central Asia by Governments, civil society organisations and UNHCR's implementing partners. Out of this number, some 79,000 cases of statelessness have been resolved either through confirmation of citizenship or naturalization (9,700 in Kazakhstan, 13,650 in Kyrgyzstan, 40,300 in Tajikistan, 5,200 in Turkmenistan and 10,200 in Uzbekistan). Members of CANS play a leading role in these countries and carry out active advocacy actions in cooperation with UNHCR, as well as assisting States at a practical level to resolve cases of statelessness. For example, the achievements of the Kyrgyz NGO, Ferghana Valley Lawyers Without Borders, in helping to resolve all identified cases of statelessness on the territory, gained important global recognition when the head of this organisation, Azizbek Ashurov, was awarded the Nansen Refugee prize in 2019 for his contributions to ending statelessness in Kyrgyzstan. This was notably the first time the award has been given to someone working solely on statelessness.

A new initiative was launched at the University of Melbourne in 2018: the Peter McMullin Centre on Statelessness was established within the Law School.[32] The main focus of the centre is to develop teaching, research and engagement project aiming to properly understand the scope, scale and reasons for statelessness to develop targeted responses; work toward reducing and eliminating statelessness and protect the human rights of stateless people in Australia, the Asia Pacific and more broadly. The Statelessness Hallmark Research Initiative, for example, has already provided valuable seed funding and partnership for a wide array of projects that are helping to advance the understanding of statelessness issues in the region and lay a firmer knowledge base for advocacy and policy reform.[33]

HAFSAR TAMEESUDDIN

"Being stateless was never our choice and it will never be anyone's choice because the right to nationality is basic human right according to UN human rights convention. In my understanding, the stateless issue of Rohingyas is very delicate, complicated and manipulated. However, we still hope we will be able to find a practical solution to end the statelessness for the Rohingyas through activism and advocacy without having any more violence against humanity."

Hafsar Tameesuddin is a human rights defender, refugee representative and refugee rights activist. Her work with various organisations has focused in particular on efforts to end the suffering of the Rohingya. Now living in New Zealand, she is Rohingya and a former refugee herself, who has become a powerful advocate for the rights of other members of the Rohingya community.

COUNTRY PROFILES

To complement the regional overview of the state of statelessness in Asia and the Pacific, this next section provides an overview of five countries where there are both

---

[32] See further https://law.unimelb.edu.au/centres/statelessness#research.
[33] See for an overview of projects https://research.unimelb.edu.au/hallmark-initiatives/home/statelessness-research-initiative#seedfunding.

challenges and interesting recent developments related to statelessness and the right to nationality for all: Brunei Darussalam, Cambodia, Iran, Kyrgyzstan and Mongolia. Two of the countries with the most significant contemporary challenges – India and Myanmar – are not featured in this section, as we take a closer look at them in Part 2 of the report.

Brunei Darussalam

According to government data, 20,863 persons, out of a total population of 421,300 in Brunei were stateless in 2018.[34] This figure has hardly changed since 2013.[35] There is no publicly available information as to the profile of the 20,863 recorded stateless persons. Further, other sources have previously estimated the stateless population to be as high as 150,000 people.[36]

Brunei is one of twenty-five countries that continues to deny women the right to confer nationality on their children on an equal basis with men. Citizenship is automatically conferred to children born to male citizens, but the Brunei Nationality Act of 1961 does not grant female citizens this same right.[37] While an application may be filed to request citizenship for a child born to a female citizen, citizenship is only granted at the discretion of the state, even if the child is stateless without acquiring his or her mother's citizenship. This denies both the mother's equal right to confer her own nationality and the child's right to acquire a nationality. Further, the Brunei Nationality Act 1961 does not allow female citizens to confer nationality on their foreign husbands. However, a foreign woman married to a male citizen can acquire Brunei Darussalam citizenship through naturalisation.

Another key cause of statelessness in the country are the discriminatory provisions, in particular article 4(1a) of the 1961 Brunei Nationality Act, which only automatically grants citizenship to the *bumiputera* (the ethnic Malay groups comprising of Bruneian Malay, Tutong, Belait, Dusun, Murut, Kedayan and Bisaya). This means that number of minority populations - such as the ethnic Chinese, who make up 15% of the population - are excluded from automatically acquiring citizenship and must apply by registration or naturalisation. Due to slow bureaucratic processes and the notoriously difficult naturalisation test, many members of the ethnic Chinese minority are 'permanent citizens', rather than

---

[34] UNHCR, 'Global Trends: Forced Displacement in 2017' (25 June 2018), available at https://www.unhcr.org/5b27be547.pdf, Annex Table 1.
[35] The stateless population was recorded as 20,524 at the end of 2013 (see UNHCR, 'Global Trends: Forced Displacement in 2013', available at https://www.unhcr.org/statistics/country/5399a14f9/unhcr-global-trends-2013.html).
[36] U.S. Department of State, 2012 Country Report on Human Rights Practices: Brunei Darussalam (19 April 2013), 9. Available at: https://2009-2017.state.gov/j/drl/rls/hrrpt/2012//index.htm.
[37] Brunei Nationality Act (Cap. 15) (No. 4 of 1961), available at http://www.agc.gov.bn/AGC%20Images/LAWS/ACT_PDF/cap015.pdf.

citizens, meaning that they can access some but not all rights.[38] Stateless persons who are not registered as permanent residents are further disadvantaged. Indigenous populations in rural areas such as the Dusun and Iban also continue to experience significant barriers in accessing birth registration, creating barriers for indigenous children in acquiring or confirming Brunei Darussalam citizenship.

Cambodia

Statelessness in Cambodia affects primarily the ethnic Vietnamese minority, which is considered to be the largest ethnic minority in the country. While some ethnic Vietnamese have integrated into society, many others live at the margins of society and face difficulties substantiating their legal status in Cambodia.[39] The NGO Minority Rights Organization (MIRO) has monitored this situation and highlighted the adverse effects of a lack of citizenship on the lives of members of these communities.[40]

The extent of statelessness in Cambodia is unknown, due to the lack of public data. In 2018 for the first time, Cambodia appeared in UNHCR's statistical reporting, which shows that 57,444 persons fall under UNHCR's statelessness mandate.[41] While this figure likely underestimates the scope of the problem, it places Cambodia as having one of the larger stateless populations in Southeast Asia. Further, civil society estimates are often higher and Cambodia's government recognises that more than 180,000 ethnic Vietnamese reside in the country[42]

In the aftermath of the 2013 national elections, Cambodian authorities adopted a new two-step policy regarding the legal status of ethnic Vietnamese populations: first an immigrant census targeting predominately ethnic Vietnamese populations which led to the deportation of thousands of individuals deemed to be 'illegal immigrants'; and second a registration process under which new immigration documents and permanent resident cards are being provided to ethnic Vietnamese residing in Cambodia, regardless of any prior status these individuals may have held under Cambodian law. Since mid-2017, this registration process has been accompanied by systematic confiscation of all documentation that authorities deem to be

---

[38] A. Tolman, 'Brunei's stateless left in a state of confusion' New Mandala (8 April 2016), available at https://www.newmandala.org/bruneis-stateless-left-in-a-state-of-confusion/.

[39] See L. Nguyen and C. Sperfeldt, 'Boat Without Anchors: A Report on the Legal Status of Ethnic Vietnamese Minority Populations in Cambodia under Domestic and International Laws Governing Nationality and Statelessness' (2012), Phnom Penh: Jesuit Refugee Service, available at http://jrscambodia.org/aboat_without_anchors.html.

[40] See C. Ang et al., 'Limbo on Earth: An Investigative Report on the Current Living Conditions and Legal Status of Ethnic Vietnamese in Cambodia' (March 2014), Phnom Penh: Minority Rights Organisation, all reports available at http://mirocambodia.org/?page_id=96.

[41] UNHCR, 'Global Trends: Forced displacement in 2018'.

[42] The Cambodian government reported that 70,000 of those are so-called 'old settlers' (Human Rights Council, Report of the Special Rapporteur on the situation of human rights in Cambodia: Comments by the State, A/HRC/39/73/Add.2 (11 September 2018), p. 23-24).

'irregular administrative documents'. The Ministry of Interior identified at least 70,000 mostly Vietnamese 'foreigners' holding such irregular documents.[43] State-sponsored relocations of Vietnamese communities on the Tonle Sap river in 2018-19 have further exacerbated the situation.

Cambodia has not ratified the two statelessness conventions, and in 2018, Cambodia amended its nationality law, without further addressing the status of stateless populations. However, in July 2019, the Ministry of Interior issued a new directive instructing sub-national authorities to expand administrative services to immigrant aliens with permanent resident cards, including the issuance of birth certificates.[44] There has been widespread reporting that Vietnamese families and children struggle to access birth registration in Cambodia.[45] This was also raised in Cambodia's 2018 Universal Periodic Review, at which a number of states recommended that Cambodia strengthen its measures for birth registration and realise the right to education for all, including minority and migrant children.[46] The issue of birth registrations also featured prominently in the 2019 report of the Special Rapporteur on the Situation of Human Rights in Cambodia, which identified persons of Vietnamese descent to be 'at risk of being left behind'.[47]

Iran

Iran is home to several populations that are either stateless or at risk of statelessness. Around three million Afghans reside in Iran, one of the largest protracted refugee situations worldwide, and an estimated 1.5 to 2 million of this population are undocumented.[48] The Khavaris, an ethnic group of Hazara origin, are at risk of statelessness because the Iranian government associates them with Afghanistan. Iran is also host to around 26,270 Iraqi refugees,[49] made up in part by the Faili Kurds, a Shia, ethnic Kurdish minority group, who were forcibly expelled from Iraq following the passing of a law in the 1980s that led to the arbitrary deprivation of

---

[43] Reported at M. Kong, 'Interior Ministry Identifies 70,000 "Improper Citizens, Mostly Ethnic Vietnamese', *Phnom Penh Post* (5 October 2017), available at https://www.phnompenhpost.com/national/interior-ministry-identifies-70000-improper-citizens-mostly-ethnic-vietnamese.

[44] Ministry of Interior Circular, 'the Issuance of Administrative Letters and Birth Certificates for Cambodian Spouses, Children, and Foreign Immigrants', No 015 (1 July 2019).

[45] Minority Rights Organization, 'Research Finding Statelessness Minority Groups in Cambodia Takeo, Kampong Chhnang, and Pursat' (2016), Phnom Penh: MIRO. All reports available at http://mirocambodia.org/?page_id=96.

[46] Minority Rights Organisation, Institution on Statelessness and Inclusion et al., 'Joint Submission to the Human Rights Council at the 32nd Session of the Universal Periodic Review: Cambodia' (12 July 2018), available at https://files.institutesi.org/UPR32_Cambodia.pdf.

[47] Report of the Special Rapporteur on the situation of human rights in Cambodia, 'Assessing protection of those at risk of being left behind', A/HRC/42/60/Add.1 (2 September 2019), paras. 47-51.

[48] UNHCR, 'Iran Needs Help to Support Afghan Refugees' (2018), available at https://www.unhcr.org/news/latest/2018/9/5b8e9f414/iran-needs-help-support-afghan-refugees-unhcr-chief.html.

[49] UNHCR statistics (2018), available at http://reporting.unhcr.org/node/2527#_ga=2.85389022.696654292.1573732048-2132637798.1571059339.

nationality of anyone deemed disloyal to Iraq. It was estimated in 2014 that the number of stateless Faili Kurds is around 8,000.[50] Particularly vulnerable are the Baluch population in the south-east of the country, an ethnic and religious minority who are believed to constitute the highest number of persons lacking proof of citizenship in Iran.[51] However, there are no reliable statistics on the total number of stateless persons in Iran.[52]

Iran is one of the 25 countries which still continues to discriminate against women in relation to the conferral of citizenship to their children. The nationality law is primarily based upon the principle of paternal *jus sanguinis,* or descent through the paternal line.[53] Up until October 2019, when the law was amended to allow Iranian mothers to pass nationality to their children, children of Iranian women and foreign national men were at a high risk of statelessness. The new law allows Iranian women married to men with foreign nationality to pass their nationality to any children aged under 18, without securing the father's consent. This means that Iranian women can now apply for citizenship for their child from birth if the father is a non-national, and even if the parents' marriage is not registered under the Iranian Civil Code (although they must be registered under Sharia Law). The law also does not require the Iranian mother to live in Iran, or the child to be born there.

Although this is a major step in the right direction, this does not completely equalise access to citizenship. While children born out of wedlock to an Iranian mother are not granted access to citizenship,[54] married women are still required to apply for citizenship for their children, subject to security checks, even though children of Iranian men are granted citizenship automatically.[55] Moreover, women are also still denied the right to confer nationality to foreign national spouses, and a marriage between an Iranian woman and a foreign national man requires government approval.

---

[50] UNHCR statistics (2018), available at
http://reporting.unhcr.org/node/2527#_ga=2.85389022.696654292.1573732048-2132637798.1571059339.
[51] United Nations High Commissioner for Human Rights, 'Situation of human rights in the Islamic Republic of Iran' (2018), available at https://www.ohchr.org/Documents/Countries/IR/A_HRC_37_24_EN.docx.
[52] European Network on Statelessness and Institute on Statelessness and Inclusion, 'Country Position Paper: Statelessness in Iran' (2019), available at https://statelessjourneys.org/wp-content/uploads/StatelessJourneys-Iran-final.pdf.
[53] European Network on Statelessness and Institute on Statelessness and Inclusion, 'Country Position Paper: Statelessness in Iran' (2019), available at https://statelessjourneys.org/wp-content/uploads/StatelessJourneys-Iran-final.pdf.
[54] European Network on Statelessness and Institute on Statelessness and Inclusion, 'Country Position Paper: Statelessness in Iran' (2019), available at
https://statelessjourneys.org/wp-content/uploads/StatelessJourneys-Iran-final.pdf.
[55] Human Rights Watch, 'Iran: Parliament OKs Nationality Law Reform' (May 2019), available at
https://www.hrw.org/news/2019/05/14/iran-parliament-oks-nationality-law-reform.

Kyrgyzstan

Kyrgyzstan has been dealing with significant challenges related to statelessness and the right to nationality since the collapse of the Soviet Union. Since then, the government has been commended for taking positive steps towards resolving statelessness. In 2014, a "door-to-door" campaign on registration and documentation of stateless persons supported by UNHCR, led to 13,707 stateless persons being identified, and13,447 being granted citizenship and obtaining proper documentation. In May 2019, there were 258 pending cases,[56] but by early July 2019, Kyrgyzstan had resolved these outstanding cases.[57] In 2019, Azizbek Ashurov, a Kyrgyz lawyer for Ferghana Lawyer Without Borders, won the Nansen Refugee Award in recognition of the instrumental role he played in assisting this entire population to obtain Kyrgyz nationality. This is the first time the award has been granted to someone working specifically on statelessness.[58]

Although this is a welcome development, there may be unidentified stateless individuals who lack the relevant protection. Moreover, it is equally important that appropriate measures are taken to prevent statelessness. Kyrgyzstan is still not party to the Statelessness Conventions. However, during the third High-Level Steering Meeting on Prevention and Reduction of Statelessness in Bishkek in December 2017, Kyrgyzstan expressed a commitment to accede to the two Statelessness Conventions and to establish a formal statelessness status determination procedure.[59] Moreover, in December 2016, an amendment of the Constitution of the Kyrgyz Republic was introduced, allowing nationality deprivation. Since then the government has initiated drafting a new constitutional law which prescribes citizenship deprivation on the grounds of participation in acts related to terrorism, funding terrorist activities, treason, espionage, separatism, extremism, and fighting as mercenaries.

Kyrgyzstan continues to apply a discriminatory approach in granting access to State registration and refugee status determination (RSD) procedures, which discriminates against, *inter alia,* Uighur refugees from China and individuals arriving from Uzbekistan. The recognition rate for applicants to the State RSD procedures is also low.[60] Moreover, over 18,000 children in Kyrgyzstan under the age of five

---

[56] Institute on Statelessness and Inclusion and Central Asian Network on Statelessness, 'Joint Submission to the Human Rights Council at the 35th Session of the Universal Periodic Review: Kyrgyzstan' (July 2019), available at https://files.institutesi.org/UPR35_Kyrgyzstan.pdf.

[57] UNHCR, 'Kyrgyzstan ends statelessness in historic first' (4 July 2019), available at https://www.unhcr.org/news/press/2019/7/5d1da90d4/kyrgyzstan-ends-statelessness-historic-first.html.

[58] UNHCR, 'Kyrgyz human rights lawyer wins UNHCR Nansen Refugee Award' (2 October 2019), available at https://www.unhcr.org/news/press/2019/10/5d937a134/kyrgyz-human-rights-lawyer-wins-unhcr-nansen-refugee-award.html.

[59] Institute on Statelessness and Inclusion and Central Asian Network on Statelessness, 'Joint Submission to the Human Rights Council at the 35th Session of the Universal Periodic Review: Kyrgyzstan' (July 2019), available at https://files.institutesi.org/UPR35_Kyrgyzstan.pdf.

[60] UNHCR, 'Submission by the United Nations High Commissioner for Refugees - Universal Periodic Review: Kyrgyzstan' (2014).

lack birth registration,[61] although 97.7% of births of children under the age of five have been registered. In 2016-2017, an analysis by the Inter-Agency Working Group revealed a number of legislative gaps that need to be addressed, including birth registration and safeguards to prevent children born and living in its territory from becoming stateless. Since then, several legal reforms (Law "On Civil Acts", Law "On Legal Status of Aliens in the Kyrgyz Republic", civil registry reform) are in progress in the area of birth registration and prevention of statelessness.[62] Moreover, in the 2019 UNHCR High-Level Segment on Statelessness, Kyrgyzstan pledged to amend nationality legislation to ensure full birth registration.

In February 2019, UNHCR and UNICEF in the Kyrgyz Republic convened a Parliamentary Roundtable on Birth Registration and Prevention of Childhood Statelessness in Bishkek. The event convened parliamentarians and experts to raise awareness of Kyrgyzstan's legislative gaps in birth registration and discuss amendments needed to prevent childhood statelessness. It resulted in an agreement to create a working group to review the draft law on civil registry acts with the aim of amending the legislation by mid-2019, but no further progress had been reported at the time of writing.[63]

Mongolia

Mongolia is not a party to either of the Statelessness Conventions, and current data on statelessness – according to which there were 17 stateless individuals as of the end of 2018 – is likely to be a gross underestimate.[64] In Mongolia, the Kazakh minority faces the highest risk of statelessness as dual nationality in Mongolia is not permitted.[65] UNHCR has reported that thousands of ethnic Kazakh Mongolians renounced their Mongolian nationality upon moving to Kazakhstan in the early 1990s, and after failing to be granted Kazakh citizenship, many returned to Mongolia, and are now stateless.[66] These individuals have since encountered difficulties in the process of acquiring Mongolian nationality. The Mongolian Immigration Agency does not consider ethnic Kazakhs to be stateless without a verification from Kazakh authorities that they are not Kazakh citizens, but the

---

[61] EEAS, 'In Kyrgyzstan as much as 18,000 children are invisible' (1 February 2019).
[62] Institute on Statelessness and Inclusion and Central Asian Network on Statelessness, 'Joint Submission to the Human Rights Council at the 35th Session of the Universal Periodic Review: Kyrgyzstan' (July 2019), available at https://files.institutesi.org/UPR35_Kyrgyzstan.pdf.
[63] UNHCR, '#IBelong' (January – March 2019 update), available at https://www.refworld.org/pdfid/5ca5bfc77.pdf.
[64] UNHCR, 'Global Trends: Forced Displacement in 2018'.
[65] UN Human Rights Council, 'Report of the Special Rapporteur on extreme poverty and human rights, Magdalena Sepúlveda Carmona, - Addendum', 23rd sess., UN Doc A/HRC/23/36/Add.2, (30 May 2013) para. 51.
[66] Ibid.

process of verification by the Kazakh government is extremely lengthy.[67] While data is unclear and often outdated, a Mongolian National Population census is planned in 2020, which could provide a better overview of the scope of the problem.

A child born to stateless parents within Mongolia may obtain Mongolian citizenship after reaching the age of 16.[68] However, this is not an automatic procedure. Instead, the child is required to apply.[69] This, in effect, leaves children stateless until they are 16 years old. Discrimination affects stateless immigrants, children who are born to persons who are not Mongolian citizens, those who have had their citizenship revoked by the state and those who already suffer from racism. This discrimination has a widespread effect on stateless individuals, as "many stateless persons do not approach the authorities or restore or acquire Mongolian nationality, because they fear the stigma of being identified as stateless".[70]

---

[67] US Department of State, Bureau of Democracy, Human Rights and Labor, '2010 Country Report on Human Rights issues – Mongolia' (8 April 2011), available at
https://2009-2017.state.gov/documents/organization/160094.pdf.
[68] Law of Mongolia on Citizenship (as amended on 7 December 2000) (5 June 1995), Article 7.
[69] Law of Mongolia on Citizenship (as amended on 7 December 2000) (5 June 1995), Article 7(5).
[70] UN Human Rights Council, 'Report of the Special Rapporteur on extreme poverty and human rights, Magdalena Sepúlveda Carmona, - Addendum', 23rd sess., UN Doc A/HRC/23/36/Add.2 (30 May 2013), para. 51.

STATELESSNESS
IN EUROPE

OVERVIEW OF STATELESSNESS IN THE REGION

Statelessness in Europe is more comprehensively mapped than in any other region. UNHCR has statistical data on statelessness for 43 out of the 49 countries that fall within the scope of their European regional bureau,[1] with the total figure in Europe at the end of 2018 reported as 533,340 persons. [2] However, the data on stateless persons in Europe is still very unreliable, due to diverging definitions and methodologies, as well as lack of awareness or capacity to effectively identify statelessness.[3] So, despite being more comprehensively mapped than other regions, the statelessness data in Europe can still be misleading, and is likely to be an underrepresentation of the actual number of stateless persons.

Most stateless persons in Europe can trace their situation back to the political upheaval of the 1990s, in particular the dissolution of the Union of Soviet Socialist Republics (USSR), but also the breakup of Yugoslavia. Indeed, over 75% of the total reported stateless population in Europe live in just four countries, all successor states of the Soviet Union: Latvia, the Russian Federation, Estonia and Ukraine, which all have stateless populations of over 10,000 persons.[4] Latvia has the largest stateless population, at 224,844, the only country in Europe with a stateless population of over 100,000.[5] Although the numbers in each of these countries are declining,[6] nearly a quarter of a century after state succession took place, 414,050 people remain stateless in these four states.[7] In the six states to emerge from the Socialist Federal Republic of Yugoslavia, a total of almost 10,000 stateless persons

---

[1] UNHCR, 'Global Trends: Forced Displacement in 2015', available at http://www.unhcr.org/576408cd7.pdf, annex 2. NB: There are only 46 out of the 49 countries in Europe included in UNHCR's Global Trends. In Monaco, Liechtenstein and Cyprus there are no figures for the stateless population.

[2] UNHCR, 'Global Trends: Forced Displacement in 2018', available at https://www.unhcr.org/5d08d7ee7.pdf. This is a drop of just under 60,000 persons in four years.

[3] Statelessness Index, 'Stateless Population Data', available at https://index.statelessness.eu/themes/statelessness-population-data.

[4] Stateless populations in Sweden, Germany and Poland also exceed 10,000 individuals.

[5] UNHCR, 'Global Trends: Forced Displacement in 2018', available at https://www.unhcr.org/5d08d7ee7.pdf.

[6] The total figure in these four countries dropped from 570,341 at the end of 2013, to 474,537 at the end of 2015. to 414,050 at the end of 2018 (Compare the UNHCR Global Trends report published in mid-2014, mid-2016, and mid-2019).

[7] UNHCR, 'Global Trends: Forced Displacement in 2018', available at: https://www.unhcr.org/5d08d7ee7.pdf.

were reported in 2015,[8] which has fallen to just under 6,000 at the end of 2018.[9] Others remain at risk of statelessness due to lack of key forms of documentation.[10]

Across Europe, the other main context in which statelessness arises is migration. In some cases, people who were already stateless in their country of origin arrive in Europe within the mixed migration flows, as migrants, trafficking victims or refugees. In other cases, people may experience citizenship problems and become stateless following their arrival, due to the loss or deprivation of nationality while they are away from their country which can occur as a result of loss or lack of proof of nationality status or family links, gaps in birth registration, and births of children to parents unable to confer nationality. With the increase in 2015 of migrants and refugees into Europe, the number of stateless persons in some receiving states has grown significantly. For instance, in Sweden, the reported figure for stateless persons in the country climbed from 20,450 at the end of 2013 to 31,062 at the end of 2015, and the figure remains above 31,000 at the end of 2018.[11] Moreover, children born in Europe to migrant or refugee parents can sometimes be exposed to statelessness as a result of discriminatory nationality laws of the country of origin or a conflict of nationality laws.

The nationality laws of many European states have been found to fail to adequately protect children born on their territory from statelessness – in fact, more than half of European parties to relevant international conventions have not properly implemented their obligations to ensure that all stateless children born in the country acquire a nationality.[12] Moreover, other factors, such as child abandonment, international surrogacy or cross-border adoption, and systemic birth registration obstacles for particular groups are also producing statelessness in Europe.

One of the main groups affected by statelessness in Europe are the Roma, a group of roughly 10 to 12 million who mainly reside in the Western Balkans and Ukraine.[13] The Roma are one of Europe's oldest minorities, and encompass a wide range of

---

[8] UNHCR, 'Global Trends: Forced Displacement in 2018', available at https://www.unhcr.org/576408cd7.pdf, annex 2. Note that no figure is reported for the Former Yugoslav Republic of Macedonia.

[9] Figures for Slovenia, Bosnia and Herzegovina, Montenegro, North Macedonia, Serbia and Kosovo, and Croatia totals 5,748 (UNHCR 'Global Trends: Forced Displacement in 2018' (available at: https://www.unhcr.org/5d08d7ee7.pdf).

[10] See for instance UNHCR, 'Persons at risk of statelessness in Serbia: Progress Report 2010-2015' (June 2016), available at http://www.refworld.org/docid/57bd436b4.html. See also *Using the CRC to help protect children from statelessness in Serbia* by Praxis Serbia, Chapter 8.

[11] UNHCR, 'Global Trends: Forced Displacement in 2018', available at https://www.unhcr.org/5d08d7ee7.pdf.

[12] European Network on Statelessness (ENS), No Child Should be Stateless (September 2015), available at http://www.statelessness.eu/sites/www.statelessness.eu/files/ENS_NoChildStateless_final.pdf. See also *An Italian recipe to address childhood statelessness* by N. Garbin and A. Weiss, and *Out of limbo: Promoting the right of undocumented and stateless Roma people to a legal status in Italy through community-based paralegals* by E. Rozzi, Chapter 12.

[13] Council of Europe, 'Glossary of terms relating to Roma issues' (May 2012), available at https://rm.coe.int/1680088eab.

"complex and multi-layered identities".[14] However, with regards to statistics on *stateless* Roma, there is a distinct lacuna, which is representative of a population who experiences systematic exclusion, discrimination and marginalisation within society, which further exacerbates their risk of statelessness. Discrimination of this kind – what has been termed 'anti-gypsyism' – is a significant challenge to statelessness in Europe.[15]

Deprivation of nationality has become an emerging concern to the statelessness scene in Europe. With recent events, the fall of the so-called 'IS caliphate', and European 'foreign fighters' pleading to return to their home countries, a number of states have adopted or broadened nationality deprivation powers in a national security or counterterrorism context. Denmark, Germany, Italy, Switzerland, Belgium, the Netherlands and the United Kingdom are among those states.[16] However, the newly implemented deprivation powers are not being used solely as a national security and counterterrorism measure. In Turkey, for example, after the failed coup in 2017, Turkey passed emergency laws that established a new procedure for nationality deprivation of citizens residing abroad and there were subsequently also reports of the denial of consular services, the cancellation and confiscation of passports and the refusal to provide nationality identity cards or passports to children born to Turkish citizens abroad.[17]

Statelessness in the European asylum system

Statelessness and (forced) migration are phenomena that can have a strong interaction: a refugee or migrant may have been stateless prior to leaving their country, but they also can become stateless as a consequence of migration or displacement. According to Eurostat,[18] of the four million people who applied for asylum in the EU in 2015-2018, approximately 115,000 were recorded as 'stateless', of 'unknown nationality', or their

---

[14] Council of Europe, 'Factsheets on Roma Culture', available at: http://romafacts.uni-graz.at/index.php/culture.1.

[15] ISI, ENS and ERRC, 'Statelessness, discrimination and marginalisation of Roman in the Western Balkans and Ukraine' (October 2017), available at https://www.statelessness.eu/sites/www.statelessness.eu/files/attachments/resources/roma-belong.pdf.

[16] A regional analysis and critique of such measures can be found in Parliamentary Assembly of the Council of Europe, *Withdrawing nationality as a measure to combat terrorism: a human rights-compatible approach?* Explanatory Memorandum, Doc. 14790 (7 January 2019) available at: http://assembly.coe.int/nw/xml/XRef/Xref-XML2HTML-EN.asp?fileid=25241&lang=en.

[17] Article 75 of Decree (KHK) 680 (6 January 2017). See further Institute on Statelessness and Inclusion, *Arbitrary deprivation of nationality and denial of consular services to Turkish citizens – Policy Brief* (2017) available at: https://files.institutesi.org/policy-brief-Turkey-arbitrary-deprivation-of-nationality_2017.pdf.

[18] Data extracted from Eurostat database "Asylum and first-time asylum applicants by citizenship, age and sex Annual aggregated data (rounded)", available at: http://appsso.eurostat.ec.europa.eu/nui/show.do?dataset=migr_asyappctza&lang=en.

nationality was recorded as 'Palestine' – equating to 3% of all asylum applications. Nevertheless, "although actors involved in the refugee response are beginning to recognise the challenge that statelessness poses in the context of current forced migration trends in Europe, little has been published on this to date and statelessness rarely appears on the migration and asylum policy agenda".[19]

These issues were explored in detail through research and consultations between 2017 and 2019, under the *#StatelessJourneys* project, a collaborative effort by the European Network on Statelessness, the Institute on Statelessness and Inclusion and many national NGO partners and experts, examining the relationship between statelessness and forced migration in Europe.[20] Whether someone is stateless was found to potentially have a heavy bearing on their journey through asylum procedures in Europe, including upon the outcome of their asylum claim. A stateless person is unlikely to have documents to prove their identity, place of birth or family links, and this impacts the registration process on arrival, the initial assessment of their protection claim, the nationality rights of their children,[21] and access to procedures such as family reunification[22] or naturalisation[23] (as well as the possibility of return)[24].

In many cases, statelessness is (incorrectly) not considered relevant to the international protection claim, which is often due to a lack of knowledge and available country of origin information about persecution faced by stateless minorities in their countries of origin, for example. The combined lack of statelessness determination procedures in Europe in general, and the non-existence of a legal framework to grant rights and protection afforded by the 1954 Convention mean that if stateless persons are denied refugee status, they are often left in

---

[19] European Network on Statelessness and Institute on Statelessness and Inclusion, 'Addressing statelessness in Europe's refugee response: Gaps and Opportunities' (2019), available at: https://statelessjourneys.org/wp-content/uploads/StatelessJourneys-Addressing_statelessness_in_Europ_refugee_response-FINAL.pdf.
[20] See further: https://statelessjourneys.org/.
[21] Stateless Journeys, 'Birth registration and children's rights', available at https://statelessjourneys.org/main-issues/birth-registration-and-the-childs-right-to-nationality/.
[22] Stateless Journeys, 'Family reunification, resettlement, and other complementary pathways to protection', available at https://statelessjourneys.org/main-issues/family-reunification/.
[23] Stateless Journeys, 'Naturalisation', available at https://statelessjourneys.org/main-issues/naturalisation/.
[24] Stateless Journeys, 'Detention and Return', available at https://statelessjourneys.org/main-issues/detention-and-return/.

legal limbo with no route to protection, and no country to return to either.[25] The determination of stateless status is therefore crucial – including where persons have already been granted refugee status – in order to grant the specific rights under international law that stateless people are entitled to, and to ensure that statelessness is not passed on down the generations. The *#StatelessJourneys* project offers a series of recommendations and tools to strengthen knowledge and capacity of key stakeholders to address statelessness within Europe's asylum and migration systems and procedures.[26]

REGIONAL STANDARDS AND INTERGOVERNMENTAL COMMITMENTS

At the core of the regional human rights system in Europe are the Council of Europe (CoE) and the European Convention on Human Rights (ECHR), which enshrines human rights and fundamental freedoms for everyone within the territory of Europe, including stateless persons and is overseen by the European Court of Human Rights (ECtHR). There are numerous cases in which stateless persons have succeeded in appealing to the Court to address a human rights violation suffered.[27] In *Kim v. Russia*, for example, the Court ruled that the detention of Mr Kim, a man who failed to acquire any nationality following the dissolution of the USSR, violated article 3 (prohibition of torture) and article 5(4) (right to judicial process in detention) of the ECHR.[28] The judgment clarified that detaining stateless persons for expulsion purposes can be characterised as arbitrary where there is no reasonable prospect of removal, and places emphasis upon determining whether a person is stateless at the earliest possible moment.[29] Building on this jurisprudence, in *Hoti v. Croatia*, the court found a violation of ECHR article 8 (right to private and family life) due to Croatia's failure to assure security of residence to Mr Hoti, a stateless man who had been living in Croatia since the late 1970s but was refused citizenship following the country's independence.[30] This judgment showed unprecedented engagement by the Court with the legal phenomenon of statelessness, as well as close consideration of international norms on statelessness. The decision has been described as

[25] Stateless Journeys, 'Status determination', available at https://statelessjourneys.org/main-issues/status-determination/.

[26] See further: https://statelessjourneys.org/resources/.

[27] These include, for example, ECtHR, *Andrejeva v. Latvia* (2009), Application no. 55707/00 (ECtHR); *Kim v. Russia* [2014] Application no. 44260/13; and *Hoti v. Croatia* (2018), Application no. 63311/14.

[28] ECtHR, *Kim v. Russia* (2014), Application no. 44260/13.

[29] A. Berry, 'Kim v. Russia – The unlawful detention of stateless persons in immigration proceedings' *European Network on Statelessness* (30 October 2014), available at https://www.statelessness.eu/blog/kim-v-russia-%E2%80%93-unlawful-detention-stateless-persons-immigration-proceedings.

[30] ECtHR, *Hoti v. Croatia* (2018), Application no. 63311/14.

"landmark" because the Court ruled that Mr Hoti was stateless despite Croatia disputing this fact and clearly "emphasised the role of statelessness in the applicant's inability to enjoy his right to private life".[31]

While the right to a nationality is not contained as a provision in the ECHR, the Court has discussed citizenship on several occasions when the circumstances for or consequences of the denial of nationality violated a separate provision under the ECHR. In *Alpeyeva and Dzhalagoniya v. Russia* (2018), the ECtHR ruled that administrative failures could not be an excuse for statelessness, which strengthened the Court's jurisprudence on the relationship between nationality rights, statelessness and article 8 of the ECHR.[32] The Court has also recognised nationality as an element of the social identity of a person, which forms part of private life as protected by article 8 of the ECHR.[33] This is a developing area of jurisprudence by the Court, with cases delivered to date focusing on the application of the principles of non-discrimination[34] and of the best interests of the child[35] in access to nationality.

In 1997, the CoE adopted the European Convention on Nationality, consolidating in a single, regional document a variety of international legal norms on nationality. This instrument contains several important safeguards directed towards the avoidance of statelessness, along similar lines to the 1961 Convention on the Reduction of Statelessness. It attracted sixteen states parties within the first decade after its adoption, at the time of writing this number had only climbed by a further five ratifications.[36] A separate CoE Convention relevant to statelessness is the Convention on the Avoidance of Statelessness in relation to State Succession, which regulates the prevention of statelessness in the specific context of state succession, but has yet to attract many states parties.[37]

The Committee of Ministers of the CoE has also adopted numerous Recommendations outlining further normative guidance on issues relating to nationality and the prevention of statelessness.[38] The Parliamentary Assembly of the Council of Europe (PACE) adopted a Resolution in March 2016 on the need to

---

[31] K. Swider, 'Hoti v. Croatia: European Court of Human Rights Landmark Decision on Statelessness' in *Statelessness and Citizenship Review,* Vol. 1(1) (2019), available at:
https://statelessnessandcitizenshipreview.com/index.php/journal/article/view/79/21.
[32] ECtHR, *Alpeyeva and Dzhalagoniya v. Russia* (2018), Applications nos. 7549/09 and 33330/11.
[33] See most prominently ECtHR, *Genovese v. Malta* (2012), Application no. 53124/09.
[34] Ibid.
[35] ECtHR, *Mennesson v. France* (2014), Application no. 65192/11 [French].
[36] This Convention had 21 states parties as of 21 January 2020. See
https://www.coe.int/en/web/conventions/full-list/-/conventions/treaty/166/signatures?p_auth=S9rHzhux.
[37] This Convention had 7 states parties as of 21 January 2020. See
https://www.coe.int/en/web/conventions/full-list/-/conventions/treaty/200/signatures?p_auth=S9rHzhux.
[38] For instance, Recommendation (99) 18 of the Committee of Ministers on the Avoidance and Reduction of Statelessness and Recommendation (2009) 13 of the Committee of Ministers on the Nationality of Children.

eradicate statelessness of children,[39] and the Council of Europe Action Plan on Migrant and Refugee Children includes an action on every child's right to a nationality.[40] In January 2019, a Resolution on nationality deprivation as a counterterrorism measure and its compatibility with human rights.[41] This resolution and the accompanying memorandum[42] reiterate the right of everyone to a nationality and the prohibition of arbitrary deprivation of nationality, and question the legitimacy of policy measures that deprive nationals suspected of involvement in terrorist acts abroad of their citizenship. Later in 2019, the Council of Europe's European Committee on Legal Co-Operation (CDCJ) launched a new initiative to improve the identification and protection of stateless people in Europe. A working group of the CDCJ reviewed Member States' protocols and procedures for determining migrants' nationalities and to resolve cases of statelessness.[43] It "identified gaps, new challenges and practical difficulties encountered by both national authorities and stateless people themselves, as well as possible activities that could be carried out by the CDCJ to address these."[44]

The current Council of Europe Commissioner for Human Rights, Dunja Mijatović, who came into this post since 2018, has followed in her predecessor's footsteps in advocating strongly for tackling statelessness in Europe.[45] Thus far, Mijatović has intervened in the case of *Emin Huseynov v. Azerbaijan* (2018), stating that "the deprivation of nationality of the applicant should not be viewed in isolation but as part of a broader pattern of intimidation of human rights defenders in Azerbaijan".[46] Moreover, she has made several recommendations to Albania regarding the Roma children and children born abroad lacking birth registration,

---

[39] PACE Resolution 2099 (2016), available at http://assembly.coe.int/nw/xml/XRef/Xref-XML2HTML-en.asp?fileid=22556&lang=en.

[40] 'Council of Europe Action Plan on Protecting Refugee and Migrant Children in Europe (2017-2019)' (2017, available at https://edoc.coe.int/en/children-s-rights/7362-council-of-europe-action-plan-on-protecting-refugee-and-migrant-children-in-europe-2017-2019.html.

[41] PACE Resolution 2263 (2019), (available at http://assembly.coe.int/nw/xml/XRef/Xref-DocDetails-EN.asp?FileID=25430&lang=EN.

[42] PACE, *Withdrawing nationality as a measure to combat terrorism: a human rights-compatible approach?* Explanatory Memorandum, Doc. 14790 (7 January 2019) available at: http://assembly.coe.int/nw/xml/XRef/Xref-XML2HTML-EN.asp?fileid=25241&lang=en

[43] CoE CDCJ Statelessness working group website, available at https://www.coe.int/en/web/cdcj/statelessness.

[44] ENS Blog, 'Fresh opportunities to tackle statelessness through a new Council of Europe led initiative' (2020), available at https://www.statelessness.eu/blog/fresh-opportunities-tackle-statelessness-through-new-council-europe-led-initiative.

[45] Previous commissioner, Nils Muižnieks, devoted attention to reviewing domestic laws and practices relating to statelessness when making country visits (see report by N. Muižnieks, Council of Europe Commissioner for Human Rights, following his visit to Latvia, from 5 to 9 September 2016, available at https://rm.coe.int/16806da9e4; Report by N. Muižnieks, Council of Europe Commissioner for Human Rights, following his visit to Croatia (25 to 29 April 2016), available at https://rm.coe.int/ref/CommDH(2016)31).

[46] Commissioner for Human Rights, 'Third party intervention by the Council of Europe Commissioner for Human Rights' (28 September 2018), available at https://rm.coe.int/third-party-intervention-before-the-european-court-of-human-rights-cas/16808e2966.

the creation of a statelessness determination procedure and accession to the 2006 Council of Europe Convention for the Avoidance of Statelessness in relation to State Succession.[47]

Besides the CoE, there is the European Union (EU), which has its own human rights document: the Charter of Fundamental Rights of the European Union. The Charter does not contain a provision guaranteeing the right to a nationality, but does provide a set of rights which are attached to EU citizenship, the special supra-national legal status enjoyed by everyone who is a national of an EU member state.[48] EU member states maintain competence in the field of nationality law and can set their own rules for acquisition and loss of nationality.[49] Due to the connection between nationality of a member state and EU citizenship, however, the Court of Justice of the European Union (based in Luxembourg), has affirmed that in relation to the loss of EU citizenship, and even when setting the conditions for acquisition of nationality, "Member States must, when exercising their powers in the sphere of nationality, have due regard to European Union law".[50] Building on this case, in March 2019, the Court of Justice of the European Union (CJEU) ruled on the Tjebbes case, determining that in order for the withdrawal of nationality to comply with EU law, an "individual examination of the consequences" is required in all cases of loss of nationality, in order to ensure that the principle of proportionality is satisfied.[51]

These two cases show that EU law may therefore have some influence on the nationality policy and practice of EU member states, including in respect to the avoidance of statelessness. The EU could also play a part in ensuring adequate protection for stateless persons on the territory of its member states through the establishment of common standards for statelessness status determination or the regulation of a residence status for stateless persons as part of its competence in the area of asylum and migration.[52] To date, there have been various regional developments at the EU level. In 2015, the European Council adopted the first ever Conclusions on Statelessness,[53] which recommended that the European Migration

---

[47] Report by Dunja Mijatović, following her visit to Albania, from 21 to 25 May 2018, available at https://rm.coe.int/report-on-the-visit-to-albania-from-21-to-25-may-2018-by-dunja-mijatov/16808d2e22, para. 58.

[48] Article 20(1), Treaty on the Functioning of the European Union (TFEU) (26 October 2012).

[49] Declaration No. 2 on Nationality of a Member State, annexed to the Treaty on European Union (1992).

[50] Court of Justice of the European Union, *Rottmann v Freistaat Bayern*, Case C-135/08 (2 March 2010), paras 32 and 56.

[51] CJEU, *Tjebbes and Others v. Minister van Buitenlandse Zaken* (2019), Case C-221/17. For more on this, see the piece further on in this report titled 'International law standards relating to the arbitrary deprivation of nationality'.

[52] K. Swider, G. Bittoni, and L. van Waas 'The evolving role of the European Union in addressing statelessness' in L. van Waas and M. Khanna (eds) *Solving Statelessness* (Wolf Legal Publishers, 2017).

[53] European Council, 'Council adopts resolution on statelessness' (4 December 2015), available at https://www.consilium.europa.eu/en/press/press-releases/2015/12/04/council-adopts-conclusions-on-statelessness/.

Network set up a dedicated platform on statelessness.[54] Moreover, in May 2018 the European Parliament introduced a resolution on the protection of children in migration[55] and another resolution passed in November 2018 on minimum standards for minorities in the EU recognised the need to end Roma statelessness.[56] Specific calls have also been made by DG NEAR to States under the 2019 Enlargement Package[57] to address the risk of Roma statelessness.[58]

In Europe, the majority of States are States parties to the Statelessness Conventions. Malta acceded to the 1954 Convention in 2019, with North Macedonia, Spain and Luxembourg acceding to the 1961 Convention in 2020, 2018 and 2017 respectively. At the time of writing, France, Switzerland, Slovenia and North Macedonia are parties to the 1954 Convention only; and Estonia, Poland, Belarus, Cyprus and Russia are parties to neither convention. Belarus did pledge to accede to both conventions on the occasion of UNHCR's High-Level Segment in October 2019. It was among just 13 European countries making pledges – a lower level of engagement with this process than some other regions. The pledges by European countries related to reform of nationality law (four countries), studies on statelessness (six countries), and the introduction or improvement of statelessness determination procedures (five countries).

Statelessness Index

In 2018, the European Network on Statelessness (ENS) launched a new comparative tool to support civil society, governments, researchers and others interested in statelessness: the Statelessness Index.[59] It is the first online platform to provide accessible, comparative information on law, policy and practice regarding the treatment of stateless people across Europe and covers 24 countries as of March 2020. These countries are assessed on the protection of stateless people and the prevention and reduction of statelessness, against international norms and good practice. Information is fed into the Index by country experts whose analysis is then reviewed by another country

---

[54] European Migration Network, 'Statelessness in the EU' (October 2016), available at
https://www.emnluxembourg.lu/wp-content/uploads/2016/11/EMN-Inform-Statelessness-in-the-EU.pdf.
[55] Council of Europe, 'Protection of children in migration' (3 May 2018) 2018/2666(RSP), available at
http://www.europarl.europa.eu/doceo/document/TA-8-2018-0201_EN.html?redirect.
[56] European Parliament, 'Minimum standards for minorities in the EU' (13 November 2018) 2018/2036(INI),
available at http://www.europarl.europa.eu/doceo/document/TA-8-2018-0447_EN.html?redirect.
[57] European Commission, 'EU Enlargement Package: 2019', available at https://ec.europa.eu/neighbourhood-
enlargement/countries/package_en.
[58] European Network on Statelessness, 'Briefing note: Addressing statelessness in Europe' (October 2019),
available at https://www.statelessness.eu/sites/www.statelessness.eu/files/attachments/resources/ENS-
Briefing_for_HLS-Sept_2019.pdf.
[59] Statelessness Index, 'About the Index', available at https://index.statelessness.eu/about.

expert to ensure reliability. The information is structured both by country and by theme.[60] Each country has a country page where the user can review its performance for all the themes and subthemes. Each theme also has a page where the user can review and compare up to four countries' performances under that theme.[61] The performance is assessed on a five-level scale from positive to negative, indicated by a visual key, which gives a quick understanding of good practices and where improvement is needed. For example, at the time of writing, a comparison of Bulgaria, Hungary, Moldova and Poland under the 'Prevention and Reduction' theme and the 'stateless born on territory' sub-theme, reveals that Bulgaria is rated as positive (every child born on the territory who cannot acquire another nationality is a Bulgarian citizen by birth), Moldova is rated as positive and negative (children born on the territory who would otherwise be stateless acquire Moldovan nationality, but only if at least one of their parents has legal residence, international protection or stateless status), and Hungary and Poland are rated as negative (in Hungary there are two partial safeguards to children born on the territory, but these are only applicable in certain cases; in Poland, there is no full safeguard to prevent childhood statelessness). This approach to comparative analysis and the simplified presentation of data has inspired conversation among civil society groups in other regions who are interested in emulating this formula with their own regional statelessness index.

CIVIL SOCIETY ENGAGEMENT

Europe has a vibrant and growing civil society community engaged on statelessness, with NGOs, scholars and others engaged in related fields such as migration, asylum and human rights taking a growing interest in the issue over the past decade and an increasing number of dedicated initiatives emerging. The establishment of the *EUDO Citizenship Observatory* in 2009 helped to build a knowledge base around nationality issues by providing important comparative analysis of the content and operation of citizenship laws in Europe, later also studying safeguards against

---

[60] Statelessness Index, 'How to Use the Index', available at
https://index.statelessness.eu/about/how-to-use-the-index.
[61] The themes are: international and regional instruments, statelessness population data, statelessness determination and status, detention, and prevention and reduction.

citizenship specifically and subsequently evolving and expanding to become the *Global Citizenship Observatory* (GLOBALCIT).[62] In 2012, the European Network on Statelessness (ENS) launched, as the first regional civil society alliance committed to addressing statelessness to be established anywhere in the world. ENS now has over 150 members covering 41 countries including, importantly, many stateless activists and grassroots organisations. ENS not only spearheads joined-up action but has become an increasingly important source of analysis on statelessness issues – most notably with the launch of the Statelessness Index in March 2018 (see above), that is helping to underpin advocacy at national and regional levels.

Since 2017, civil society in Europe has continued to organise and engage in coordinated advocacy to address statelessness across the region. Campaigns and initiatives spearheaded by ENS have included those aimed at addressing Roma statelessness (#RomaBelong),[63] protecting stateless people from arbitrary detention (#LockedInLimbo),[64] and addressing childhood statelessness (#StatelessKids).[65] The #StatelessJourneys knowledge hub, launched by ENS in partnership with ISI in 2019, hosts bespoke tools designed to equip refugee response actors to better identify and address the protection needs of stateless people on the move and provides an important foundation for further capacity building in this area.[66] Civil society action also contributed to 33 pledges being made by 12 European countries at UNHCR's High-Level Segment on Statelessness in October 2019. In seeking to build on recent efforts, ENS and its members will be guided by a new five-year strategic plan (2019-23) 'Solving Statelessness in Europe'.[67] At local and country level, NGOs across the region have been stepping up their campaigning, litigation and capacity building efforts. In late 2019, a dedicated new civil society organisation was launched in Sweden – the Swedish Organization Against Statelessness – with the aim of amplifying the voices of stateless people in the country and ensuring more effective advocacy for both legal and policy change around the protection of the stateless and the realization of the right to a nationality.[68] It will be interesting to see whether further statelessness-specialist organisations such as these are established in the coming years.

---

[62] See http://globalcit.eu/.

[63] '#Roma Belong', available at https://www.statelessness.eu/romabelong.

[64] '#LockedinLimbo', available at http://www.lockedinlimbo.eu/.

[65] '#StatelessKids', available at https://statelesskids.eu/.

[66] 'StatelessJourneys', available at https://statelessjourneys.org/.

[67] European Network on Statelessness, 'Solving Statelessness in Europe', available at https://www.statelessness.eu/sites/www.statelessness.eu/files/attachments/resources/ENS-Strategic-Plan-2019-23.pdf.

[68] J. Al-Moushahidi, 'New joint efforts towards ending statelessness in Sweden', *European Network on Statelessness* (13 December 2019) available at: https://www.statelessness.eu/blog/new-joint-efforts-towards-ending-statelessness-sweden.

ELVIS BERIŠA

"Due to disintegration of Yugoslavia, thousands of Roma in the Western Balkans are still bearing the costs of being displaced by war in the late 1990s, as well as their children, many of whom are born without a nationality, and are in a legal limbo. The UN's 2030 Agenda for Sustainable Development states that a primary goal is "to leave no-one behind". I believe that it is time to start to combat anti-gypsyism as the main cause of exclusion of Roma community and the fact that a large number are stateless or at risk of becoming stateless in Europe, especially in the Western Balkans."

Elvis Beriša was born in Podgorica, Montenegro and graduated with a degree in Criminology from the Faculty of Law at the University of Montenegro. He is the founder and CEO of Roma youth organisation, Walk with us – 'Phirenamenca', human rights activist, journalist and director of First Roma web portal in Montenegro 'RomaNet.' Being a member of Roma community himself and speaking Romanes and Albanian gives Elvis both access and understanding of the issues which often tend to be hidden from the eye of an outsider. He is actively working on combating anti-gypsyism in Montenegro, and with others, is helping the Roma community to gain legal status, especially those who are stateless or who are at risk of becoming stateless. He has also attended national and international conferences on statelessness in order to contribute by sharing his experience and knowledge on this topic.

COUNTRY PROFILES

To complement the regional overview of the state of statelessness in Europe, the following sections explore the situation at national level in greater detail, in five countries where there are significant challenges and interesting recent developments, in fulfilling the right to a nationality for all: Albania, Bulgaria, Cyprus, the Netherlands and Spain.

Albania

Albania has ratified both statelessness conventions and has a largely unproblematic nationality law, yet it still has a significant population at risk of or experiencing statelessness and it also lacks a statelessness determination mechanism.[69] Although estimates vary, UNHCR recorded 4,160 stateless persons in Albania at the end of 2018. This figure refers to a census from 2011 and has been adjusted to reflect the number of persons with undetermined nationality who had their nationality confirmed in 2011-2018.[70] The two major issues that Albania reportedly faces when it comes to statelessness relate to access to nationality for children born abroad and the risk of statelessness facing Albania's Roma and Egyptian communities.[71]

Nationality law in Albania combines *jus soli* and *jus sanguinis* and provides that every child born (within Albania or abroad) of at least one Albanian citizen parent, as well as every child born within Albania to lawfully resident non-Albanian parents, can acquire Albanian citizenship. However, there are significant shortcomings in the law's implementation. The administrative and judicial procedures for accessing citizenship are often costly and lengthy, especially when it comes to obtaining birth registration. A joint report by UNHCR and Tirana Legal Aid Society found that out of the 1,031 persons identified to be at risk of statelessness, 97% were children.[72] Children born outside of Albanian territory especially struggle to have their citizenship recognised.

Moreover, statelessness disproportionately affects Albania's Roma and Egyptian communities. These communities represent only 0.4-3.3% of the population, but they constitute half of all cases of those at risk of, or experiencing, statelessness.[73] Although statelessness exacerbates pre-existing discrimination, marginalisation and barriers to accessing equal rights, it is difficult to disentangle lack of citizenship from the wider structures of discrimination. Furthermore, it is difficult to measure full the scope of the issue as stateless people are often legally invisible.[74]

Positively, the Albanian government in 2017 acknowledged the Roma community as a national minority.[75] The Egyptian community, on the contrary, to date has not

---

[69] UNHCR, 'Mapping of the population at risk of statelessness in Albania' (May 2018), available at http://www.un.org.al/sites/default/files/Mapping%20of%20the%20population%20at%20risk%20of%20statele ssness_%20ENGLISH.PDF.

[70] UNHCR, 'Global Trends: Forced Displacement in 2018'.

[71] Tirana Legal Aid Society, Institute on Statelessness and Inclusion et al., 'Joint Submission to the Human Rights Council at the 33rd Session of the Universal Periodic Review: Albania' (4 October 2018), available at https://files.institutesi.org/UPR33_Albania.pdf.

[72] UNHCR, 'Mapping of the population at risk of statelessness in Albania' (May 2018), available at http://www.un.org.al/sites/default/files/Mapping%20of%20the%20population%20at%20risk%20of%20statele ssness_%20ENGLISH.PDF.

[73] Ibid.

[74] ERRC, 'Roma Belong: Statelessness, discrimination and marginalisation of Roma in Albania' (February 2018), available at http://www.errc.org/uploads/upload_en/file/4993_file3_roma-belong-albania-english-language.pdf.

[75] Ibid.

been acknowledged as such.[76] Furthermore, in October 2018, the parliament accepted amendments which serve to remove barriers from the birth registration procedure.[77] Albania made several pledges on the occasion of the UNHCR High-Level Segment on statelessness in 2019, including to fully implement the amendments passed in 2018 and to further align the nationality law with the 1961 Convention standards as well as to adopt a statelessness determination procedure by 2020.[78]

Bulgaria

UNHCR reported that there were 92 stateless persons in Bulgaria at the end of 2018,[79] although these statistics may not be reliable or complete because the issue has never been comprehensively mapped in the country and government sources may be underreporting the numbers because country of origin and nationality are sometimes conflated in practice by officials.[80] Importantly, in December 2016, Bulgaria introduced a statelessness determination procedure (SDP), outlined in the Law on Foreign Nationals in the Republic of Bulgaria (Закон за чужденците в Република България). In April 2019, Bulgaria further amended its statelessness law to provide for the right to a continuous residence permit (for a renewable period of up-to one year) for holders of stateless status. However, stateless persons with a continuous residence permit are not given access to the labour market and cannot sign a labour contract; moreover, they are outside the scope of the health insurance system and are therefore not covered by the National Health Insurance fund.

There is no time limit for access to the SDP, no fee, the right to an interview and an appeal, free legal aid which is provided by NGOs, and cooperation between asylum and SDP decision-makers. However, Bulgarian civil society has raised serious concerns about remaining shortcomings. An application can only be made in Bulgarian, and the burden of proof - which is higher than in asylum procedures - lies with the applicant. Decisions are given in writing within six months, and although reasons are usually stated, there have been cases of 'silent rejections' where no acknowledgement or extension is communicated within the timeframe. Moreover, there is no protection during the SDP so applicants have no access to basic services and may be detained during the procedure. There have also been

---

[76] Minority Rights Group International, 'Egyptians', available at
https://minorityrights.org/minorities/egyptians/.
[77] UNHCR, 'Coalition efforts lead to the adoption of legal amendments to civil status law by the Parliament of Albania', available at https://www.unhcr.org/ibelong/parliament-of-albania-adopts-legal-amendments-to-civil-status-law/.
[78] UNHCR, Results of the High-Level Segment on Statelessness – Albania (2019) available at:
https://www.unhcr.org/ibelong/results-of-the-high-level-segment-on-statelessness/.
[79] UNHCR, 'Global Trends: Forced Displacement in 2018'.
[80] European Network on Statelessness, 'Statelessness Index: Bulgaria – Statelessness population data' available at:
https://index.statelessness.eu/country/bulgaria.

cases of the competent authorities issuing return orders to irregularly residing stateless persons when they apply for stateless status.

Bulgaria also has relatively strong safeguards in its nationality law to prevent childhood statelessness: children born on the territory automatically acquire Bulgarian nationality if they would otherwise be stateless, and children born to Bulgarian parents abroad (and foundlings) also acquire citizenship at birth automatically. However, in the case of adoption of a foreign child by Bulgarian nationals, there is a potential risk of statelessness, as the child does not automatically acquire Bulgarian nationality but must apply for nationality before the age of 18.[81]

Cyprus

Cyprus (RoC) is not party to either Statelessness Convention and has a very weak legal framework for protecting stateless persons. There are also problems with the fulfilment of the right to a nationality in Cyprus: while children born to two RoC parents acquire nationality automatically, whether born within the country or abroad, there is no safeguard to prevent children being born stateless in Cyprus, nor to grant citizenship to foundlings.[82] Where a child is born in Cyprus to parents of mixed marriages – to one Cypriot and one non-Cypriot – if one parent entered or stayed in the country illegally, the child will not be granted nationality.[83]

People born in the Turkish Republic of Northern Cyprus (TRNC) experience particular difficulties accessing citizenship, as a result of the conflict over this part of the island. Everyone who enters the island on the north side is considered by RoC to have entered the country illegally.[84] Although many have 'TRNC nationality', the TRNC is not an internationally recognised state and so their nationality is not valid from an international legal perspective, nor from the RoC's perspective. Children of one Turkish parent and one 'original Cypriot' parent[85] are denied citizenship upon application, and grandchildren who have one Turkish grandparent and three Cypriot grandparents can also not acquire nationality.[86] Officially, these people are not 'denied' citizenship by the ministry of interior; rather, their

---

[81] For a full overview of the state of statelessness in Bulgaria, see European Network on Statelessness and Foundation for Access to Rights, 'Country briefing: Bulgaria' part of the *Statelessness Index* (November 2019) available at:
https://index.statelessness.eu/sites/statelessindex.eu/files/Index%20Country%20Briefing%20Bulgaria_2019_EN%20reformatted.pdf.
[82] European Network on Statelessness, 'Cyprus', available at https://index.statelessness.eu/country/cyprus.
[83] 1967 Republic of Cyprus Citizenship Law (updated in 2000), articles 3(1) and 2(a).
[84] Cyprus visa, available at http://www.cyprusvisa.eu/cyprus-admission-restrictions.html; Cyprus embassy, 'Entry regulations for Cyprus', available at
https://cyprusembassy.fi/main/filemanager/EntryregulationsCyprus.pdf.
[85] Referring to anyone who was a RoC national before 1974.
[86] M.J. Hopman, A.E. Borne, C. Bruchi, R. Nys, F. Pircher & N. Trip, 'Deleted off the map: The child's right to nationality in the Turkish Republic of North Cyprus' (2018) available at: http://kinderrechtenonderzoek.nl/wp-content/uploads/2018/10/1784-Universiteit-Maastricht-Rapport-Noord-Cyprus-UK_WEB-spread.pdf.

applications are marked as 'pending', some for up to 14 years.[87] Exceptions are also made based on gender - if the child was born between 1960 and 1999, only the Cypriot father, not the mother, can pass on nationality.[88] Although it is difficult to estimate how many people are affected by these difficulties, estimates suggest between 15,000-25,000 people.[89]

Exacerbating the challenges around acquisition of nationality highlighted above, are gaps relating to statelessness status determination and birth registration. The RoC does not have a statelessness determination procedure in place, and this can result in the exclusion and denial of rights, particularly to migrants and failed asylum seekers, who nonetheless are stateless.[90] Moreover, there are problematic birth registration practices, which further heighten the risk of statelessness. In particular, "undocumented parents, including stateless people, may face difficulties registering births in practice as there have been cases where they were asked to present passports or other documentation as a condition for registration, and they may fear being detected as irregular residents", a problem which has raised complaints before the Children's Commissioner.[91]

The Netherlands

In 2019, the National Statistics Bureau (CBS) reported that around 55,000 people residing in the Netherlands experience nationality problems, with just under 13,000 registered as stateless and the rest with an 'unknown nationality'.[92] This is in stark contrast with the 1,951 stateless persons reported by UNHCR, and reveals the true scale of the issue.[93]

---

[87] Ibid.

[88] The law was changed in 2000 to align national legislation with EU standards, as part of the process of Cyprus joining the EU.

[89] In a PRIO research report, it is estimated that of the "TRNC citizen population", 12,000-15,000 are of mixed parentage (one Cypriot parent). See M. Hatay (2017), p. 32. Taking into account that the issue not only concerns children of mixed parents (here based on birth place), but also the grandchildren of these couples, we estimate that the number of people not able to pass on their nationality is in fact higher. Another factor is that elsewhere it is estimated that there are 17,000 mixed marriages in northern Cyprus. See for example 'Cyprus denies ID cards for children of mixed marriages with Turks' *Tornos News* (30 November 2017), available at http://www.tornosnews.gr/en/greek-news/politics/28519-cyprus-denies-id-cards-for-children-of-mixed-marriages-with-turks.html.

[90] Institute on Statelessness and Inclusion and Research Team from Maastricht University, 'Joint Submission to the Human Rights Council at the 32nd Session of the Universal Periodic Review' (12 July 2018), available at https://files.institutesi.org/UPR32_Cyprus.pdf.

[91] European Network on Statelessness, 'Statelessness Index: Cyprus – Prevention and Reduction' available at: https://index.statelessness.eu/country/cyprus.

[92] P. Vissers, 'Municipalities no longer want to wait for legislation and will help people without a passport themselves' *Trouw* (June 8 2019), available at https://www.trouw.nl/nieuws/gemeenten-willen-niet-langer-wachten-op-wetgeving-en-gaan-mensen-zonder-paspoort-zelf-helpen~b45cb795b/?mc_cid=24df302e1c&mc_eid=52b81a63d2.

[93] Institute on Statelessness and Inclusion, 'Statelessness in Numbers: 2019' (July 2019), available at https://files.institutesi.org/ISI_statistics_analysis_2019.pdf?mc_cid=24df302e1c&mc_eid=52b81a63d2.

The large number of people with 'unknown nationality' is the result of the lack of a statelessness determination procedure. In 2014, the Dutch government announced its intention to address the gaps in domestic law and policy, but the draft bill published in 2016 was heavily criticised for falling short of international standards.[94] The legislative process has since stalled, but other avenues are being explored, with a number of Dutch cities announcing their intention to better identify and assist stateless residents.[95] None of these (proposed) initiatives addresses the problem of lack of access to residence status for stateless migrants who do not qualify for any other immigration status or procedure and they remain in limbo with a significant risk of lengthy and arbitrary detention.[96] Stateless children born in the Netherlands are also not always able to claim their right to a nationality because the law currently excludes children without a lawful residence status from using the special procedure that provides access to Dutch nationality and in practice even stateless children who meet the residence criteria may not be able to gain citizenship because they have not been officially recognised as stateless (but are registered as having an 'unknown nationality' instead).[97]

Since 2010, there has been a gradual expansion of the powers to revoke nationality under the Dutch Nationality Act (DNA), with new grounds added in 2010, 2016 and 2017. The most recent of these allows for the revocation of nationality without the need for a criminal conviction, if a person voluntarily enters the foreign military service of a State involved in hostilities against the Netherlands (article 14(3)) or joins an organisation that is listed as constituting a threat to national security (article 14(4)).[98] Between December 2017 and March 2019, the nationality of 13 persons was revoked.[99] In two cases, the revocation was reversed because it violated

---

[94] Rijksoverheid, 'Letter to Parliament with the Cabinet's first reaction to the ACVZ's recommendation on statelessness' [Dutch], available at
https://www.rijksoverheid.nl/documenten/kamerstukken/2014/09/11/eerste-reactie-van-het-kabinet-op-het-advies-van-de-acvz-inzake-staatloosheid; Overheid, 'Statute Statelessness Procedure' [Dutch], available at:
https://index.statelessness.eu/sites/statelessindex.eu/files/INDEX-Country_Briefing_Netherlands_ENG_update%20July%202019_0.pdf.
https://www.internetconsultatie.nl/staatloosheid/details?mc_cid=24df302e1c&mc_eid=52b81a63d2.
[95] P. Vissers, 'Municipalities no longer want to wait for legislation and will help people without a passport themselves' [Dutch] *Trouw* (June 8 2019), available at https://www.trouw.nl/nieuws/gemeenten-willen-niet-langer-wachten-op-wetgeving-en-gaan-mensen-zonder-paspoort-zelf-helpen~b45cb795b/?mc_cid=24df302e1c&mc_eid=52b81a63d2.
[96] European Network on Statelessness and ASKV Refugee Support, Country briefing: The Netherlands' part of the *Statelessness Index* (July 2019) available at
[97] Netherlands Institute for Human Rights, 'Report To the 84th session of the Committee on the Rights of the Child pre-sessional working group for adoption of the list of issues prior to reporting for the Kingdom of The Netherlands' (June 2019) available at: https://publicaties.mensenrechten.nl/file/16566ee4-c146-467e-bc1a-1764d233752f.pdf.
[98] Overheid, 'National Act of 10 February 2017, amending the National Act on Dutch Nationality in connection with the withdrawal of Dutch nationality in the interest of national security' [Dutch} (2017), available at https://zoek.officielebekendmakingen.nl/stb-2017-52.html.
[99] National Coordinator of Counterterrorism and Security, 'Report Integrated Approach Terrorism' [Dutch} (2019), p.11.

procedural due process standards (namely non-retroactivity),[100] which led to a further five cases of reinstatement of nationality for individuals in similar circumstances. In July 2019, the Minister for Security and Justice reported that although an estimated 100 dual nationals may fall within the scope of article 14(4) DNA and could be subject to revocation of nationality, evidential issues mean it is unlikely that the Netherlands will proceed to deprivation of nationality in many more cases.[101]

Only dual nationals may be subject to deprivation of nationality under the aforementioned provisions. The UN Special Rapporteur on Racism, Tendayi Achiume, has raised concerns that this policy discriminates between mono and dual citizens, and disproportionately affects dual nationals of "non-Western origin" – in particular Dutch-Moroccan and Dutch-Turkish dual nationals.[102]

Spain

According to UNHCR, there were 2,455 stateless persons in Spain at the end of 2018.[103] Spain is a party to both Statelessness Conventions,[104] as well as numerous human rights treaties that contain provisions pertaining to statelessness.[105] According to Spain's Constitution, "validly concluded international treaties once officially published in Spain, shall be part of the internal legal system",[106] meaning that these are incorporated into national law without the need to implement separate legislation. However, Spain has not acceded to the European Convention on Nationality and the Council of Europe Convention on the avoidance of statelessness in relation to State succession, despite various recommendations to do so.[107]

---

[100] *B v. State Secretary of Justice and Security* (2019), Ruling 201806104/1/V6; *Z v. State Secretary of Justice and Security* (2019), Ruling 201806107/1/V6.

[101] Rijksoverheid, 'Letter to Parliament on the implementation of the motion on the withdrawal of Dutch nationality' [Dutch] (2019), available at
https://www.rijksoverheid.nl/documenten/kamerstukken/2019/07/15/tk-uitvoering-motie-laan-geselschap-en-van-toorenburg-over-de-intrekken-van-het-nederlanderschap.

[102] UN, 'Amicus Brief' (23 October 2018), available at:
https://www.ohchr.org/Documents/Issues/Racism/SR/Amicus/DutchImmigration_Amicus.pdf. See also the HRC-CCPR in CCPR/C/NLD/QPR/5, para. 10.

[103] UNHCR, 'Global Trends: Forced Displacement in 2018', available at
https://www.unhcr.org/statistics/unhcrstats/5d08d7ee7/unhcr-global-trends-2018.html.

[104] Spain recently acceded to the 1961 Convention in September 2018.

[105] Such as the International Covenant on Civil and Political Rights, the International Convention on the Elimination of All Forms of Racial Discrimination, the Convention on the Elimination of All Forms of Discrimination against Women, and the Convention on the Rights of Persons with Disabilities.

[106] Spanish Constitution (1978), available at: http://cort.as/4DRJ.

[107] See Institute on Statelessness and Inclusion, 'Analysis of the Committee's recommendations on the right to a nationality, statelessness and birth registration', Committee on the Rights of the Child 77th Session, (15 January - 2 February 2018), available at: http://www.statelessnessandhumanrights.org/assets/files/crcanalysis_77.pdf.

Spain's nationality law incorporates mainly *jus sanguinis* provisions, but it also offers access to citizenship via *jus soli* where there is a risk of statelessness – for example in the case of children of stateless parents or parents who cannot pass on their nationality and for foundlings. Spain mandates that all births on the territory must be registered, which protect the child's right to a nationality and acts as a safeguard against childhood statelessness. However, despite the relatively strong protections against statelessness in the citizenship regime, stateless persons are still not granted access to facilitated naturalisation, in contrast with refugees,[108] meaning that naturalisation can only happen after 10 years and involves a compulsory language and civic test, as prescribed by Law 19/2015.[109] Moreover, in February 2019, Spain announced that it would reject registration of babies born to surrogate mothers in Ukraine, putting children born from such arrangements at risk of statelessness.[110]

Spain has a dedicated statelessness determination procedure, but it contains various bureaucratic obstacles, and does not protect the person from detention during the process. There are also no procedures in place that prevent stateless persons from being detained for removal, and statelessness is not taken into consideration when assessing vulnerabilities.[111] The majority of applicants for statelessness status are Sahrawis – persons of West Saharan origin – who were previously living in refugee camps in Tindouf, Algeria.[112] Since 2013, when Spain recognised a person of Sahrawi origin as stateless for the first time,[113] Spain has recognised the statelessness status of an increasing number of individuals. In 2016, the Asylum and Refugee Office decided on 2,151 applications for statelessness protection status, with 1,871 positive outcomes and 280 rejections.

The numbers were lower in 2017 and 2018, with 691 decisions (585 positive) and 932 decisions (859 positive) respectively – the recognition remaining high at between 87-92% of applicants.[114]

---

[108] Report of the Working Group of Experts on People of African Descent on its mission to Spain' (2018), A/HRC/39/69/Add.2, para 67.

[109] F. Pasetti, 'The politics and policies of citizenship in Italy and Spain, an ideational account' *Journal of Ethnic and Migration Studies* (2018), available at https://doi.org/10.1080/1369183X.2019.1611422.

[110] M. R. Martinez, 'Spain to reject registration of babies born to surrogate mothers in Spain' *EuroNews* (20 February 2019), available at https://www.euronews.com/2019/02/20/spain-to-reject-registration-of-babies-born-to-surrogate-mothers-in-ukraine.

[111] See further Fundación CEPAIM, European Network on Statelessness and Institute on Statelessness and Inclusion, 'Joint Submission to the Human Rights Council at the 35th Session of the Universal Periodic Review: Spain' (July 2019), available at https://files.institutesi.org/UPR35_Spain.pdf.

[112] V. Cherednichenko, 'A ray of hope for stateless Sahrawis in Spain?' *European Network on Statelessness* (22 October 2013), available at https://www.statelessness.eu/blog/ray-hope-stateless-sahrawis-spain-1.

[113] 'Spain recognises statelessness claims of two individuals from Western Sahara', *Citizenship Rights in Africa Initiative* (1 January 2014), available at http://citizenshiprightsafrica.org/spain-recognises-statelessness-claims-of-two-individuals-from-western-sahara/.

[114] All figures from Ministerio del Interior. *Asilo en cifras,* available at: http://www.interior.gob.es/web/archivos-y-documentacion/documentacion-y-publicaciones/publicaciones-descargables/extranjeria-y-asilo/asilo-en-cifras.

STATELESSNESS IN THE MIDDLE EAST AND NORTH AFRICA (MENA)

OVERVIEW OF STATELESSNESS IN THE REGION

Statelessness is an extremely prevalent issue across the Middle East and North Africa (MENA). UNHCR's 2018 statistics indicate that there are 370,761 recorded stateless persons in the region – a decrease of only around 3,500 from previous years.[1] However, statelessness is poorly mapped, and no reliable figures are available for the stateless populations in the majority of countries, even though it is well known that many of these states have significant stateless populations. This is partly due to the diversity of the groups affected and the underlying causes, as well as the high political sensitivity of questions of demography and citizenship in many countries. The figures that do exist, such as those collated by UNHCR, present a significantly lower estimate of what is likely to be the actual size of the stateless population in the region. Palestinians under UNRWA mandate[2] and stateless refugees in general are not included in UNHCR's global data on statelessness.[3] This means that large populations who are affected by statelessness are not accounted for in these statistics. Moreover, conflict and instability have spread across the region over the last few years, displacing millions of persons and creating new risks for the emergence of statelessness.

Among the groups affected by statelessness in the region are: Kurds in Syria, Iraq and in smaller numbers in Lebanon; Bidoon (or Bidun, literally, without nationality or *bedun jinsiya*) in Kuwait, Saudi Arabia, the UAE and Iraq; Palestinians displaced throughout the region, whose opportunities to naturalise in the host states are extremely limited; Rohingya who have settled in the MENA, in particular in Saudi Arabia; and other communities that have either been denied or stripped of citizenship in countries across the region such as Lebanon and Qatar.

---

[1] UN High Commissioner for Refugees (UNHCR), 'Global Trends, Forced Displacement in 2018' (2018), available at https://www.unhcr.org/5d08d7ee7.pdf. In 2015, the number was 374,237.

[2] UNHCR Statistical online population database, 'General Notes' (2013), available at www.unhcr.org/uk/statistics/unhcrstats/4a01417d6/unhcr-statistical-online-population-database-general-notes.html.

[3] For a detailed analysis of the challenges and gaps related to statistical reporting on statelessness in the world, see Institute on Statelessness and Inclusion, 'The World's Stateless' (2014), available at http://www.institutesi.org/worldsstateless.pdf.

Various historical factors have contributed to the prevalence of statelessness in the region today. Many stateless persons can trace their statelessness back to the formation of states, which mostly occurred with the dissolution of the Ottoman Empire and, later, the end of colonisation. When the borders were (re)drawn, the new states were faced with the task of defining who their citizens were. In Kuwait for example – which has a reported stateless population of 92,00 persons[4] although other sources estimate the number as many as 130,000[5] – the genesis of statelessness was the failure to comprehensively identify and register all persons who should have been recognised as citizens during the post-colonial period of state formation.[6] The government now wholly classes this community as 'illegal residents' and has imposed severe restrictions on rights and access to services since the mid-1980s.[7] Similarly, in Lebanon, a census that took place in the 1930s after the establishment of the state 'locked in' those who were entitled to nationality (and the delicate religious balance of the state), and left others out.[8] Since the Kuwaiti and Lebanese citizenship systems, like those of the other countries in the region, are based on *jus sanguinis,* statelessness is an intergenerational problem that today also affects the children, grandchildren and great-grandchildren of those who historically were denied nationality.

Flawed and discriminatory nationality laws also create new cases of statelessness and prolong protracted ones across the region. MENA is the region with the highest concentration of gender discriminatory nationality laws, with roughly half of the 25 countries that deny women equal rights to pass nationality to their children located in the region.[9] In Qatar, for example, the law does not allow mothers to confer nationality to their children, without exception, even if this would result in statelessness. Discrimination based on religion, race, and disability is also prevalent

---

[4] UNHCR, 'Global Trends, Forced Displacement in 2018' – Table 7 (2018), available at https://www.unhcr.org/5d08d7ee7.pdf.

[5] Human Rights Council, Written statement submitted by Conseil International pour le soutien à des procès équitables et aux Droits de l'Homme, (19 February 2019) A/HRC/40/NGO/132, available at https://documents-dds-ny.un.org/doc/UNDOC/GEN/G19/044/06/PDF/G1904406.pdf?OpenElement.

[6] For more information on this population see Human Rights Watch, 'Prisoners of the Past, Kuwaiti Bidoon and the Burden of Statelessness' (2011) available at https://www.hrw.org/report/2011/06/13/prisoners-past/kuwaiti-bidun-and-burden-statelessness; and Amnesty International, 'The Withouts of Kuwait' (2013), available at https://www.amnesty.org/en/documents/MDE17/001/2013/en/

[7] MENA Rights Group and Institute on Statelessness and Inclusion, 'Report submitted to the United Nations Human
Rights Council in the context of the third periodic review of Kuwait' (July 2019) available at https://files.institutesi.org/UPR35_Kuwait.pdf.

[8] Frontiers Ruwad Association, 'Statelessness in Lebanon: Submission in view of Lebanon's Second Periodic Review by the Human Rights Council' (March 2015) available at https://frontiersruwad.files.wordpress.com/2015/03/upr-lebanon-2015_frontiers-association-submission-on-statelessness_f.pdf.

[9] See UNHCR, 'Background Note on Gender Equality, Nationality Laws and Statelessness' (2019), available at https://www.refworld.org/pdfid/5c8120847.pdf.

in the nationality legislation of various countries across the region.[10] Even countries such as Lebanon and Syria, which have safeguards to protect children from being born stateless on their territories, rarely implement these safeguards.[11] These problems are exacerbated by challenges relating to civil registration that leave many children without proof of where they were born and of parentage. Children born out of wedlock, for example, are often not legally recognised, and in most countries in the region valid marriage certificates are required to register the births of children.[12] Migrant and refugee parents also face particular difficulties in registering births, which may put their children at risk of statelessness.[13]

These discriminatory nationality laws and challenging civil registration practices are of particular problem given the recent upsurge of conflict in the region. Forced migration has been and remains a fundamental cause of statelessness. Historically, due to the upheaval of hundreds of thousands of Palestinians in the wake of the establishment of Israel, millions of Palestinians remain stateless today. Neighbouring countries do not grant citizenship to Palestinians, and therefore many live in an intergenerational and protracted state of statelessness. The ongoing conflicts in Yemen and Syria have meant that refugees fleeing into neighbouring countries are at risk of statelessness, given the difficulty of accessing documents. Children born to refugees are particularly at risk, as birth registration rates are low. Since only fathers can confer their citizenship in many countries, under certain conditions, an absent father precludes registration and may leave a child stateless. Moreover, displacement or forced migration means that countries are directly confronted with the problem of statelessness, even if this previously was not a significant issue within their territory.

The region has also witnessed many cases of arbitrary deprivation of nationality by states. Mauritania, Iraq, and Syria are three countries in the region that in recent history have arbitrarily deprived large numbers of persons their nationality due to race and ethnicity.[14] More recently, there has been a rise in the deprivation of nationality of individuals in the Gulf region, where nationality is being used as a tool

---

[10] Z. Albarazi, 'Regional Report on Citizenship: The Middle East and North Africa (MENA)' Global Citizenship Observatory (2017) available at
https://cadmus.eui.eu/bitstream/handle/1814/50046/RSCAS_GLOBALCIT_Comp_2017_03.pdf.
[11] Ibid.
[12] B. Fisher, 'Why Non-Marital Children in the MENA Region Face a Risk of Statelessness' *Harvard Human Rights Journal* (2015) available at https://harvardhrj.com/2015/01/why-non-marital-children-in-the-mena-region-face-a-risk-of-statelessness/.
[13] See, for instance, B. Manby, 'Preventing Statelessness among Migrants and Refugees: Birth Registration and Consular Assistance in Egypt and Morocco' *LSE Middle East Centre Paper Series 27* (June 2019) available at http://eprints.lse.ac.uk/101091/26/PreventingStatelessnessAmongMigrants.pdf.
[14] Z. Albarazi, 'Stateless Syrians' (2013), available at
https://papers.ssrn.com/sol3/papers.cfm?abstract_id=2269700; Open Society Foundations, 'We Are Mauritanians' (2009), available at https://www.opensocietyfoundations.org/multimedia/we-are-mauritanians; Refugees International, 'The Failli Kurds of Iraq' (2010), available at http://reliefweb.int/report/iraq/faili-kurds-iraq-thirty-years-without-nationality.

of political control and to exclude persons from membership.[15] For example, in April 2019, Bahrain sentenced 139 people to prison, with 138 of those having their citizenship revoked.[16] Furthermore, in the majority of countries across the region, nationality disputes are not considered to fall under the jurisdiction of national courts, and therefore any arbitrary denial or deprivation cannot be legally challenged.

Palestinians and statelessness

The term "Palestinian" describes people who share a common heritage and attachment to "Palestine", but who are now dispersed across different countries and territories in the MENA region and around the world. Not all Palestinians are similarly situated in terms of their legal status, including citizenship. The large-scale displacement of Palestinians, at various times, means that their legal status and enjoyment of nationality is affected by the policy of different host countries. Historically, from 1919 to 1948, all persons who legally resided, were registered, born, or naturalised in Palestine under the British Mandate were considered to be British Protected Persons and held British Palestine passports. The UN Partition Plan for Palestine of 1947 (General Assembly Resolution 181), sought to regulate future citizenship in the proposed Jewish and Arab states. However, when Britain withdrew from the territories of Historic Palestine on 15 May 1948, in effect the question of establishment of nationality was left to the new successor state, Israel. Some Palestinians gained Israeli citizenship but, especially in light of the rejection of the Partition Plan and the mass displacement that accompanied the 1948 conflict (and later the 1967 hostilities), the majority did not. Today, the question of the nationality or statelessness of Palestinians is inextricably linked to the larger issue of Palestinian statehood[17] and of a Palestinian

---

[15] For discussion on using the political usage of citizenship in the region see Z. Albarazi and J. Tucker, 'Citizenship as a Political Tool: the recent turmoil in the MENA and the creation and resolution of statelessness' in T. Bloom, K. Tonkiss, P. Cole, *Understanding Statelessness* (2017).

[16] 'Bahrain revokes citizenship of 138 people after mass trial' *BBC News* (16 April 2019), available at https://www.bbc.com/news/world-middle-east-47947036.

[17] In 2011, Palestine was admitted to UNESCO and in November 2012, the UN General Assembly passed a resolution which accorded Palestine the status of "non-member observer state" of the United Nations. In 2014, Palestine acceded to numerous multilateral treaties which are open to accession by States, including treaties relating to diplomatic and consular relations. A majority of the world's governments had recognised Palestine as a state prior to these latest developments and at the time of writing Palestine enjoyed bilateral recognition from 137 States. See https://palestineun.org/about-palestine/diplomatic-relations/.

nationality policy,[18] neither of which are straightforward. Access to nationality in countries in the region that host Palestinian refugees is highly restricted as a result of a policy aimed at preserving their 'right to return'.[19] The implication of the 1965 "Casablanca Protocol", in particular, is to deny Palestinians naturalization – allowing access to rights and services as well as the issuance of Refugee Travel Documents as a way to facilitate travel, without conferring citizenship.[20] Given that countries in the MENA region grant nationality via *jus saguinis* (parental decent, often only from a father who is a national), Palestinians also cannot access nationality at birth even if they are the second or third generation born in the host country. In the absence of a Palestinian nationality law and without access to nationality in the other countries in the region, it is likely that the majority of Palestinians would technically meet the definition of a stateless person under article 1 of the 1954 Convention relating to the Status of Stateless Persons.

Many Palestinians – specifically 'Palestine Refugees' and 1967 Palestinian 'displaced persons' – fall under the mandate of the United Nations Relief and Works Agency for Palestinian Refugees in the Near East (UNRWA), which operates in Lebanon, Jordan, Syria, the West Bank and the Gaza Strip. UNRWA has estimated that over 5 million Palestinians qualify for UNRWA services.[21] So long as they are receiving protection or assistance from UNRWA, Palestinians who are stateless for the purposes of international law are nevertheless excluded from the scope of the 1954 Convention (as well as the 1951 Refugee Convention).[22] However, this does not mean that they should not be considered stateless for the purposes of the application of other international norms, including under the 1961

---

[18] The recognition of Palestine as a state has not yet translated into the resolution of issues regarding nationality. There is currently no single authoritative source on the rules relating to acquisition or loss of Palestinian nationality, nor is it clear which persons of Palestinian origin are deemed eligible to be recognised as nationals of the state of Palestine.

[19] In Jordan, a large number of Palestinians were naturalised – around 2 million persons – but this policy later changed, reportedly due to a fear that the continued acceptance of Palestinians as Jordanian nationals may give rise to the identification of Jordan as an alternative homeland for Palestinians ('Jordan Queen's Decree stirs tempest' *Christian Science Monitor* (17 December 2002), available at https://www.globalpolicy.org/component/content/article/173-sovereign/30394.html.

[20] League of Arab States, 'Protocol for the Treatment of Palestinians in Arab States' ("Casablanca Protocol") (11 September 1965), available at https://www.refworld.org/docid/460a2b252.html.

[21] UNRWA, 'Palestinian Refugees', available at https://www.unrwa.org/palestine-refugees.

[22] Article 1, paragraph 2(i) of the 1954 Convention relating to the Status of Stateless Persons.

Convention on the Reduction of Statelessness.[23] It should be noted that Palestinians who are receiving assistance from UNRWA, as well as Palestinians who are not in an UNRWA area of operation but who are refugees for the purposes of international law, are not included within UNHCR's global data on persons under its *statelessness* mandate. Nevertheless, the UNHCR statelessness data for some countries may include Palestinians who have been recognised or registered as stateless in the population data of those countries.[24] In recent years, the question of the nationality or statelessness of Palestinians has gained fresh attention as a result of the secondary displacement of many Palestinians due to further conflicts in the region – most notably from Iraq and later Syria. For example, in the European migration and asylum context, the inconsistency of practices relating to the identification and treatment of Palestinians as stateless has been flagged as causing problems with respect to protection procedures, naturalisation and the avoidance of childhood statelessness.[25]

REGIONAL STANDARDS AND INTERGOVERNMENTAL COMMITMENTS

There is a weak regional human rights framework in the MENA region. Both the Arab Charter on Human Rights and the Covenant on the Rights of the Child in Islam protect the right to a nationality.[26] However, these are not binding frameworks and there is no human rights mechanism or regional court to monitor implementation or to hear individual complaints under these treaties. The League of Arab states (LAS), a regional organisation of Arab states, has recently shown some interest in statelessness-related issues, developing a ministerial declaration in 2018 to strengthen rights to legal identity, including nationality, family unity and birth

---

[23] As is set out in UNHCR Guidelines no. 4 on the interpretation of articles 1-4 of the 1961 Statelessness Convention: "*The exclusion provisions set out in Article 1(2) of the 1954 Convention limit the scope of the obligations of States under that Convention. They are not relevant, however, for determining the applicability of the 1961 Convention to particular individuals*". The guidelines are available at https://www.refworld.org/docid/50d460c72.html.

[24] See further Institute on Statelessness and Inclusion, *The World's Stateless – Chapter 3.VIII* (2014) available at https://files.institutesi.org/worldsstateless.pdf.

[25] See in particular European Network on Statelessness, Institute on Statelessness and Inclusion and ASKV Refugee Support, 'From Syria to Europe: Experiences of Stateless Kurds and Palestinian Refugees from Syria Seeking Protection in Europe' (2019) available at: https://statelessjourneys.org/wp-content/uploads/2019/01/ENS-ISI-From_Syria_to_Europe_Jan-2019.pdf.

[26] Article 24 of the Arab Charter on Human Rights (1994); Article 24 of the Covenant on the Rights of the Child in Islam (2004).

registration. The declaration also calls for gender equal nationality laws in all LAS Member states, as well as children's right to a legal identity.[27]

However, substantive engagement and progress in the field of statelessness remains low. There are also only two countries in the region that have acceded to both the 1954 and the 1961 Statelessness Conventions: Libya and Tunisia; while Algeria and Israel are State parties to the 1954 Convention. The level of accessions in the region has not changed for many years and with the majority of the States not having ratified the 1951 Refugee Convention either, there has been little push or expectation to encourage more accessions. Moreover, in UNHCR's High-Level Segment on Statelessness in October 2019, there was very little engagement by MENA States, with only one country (Mauritania) making a pledge, which focused on birth registration, refugee registration and accession to the 1961 Convention.

It is important to note that, despite slight variations from state to state, in general, the rights of stateless persons are rarely protected in the region. There is not a single country in the region that has a statelessness determination procedure, nor a specific protection status for stateless persons. This means that stateless persons are treated as non-nationals - often under immigration law, or *ad hoc* measures - which can massively hinder the process of applying for documents.[28] The lack of legal status, and associated difficulty of applying for a legal status, means that a stateless person will remain legally invisible and unable to access a host of various rights. Despite this, the countries in the region have a reasonably high accession rate to human rights conventions – all, for example, are parties to the CRC, the ICCPR and CEDAW.[29]

Fighting for women's equal nationality rights

Although the MENA region has the highest concentration of gender discriminatory nationality laws, there has been some recent progress on this issue. In 2018 alone, the following developments were reported in the region: in Saudi Arabia, the Shura Council approved the study of two proposals to amend the nationality law to allow women to pass nationality to their children;[30] Morocco announced its intention to pass law reform

---

[27] League of Arab States, 'Arab Declaration on Belonging and Legal Identity' (28 February 2018), available at https://www.refworld.org/docid/5a9flbd04.html.

[28] L. van Waas, 'The situation of stateless persons in the Middle East and North Africa' *UNHCR* (October 2010), available at https://www.unhcr.org/4ce63e079.pdf, p. 3.

[29] However, many states have put in reservations to various articles in these conventions, specifically Article 9 of the CEDAW prohibiting discrimination against women in nationality law.

[30] H. Toumi, 'Saudi Shura Council approves citizenship amendment study' *World Gulf* (7 February 2018), available at https://gulfnews.com/world/gulf/saudi/saudi-shura-council-approves-citizenship-amendment-study-1.2169819.

which would grant women the right to transmit nationality to their foreign husband;[31] and in Syria, the parliamentary council has approved the issuance of a law granting Syrian nationality to children of a Syrian woman if the paternal descent is unknown, which would be welcome progress given the situation of many children who are unable to establish the identity of their father, due to the Syrian crisis.[32] In 2019, the United Arab Emirates changed its policy to allow Emirati women married to foreign fathers to apply for UAE citizenship for their children when they turn six years old, with three thousand children retroactively being granted citizenship;[33] and in Lebanon, the foreign minister announced his intent to amend the law so that Lebanese women can pass on their nationality to their children.[34] Although this is certainly promising, aside from the UAE, no proposed laws or amendments have been enforced, so time will tell whether these developments are substantive, or merely paying lip service to the recognition of women's equal nationality rights. Moreover, in Iraq, proposed amendments to the nationality which would have allowed Iraqi women married to foreigners, as well as unmarried foreigners who have lived in Iraq for only one year to apply for Iraqi citizenship were rejected on the grounds that "the Iraqi nationality law in force is good and authentic", showing that the issue continues to be a contentious one.[35]

CIVIL SOCIETY ENGAGEMENT

There are few civil society organisations or academic bodies in the MENA region working on aspects of statelessness or the promotion of nationality rights. There is

[31] S. Kasrouai, 'Moroccan women will soon be able to pass citizenship to non-Moroccan spouses' *Morocco World News* (March 7 2018), available at https://www.moroccoworldnews.com/2018/03/242601/moroccan-women-will-soon-able-pass-citizenship-non-moroccan-spouses/.

[32] H. Ghanem, 'The People's Assembly approves granting of citizenship of unknown descent' (Wed June 2018), available at http://alwatan.sy/archives/154859.

[33] 'Thousands of children granted UAE citizenship' *Gulf Business* (28 May 2019), available at https://gulfbusiness.com/thousands-children-granted-uae-citizenship/.

[34] 'Lebanon nationality law set to change, but critics say doesn't go far enough' *Middle East Eye* (3 April 2019), available at https://www.middleeasteye.net/news/lebanon-nationality-law-set-change-critics-say-doesnt-go-far-enough.

[35] 'Iraq Parliament rejects proposed changed to nationality law' *Middle East Monitor* (27 March 2019), available at https://www.middleeastmonitor.com/20190327-iraq-parliament-rejects-proposed-change-to-nationality-law/amp/?__twitter_impression=true.

also no cross-regional network that provides a focal point for civil society activities (as there is in other regions of the world) – although the UNHCR-led Middle East & North Africa Civil Society Network for Displacement has had a role in helping civil society organisations to connect and the women's rights organizations across the region that have been campaigning for equal citizenship rights for over a decade also coordinate some of their work through the Global Campaign for Equal Nationality Rights.[36]

Much of the work on statelessness in the MENA region is done by individual lawyers or informal groups of affected individuals. One of the exceptional actors that is well established in the region is Ruwad al-Houkouk in Lebanon. There, Ruwad provides legal assistance for statelessness cases, and engages in advocacy with government ministries.[37] Responding to the significant needs to prevent risks of statelessness for Syrians, Iraqis, Palestinians and other groups within the Middle East region, the Norwegian Refugee Council's Information, Counselling and Legal Assistance (ICLA) programme is helping displaced persons obtain legal identity and civil documentation, including birth certificates and national IDs.[38] Other organisations campaign on specific issues, such as gender discrimination in nationality laws.

In the Gulf, civil society space for mobilisation on statelessness remains particularly limited. Diaspora-based organisations such as Salam for Democracy and Human Rights, Gulf Institute for Human Rights, alongside individual activists, have worked to fill this gap by highlighting the ongoing violations relating to deprivation of citizenship, and particularly the ongoing violations against Bidoon in Kuwait. Indeed, in some cases, organisations both in and outside the MENA region campaign on community recognition and rights, such as stateless Syrian Kurds or Kuwaiti Bidoon. Individual members of the Kuwaiti Democratic Forum, a political group, also campaign for the rights of the Bidoon.[39]

At the regional level, the 2018 adoption of the Arab Declaration on Belonging and Legal Identity by Arab League states (through facilitation by the state of Tunisia) provides a key tool with potential for further advocacy and accountability. In recent years, a number of academic and stakeholder roundtables have also been held in the region, leading to a coalescence between actors, activists and academics working on statelessness as a regional issue. In 2019, for example, the Center for Migration and Refugee Studies (CMRS) at the American University in Cairo and the Association marocaine d'études et de recherches sur la migration (AMERM) in

---

[36] See https://equalnationalityrights.org/countries/middle-east-north-africa.
[37] See http://www.frontiersruwad.org/. It both provides legal support for and advocacy on behalf of refugees, asylum-seekers and stateless persons.
[38] See also http://www.syrianationality.org/.
[39] 'Government lacks real program by which it can operate: Kuwait Democratic Forum' *Kuwait Times* (17 November 2019) available at: https://news.kuwaittimes.net/website/government-lacks-real-program-by-which-it-can-operate-kuwait-democratic-forum/.

Rabat, Morocco collaborated with the London School of Economics in a research publication issued in June 2019 on the risk of statelessness in relation to children born to migrant and refugee parents.[40] In January 2020, the American University in Cairo ran a Short Course on statelessness, further signalling a growing interest in capacity development on the issue.

HABIBA AL-HINAI

"When my son was born premature, he had to be in an incubator... I suddenly received a heavy bill that I had to pay. I told them "I am Omani it's free medical care" and they responded "you have a foreigner child...this creature is a foreigner, so you have to pay the bill"

Following the birth of her son, Habiba came to learn that women were unable to confer their nationality to their children on an equal basis to men. Her non-Omani husband was unable to pass his nationality to their child, and she, as a woman could not either. Her child was, as a result, born stateless, and as he was not considered an Omani citizen, Habiba was landed with steep medical bills. Habiba has since dedicated her life to gender equality and overturning the discriminatory laws in Oman which prevent women from conferring her nationality.

COUNTRY PROFILES

To complement the regional overview of the state of statelessness in MENA, the following sections explore the situation at national level in greater detail, in four countries where there are significant challenges and interesting recent developments, in fulfilling the right to a nationality for all: Kuwait, Qatar, Saudi Arabia and Syria.

---

[40] B. Manby, 'Preventing Statelessness among Migrants and Refugees: Birth Registration and Consular Assistance in Egypt and Morocco' *LSE Middle East Centre Paper Series 27* (June 2019) available at http://eprints.lse.ac.uk/101091/26/PreventingStatelessnessAmongMigrants.pdf.

Kuwait

The stateless population in Kuwait was estimated to be 92,000 persons at the end of 2018,[41] although other sources estimate the number 130,000 or more.[42] These figures relate to Kuwait's Bidoon (or Bidun) population whose name in Arabic means 'without' (nationality). Kuwait is also one of the 25 countries with gender discriminatory nationality laws, and is home to around 80,000 Palestinians. The Bidoon have suffered from statelessness since 1961 when the country gained independence, and have been considered by the government as 'illegal immigrants' and a security threat since the mid-1980s, after which their position in society deteriorated dramatically.[43] In 2011, following protests demanding access to rights, including the right to a nationality, the government announced that certain rights, such as access to education, registration, and healthcare, would be reinstated to the Bidoon. However, little has been done to fulfil these promises; instead, there has been an increase in arrests and harassment, with attempts to block public and civil society efforts to advocate for their rights.[44] Worryingly, in 2016 the Kuwaiti government offered to buy them citizenship to the Comoros Islands.[45] For Kuwait, this presents an opportunity to absolve itself of legal responsibility, yet it would result in affiliating the Bidoon with a country that they lack ethnic, historical and cultural ties to – a country that they may not even have a right to settle in.[46] Although there have been reports of individuals obtaining this citizenship, the exact figures are unclear.[47]

In early 2019, the UN Special Rapporteur on the right of persons with disabilities expressed concern at the treatment of the Bidoon, especially with regards to obtaining an ID card that can remedy the status of illegal residents, which is essential to access any services. Later on in 2019, the suicide of 20-year-old Bidoon Ayed Hamad Moudath, who ended his life after the government denied him the civil documentation he needed for study and work, sparked a series of peaceful

---

[41] UNHCR, 'Global Trends, Forced Displacement in 2018' – Table 7 (2018), available at https://www.unhcr.org/5d08d7ee7.pdf.

[42] Open Justice Society Initiative, 'Stateless in Kuwait: Who Are the Bidoon?' (March 2011), available at https://www.justiceinitiative.org/voices/stateless-kuwait-who-are-bidoon; Human Rights Council, Written statement submitted by Conseil International pour le soutien à des procès équitables et aux Droits de l'Homme, (19 February 2019) A/HRC/40/NGO/132, available at https://documents-dds-ny.un.org/doc/UNDOC/GEN/G19/044/06/PDF/G1904406.pdf?OpenElement.

[43] European Network on Statelessness and Institute on Statelessness and Inclusion, 'Statelessness in Kuwait: County Position Paper' (May 2019).

[44] European Network on Statelessness and Institute on Statelessness and Inclusion, 'Statelessness in Kuwait: County Position Paper' (May 2019).

[45] A. Taylor, 'The controversial plan to give Kuwait's stateless people citizenship of a tiny, poor African Island' Washington Post (17 May 2016), available at https://www.washingtonpost.com/news/worldviews/wp/2016/05/17/the-controversial-plan-to-give-kuwaits-stateless-people-citizenship-of-a-tiny-poor-african-island/?utm_term=.c20d7e473934.

[46] A. A. Abrahamian, 'Who loses when a country puts citizenship up for sale?' New York Times (January 5 2018), available at https://www.nytimes.com/2018/01/05/opinion/sunday/united-arab-emirates-comorans-citizenship.html.

[47] A. A. Abrahamian, *The Cosmopolite: The Coming of the Global Citizen* (Columbia Global Reports 2015).

demonstrations calling for equal rights by members of the Bidoon. This led to a number of unlawful arrests and imprisonments, including prominent human rights defender Abdulhakim al-Fadhli. In reaction, the group went on a hunger strike, protesting their unlawful detainment and the human rights abuses of the Bidoon in general.[48] 15 stateless Bidoon activists remain in prison until early 2020 when, on 28 January, a Kuwaiti court sentenced three of the protesters (one in absentia) to between 10 years and life in prison. The other 13 individuals who were also arrested were finally ordered released: 12 subject to a pledge of good conduct for two years, five of whom were ordered to pay a bail payment of 1,000 Kuwaiti dinars ($3,300) and one individual was fully acquitted.[49]

Qatar

The size of the stateless population in Qatar is unclear. UNHCR reports 1,200 stateless persons at the end of 2018, but this number has not changed since 2008.[50] There are three main issues in Qatar related to statelessness: gender discrimination in the nationality law, statelessness among the Bidoon and al-Ghufran communities, and deprivation of citizenship.

Qatar does not allow women to confer nationality to their children or spouses under any circumstances, and does not show any steps in changing this. In October 2018, Qatar adopted 'Law 10/2018 on Permanent Residency', enabling children of Qatari women with foreign spouses to obtain permanent residence in the State party, which allows them to gain access to education and health care and to own property.[51] However, this does not put them on an equal footing with Qatari nationals, and the law also requires that the child's parents be married under Qatari law. Moreover, gender discrimination in the nationality law is not addressed, and Qatar still has in force a reservation to CEDAW Article 9, which affirms women's equal nationality rights.

Members of the Bidoon community and the al-Ghufran clan continue to be affected by statelessness. Mostly descendants of nomadic groups in the Arabian Peninsula, the Bidoon are stateless as they were not registered as citizens at the time of Qatar's state-formation in 1971, and children born to Bidoon parents have systematically

---

[48] Global voices, 'The plight of Kuwait's stateless community: silenced and deprived of human rights' (September 2019), available at https://globalvoices.org/2019/09/03/the-plight-of-kuwaits-stateless-community-silenced-and-deprived-of-human-rights/.

[49] Amnesty International, 'Kuwait: Heavy prison sentences of activists demanding rights of citizenship' (28 January 2020) available at https://www.amnesty.org/en/latest/news/2020/01/kuwait-heavy-prison-sentences-of-activists-demanding-rights-of-citizenship/

[50] UNHCR, 'Persons of concern', available at http://popstats.unhcr.org/en/persons_of_concern.

[51] Committee on the Elimination of Discrimination against Women, 'Concluding Observations: Qatar', CEDAW/C/QAT/CO/2, (July 2019), available at https://tbinternet.ohchr.org/_layouts/15/treatybodyexternal/Download.aspx?symbolno=CEDAW/C/QAT/CO/2&Lang=En; UNHCR, 'UNHCR Submission on Qatar: 33rd UPR Session' (May 2019), available at https://www.refworld.org/docid/5ccad3d07.html.

been denied the right to a nationality. Qatar has made no attempts to resolve their statelessness nor ensure that their access to rights in the country are protected. Members of the al-Ghufran clan are stateless as a result of being deprived of their citizenship on 1 October 2004 on allegations of their holding second nationality. Later, government officials demanded or induced thousands to leave Qatar. An indeterminate number have regained rights in Qatar in recent years and it is unclear how many continue to be stateless in 2019.[52]

The State of Qatar continues to arbitrarily deprive citizens of Qatari nationality. Often, this is pretexted on the enforcement of the prohibition of dual nationality, but it has also become mechanism to target political opponents or human rights defenders. In September 2017, following the diplomatic crisis between the Gulf Cooperation Council states, Qatar withdrew citizenship from individuals who were deemed sympathetic to Saudi Arabia – specifically members of the Al Murra tribe. This included, among others, a tribal leader and a well-known poet.[53]

Saudi Arabia

Saudi Arabia has a stateless population of 70,000 people, according to UNHCR.[54] It is not clear who is 'counted' under this figure, but Saudi Arabia is known to be home to a large Bidoon population, like the other countries in the Gulf. Other estimates have placed the number of Bidoon to be as high as 250,000.[55] Since 2009, the Bidoon have been issued renewable identity documents known as 'black cards' which serve as five-year residence permits. However, in September 2019 several cases were reported of problems acquiring identity paper, which affected Bidoon children's attendance of school. In response, the Ministry of Education issued a resolution that allowed these children to be admitted to schools. However, the Bidoon are still deprived of many rights, such as the right to work and higher education,[56] and the Saudi government continues to put pressure on human rights activists defending Bidoon issues through arrests.[57] It has also been reported that in 2020, the Bidoon will be required to prove their origin. The consequences of failing to do so are still unclear.[58]

---

[52] Institute on Statelessness and Inclusion, Rights Realisation Centre and Global Campaign on Equal Nationality Rights, 'Joint Submission to the Human Rights Council at the 33rd Session of the Universal Periodic Review: Qatar' (4 October 2019), available at https://files.institutesi.org/UPR33_Qatar.pdf.

[53] 'Qatar revokes famous poet's citizenship' *Gulf News*, (1 October 2017), available at https://gulfnews.com/news/gulf/qatar/qatar-revokes-famous-poet-s-citizenship-1.2098844.

[54] UNHCR, 'Population Statistics', available at http://popstats.unhcr.org/en/overview.

[55] ESOHR, 'Deprivation of Nationality in Saudi Arabia' (April 2016), available at http://www.esohr.org/en/wp-content/uploads/2016/03/Deprivation-of-nationality-in-Saudi-Arabia.pdf.

[56] ESOHR, 'Bidoon Victims of Unjust Practices and Laws: Temporary Solutions do not Protect Rights' (5 September 2019), available at https://www.esohr.org/en/?p=2546.

[57] Id.

[58] Id.

According to the nationality law, Saudi men can confer their nationality to their children regardless of their birthplace, but Saudi women cannot unless the father is unknown. Saudi women are also prohibited from passing their nationality onto a non-national spouse, a right reserved only for Saudi males.[59] Children of Saudi mothers do have the option of applying for nationality at age 18, but subject to conditions such as permanent residency, 'good behaviour' and fluency in Arabic. Although this provision offers an avenue towards citizenship, children of Saudi mothers continue to be denied access to many rights during their childhood. Saudi nationality law also contains no safeguard against statelessness at birth.[60] This, combined with the gender discriminatory *jus sanguinis* rules, aggravates the problem of intergenerational statelessness in the country.

A large population of stateless Rohingya also resides in Saudi Arabia, estimated at over half a million.[61] In early 2017, Saudi Arabia issued 190,000 four-year residence permits for members of the Rohingya population.[62] However, reports in 2019 have brought to light systematic detention and deportation of hundreds of Rohingya, including women and children who remain detained indefinitely and without charge at the Shumaisi detention centre in Jeddah.[63] In April 2019, many stateless Rohingya detained inside Shumaisi went on hunger strike to demand an end to their indefinite detention and potential deportation to Bangladesh, from where some Rohingya obtained faked passports to travel to Saudi Arabia.[64] Protesters were reportedly faced with retributive measures from the Saudi authorities.[65]

Up to 287,000 Palestinians also live in Saudi Arabia. Most of them have residence status but are excluded from naturalisation procedures.[66] Moreover, since they are dependent on sponsorship to ensure their continuous residency, they remain in a

---

[59] Institute on Statelessness and Inclusion, the Global Campaign for Equal Nationality Rights and the European Saudi Organization for Human Rights, 'Joint Submission to the Human Rights Council at the 31st Session of the Universal Periodic Review: Saudi Arabia' (29 March 2018), available at https://files.institutesi.org/UPR31_SaudiArabia.pdf.

[60] Ibid.

[61] Institute on Statelessness and Inclusion et al., 'Joint Submission to the Human Rights Council at the 31st Session of the Universal Periodic Review: Saudi Arabia' (29 March 2018).

[62] '190,000 Myanmar nationals' get residency relief in Saudi Arabia' *Al Arabiya* (25 January 2017), available at http://english.alarabiya.net/en/News/gulf/2017/01/25/Over-190-000-Myanmar-nationals-granted-Saudi-residency.html.

[63] A. Ullah, 'Hundreds of Rohingya imprisoned 'indefinitely' in Saudi Arabia' *Middle East Eye* (13 November 2018), available at https://www.middleeasteye.net/news/revealed-hundreds-rohingyas-imprisoned-indefinitely-saudi-years-1365716422.

[64] A. Ullah, 'Saudi Arabia continues to deport scores of Rohingya to Bangladesh' *Middle East Eye* (25 January 2019), available at https://www.middleeasteye.net/news/saudi-arabia-continues-deport-scores-rohingya-bangladesh.

[65] A. Ullah, 'Saudi Arabia accused of torturing Rohingya detainees to end hunger strike' *Middle East Eye* (17 April 2019), available at https://www.middleeasteye.net/news/saudi-arabia-accused-torturing-rohingya-detainees-end-hunger-strike.

[66] A. Shiblak, 'Stateless Palestinians', FMR 26, available at http://www.fmreview.org/sites/fmr/files/FMRdownloads/en/palestine/shiblak.pdf.

vulnerable situation, ineligible for public services and at risk of being deported.[67] Since UNRWA has no presence in Saudi Arabia it does not formally recognise or assist them.[68]

Syria

Syria has a long history of statelessness, even prior to the outbreak of the civil war in 2011. According to UNHCR, the stateless population pre-civil war was 300,000,[69] dropping to 160,000 at the end of 2013.[70] This figure refers to the population of stateless Kurds who were stripped of their nationality following a controversial 'arabisation' census in 1962.[71] The reduction in numbers is not explained, but is likely to be attributable in part at least to reported naturalisations on the basis of a Decree passed in April 2011 that created a pathway to citizenship for Syria's stateless *Ajanib* Kurds (but not the stateless *Maktoumeen* Kurds).[72] Indeed, in mid-2013, UNHCR reported that 104,000 individual Kurds had acquired citizenship through this new process.[73] However, during the same period in which the reduction in the number of stateless people can be observed, the conflict in Syria was beginning to cause mass displacement and this may have affected the statistical reporting on statelessness where stateless persons were (instead) accounted for among IDP and refugee populations. This figure has not been updated since and it remains a challenge to estimate how many people from Syria are affected by statelessness given the conflict and displacement. As of the end of 2018, there were an estimated 6.3 million refugees from Syria residing abroad and 6.2 million internally displaced, [74] but there is no comprehensive disaggregation of data on the basis of statelessness.[75] UNHCR has reported that 0.2% of refugees registered in Lebanon are stateless, which translates to several thousand persons *just in Lebanon*,

---

[67] S. Aziza, 'A Palestinian refugee in Saudi Arabia: 50 Years of lost dreams' *Middle East Eye* (1 March 2016), available at http://www.middleeasteye.net/columns/palestinian-refugee-saudi-arabia-civic-immobility-and-lost-dreams-344102002.

[68] Institute on Statelessness and Inclusion et al., 'Joint Submission to the Human Rights Council at the 31st Session of the Universal Periodic Review: Saudi Arabia' (29 March 2018).

[69] UNHCR, 'Global Trends: Forced Displacement in 2009', available at https://www.unhcr.org/4c11f0be9.pdf, p. 26.

[70] UNHCR, 'Global Trends: Forced Displacement in 2018', available at https://www.unhcr.org/5d08d7ee7.pdf, p. 67.

[71] Some estimates place the figure at around 500,000 before 2011. Syrians for Truth and Justice, 'Syrian Citizenship Disappeared: How the 1962 Census destroyed stateless Kurds' lives and identities' (15 September 2018), available at: https://www.stj-sy.com/en/view/745.

[72] See further European Network on Statelessness and Institute of Statelessness and Inclusion, 'Country Position Paper: Statelessness in Syria' (August 2019), available at https://statelessjourneys.org/wp-content/uploads/StatelessJourneys-Syria-August-2019.pdf.

[73] UNHCR, Global Report 2012 – Syrian Arab Republic, 19 June 2013, available at: http://www.unhcr.org/51b1d63cb.html.

[74] UNHCR, 'Global Trends: Forced Displacement in 2018', available at https://www.unhcr.org/5d08d7ee7.pdf, p. 67; p. 14.

[75] Institute on Statelessness and Inclusion, 'The World's Stateless' (December 2014), available at https://files.institutesi.org/worldsstateless.pdf, p. 10.

not including other host countries.[76] The full effect of the 2011 Decree and the implications of the conflict and displacement for statelessness among Syria's Kurdish population remain unclear. Meanwhile, historically-rooted structural ethnic discrimination against Kurds persists.[77]

Nationality and statelessness problems in Syria are aggravated by the gender discriminatory provisions in the 1969 nationality law, which is based upon paternal *jus sanguinis*. This means that the acquisition of nationality at birth depends on the father being a Syrian citizen. There are very few provisions for a mother transmitting her nationality, and they do not apply if the child is born out of wedlock, or if the child is born abroad.[78] This is of even greater concern in the context of mass forced displacement,[79] since it becomes very difficult for a child born abroad to establish a legal link to the father.[80] Moreover, the civil war has also resulted in many barriers to civil registration access, both for those still in Syria and refugees abroad. Statelessness poses a major obstacle for IDPs within Syria, who are considered ineligible for most forms of social services, including food subsidies.[81] According to a 2019 survey, there were civil documentation problems in 59% of the communities assessed.[82] This is due to a variety of reasons, including difficulty accessing civil registry offices, a lack of offices, non-recognition of documents or security concerns.[83]

The Syrian Government also has considerable discretion in depriving people of nationality if it is deemed "in the interests of security and safety of the country".[84] For example, the government reserves the right to withdraw nationality if a citizen resides in a State that is at war with Syria, joins the military service of another State,[85] or has been outside the country for more than three years and does not

---

[76] Norwegian Refugee Council/Internal Displacement Monitoring Centre (NRC/IDMC), 'Understanding statelessness in the Syria refugee context' (2016) available at https://www.refworld.org/docid/584021494.html, p. 44 [accessed 3 December 2019]

[77] International Crisis Group, 'Syria's Kurds: A Struggle within a Struggle' (2013).

[78] European Network on Statelessness and Institute of Statelessness and Inclusion, 'Country Position Paper: Statelessness in Syria' (August 2019), available at https://statelessjourneys.org/wp-content/uploads/StatelessJourneys-Syria-August-2019.pdf.

[79] Ibid.

[80] Institute on Statelessness and Inclusion and The Global Campaign for Equal Nationality Rights, 'Submission to the Human Rights Council at the 26th Session of the Universal Periodic Review: Syrian Arab Republic' (24 March 2016), available at https://equalnationalityrights.org/images/zdocs/ISI-GCENR---UPR-Submission-Syria---March-2016-Final.pdf.

[81] Ibid.

[82] Strategic Steering Group (SSG) and humanitarian partners working under the Whole of Syria (WoS) framework, '2019 Humanitarian Needs Overview (HNO)' (March 2019), available at https://reliefweb.int/sites/reliefweb.int/files/resources/2019_Syr_HNO_Full.pdf, p. 28.

[83] European Network on Statelessness and Institute of Statelessness and Inclusion, 'Country Position Paper: Statelessness in Syria' (August 2019), available at https://statelessjourneys.org/wp-content/uploads/StatelessJourneys-Syria-August-2019.pdf.

[84] Nationality Law [Syrian Arab Republic], 'Legislative Decree 276' (24 November 1969) Article 21F, available at https://www.refworld.org/docid/4d81e7b12.html.

[85] Nationality Law [Syrian Arab Republic], 'Legislative Decree 276' (24 November 1969) Articles 21B and E, available at https://www.refworld.org/docid/4d81e7b12.html.

respond to requests to return to Syria within three months.[86] This raises potential concern in the context of the conflict and related displacement, although there is no information on State practice in this regard. There have been several cases of citizenship stripping of foreign fighters who came to Syria from Western nations, by their own governments, as a counter-terrorism measure – such as Denmark[87] and the UK.[88] In some cases, this has rendered individuals stateless[89], preventing them from returning home and leaving them at the mercy of Syrian courts where they could face the death penalty.

It is important to note that the UNHCR estimate for the number of persons under its statelessness mandate in Syria does not include Palestinian refugees.[90] In 2014, approximately 550,000 Palestinians were registered by UNRWA as living in Syria. Due to the country's restrictive naturalisation laws, the vast majority of Palestinians in Syria are believed to be stateless.[91] The current crisis has exacerbated the vulnerability of Palestinians due to their precarious legal status and led to problems in accessing protection in the context of secondary displacement from Syria.[92]

---

[86] Nationality Law [Syrian Arab Republic], 'Legislative Decree 276' (24 November 1969), Article 21G, available at https://www.refworld.org/docid/4d81e7b12.html. Note, it is not clear whether these provisions are enforced in practice.

[87] 'Government to fast-track stripping foreign fighters of citizenship', CPH Post (15 October 2019), available at http://cphpost.dk/news/government-to-fast-track-stripping-foreign-fighters-of-citizenship.html.

[88] 'Jihadi Jack: IS recruit Jack Letts loses UK citizenship', BBC News (18 August 2019), available at https://www.bbc.co.uk/news/uk-49385376.

[89] See K. Rawlinson and V. Dodd, 'Shamima Begum: Isis Briton faces move to revoke citizenship', The Guardian (19 February 2019), available at https://www.theguardian.com/world/2019/feb/19/isis-briton-shamima-begum-to-have-uk-citizenship-revoked; 'High Court backs removal of UK man's citizenship over joining Islamic State group', Middle East Eye (8 August 2019), available at https://www.middleeasteye.net/news/removal-uk-mans-citizenship-over-joining-backed-first-high-court-judgement.

[90] UNRWA, 'Syria Regional Crisis - Emergency Appeal' (2018), available at https://www.unrwa.org/sites/default/files/content/resources/2018_syria_ea_final_web_0.pdf, p. 1. However, other sources suggest that this figure was 526,744. See for example: Australian Department of Foreign Affairs and Trade, 'Thematic Report on Conditions in Syria' (23 October 2017), available at https://dfat.gov.au/about-us/publications/Documents/country-information-report-syria.pdf.

[91] Institute on Statelessness and Inclusion, The World's Stateless (2014).

[92] Norwegian Refugee Council and Institute on Statelessness and Inclusion, 'Understanding statelessness in the Syria refugee context' (2016) available at https://www.refworld.org/docid/584021494.html; European Network on Statelessness, Institute on Statelessness and Inclusion and ASKV Refugee Support, 'From Syria to Europe: Experiences of Stateless Kurds and Palestinian Refugees from Syria Seeking Protection in Europe' (2019) available at: https://statelessjourneys.org/wp-content/uploads/2019/01/ENS-ISI-From_Syria_to_Europe_Jan-2019.pdf.

PART II

DEPRIVATION OF NATIONALITY

THE POWER TO DEPRIVE

INTRODUCTION

> **The growing practice of citizenship deprivation… is a stain against the claim of liberal democratic states to be communities where all enjoy freedom and equality before the law. The practice undermines equality among citizens, damages their commitment to uphold human rights, and unfairly excludes from membership people who became the people they are within the community that now seeks to banish them."**

Christopher Bertram

The power to deprive citizenship is as old as the power to grant citizenship. In fact, the choices that are made when determining and implementing the rules of citizenship, are influenced as much by who (when and upon what terms) to 'exclude', as they are by who (when and upon what terms) to 'include'.

Over the course of modern history, we have witnessed the most egregious and shocking consequences of the power to deprive, when concentrated in the hands of a few, unchecked by democratic institutions, and targeted at vulnerable minorities. Deprivation of citizenship was a necessary precursor to the Holocaust, just as it was to the genocide of the Rohingya. In both contexts, highly militarised and authoritarian states, obsessed with the notion of ethnic and racial purity, targeted unwanted minorities to be disenfranchised and persecuted.

The post-World War moment, one of great introspection and despair, saw a hitherto unprecedented coming together of states to shape a rules-based order premised on individual rights and a global commitment to peace. This brave new world recognised the centrality of protecting everyone's right to a nationality (Article 15 of the UDHR), while also protecting those who had no nationality or protection of the state (the Refugee and Statelessness Conventions). However, the promise of this era has – at best – been only half delivered. We have stronger rules and institutions in place to protect the right to nationality, but the wielders of power continue to find new ways to circumvent the trappings of the law, justify their actions and shield themselves from scrutiny.

After WWII, citizenship stripping was no longer seen as democratic and the prohibition of arbitrary deprivation of nationality became anchored in international human rights law; today, while most states resist increasing these powers, the policy is regaining traction and deprivation of nationality is in active use across a range of contexts. In this new era of rising authoritarianism, growth of the security state, genocide, and increasing populism, xenophobia and racism, citizenship is under threat in ways not seen for generations. As more states instrumentalise nationality and treat it as a privilege that can be taken away, members of minority communities, human rights defenders, dissidents and suspected terrorists are all more likely to be stripped of their nationality – facing acute human rights depravations as a result. The growing (mis)use of citizenship stripping powers to target some, undermines the sanctity of citizenship for all.

Since ISI was first established, we have been reflecting on and trying to respond to this alarming trend, through our research, advocacy and other activities. We began working on these issues in a more concerted manner in 2017, when we convened a group of experts to discuss the phenomenon of citizenship deprivation. This marked the beginning of a 30-month (to-date) collaboration with Open Society Justice Initiative, the Asser Institute and Ashurst LLP, of research and consultations on trends of deprivation, the effectiveness of such measures and the international standards and norms which limit and shape state action in this area. Through this process, guided by over 60 leading experts in the fields of human rights, nationality & statelessness, counter-terrorism, refugee protection and other related areas, we developed the **Principles on Deprivation of Nationality as a National Security Measure**.

These Principles, which are included at the very end of this World's Stateless Report, articulate the international law obligations of states and apply to all situations in which states take or consider taking steps to deprive a person of nationality as a national security measure. They do so by restating or reflecting international law and legal standards under the UN Charter, treaty law, customary international law, general principles of law, judicial decisions and legal scholarship, regional and national law and practice. The launch of the Principles and this World's Stateless Report in March 2020, also mark the launch of a **Year of Action Against Citizenship Stripping**, which provides a unifying banner under which all actors opposed to the instrumentalisation of nationality and deterioration of the institution of citizenship may come together to raise awareness, strengthen discourse and advocate for states to align their laws, policies and practices with their international legal obligations. The Principles remain open for institutional and individual endorsement throughout the Year of Action.

As such, the 2020 World's Stateless Report – unlike previous editions – serves both to further unpack a particular theme related to statelessness (citizenship deprivation for this edition) and as a resource for an active campaign to strengthen awareness and encourage reform. This departure is reflective of the urgency with which we feel this issue must be addressed, in order to prevent the further erosion of the institution of citizenship, a cornerstone upon which democratic societies have been built. The more we are able to keep state power to deprive in check today, the better equipped we will be to prevent the atrocities of tomorrow.

But it's not only about taking action. It's also about understanding and reflecting on the history and motivations as well as the standards at issue. This is exactly what we aim to do through Part 2 of this report. Below are four reflections and observations of ours – which resonate in different ways through Part 2 of the report:

DEPRIVATION – THE AGENDA OF THE POWERFUL

As set out in the Principles on Deprivation of Nationality:

"Deprivation of nationality refers to any loss, withdrawal or denial of nationality that was not voluntarily requested by the individual. This includes where a State precludes a person or group from obtaining or retaining a nationality, where nationality is automatically lost by operation of the law, and where acts taken by administrative authorities result in a person being deprived of a nationality."[1]

Deprivation can target entire communities as well as individuals. The power to deprive citizenship as a national security measure, the power to deny citizenship to minority communities and the power to withdraw citizenship of political dissidents are not accidents of history. These powers exist, not necessarily because they serve legitimate purposes, or are proportionate or fair, but because they serve the agendas of the powerful. Such powers are likely to be discriminatory in their origin and their impact, demonstrating an inextricable link between citizenship deprivation and discrimination. In the UK for example, as elaborated in Amanda Weston's reflection from a British Litigator's Perspective, citizenship deprivation powers target dual nationals and naturalised citizens, thereby discriminating against minorities and those of migrant heritage. The legal frameworks under which Rohingya and Dominicans of Haitian origin were deprived of their nationality, meanwhile clearly discriminate against minorities. Reflecting on this trend, Special Rapporteur Tendayi Achiume observes in her interview:

One way to understand denationalisation is as a tool that governments have long used to ethnically purify their nation states. It is a very convenient and easy way to do so,

---

[1] Principles on Deprivation of Nationality as a National Security Measure. Principle 2.2.1, see page 288.

> **sometimes by explicitly identifying groups that are understood to be foreign or outside of the nation."**

Citizenship deprivation is also a powerful tool through which to silence voices of opposition and punish dissidents. Jawad Fairooz, a human rights activist who was stripped of his Bahraini citizenship, reflects on the abuse of power he was at the receiving end of as follows:

> **Is security really being achieved by this inhuman and unlawful act? By targeting civil society, the pillars of a healthy society are eroded, paving the way for further insecurity. By revoking the citizenships of peaceful dissidents under the 2006 law, the Bahraini government is equating human rights defenders with violent terrorists. By excluding individuals in this way and denying them countless human rights, the seeds of a deep mistrust are sown."**

THE NARRATIVES AND THE OBJECTIVES BEHIND DEPRIVATION

Related to the above, is the often complex and muddled relationship between the narratives related to citizenship deprivation and the real objectives of those who wield the power to deprive. International law imposes significant limits on the utilisation of citizenship deprivation by states. Consequently, there is a greater onus on states to justify, both internally and externally, the introduction, expansion and utilisation of citizenship deprivation powers. The 'real' objectives often cannot be stated, as these would not withstand the scrutiny of courts and other forms of oversight. And so, proxy reasons and narratives are often woven into discourse, to build the argument for citizenship deprivation. Narratives – through which deprivation is justified, rationalised and normalised – tend to embrace themes such as 'national security and counter-terrorism', 'patriotism and loyalty', and 'belonging and identity'. They invoke the idea that the State serves the nation, and anyone who is not part of the nation or is disloyal to it, has no place in it. These narratives thrive on populism, the othering of minorities and those with migrant backgrounds, and insularity. Recognising the danger of such narratives, diplomatic expert Laetitia van den Assum reflects that:

> **The arguments governments put forward to denationalise individuals show that citizenship is at risk of being seen as a privilege, rather than a fundamental right to belong to a nation. Accepting these arguments implies the devaluation**

**of everyone's citizenship – not just the citizenship of those
who lose it and are thus at risk of statelessness."**

The underlying objectives for citizenship deprivation on the other hand, are more likely to be about plastering over the failures of government or concentrating power and resources. Citizenship deprivation is a symbolic gesture to show that the state is being hard on terrorism, even if this is not an effective measure. It is about the scapegoating of minorities, who can be blamed for economic and other failures. It is about punishing dissent, to keep the people in check.

The more confident a state becomes, the more the gap between narratives and objectives can begin to close. A government which has retained power through a populist, racist and xenophobic agenda, has less reason to hide its own racist motivations for citizenship deprivation, as is currently playing out in India. Similarly, a government that has successfully cracked down on dissent, has less reason to hide behind the façade that it is only terrorists who need to fear the consequences of citizenship deprivation. And so, in a strange paradox, states can become more 'honest' about their intentions the more they believe their actions will go unchallenged. In these situations, governments may benefit in the short term by preying on the disenfranchised and strengthening their narratives of othering. However, in no such situation has a country truly benefited. Mass disenfranchisement does not bring with it economic progress, development or peace. Narratives of blame, fear and scapegoating are propagated for short-sighted political gain.

THE VIOLENCE OF BUREAUCRACY

It is often easier to get away with deprivation of nationality by imposing unsurmountable bureaucratic barriers, than by explicitly targeting particular groups under the law. Unfair evidentiary burdens, indirect discrimination through the imposition of proxy measures, arbitrary, corrupt and inefficient processes can all lead to the deprivation of nationality, which disproportionately impacts on minorities and other target groups. Seemingly bureaucratic processes have cloaked and facilitated racist, xenophobic and discriminatory motivations and actions throughout the world and over history. The resultant disenfranchisement and exclusion of entire communities and the human rights deprivations faced by millions has destabilised societies, undermined economic progress, escalated conflict and caused immeasurable pain and suffering.

Commenting on some of these themes, Kipling Williams and Andrew Hales, in presenting their psychologists' perspective on 'statelessness as social ostracism', state as follows:

> **Statelessness is a condition that has many of the same characteristics as chronic social ostracism, which has been empirically shown to predict depressive symptoms, feelings of alienation, worthlessness, and learned helplessness... the finding that ostracism activates brain regions associated with physical pain makes Chief Justice Warren's statement that statelessness is "A form of punishment more primitive than torture" seem slightly less hyperbolic."**

At present, this type of bureaucratic nightmare is playing out in India, as explored in the contribution by José Arraiza, Marina Arraiza Shakirova and Phyu Zin Aye. Laura Bingham also explores abuse of bureaucratic procedures related to fraud in the U.S.A. as violence. As Bingham elaborates:

> **Recent examples of U.S. born Americans caught up in immigration raids, deported, denied vital documentary proof of citizenship and deprived of U.S. passports following fraud investigations, share common equally intertwined drivers: nationalism and the criminalisation of the U.S. immigration system. All of the 'errors' listed above disproportionately impact Americans who identify with or are identified with communities that are heavily profiled for immigration enforcement under a growing array of civil and criminal immigration laws."**

Historically, we have witnessed and responded to the fallout of such 'bureaucratic processes' with regard to the Rohingya in Myanmar, the Dominicans of Haitian descent, the Lhotshampa of Bhutan, Kenyan minorities forced to undergo 'vetting', Syrian Kurds and the Erased of Slovenia (to name but a few). In all of these situations of manufactured statelessness, individuals and minority communities have experienced the brunt of the impact.

FALSE DICHOTOMIES AND INTERNATIONAL STANDARDS

Nationality deprivation – perhaps like no other issue – elicits arguments about state sovereignty and the alleged overreach of international law. As Tendayi Achiume articulates:

> **The trouble is that States often want to characterise decisions around nationality as being within their domestic**

jurisdiction as sovereign nation states, meaning that they reserve the right to exercise discretion over who they include and exclude. However, it is important to remember that even those kinds of decisions, sovereign decisions, are constrained by principles and laws within the international framework that apply in this realm as well."

This perceived tension between the states' right to decide who belongs, and the human right of every person to a nationality, lies at the heart of many a debate, with minorities at the fault-line. But it is important to acknowledge that states also exercise their sovereignty when they accede to international treaties, participate as member states of the UN and incorporate international norms into domestic law. This is not a clash, but a reinforcement. And so, perhaps this tension is not as strong as sometimes portrayed. Further, even where there may be a tension, it is only in a few fundamental ways that international law limits how a state may shape its nationality law. Everyone has the right to a nationality, the arbitrary deprivation of nationality is prohibited, statelessness should be avoided, nationality laws should not discriminate and the best interests of the child should always be a primary consideration in decisions or actions affecting children. These are some of the basic principles which limit state discretion, and, which we all should be able to agree, benefit us all.

Just as there is a perceived tension between state sovereignty and individual rights, there can also be a perceived tension between some of these different rights. The idea that you can either avoid statelessness or prevent discrimination, but cannot do both, resonates with many states. The argument is that if you cannot make someone stateless, you can only deprive nationality of dual citizens. Doing so creates a hierarchical citizenship structure, in which those with only one citizenship are more secure than those with multiple citizenships. Such structures are inherently discriminatory against minorities and those of migrant heritage, who are more likely to hold more than one citizenship. The correct interpretation of these international standards – as set out in the Principles on Deprivation of Citizenship – is that both standards must be met. This makes it more difficult for states to deprive nationality, not less.

Despite these strong international standards, as Matthew Gibney observes, *"not only have deprivation powers spread… the courts have done little to limit their development and impact."* As Gibney states, there is a chance that we are *"in the midst of a radical revision in the way that citizenship is conceived, one that puts an increasing emphasis on obligations rather than rights."* And so, we must take his warning seriously, that:

"A new era of banishment may be only just beginning."

What follows in Part 2 of this report, is a series of interventions which relate to different aspects of the issue of citizenship deprivation, and from different perspectives. Part 2 covers a lot of ground to give us a sense of the wider citizenship deprivation landscape: from a closer analysis of legal standards, to an overview of current trends; a look at situations of mass deprivation of nationality, to an unpacking of the effectiveness of citizenship deprivation as a national security measure; an exploration of some of the more idiosyncratic aspects of the problem like quasi loss and retroactive denial, to a critique of justifying deprivation on the grounds that nationality was acquired by fraud. Interspersed between these interventions, are a series of 'Perspectives' - reflections by experts from different backgrounds (historians, philosophers, legal practitioners, psychologists, security experts and victims of citizenship deprivation, to name but a few), which serve to provoke thought by challenging us to view this issue through different lenses. Part 2 also includes an exclusive interview with the UN Special Rapporteur on contemporary forms of racism, racial discrimination, xenophobia and related intolerance. The report ends with the Principles on Deprivation of Nationality as a National Security Measure.

Collectively, these contributions present a range of expertise, analysis and coverage on the subject, which, to our knowledge, has never been collected in one place before. We are delighted to be able to bring to you. In this era of othering, in which citizenship is under threat, we hope this contribution will enrich discourse and catalyse action towards the much-needed course correction to protect everyone's right to acquire and preserve their nationality, by depriving states of the power to deprive.

STATE TERRORISM: REVOKING THE NATIONALITY OF CITIZENS IN BAHRAIN: *AN AFFECTED PERSON'S PERSPECTIVE*

BY JAWAD FAIROOZ[*]

Most of us take our citizenship for granted. From birth we belong to one, or in some cases, two states. This belonging represents a significant part of our identity and enables us to maintain our daily life under the protection of the state. But, imagine if one morning, you suddenly woke up stateless.

It has been seven years since I was stripped of my Bahraini nationality and officially became stateless. I was one of the first victims of Bahrain's revocation of citizenship programme, but I am not the only one. Since 2012, one year after the pro-democracy uprising began, the Bahraini government has used citizenship as a weapon for political punishment. On 7 November 2012, the Ministry of Interior revoked the nationality of 31 citizens without any justification being given. This included me and my brother, Jalal Fairooz, also a former member of parliament. In 2015, another 208 citizens were denaturalised and in 2018, a further 298. In total, around 990 Bahraini nationals have had their citizenship revoked in the past eight years,[1] which amounts to 0.15% of the population. If the same percentage had their citizenship revoked in the United States, this would amount to nearly half a million people.

REASONS FOR REVOCATION

The justification the Bahraini authorities use to carry this out is nearly always the same - to protect the country and its citizens from extremists and terrorists. The legal basis which allows for this practice dates back to August 2006, when Bahrain adopted an anti-terrorism law.[2] The government's powers were expanded further in

---

[*] **Jawad Fairooz** is a former Bahraini Member of Parliament and chair of Salam for Democracy and Human Rights Organization (SALAM DHR). He is an Advisory Council member of ISI.

[1] http://www.anabahraini.org/

[2] Law No.58 (2006) On Protecting Society from Terrorist Acts [online] available at: http://www.vertic.org/media/National%20Legislation/Bahrain/BH_Law_No_58_Protection_Community_aga inst_Terrorist_Acts.pdf

2013 when deprivation of nationality was included as an additional penalty for those who commit so called "terrorist crimes".

But how can we define terrorist crimes? Bahrain's Penal Code[3] already has a number of articles that detail terrorism-related crimes, including articles 112-129. However, the terrorist acts listed in the new 2006 law are extremely broad, extending to non-violent acts such as "disrupting the public order", "threatening the Kingdom's safety and security", and "damaging national unity". However, rather than fighting 'terrorism', the law has instead been used to target activists, politicians, clerics and any peaceful dissidents.

Such broad definitions are not compatible with international human rights law, neither is the act of making a person stateless, with Article 15 of the Universal Declaration of Human Rights (UDHR) stating that "Everyone has the right to a nationality" and "No one shall be arbitrarily deprived of his nationality."[4] Yet in Bahrain, hundreds of individuals have been, and continue to be, arbitrarily deprived of their nationality.

CONSEQUENCES OF REVOCATION

Citizenship is the most basic and fundamental right of every individual. It is a 'right of rights': a right which unlocks other rights, the absence of which erodes the enjoyment of all rights and protection. Losing one's nationality can thus be described as a form of social death.

Once someone is stripped of their citizenship, they are stripped of a whole host of human rights. Denaturalisation often follows and is followed by arrest, interrogation and detention causing multiple rights violations. The practice also leaves individuals unable to access many basic services, from healthcare and education to housing and finance.

This social death means total exclusion from public life and can often result in poverty and mental illness. It does not just affect the individual, but the entire family, and it will not just affect the present generation, but future generations too as the new-born children of those who have had their nationality revoked are also at risk of statelessness and its associated negative impacts. The possible long-term effects of this are hard to fathom.

---

[3] Bahrain Penal Code (1976) [online] available at:
https://www.unodc.org/res/cld/document/bhr/1976/bahrain_penal_code_html/Bahrain_Penal_Code_1976.pdf
[4] Article 15 UDHR (1948) [online] available at:
https://www.ohchr.org/EN/UDHR/Documents/UDHR_Translations/eng.pdf

Is security really being achieved by this inhuman and unlawful act? By targeting civil society, the pillars of a healthy society are eroded, paving the way for further insecurity. By revoking the citizenships of peaceful dissidents under the 2006 law, the Bahraini government is equating human rights defenders with violent terrorists. By excluding individuals in this way and denying them countless human rights, the seeds of a deep mistrust are sown.

WHAT WENT WRONG?

The Bahraini government is the prime actor responsible for this practice. Intending to completely crack-down on dissent, the government has used the banner of 'terrorism' to mask this goal, and the revocation of citizenship as the latest tool to carry out its repression. The practice should be seen as one of a number of methods used to spread fear and punish dissent, akin to the death penalty and the use of torture.

But, more surprisingly, how has the international community allowed it to foster? The problem is that certain bodies have been slow to act and recognise the scope of the problem. In 2014, the UN High Commissioner for Refugees (UNHCR) launched a campaign "#IBelong", in a bid to end statelessness. While this was welcome, the campaign failed to include those who have become stateless through citizenship revocation, like the hundreds of Bahrainis. NGOs have also been slow to address the issue. Aside from thematic organisations, like the Institute on Statelessness and Inclusion (ISI) and the European Network on Statelessness (ENS), other international organisations have been playing catch up. A conference on citizenship revocation held at Amnesty International in 2016 and the ISI World Conference on Statelessness and Inclusion in 2019 were both an exception to this and led to transnational action in the Gulf region, such as the creation of an All-Party Parliamentary Group (APPG) on human rights in the Gulf.

There are signs that the international community is waking up. When the Bahraini government revoked the nationality of 138 people in a mass trial in April 2019, there was a huge backlash. Soon thereafter, Bahrain announced that 551 individuals would have their nationality reinstated. This marks a point from which further change can emerge, however the most prominent activists and politicians have not been included in this decision. This is nowhere near sufficient for full remedy, justice and reparation to be attained.

HOW TO END THE PRACTICE?

Ending the inhuman and unlawful practice of arbitrary deprivation of citizenship can and must be a straightforward goal. Continuous international pressure on the Bahraini government is needed. The recent reinstatement of citizenship shows that international pressure can be effective, but this pressure must be sustained and increased in order to secure long-term change, including ending the practice, reinstating all citizenships revoked for politically motivated purposes and scrapping the 2006 anti-terrorism law.

In order to achieve this, further work also needs to be done on a thematic basis around the issue of statelessness and citizenship revocation including for example the establishment of specific UN guidelines. Increased cooperation between international bodies, including those at the UN level, is also crucial in order to effectively combat this practice both in Bahrain and internationally.

If you lose your citizenship, as in my case, you will immediately lose your job, will be unable to access public services, will face restrictions on travel, and will be unable to vote. Your identity papers become invalid meaning that you are basically an invisible person in the eyes of the law. You no longer feel personal security and may be considered an illegal immigrant and treated like a criminal in your own country. You are more likely to be forced to leave the country where you were born, raised and lived for your whole life, leaving your beloved ones behind at home.

Citizenry is above the government, not vice versa, and citizenship revocation powers only serve to enhance the discretionary and arbitrary power of the executive authority. The possession of citizenship should not be understood as a privilege or rewarded for allegiance and its revocation should not be wielded as a weapon of control and oppression.

DEPRIVATION OF NATIONALITY:
A DIPLOMAT'S PERSPECTIVE

BY LAETITIA VAN DEN ASSUM*

Are we living on the edge? On the divide between a rules-based order - with widely shared principles and consensus about the importance of multilateralism - and an unknown world?

The future will only present itself gradually, but it is already clear that persistent conflict and climate change are here to stay, forcing us to come to terms with growing human insecurity and massive population movements. Higher human mobility will compel us to safeguard existing rights, norms and standards related to citizenship, nationality and identity. Adjustments may have to be made, not in a haphazard manner but with safeguards to ensure that a comprehensive and rational framework with due regard for inclusion remains in place.

The aftermath of World War II was marked by chaos, trauma and massive population movements. Millions were on the move in a world that had undergone major changes. It was no accident that, after the 1948 Universal Declaration of Human Rights and the Genocide Convention, the 1951 Refugee Convention and the 1954 Convention on the Status of Stateless Persons were among the first major human rights treaties to be concluded. Large scale population movements had demonstrated the need for greater clarity about refugee status, statelessness and internal displacement.

But now, 75 years on, the sands have started to shift again. We started to see changes from 9/11 onwards but continue to feel distinctly uncomfortable because we still don't have a good sense of what the future will bring. It is obvious that important chapters of the present international order have to be examined on a regular basis. Determining whether, for example, nationality laws are still fit for purpose and adjusting them where necessary, will ensure their continued domestic relevance and acceptance as well as their practicality in international relations.

We are, however, seeing a tendency to give more weight to domestic political acceptability than to maintaining a generally accepted and tested international

---

* **Laetitia van den Assum** is an expert in international diplomacy who serves on the Advisory Council of ISI. She previously served as Ambassador of the Netherlands on four different continents. She was also a member of the Rakhine Advisory Commission, which was chaired by Kofi Annan.

system that favours predictable outcomes. Although the rights and duties afforded by nationality laws to individuals differ from state to state, the accepted basic principle is that nationality gives the state jurisdiction over a person and affords him or her the protection of the state. Although this principle has generally served us well, cracks are appearing.

The recent ambiguity around the legal status and nationality of IS fighters and their families is a case in point. Some countries of origin have shown willingness to repatriate them, thus recognising their protection duty towards their nationals. Others, mostly western countries, have an approach in which fear and security concerns are major drivers. They are reluctant to accept their duty of protection. While the fear factor should not be downplayed, it is difficult to capture it in legal terms. It invites ambiguity and arbitrary decisions. Will the exclusionary attitude towards IS fighters remain an exception to the rule, or will others follow?

The arguments governments put forward to denationalise individuals show that citizenship is at risk of being seen as a privilege, rather than a fundamental right to belong to a nation. Accepting these arguments implies the devaluation of *everyone's* citizenship – not just the citizenship of those who lose it and are thus at risk of statelessness.

The practice of nationality deprivation is of particular concern when it takes place without due process and without a judicial determination that such drastic action is warranted. Another worrying aspect is countries' reluctance to take back children who are their nationals, the most striking example of a state's neglect of its duty to protect its citizens.

Shifting the burden to the authorities in areas where fighters are being held however is not a solution. It undermines the present rules-based system which holds a reasonable guarantee that countries of origin take responsibility for their nationals. It also places a severe and unfair burden on countries struggling to recover from years of savage violent conflict, who lack even the basic capacity to look after their own people.

We are at the mid-point of UNHCR's decade-long #IBelong campaign to end statelessness by 2024. Progress has been made. Not only has awareness of statelessness grown, many countries have taken bold steps to reduce the number of stateless people. Colombia and Kyrgyzstan are among those who have led the way. But this progress may be reversed unless we guard against efforts to increase statelessness.

The Rohingya of Myanmar make up the world's largest group of stateless people. Since the 1980s they have gradually lost their claim to Myanmar citizenship and in 2015 the government declared their temporary papers invalid. Since then, the number seeking refuge in Bangladesh has swollen to 1.1 million. A similar number have fled to other countries as far afield as Saudi Arabia, Pakistan and Malaysia. The Rohingya have experienced a gradual 'othering' or alienation, based on their ethnicity and religion. Othering is a process of expressing prejudice on the basis of group identity. It leads to a group's inequality and marginalisation with rejection as its ultimate conclusion. For the Rohingya, rejection included statelessness.

Othering is on the rise around the world. Linked to the rise of nationalism, it is among the most pressing problems of the 21st century. Growing Hindu nationalism in India has given rise to census-driven efforts to identify people who are said to disqualify for citizenship. In Assam alone, 1.9 million people are at risk of losing citizenship, most of them Muslim. Fears have also grown about Sri-Lanka, where a president with a history of authoritarian abuse and ethnic and religious division took over in late 2019. India and Sri-Lanka are however by no means alone. Incompatible perceptions of identity and belonging are a major cause of disunity and rejection around the world. Unless checked, conflict may give rise to new migration and refugee flows. Once mobility increases, the threat of statelessness is never far away.

We are best served by a rules-based system that minimises the opportunity for *ad hoc* interpretation. If greater allowance is made for exceptions, governments will feel comfortable prioritising short-term domestic political expediency over the maintenance of a functioning international system, and chaos will be just around the corner. Close international collaboration is the only solution.

STATELESSNESS AS SOCIAL OSTRACISM: A PSYCHOLOGIST'S PERSPECTIVE

BY KIPLING D. WILLIAMS*
AND ANDREW HALES*

People who are stateless are faced with a wide range of negative practical impacts that are well detailed in this report and elsewhere. They have less access to rights and less access to various educational, health, employment and legal resources. This alone is reason for concern. We suggest, however, that on top of these practical consequences, it is likely that deprivation of nationality also induces the same negative psychological effects that result from social ostracism more generally.

A robust understanding of social ostracism's consequences has been developed in recent decades.[1] We are not aware of research addressing the psychological effects of statelessness directly, however, simple extrapolation from the large body of research on ostracism as a general phenomenon suggests that statelessness very likely produces similar negative psychological consequences.

In experiments involving over 10,000 participants[2], research on ostracism finds again and again that being ignored and excluded not only causes sadness and anger, but also threatens four fundamental human needs: belonging, self-esteem, control and meaningful existence. Ostracised individuals feel less connected to others, badly about themselves, unable to do anything about it and invisible and unworthy of

---

* **Kipling D. Williams** is Distinguished Professor of Psychological Sciences at Purdue University, where he has taught since 2004. Previously, Williams was on faculties at Macquarie University and University of New South Wales (both in Sydney, Australia), University of Toledo (Ohio), and Drake University (Iowa). He is a pioneer and world-leading expert on social and psychological dynamics of ostracism. In addition to his authored book, *Ostracism: The Power of Silence* (Williams, 2001), he has edited nine books on related topics.

* **Andrew Hales** is a researcher in the Frank Batten School of Leadership and Public Policy at the University of Virginia. Starting in Autumn 2020 he will be in the Department of Psychology at the University of Mississippi. Andrew studies how people respond to ostracism. Specifically, he is interested in interventions that either intensify or dull the momentary pain of ostracism.

[1] K.D. Williams 'Ostracism' (2007) Annual Review of Psychology, 58, 425-452; K.D Williams 'Ostracism: A temporal need-threat model' (2009) In M. Zanna (Ed), *Advances in Experimental Social Psychology* 41, NY: Academic Press.

[2] C.H.J Hartgerink, I. van Beest, J.M. Wicherts, & K.D. Williams, 'The ordinal effects of ostracism: A meta-analysis of 120 Cyberball studies' (2015) PLOS ONE, 10. e0127002.

attention. Recent research also finds that ostracism diminishes an individual's sense of self-clarity: they are less certain about who they are and what they stand for.[3] Moreover, the pain of ostracism is not just metaphorical. Brain imaging research finds that being ostracised activates brain regions that detect and sense physical pain.[4] What is perhaps most surprising about these findings on the negative effects of ostracism is that they are largely from experiments in which the ostracism was designed to be as innocuous as possible: mere strangers connected through the internet excluding participants from a low-stakes ball tossing game for two minutes. The participants in these experiments had not met the others, nor did they expect to meet them. They were unknown strangers never to be encountered again. Nevertheless, the impact was strong and consistent across hundreds of studies. If effects such as these occur after two minutes, imagine the impact from being ostracised daily by (former) friends, teachers, administrators and the government itself.

Indeed, humans have a fundamental need to belong – to have at least a few deep and meaningful social connections. Of course, this need can be met in the context of statelessness (it's not as if statelessness necessarily entails social isolation). But research on being out of the loop, a form of partial ostracism in which individuals belong and are acknowledged in some realms, but not in others, has also been shown to threaten fundamental needs, so total isolation is not necessary for these effects to occur.[5] We speculate, that the ever-present knowledge of one's deprived citizenship causes a low-hum, but constant, threat to psychological needs for self-esteem (by making a person feel unworthy of inclusion into a national community); control (by denying access to services, resources and even basic legal recourse); meaningful existence (by suggesting that the country does not need them) and finally, a feeling of certainty (by creating bureaucratic ambiguities that one must navigate to participate in public life).

In short, statelessness is a condition that has many of the same characteristics as chronic social ostracism, which has been empirically shown to predict depressive symptoms, feelings of alienation, worthlessness, and learned helplessness. Finally, the finding that ostracism activates brain regions associated with physical pain makes Chief Justice Warren's statement that statelessness is "A form of

[3] A.H. Hales and K.D. Williams 'Marginalized individuals and extremism: The role of ostracism in openness to extreme Groups' (2018) Journal of Social Issues, 74, p.75-92.

[4] N.I. Eisenberger, M.D. Lieberman, and K.D. Williams 'Does rejection hurt? An fMRI study of social exclusion' (2003) Science, 302, p.290-292; E. Kross, M.G. Berman, W. Mishel, E.E. Smith, and T.D. Wager 'Social rejection shares somatosensory representations with physical pain (2011) Proceedings of the National Academy of Sciences, 108, p.6270-6275

[5] E.E. Jones, A.R. Carter-Sowell, J.R. Kelly and K.D. Williams 'What you don't know can hurt: Effects of being out of the loop' (2009) Group Processes and Intergroup Relations, 12, p.157-174

punishment more primitive than torture" seem slightly less hyperbolic.[6]

The negative effects of ostracism are not only felt by the targeted individual. Ostracism has been shown to provoke aggressive responses towards others.[7] People who are ostracised may come to feel that it is more important to be noticed than to be liked, and aggression is one way to assert control and demand acknowledgement from others. Statelessness could potentially contribute to this dynamic. Further, the global decline in violence across human history has been attributed, at least in part, to the growth and development of effective governments that harness the use of legitimate power to administer justice and punish wrongdoing (thereby removing the need for victims of violence to respond in kind, and perpetually even-the-score[8]). Excluding people from that system, even partially, could potentially provoke greater aggression.

Our recent work also suggests that individuals experiencing chronic ostracism may be especially susceptible to recruitment efforts by extreme groups.

Compared to moderate groups, extreme or radicalised groups are perceived to be more cohesive, supportive while feeling superior to other groups, impactful and noticeable. They are also perceived to be clearer as to their sense of mission. All of these perceived benefits provide an attractive solution to the despair of ostracism and marginalisation.[6]

The psychological consequences of statelessness deserve greater empirical attention (as do related questions regarding the effects of the international community not acknowledging certain states, for example). However, based on current ostracism research and theory, it is reasonable to expect deprivation of nationality to have meaningful negative psychological consequences for those who experience it.

---

[6] *Trop v. Dulles*, 356 U. S. 86 (1958).

[7] K.D. Williams, and E.D Wesselmann 'The link between ostracism and aggression' (2011) In J. P. Forgas, A. W. Kruglanski and K. D. Williams (Eds.), *The Psychology of Social Conflict and Aggression* (New York, NY: Psychology Press).

[8] S. Pinker *The better angels of our nature: Why violence has declined* (NY: Viking 2011).

STATELESSNESS AND THE DEPRIVATION OF NATIONALITY: *A HISTORIAN'S PERSPECTIVE*

BY LAURA ROBSON*

The idea of "deprivation of nationality" is, above all, a twentieth century idea that would have seemed rather nonsensical in most political contexts prior to the First World War. Before about 1918, neither nationality nor its corollary, statelessness, had much meaning; subjecthood and (to a lesser extent) citizenship were not generally understood as guarantors of political, economic, or civil rights. It was only with the fairly recent rise of the modern nation-state that rights came to reside almost solely in the framework of nationality, rendering a loss or lack of nationality a fundamental political problem.

Indeed, statelessness was a relatively normal condition across the globe – including in Europe – until the twentieth century, and nationality, to the extent that it could be identified at all, was often flexible and mutable in surprising ways. First of all, nationality was not necessarily territorially bound nor ethnically, religiously, or linguistically defined. This can be seen from the multifarious communities – Indian, Armenian, Orthodox Christian, Jewish – claiming British or Ottoman imperial subjecthood from Delhi to Ceylon to Baghdad to Cairo. Second, although nationality might have conferred a degree of economic protection and some useful contacts – to merchant communities, for instance – it offered little in the way of political or civil rights. As a consequence, nationality and its various proofs were, for most of the nineteenth century, tested and confirmed or denied mainly in the context of commercial travel. In the relatively rare instances where subjects were denied rights on the grounds of an individual action placing them outside the framework of state-granted rights, the consequences were mostly material: forfeiture of property and denial of inheritance. The practice of 'civil death,'[1] was also occasionally deployed in various places as a punishment for criminal acts or unsanctioned religious conversions.

---

* **Laura Robson** is a professor of modern Middle Eastern history at Portland State University in Portland, Oregon, specialising in histories of forced migration, the construction of refugee and asylum policies, and decolonisation and mass violence. She is the author or editor of several books, including *States of Separation: Transfer, Partition, and the Making of the Modern Middle East* (University of California Press, 2017), which explores the history of forced migration, population exchange, and refugee resettlement in Iraq, Syria, and Palestine during the interwar period.

[1] The loss of some or all civil rights usually as a result of criminal conviction or as an act by government.

The First World War changed this situation. With the sudden and unexpected demise of four great multinational land empires in Europe: the Austro-Hungarian, German, Ottoman and Russian, the stage was set for the introduction of a new Allied-dominated global order: the nation-state, in which ethno-national identity (linguistic, religious, cultural) would align with the political borders of the state. The enforcement of such a political order in the profoundly pluralistic lands of Eastern and Central Europe and the Middle East would, of course, require considerable violence in the form of mass deportations, population 'exchanges', and large-scale killings; and still it left behind enormous numbers of people now categorised as 'minorities' in majoritarian ethno-national states. Now, belonging to a nationality represented a new guarantee of rights, and existing outside the nation – whether as a stateless person or as a legal 'minority' – rendered a person newly vulnerable in this emerging national and global order.

It should not surprise us, then, that this was the moment when the modern era's refugee problem was born. Although mass migration of displaced peoples had characterised wartime prior to the twentieth century, the First World War marked the beginning of a new international approach to refugees who understood their role in the context of a global order of nation-states.

Refugees were victims of the new system, but they also helped to constitute nationality by clearly demarcating its borders: their political and geographical exclusion helped define the nature of citizenship and political rights within individual nation-states and, more broadly, within the global *system* of nation-states.

Further, they offered a rationale for and legitimisation of new kinds of imperial authority in the guise of internationalism. Their plight as citizens of nowhere served to promote the notion of the League of Nations – which would largely serve, in practice, as a venue for British and French imperial management, and as an international necessity in the post-1918 world.

In the years following the war, League officials broadcast this notion both to refugees themselves and to an emerging network of international funders through the institutionalisation of refugee camps for newly stateless peoples. The maintenance of refugee settlements as quasi-sovereign spaces run by international authorities, from which refugees could not assimilate or engage politically with their host countries (an arrangement, we should note, made possible mainly by the military occupation of these spaces), served as a public display of the international community's ideological commitment to locating political rights solely in nationality. This is the context in which Hannah Arendt's famous statement about the "right to have rights" was born: in a world of nation-states, where the only guarantee of civil or political rights lay with the state, to exist outside of a nationality meant to enjoy no rights at all. By seeking to remake the pluralistic politics of multinational empires into a modern politics of exclusionary nation-states, the Allied powers had deliberately removed the possibility of accessing rights outside a framework of national belonging.

Even as the new United Nations – in theory, and in some ways in practice, a more inclusive organisation than its predecessor – declared that human rights did indeed exist outside a national frame, it continued to assure its members that the national state was the only viable venue for their enforcement and guarantee. Thus, the 1948 United Nations Universal Declaration on Human Rights specifically posited a "right to a nationality" as a basic human right – formally stigmatising and pathologising a condition that had been common, if not normative, throughout most of human history. Statelessness became a political problem only when nationality was invested with a "right to have rights" that could be accessed in no other way. It is worth noting that this entangled relationship between nationality and rights remains problematic not just for stateless persons but also for many millions whose nationality lies in states unwilling, or unable, adequately to guarantee civil and political rights to their citizens. From an historical perspective, then, we might say that the problem of "deprivation of nationality" is not so much the deprivation as the nationality itself.

INTERVIEW
WITH TENDAYI ACHIUME*

INTERVIEWED BY AMANDA BROWN, 15 NOVEMBER 2019

How should we understand the nexus between xenophobia, racism and the deprivation of nationality?

"It is a very complicated nexus, and I think that we need to approach it with a sense of humility and recognition of the complex nature of the relationship. One thing we know for sure is that the deprivation of nationality has played out, both historically and in a more contemporary context, along racialised and xenophobic lines. So, while there may be many different causes and factors that lead to denationalisation, racism and xenophobia are a very big part of it.

I think one way to understand denationalisation is as a tool that governments have long used to ethnically purify their nation states. It is a very convenient and easy way to do so, sometimes by explicitly identifying groups that are understood to be foreign or outside of the nation. You can think about what recently happened with Haitians in the Dominican Republic; you can think about the Rohingya in Myanmar; you can think about Jews in Nazi Germany. There are many places where there has been an explicit project that identifies a group and claims they are outsiders to the nation. Sometimes it is done in more implicit, but nonetheless, effective ways, such as gendered restrictions on women which prevent them from passing their nationality on to their children. You might see it in the context of counter-terrorism law and policy, where there are measures that strip people of nationality, ostensibly on national security grounds, but which nonetheless have racially, ethnically or religiously specified targets, that are also being identified in other discourses as threats to the nation.

And so, one relationship that I think is absolutely important to highlight is the use of denationalisation as a tool to achieve ethnonationalist ends. We should always be on the lookout for this particular dynamic. This is not to say that all

---

* **Tendayi Achiume** is the UN Special Rapporteur on Contemporary Forms of Racism, Racial Discrimination, Xenophobia and Related Intolerance. She is also Professor of Law at the University of California, Los Angeles School of Law, where she is the faculty director of the Promise Institute for Human Rights. She is also research associate of the African Center for Migration and Society at the University of Witwatersrand in South Africa and an Advisory Council member of ISI.

denationalisation is taking place as the result of implicit or explicit ethnonationalist projects, but there is certainly reason to be deeply suspicious."

Can deprivation of nationality constitute racial discrimination? If so, what is the legal foundation for this?

"Absolutely, I really think that it can constitute racial discrimination, and there are different legal foundations for making this argument, some that are clearer than others. Part of the important work that the Institute on Statelessness and Inclusion (ISI) is doing, is trying to map out the doctrinal foundations or the doctrinal restrictions that exist in public international law, and how you deprive people of nationality if you're going to do so.

Arbitrary deprivation of nationality is prohibited in international law, and there are several grounds upon which racial discrimination can constitute an arbitrary ground for nationality stripping. There are multiple norms that already exist within the human rights framework that prohibit racial discrimination that would not permit it in the context of stripping of nationality. But in terms of the sources of the principles, there are many, including the *jus cogens* prohibition on racial discrimination, and the International Convention on the Elimination of All Forms of Racial Discrimination.

The trouble is that States often want to characterise decisions around nationality as being within their domestic jurisdiction as sovereign nation states, meaning that they reserve the right to exercise discretion over who they include and exclude. However, it is important to remember that even those kinds of decisions, sovereign decisions, are constrained by principles and laws within the international framework that apply in this realm as well.

So, in short, there is a legal foundation for construing deprivation of nationality as racial discrimination. Organisations like ISI are doing important work in clarifying and raising awareness of these legal norms."

Could you share any examples of how this nexus has manifested in State laws, policies or practices?

"There are many different examples of where you see this happening, and I think some of them are some more explicit than others. In the United States, the Open Society Justice Initiative, for example, has done important work to publicise the way in which US citizens are being stripped of nationality on an ethnic and racial basis, and how the current US administration has exacerbated this policy. In this case, you can see an ethnonationalist project that has been articulated in political terms which is now finding legal and policy manifestations.

Some countries in the European Union, in the context of their counterterrorism policies, have rules that permit nationality stripping of individuals who are dual nationals. Significantly, in most of these places, another EU nationality does not count as an additional nationality that makes an individual eligible for nationality stripping. Rather, it is North African and other so-called "non-western" nationalities that are targeted. These measures predictably and disproportionately target racial and ethnic minority communities in a way that means an EU citizen with North African ancestry suspected of Islamic extremism is subject to nationality stripping, whereas an EU citizen with European ancestry and who engages in extreme right-wing terrorism can be fully guaranteed to be shielded from nationality stripping.

Other examples include the Rohingya in Myanmar, and the religiously and ethnically targeted process of citizenship-stripping underway in Assam, India. I think the cases I mention, which are sometimes treated as discrete and separate from each other, should be understood as being on a continuum."

Do you think that deprivation of nationality, including its intersections with racism and xenophobia, has received the attention in the UN System that it deserves? What are some of the challenges?

"No, I don't think so, but to be fair, there are many human rights issues that don't receive the attention that they deserve. I think the problem in this case is that the issue seems to interfere more directly with the ways in which States understand their sovereignty. This is an area that States are very protective of, which may explain why they are not investing the time that is required to deal with this problem seriously.

I think there has been a lot of momentum within the UN to consolidate counterterrorism and counter-extremism collaboration in ways that are directly in tension with concerns surrounding citizenship stripping. In my opinion, this momentum has been moving in the wrong way rather than in the right way. However, I generally find that this happens with most issues that relate to racial discrimination. I wouldn't be surprised if the conversation surrounding citizenship stripping continues to be divorced from concerns about racism, religious intolerance and other forms of intolerance.

More urgent work needs to be done in this space, in a way that links conversations around citizenship stripping to the entire spectrum of methods in which States are excluding people from their nations on a racial, religious or ethnic basis. Citizenship Stripping is just one mechanism through which it's happening, and again, organisations like ISI are well poised to ensure that conversations around statelessness, citizenship stripping, refugees, as well as the multitude of other ways in which race or ethnicity can make you vulnerable when it comes to political membership should be understood and treated as part of a shared picture."

Can you reflect a little more on the historic and potential future use of deprivation of nationality by States?

"Among other approaches, we should also have a functional approach to understanding what citizenship stripping is about. I really do think that one of the functions it plays is this ethnic or racial purging of political communities. I believe we should be monitoring citizenship stripping as a tool that is very effective at policing the ethnic, racial and other boundaries of the nation.

It will likely remain a handy tool for racially engineering political communities in the future, which means that it is extremely important to think about it right now. It is essential that we continue to discuss how the principles that govern citizenship stripping should include consideration of racial discrimination, putting pressure on States to both prioritise and adopt them."

What gives you hope in this space?

"What gives me hope is the civil society energy around these issues. In the last few years, as migration has become one of the ground zeroes for understanding equality and determining equality in different parts of the world, it has been heartening to see that both big traditional NGOs and smaller ones are beginning to realise that this is an issue that requires attention. This has to be something that is sustained.

I think we are in a moment, even within the UN system, where ignoring racism, xenophobia and related intolerance is increasingly difficult because of right-wing actors who explicitly espouse these views. It is no longer something that we can deny; although it is still something that we can choose to ignore. This, however, provides an opportunity for people who believe in equality and non-discrimination to really insist on a discourse that prioritises these issues. So, there is a moment of openness and possibility. However, I'm not quite sure whether I'm hopeful or not, because we are still unsure as to how this will unfold. ISI's upcoming Draft Principles on Deprivation of Nationality as a Counterterrorism and National Security Measure will be a litmus test.

The crucial question is whether the people with power actually take the opportunity, or will they continue to profess a commitment to liberalism that fails to take seriously issues of racial equality? I think we are about to see how this is going to unfold. So, I'm optimistic that there is an opportunity, but whether or not that opportunity will be taken, remains to be seen."

ARBITRARY DEPRIVATION OF NATIONALITY AS A MATTER OF INTERNATIONAL CRIMINAL LAW: *AN INTERNATIONAL CRIMINAL PROSECUTOR'S PERSPECTIVE*

BY CÓMAN KENNY[*]

Having a legal status, whether it is classified as nationality or citizenship, is the fundamental basis of human rights. The damaging consequences of its absence are pervasive and debilitating. Statelessness affects every aspect of life, from enjoyment of economic, social and cultural rights, to access to judicial and political processes.[1] Yet, despite statelessness being a cause of major human rights deprivations, the relevance of individual criminal responsibility for those who have caused it is overlooked. This is likely because the question of who is a national of a state is within each state's sovereign authority to decide, albeit within the bounds of international law.[2]

There are many causes of statelessness and individual criminal responsibility does not apply to most. However, in the case of discriminatory nationality laws, the application of international criminal law is not only relevant but, arguably, necessary. Discriminatory nationality laws are a significant source of statelessness[3] and have been used as a tool to target minorities within a state. Under the veil of the sovereign act of legislating for citizenship, states have implemented or maintained legislation designed to exclude specific populations from society[4] and

---

[*] **Cóman Kenny** is an Irish barrister currently serving as an Assistant Prosecutor at the UN assisted Extraordinary Chambers in the Courts of Cambodia. He previously worked as a prosecution lawyer at the International Criminal Court and the Special Court for Sierra Leone, and as a defence lawyer at the International Criminal Tribunal for the former Yugoslavia. He has published widely on issues of international criminal justice and public international law. *The views expressed herein are those of the author alone and do not reflect the views of any institution to which he is affiliated.*

[1] See e.g., UN Human Rights Council, 'Human Rights and Arbitrary Deprivation of Nationality', A/HRC/RES/32/5 (15 July 2016), p. 3; Guidance Note of the U.N. Secretary-General, 'The United Nations and Statelessness' (June 2011), p. 2.

[2] See e.g., ILC, 'Special Rapporteur Maurice Kamto, Fourth Report on the Expulsion of Aliens', A/CN.4/594 (24 March 2008), para. 4.

[3] UN Human Rights Council, 'Report on discrimination against women on nationality-related matters, including the impact on children', A/HRC/23/23 (15 March 2013), para. 7.

[4] UN Human Rights Council, 'Promotion and Protection of all Human Rights, Civil, Political, Economic, Social and Cultural Rights, Including the Right to Development, Report of the Independent Expert on Minority Issues', A/HRC/7/23 (28 February 2008), para. 56.

deprive them of their rights.[5] This has occurred due to discrimination on racial, ethnic, religious, linguistic or presumed national origin grounds.[6]

Where groups are discriminatorily targeted, it can cause both privations that are suffered by individual group members, and cumulative human rights violations occasioned by statelessness, particularly where inter-generational. These are extremely serious and can result in the denial of a group's minority rights. This can include protection of collective cultural identity, such as recognition and use of minority languages, or the freedom to practice minority religions.[7] Marginalisation of this kind can be used to dehumanise members of a group and may ultimately threaten a group's very existence.

Significantly, in terms of international criminal law, where the targeted deprivation of nationality of a minority group is set against or accompanied by xenophobia, statelessness can be the precursor to mass atrocity.

Given the human rights effects on those impacted, arbitrary deprivation of nationality targeting a minority group may, depending on the factual circumstances, be legally characterised as an international crime. It could, for example, constitute apartheid – as an act committed in the context of an institutionalised regime of systematic oppression by one racial group over another.[8] It could be considered as an act of persecution – amounting to an intentional and severe deprivation of the fundamental rights of a group on discriminatory grounds.[9] Furthermore, it could be deemed an "other inhumane act" – meaning an act which intentionally causes great suffering or serious injury to the body or to mental or physical health and is of a similar nature to other crimes against humanity.[10] Additionally, arbitrary deprivation of nationality could potentially constitute an underlying element of other crimes, such as forcible transfer or deportation – when deemed a coercive act that forces the displacement of persons from the area in which they are lawfully present.[11] It could even be characterised as an act of genocide – where it causes serious bodily or mental harm to members of a national, ethnical, racial, or religious group and is committed with the intent to destroy the group, in whole or in part.[12]

---

[5] UN Human Rights Council, 'Background document by the independent expert on minority issues', A/HRC/FMI/2009/3 (8 October 2009), para. 37.
[6] Guidance Note of the U.N. Secretary-General, 'The United Nations and Statelessness' (June 2011), p. 7.
[7] UN Human Rights Council, 'Human rights and arbitrary deprivation of nationality', A/HRC/19/43 (19 December 2011), para. 43.
[8] For the full legal definition see Article 7(j) of the Rome Statute.
[9] For the full legal definition see Article 7(h) of the Rome Statute.
[10] For the full legal definition see Article 7(k) of the Rome Statute.
[11] For the full legal definition see Article 7(d) of the Rome Statute.
[12] For the full legal definition see Article 6 of the Rome Statute.

There is precedent for considering arbitrary deprivation of nationality resulting in statelessness as a matter for international criminal law. Perhaps the most notorious historical example of discriminatory denationalisation is that of the Jews in Germany and German-occupied territories under the Nazis. The Reich Citizenship Law, which deprived Jews of German citizenship, was one of the infamous 'Nuremberg Laws' of September 1935.[13] Following the end of World War II, the International Military Tribunal at Nuremberg, which tried major political and military leaders, held that the discriminatory laws restricting the rights of citizenship amounted to the crime of persecution.[14] Stripping Jews of their citizenship was also, of course, the foundation for one of the worst barbarities of the twentieth century.

A contemporary example of a state using the arbitrary deprivation of citizenship to target a minority group is that of the Rohingya in Myanmar. The Rohingya are the largest stateless population in the world, having effectively been made stateless by a citizenship law in 1982.[15] In the subsequent decades, profound discrimination and human rights abuses have been accompanied by a "hate campaign" emanating from the highest echelons of the Myanmar state.[16] In 2017, concerted violent repression resulted in hundreds of thousands of Rohingya fleeing to Bangladesh and gave rise to allegations of genocide, crimes against humanity, and war crimes against senior Myanmar officials.[17]

> **Notably, the UN's independent international fact-finding mission declared that "the cornerstone" of the oppression of the Rohingya was their "lack of legal status".[18] This again serves to link arbitrary deprivation of nationality with perpetration of violent crimes against those made stateless.**

Most recently, the UN High Commissioner for Refugees has raised alarm about the risk of statelessness for minority populations in India's north-eastern state of Assam, after a National Register of Citizens (NRC) omitted some 1.9 million people.[19] While it is too early to tell what the legal status of these people will ultimately be, following other citizenship measures currently being adopted which are fundamentally

---

[13] Judgment of the International Military Tribunal, vol I (14 November 1945 – 1 October 1946), p. 180-181.

[14] Judgment of the International Military Tribunal, vol I (14 November 1945 – 1 October 1946), p. 248.

[15] UN Human Rights Council, 'Promotion and Protection of all Human Rights, Civil, Political, Economic, Social and Cultural Rights, Including the Right to Development, Report of the Independent Expert on Minority Issues', A/HRC/7/23 (28 February 2008), para. 59.

[16] UN Human Rights Council, 'Report of the detailed findings of the Independent International Fact-Finding Mission on Myanmar', A/HRC/39/CRP.2 (17 September 2018), para. 696.

[17] UN Human Rights Council, 'Report of the independent international fact-finding mission on Myanmar', A/HRC/39/64 (12 September 2018), paras 87-89.

[18] *Ibid.*, para, 21.

[19] UN High Commissioner for Refugees expresses alarm at Statelessness Risk in India's Assam (1 September 2019).

discriminatory in nature[20], there is concern that the NRC may be used to deprive Muslims in India of citizenship.[21]

In sum, though nationality matters are the sovereign prerogative of a state, this power is constrained by the framework of international human rights law. While violations of human rights do not automatically give rise to international criminal responsibility, there may be situations where the resulting harm is of sufficient gravity to meet the necessary definitional elements of international crimes. Arbitrarily depriving a minority group of nationality and making its members stateless involves the intentional imposition of a dire human rights situation on some of the most vulnerable people in society. Given the scope of the injury suffered by a minority group that is made stateless, the possible individual accountability under international criminal law of those state or government figures responsible for the imposition or continuation of such devastating policies should most certainly be examined.

---

[20] Spokesperson for the UN High Commissioner for Human Rights, 'Press Briefing on India' (13 December 2019).
[21] *id.*

STATELESSNESS MOTIVATED BY NATIVISM, RACISM AND XENOPHOBIA: A COMPARISON OF MYANMAR, THE DOMINICAN REPUBLIC AND INDIA

BY JOSÉ MARÍA ARRAIZA*,
MARINA ARRAIZA SHARIKOVA*
AND PHYU ZIN AYE*

INTRODUCTION

The overwhelming majority of stateless persons belong to impoverished minority communities. Statelessness is inflicted as a discriminatory act, and then becomes the basis for further discrimination. It can escalate into physical segregation, displacement and (as in Myanmar) crimes against humanity or even genocide.

One of the basic tenets of xenophobia include ascribing a group (the 'other') with negative traits in order to construct a positive vision of one's own group by opposition. Such narratives of the evil stranger follow a simple logic where "unless we hate what we are not, we cannot love what we are", or in Carl Schmitt's ultraconservative terms: "we don't know who we are, if we don't know our enemies".[1] Both xenophobia and racism tie closely to the ideology of nativism. understood as a unity of culture and even 'blood', meaning that nativism links more closely to the concept of citizenship. Historian, John Higham, described it in the US context as "intense opposition to an internal minority on the grounds of its foreign

---

* **José María Arraiza** is based in Madrid and holds a PhD from Åbo Akademi University. He is a researcher on minority issues specialising in legal identity rights. He has worked in the humanitarian field in research and peace-keeping since 1998, in conflict and post-conflict contexts such as Kosovo, East Timor and Myanmar.

* **Marina Arraiza Shakirova** is based in Pamplona, Spain. She holds an LLM from Maastricht University. She is a jurist researching citizenship and statelessness. In 2019, she received the "Jaime Brunet" award from the Public University of Navarra on human rights and development for her research on the situation of the Rohingya from a legal perspective.

* **Phyu Zin Aye** is a PhD student at Mahidol University, Thailand. She focuses on citizenship, statelessness and refugees from a non-discrimination perspective. She also currently works at OXFAM and has previously worked on statelessness, displacement and minority rights issues with UNHCR and the Norwegian Refugee Council in Myanmar.

[1] P. Hervik, 'Nativism and Xenophobia', International Encyclopedia of the Social & Behavioral Sciences (2015), Second Edition, p. 796–801.

(*i.e.*, 'unamerican') connections".[2] Nativism, therefore, makes xenophobia a *national* project.[3]

The targeting of minorities which results in their statelessness is often motivated by nativism. Rejecting those considered to be the illegitimate 'others', who are regarded as undeserving of citizenship despite strong links with the state, is sometimes directly engrained in citizenship legislation and policies. In other cases, citizenship deprivation may take place in practice, despite legally entrenched rights. From a broader perspective, as Rogers Brubaker noted, "citizenship is a powerful instrument of social closure, shielding prosperous states from the migrant poor".[4] Hence, classism also plays a role in undermining legitimate claims to citizenship, which, combined with a mixture of xenophobia, racism and nativism serves to systematically exclude impoverished migrants and their descendants from citizenship.

With this frame in mind, this chapter analyses and compares three case studies - Rakhine in Myanmar, Assam in India and the Dominican Republic - all cases where nativism has influenced citizenship deprivation.

I. MYANMAR

> **You may have tried in every possible way to erase our existence. But we exist and we will continue to strive and exist in honour of our people who have been murdered and who have lost everything. Our souls shall never rest until what has been taken away from us will be given back to us with dignity and respect."**
>
> *Hafsar Tameesuddin,*
> *Rohingya activist*

In Myanmar, various ethnic and religious minorities have been gradually excluded over the years, either being stripped of their citizenship (as in the case of the Rohingya) or demoted to a second-class citizenship status (through 'naturalised' and 'associated' citizenship status being imposed on persons of Indian, Pakistani, Nepali, Bangladeshi or Chinese descent). Such a process has been intimately interconnected with a nativist narrative which places the 135 *Taingyintha* (recognised national ethnic

---

[2] J. Higham, *Strangers in the Land, Patterns of American Nativism (1860-1925)*, (Rutgers University Press 1983), p. 4.

[3] D. Haekwon Kim and R. Sundstrom, 'Xenophobia and Racism', Critical Philosophy of Race, 2(1) p. 20–45; p. 31.

[4] R. Brubaker, *Citizenship and Nationhood in France and Germany*, (Harvard University Press, Cambridge, 1992).

groups), as the primary group entitled to full citizenship and designates these 135 groups as legitimate members of Burmese society. The corollary is that any persons who do not belong to the 135 ethnic groups are illegitimate. The basic tenet of this narrative is openly racist as it differentiates between those of so-called 'pure' and 'mixed' blood. The *Taingyingtha* are considered legitimate, genuine citizens, whose blood is 'pure';[5] in contrast, the 'others' - be they Rohingya, or those of Chinese or Indian descent - are of 'mixed blood', and therefore legally considered either second-class citizens or as outright stateless.

Background

Since the 1930s, Burmese nationalism struggled to define the identity of what would later become independent Burma. The idea of one nation, one language and one state manifested as a Buddhist and Bamar centred national project. Such a vision contrasted with a highly diverse society comprised of a variety of ethnic groups, as well as persons of Chinese, Malaysian, Nepali or Indian ancestry, colonial workers and their descendants.

The need to ensure peace and accommodate diverse ethnic groups in the territory led to the recognition of other groups and their administrative territories in the first Constitution. Most importantly, the 1948 Citizenship Act recognised the Arakanese, Burmese, Chin, Kachin, Kayah, Kayin, and Shan, together with any other group which had settled in the territory before the First Anglo Burmese War (1823), as "indigenous races".[6] Between 1948 and 1982, Burmese citizenship legislation allowed for the naturalisation of all persons legitimately entitled to Burmese nationality through *jus soli* provisions[7] and other rules.[8]

In 1962, a military coup led by General Ne Win saw the Burmese government fall under the control of a military regime. The military, in one form or another, still retains power under provisions stipulated in the 2008 Constitution which provides the army (*Tatmadaw*) three ministers, one third of the parliamentary seats and parliamentary veto powers. In 1982, General Ne Win presented a new citizenship law which erased most *jus soli* provisions and established a second-class category of citizenship for persons not belonging to the recognised national races. This law denies the status of 'full citizen' to individuals who do not belong to one of the 135 'national ethnic groups' which have been arbitrarily determined by the state. The

---

[5] As General Ne Win put it: "racially, only pure-blooded nationals will be called citizens", speech by General Ne Win, *The Working People's Daily* (9 October 1982).
[6] Article 3(1), Union Citizenship Act, 1948 (Act No. LXVI of 1948).
[7] Citizenship through birth on the territory.
[8] Articles 4, 5, Union Citizenship Act, 1948 (Act No. LXVI of 1948).

1982 Citizenship Law, which discriminates on the grounds of ethnicity and religion,[9] is still in force today.

The Rohingya and Rakhine State

The Rohingya are an ethnic group with a distinct language and culture, historically present in Rakhine State and across today's border with Bangladesh. Rakhine State is a highly diverse territory, inhabited by large groups such as the Rakhine, one of Myanmar's four main Buddhists ethnic groups, and smaller minorities such as the Daingnet, Khami, Marmagyi, Mro and Thet. Rakhine state is also one of the least developed states in Myanmar, and the Rohingya, as well as the other ethnic groups, suffer the associated consequences of poverty and conflict. During the 1970s, the Rohingya were used as a scapegoat by the military regime in an attempt to gain legitimacy by mobilising the masses against the alleged external threat of 'illegal' migration from the newly created Bangladesh.

From a legal standpoint, between 1948 and 1982, the Rohingya were considered citizens. Similar to the rest of the Burmese population, the majority of the Rohingya did not possess Union Citizenship Certificates (which were rarely applied for), but rather 'National Registration Cards' as their civil documentation. Contrary to the provisions of the 1982 Citizenship Law, the government arbitrarily denied the Rohingya the new 'Citizenship Scrutiny Cards', despite the fact that the law provided for the issuance of Naturalised Citizenship Cards, Associate Citizenship Cards or full Citizenship Scrutiny Cards depending on their situation.[10] During this denationalisation process, immigration officials insisted that the Rohingya officially self-identify as "Bengali" (implying foreign descent). As a result, approximately one million persons were rendered stateless.

In addition to being deprived of nationality, a quasi-apartheid regime was imposed in Rakhine during the seventies and continues to this day, characterised by undue restrictions on freedom of movement and the discriminatory denial of services.

Forcible Displacement

This progressive denationalisation of the Rohingya was followed by forcible displacement across the border to Bangladesh. The establishment of an independent Bangladesh increased fears of irregular migration and led the government to implement the restrictive Emergency Immigration Act and require all Rakhine inhabitants to carry their identity documents. Any person suspected of being a

---

[9] *See* International Commission of Jurists, 'Citizenship in Myanmar: Why a Law Reform is Necessary and Urgent', (ICJ, 2019); for gender aspects *see* 'A Gender Analysis of the Right to a Nationality in Myanmar' (NRC, UN Women and UNHCR, 2018).
[10] Arts. 4-8 and Chapters III and IV, 1982 Citizenship Law.

foreigner could be arrested, imprisoned and/or deported, with the burden of proving his or her citizenship laying with the individual. In 1978, the implementation of the 'Operation *Naga Min*' (Dragon King), which aimed to officially identify 'illegal' migrants and counter the armed activities of the Rohingya Solidarity Organisation (RSO), led to the displacement of over 200,000 Rohingya to Bangladesh.

A similar scenario occurred in 1991, when 'Operation Clean and Beautiful country' (*Pyi Thaya*) led to over 250,000 persons being displaced across the border. In 2012, a series of incidents between the Rohingya and Rakhine led to riots which resulted in the internal displacement of approximately 125,000 Rohingya, as Bangladesh closed its border and pushed back fleeing refugees. These Internally Displaced Persons (IDPs) were housed in detention camps which are still in operation, despite commitments from the Government to implement the recommendations of the Final Report of the Advisory Commission on Rakhine State.[11]

In November 2016 and August 2017, following attacks by the Arakan Rohingya Salvation Army (ARSA)[12], the Tatmadaw launched an indiscriminate and excessively violent offensive that led to the displacement of over 750,000 Rohingya civilians to Bangladesh. The scale of the violence used, including rape, torture, burning, killings and other atrocity crimes, led to claims that have been echoed by the Rohingya community, NGOs, journalists and independent UN experts, that the Burmese authorities were committing crimes against humanity and genocide.

The internal displacement within Rakhine or expulsion of Rohingya to Bangladesh in 1978, 1991-1992, 2012, 2016 and 2017 have shown the linkages between deprivation of nationality and international crimes such as persecution, crimes against humanity and genocide.

Latest Developments

In February 2019, the conflict between another Rakhine State based EAG, the Arakan National Army (an ethnic Rakhine armed group fighting for the independence of the territory) and the Tatmadaw escalated, leading to the displacement of thousands of ethnic Rakhine and an overall deterioration of conditions in the state.[13] The Burmese authorities also implemented an internet

---

[11] Final Report of the Advisory Commission on Rakhine State (25 August 2017).

[12] ARSA is an Ethnic Armed Group (EAG) from Rakhine State.

[13] International Crisis Group, 'A New Dimension of Violence in Rakhine State' (January 2019), available at https://www.crisisgroup.org/asia/south-east-asia/myanmar/b154-new-dimension-violence-myanmars-rakhine-state.

shutdown which affected the delivery of humanitarian assistance as well as access to basic services of the population.[14]

As the situation continues to worsen, the Rohingya have gained increasing international attention, and the body of evidence and documentation of the crimes perpetrated against the community has grown. The UN-Fact-Finding Mission published its final report to the Human Rights Council in August 2019, detailing the massive violations by the military in Rakhine, Kachin Chin and Shan States. The Mission's work will be continued by the Independent Investigative Mechanism for Myanmar once it becomes operational. The Pre-Trial Chamber of the International Criminal Court (ICC) also recently authorised its Prosecutor to proceed with an investigation into the crimes of deportation and persecution committed against the Rohingya in Bangladesh.[15] On 11 November 2019 The Gambia filed a lawsuit against Myanmar before the International Court of Justice (ICJ) for acting in contravention of its obligations under the 1948 Genocide Convention.[16] There has also been a case filed in Argentina under the principle of 'universal jurisdiction', which allows for the prosecution of international crimes committed anywhere in the world. This case marked the first time that legal action has been taken directly against Myanmar's *de facto* leader, Aung Sang Suu Kyi.[17]

II. DOMINICAN REPUBLIC

 **This is the consequence of slavery and colonial systems, until today manifested in modern and neoliberal forms, kept in laws, measures, practices and judgments"**

Elena Lorac
Reconocido Movement Coordinator

Since its independence from Haiti in 1844, there has been a concerted effort to build the Dominican identity in opposition to Haiti.[18] Hence, during the 20th Century, the

---

[14] Amnesty International, ´Myanmar: End Internet Shutdown in Rakhine and Chin States´ (June 2019), available at: https://www.amnesty.org/en/documents/asa16/0604/2019/en/

[15] International Criminal Court, 'ICC judges authorise opening of an investigation into the situation in Bangladesh/Myanmar' (November 2019), available at https://www.icc-cpi.int/Pages/item.aspx?name=pr1495.

[16] International Court of Justice, *Republic of the Gambia v. The Republic of the Union of Myanmar* (2019); Human Rights Watch, 'Gambia Brings Genocide Case Against Myanmar' (November 2019), available at https://www.hrw.org/news/2019/11/11/gambia-brings-genocide-case-against-myanmar.

[17] The Telegraph, 'Aung San Suu Kyi faces first legal action over 'existential threat' to Rohingya' (14 November 2019), available at https://www.telegraph.co.uk/news/2019/11/14/aung-san-suu-kyi-faces-first-legal-action-existential-threat/.

[18] S. Rodrigues Pinto, 'Anti-Haitianismo en la República Dominicana: de Sánchez Valverde hasta Balague'", in Matías Bosch Carcuro et al, *Masacre de 1937. 80 años después. Reconstruyendo la memoria.* CLACSO (2018), p. 25–45.

ideology of *antihaitianismo* was fed by the political elites, promoting a European and Hispanic identity and denying any African roots.[19] One example of this delegitimisation of African heritage is the omission in history books of any reference to the contribution of African slaves and their descendants to the Dominican culture. Another, was the creation of a civil registry system that classified Dominicans according to their Hispanic or Amerindian roots, denying any connection to Haiti.[20] This nativist 'otherisation' produced a history of violence, exemplified by the 1937 massacre of thousands of ethnic Haitians in the northwest of the country, ordered by the then President Trujillo's forces.[21]

The 1844 Constitution of the Dominican Republic recognised as Dominicans all individuals who had Dominican nationality at the time the Constitution entered into force, as well as persons born to Dominican parents in its territory. It excluded those Haitians who had invoked their status as foreigners to avoid fighting for independence. Dominican nationality, therefore, implied a combination of birth in the Dominican Republic and belonging to the Dominican/Spanish culture.[22] The next Constitution of 1865 introduced the acquisition of nationality through *jus soli* regardless of the nationality of the parents.[23] The 1908 Constitution introduced the controversial 'in transit' clause which restricted the application of *jus soli* to persons who were permanently settled in the country.[24] The interpretation of this provision has been at the crux of deprivation of nationality for persons of Haitian descent.

From 1916 until 1924, the Dominican Republic was occupied by the US, and Haitian migration increased as cheap labour for the sugar industry. Haitian migrants were not only tolerated by the Dominican authorities but were also documented in civil registries until 1986. Between the 1950s and the 1990s, many Dominicans of Haitian descent were recognised as citizens. However, the dictatorship of Trujillo between 1930 and 1961 led to a shift towards *antihaitianismo*, while the country still profited from migration. During Trujillo's leadership, immigration was encouraged, while hostility and outright violence towards immigrants was simultaneously exercised. The fact that the 1937 massacre took place during this period is a sign of these contradictory policies.[25]

During this time, citizenship policies were derived from the 1924 Constitution, which applied until 1934. It provided nationality to individuals born to Dominican parents and those born to foreigner parents in the territory, among others. In

---

[19] B. Wooding, 'Upholding birthright citizenship in the Dominican Republic. Iberoamericana' (2014), Nordic Journal of Latin American and Caribbean Sutidoes XLIV(1-2), (99-199), p. 99.

[20] M. Paz Bermejo Pérez, 'Políticas de Inmigración y Ciudadanía y el Estado Dominicano: un Desafío de Gobernanza Democrática' (2018), Universidad Complutense Madrid, p. 124.

[21] E. Sagás, *Race And Politics In The Dominican Republic* (University Press of Florida 2000), p. 46.

[22] E. Sagás, 'Report on Citizenship Law: Dominican Republic' (2017), p. 3.

[23] Article 5(1), 1865 Constitution of the Dominican Republic.

[24] Article 7, 1908 Constitution of the Dominican Republic.

[25] E. Sagás, *Race and Politics in The Dominican Republic* (University Press of Florida 2000), p. 46.

addition, Naturalisation Law 1683 of 1948, which is currently in force, allowed foreigners to naturalise on the basis of residence or marriage, with the presentation of documents to certify them. It also provided a privileged manner of naturalisation on the basis of services provided to the Republic.

The fall in sugar prices from the mid-1980s led to an increase in the arrival of unauthorised migrant workers in other sectors of the labour market. Political leaders and social elites instigated fears of a 'peaceful invasion' of Haitians.[26] Subsequently, in the 1990s, Dominicans of Haitian origin were increasingly denied documents, a process which took place within a nationalist movement that promoted a restrictive interpretation of the term 'in transit'. This led to children of undocumented Haitian migrants being denied birth registration on a discriminatory basis. In 2004, the General Migration Law 285-04 designated undocumented immigrants, notwithstanding how long they had lived in the country, as non-residents ('in transit'). Three years later, in 2007, the Central Electoral Board started issuing administrative resolutions to cancel and suspend identity cards and birth certificates issued to children before the 2004 law entered into force.

In 2005, a landmark judgment of the Inter-American Court on Human Rights rejected these discriminatory practices. In *Yean y Bosico vs. República Dominicana*, the Court concluded that the discriminatory application of Dominican laws concerning access to civil documents and nationality violated the right to a nationality and equality.[27] Unfortunately, the case did not put an end to discrimination.

Jus soli was further eroded through the 2010 Constitution, whose Article 18(3) established that individuals born in the Dominican Republic of parents residing illegally in the Dominican Republic were not entitled to nationality by birth.

Latest Developments

In 2013, the Constitutional Tribunal delivered its judgment 168-13. This judgment stated that the interpretation of the Constitutions from 1929 to 2010 could be retroactively changed so that children of migrants born in Dominican territory in an 'irregular migratory situation'[28] were not entitled to Dominican nationality. Then, the Naturalisation Law 169-14 created two categories of individuals: those listed in the Civil Registry (group A), eligible for recognition as nationals, and those

---

[26] B. Pérez (2018), p. 118, 137; Richard Lee Turits, *Foundations of Despotism. Peasants, the Trujillo Regime, and Modernity in Dominican HIstory* (Stanford University Press, 2003), p. 172.

[27] Inter-American Court of Human Rights, *Caso de las Niñas Yean y Bosico vs. República Dominicana* (8 de Septiembre de 2005).

[28] Irregular migratory situation refers to children who were issued birth certificates even if their parents had never been registered in the Dominican Republic due to the lack of proof of documents certifying their authorised stay in the country. They are considered to have been irregularly registered in the Civil Registry and therefore in an "irregular migratory situation".

who were not (group B), who need to apply for naturalisation. The procedure included numerous obstacles and thousands of individuals are still awaiting naturalisation. In addition, after the end of the official regularisation plan in 2015, there were tens of thousands of irregular expulsions and undue pressures on persons of Haitian descent to leave the Dominican Republic.[29]

III. ASSAM (INDIA)

 **The branding of minorities as illegal foreigners done randomly in Assam in the last thirty years became a hasty process in the form of NRC; now millions are excluded and at risk of statelessness"**

Iftikar Hussain Siddique,
Activist

As with Myanmar and the Dominican Republic, following India's independence in 1948, the Assam region of Northeast India also underwent a process of nation-building characterised by a rejection of the 'other'. In this case, the 'other' was identified as the Bengali Muslim and, to a lesser extent, Hindu Bengali communities. These groups, considered by their detractors to mainly comprise irregular migrants from Bangladesh, were henceforth marked as a target for denationalisation. Recently, there has been an alignment of historical Assamese nationalism with the Hindu nationalism espoused by India's Bharatiya Janata Party (BJP) government led by Prime Minister, Modi.[30]

Background

The roots of inter-ethnic conflict in Assam can be traced back to the mid-19th Century, when British colonisers sponsored the migration of Bengali speaking Muslims to work in the tea industry. By the beginning of the 20th Century, migrants made up close to one third of Assam's population.[31] Thus, Assamese nationalist sentiment grew against a population they considered to be a threat: Bengali-speaking Hindus and Muslims.

---

[29] Amnesty International, 'Where are we going to live? Migration and Statelessness in Haiti and the Dominican Republic' (2016), available at: https://www.amnesty.org/en/documents/amr36/4105/2016/en/.

[30] N. Kaul, "Rise of the Political Right in India: Hindutva-Development Mix, Modi Myth, and Dualities (2017), 20 Journal of Labor and Society, p. 523–548.

[31] S. Baruah, *India Against Itself: Assam and the Politics of Nationality* (Philadelphia: University of Pennsylvania Press 1999), p. 46, quoted in M. Encinas, 'Migrant Rights and Extraordinary Law in India: The Cases of Assam and Jammu & Kashmir' (2017), 40:3 South Asia: Journal of South Asian Studies, 40(3), p. 463-480; p. 465.

Xenophobia against real or perceived migrants in Assam continued after independence and was the cause of major outbreaks of inter-ethnic violence. The reaction of the authorities was primarily repressive. For example, between 1961 and 1967, Assam implemented a 'detect and deport' policy which saw the deportation of 66,000 persons to East Pakistan. After the independence of neighbouring Bangladesh from Pakistan in 1971, there was an additional large influx of refugees into Assam, accompanied by further anti-Bengali riots.[32]

The tensions grew steadily. In 1979, it was discovered that 45,000 undocumented Bangladeshi migrants had been listed on the electoral rolls, sparking further unrest led by the All Assam Students Union (AASU). In 1983, during elections, Assamese nationalists perpetrated the 'Nellie Massacre', which killed at least 2,000 persons, mostly Bengali Muslims.[33]

Continuous pressure by Assamese nationalists led to the signing of the 'Assam Accord' in 1985. This agreement provided that:
- All persons who came to Assam from present-day Bangladesh prior to 1 January 1966, including those whose name appeared on the electoral rolls used in the 1967 elections, would be regularised as citizens.
- Detected foreigners who had arrived between 1 January 1966 and 24 March 1971 could access naturalisation and their voting rights would be suspended for a period of ten years.[34]
- Any detected foreigner coming to Assam on or after 25 March 1971 would be detained and expelled.

Such rules were further elaborated and entrenched as an amendment (Article 6A) to the Citizenship Act of India.

The National Register of Citizens (NRC)

In 2005, in *Sarbananda Sonowal vs. Union of India*, the Supreme Court observed an alleged "silent and invidious demographic invasion of Assam". It also controversially identified this alleged mass influx as an act of "external aggression" as per Article 355 of the Constitution.[35] The judgment struck down the 1983 Illegal Migrants (Determination by Tribunals) Act, removing its guarantees and placing the burden of proving citizenship back on the individual.

Then, in 2009, an NGO called Assam Public Works requested that the Supreme Court remove the names of undocumented migrants from the voters' list and

---

[32] M. Encinas, ibid., p. 464-467.
[33] M. Kimura, *The Nellie Massacre of 1983, Agency of Rioters*, (Sage Publications 2013).
[34] Article. 5, Assam Accord.
[35] Supreme Court of India, *Sarbananda Sonowal vs Union of India & Anr* (12 July, 2005).

demanded an update of the 'National Registry of Citizens' (NRC). The NRC is a registry of all citizens of Assam which had been first attempted in 1951.

The writ was heard in 2013 and the Supreme Court directed the government to start the process of updating the NRC in 2013. In 2015, the Assam state government initiated a process of updating the NRC, requiring every resident of Assam who claimed Indian citizenship to submit proof of their ancestry (or birth) in the country pre-dating 1971. The final NRC list was published on 31 August 2019. It excluded as many as 1.9 million Assam residents, predominantly Muslim (but also Hindus and others) leaving them at risk of statelessness (as there is now an appeal process available).

Foreigner Tribunals

All residents not appearing in the published NRC had 120 days to appear before 'Foreigner Tribunals' which would ascertain whether they were nationals (with detected non-nationals subject to detention and expulsion). The number of Foreigner Tribunals has increased exponentially, and the standard criteria of legal experience and the quality of their procedures has been lowered. Overall, the procedure followed is highly discriminatory against Muslims of Bengali descent and was condemned by 125 civil society organisations in September 2019 in a joint statement who argued the NRC process contravenes international human rights law.[36]

A month earlier, in August 2019, the Supreme Court held in its decision on *Assam Public Works vs. India* that the deprivation of nationality also covered the children of 'doubtful voters', persons declared foreigners and persons with pending cases before the Foreigner Tribunals. Moreover, children born after 3 December 2004, to a parent belonging to one of these three categories, would be excluded from the NRC, regardless of the nationality of the second parent. This breached both retroactivity principles and the nationality provisions of the Convention on the Rights of the Child.[37]

Latest Developments

In November 2019, the Modi Government proposed expanding the implementation of the NRC to the whole of India, sparking fears for Muslim minorities across the country. Moreover, the government continues to pursue an amendment to the Citizenship Act which would make irregular migrants who are

---

[36] 'The biggest mass-disenfranchisement of the 21st Century – Joint Statement: 125 Civil Society Organisations condemn the exclusion of 1.9 million people from the Assam NRC and call for urgent action to protect everyone's right to a nationality', available at
https://www.institutesi.org/news/cso-joint-statement-on-assam-nrc
[37] *Ibid*, p. 15.

Buddhist, Christian, Jain, Hindu, Parsi and Sikh from Afghanistan, Bangladesh and Pakistan, eligible for citizenship under easier naturalisation procedures than those who do not belong to these religions (such as Rohingya escaping persecution in Myanmar). The amendment seeks to ensure that the discriminatory measures against Muslims are not suffered by recognised 'others.' It is likely that this act will be used to naturalise Hindu Bengalis who have been excluded from the NRC.

COMPARATIVE ANALYSIS OF MYANMAR, THE DOMINICAN REPUBLIC AND INDIA

These three cases show that denationalisation is usually a process: a series of discriminatory and arbitrary acts, whose cumulative effect is to make people stateless, deny their belonging and rights, and ultimately expel them from the territory. This cumulative effect makes it more difficult to remedy the situation. Moreover, deprivation of nationality is often exercised through the administrative violence of bureaucracy, where procedures are implemented in an arbitrary and discriminatory manner.

India, Myanmar and the Dominican Republic also exhibit a nativist re-imagination of history, sometimes in the framework of post-colonial nation building and military or highly nationalistic governments. The erosion of minority identity is present in all three cases. Mass deprivation is often coupled with hate speech: for example, in India, minorities have been referred to as "infiltrators" and "termites". In Myanmar, Rohingya have been qualified as "poisonous plants", "catfish" and a "black tsunami" accused of conducting a "slow invasion".[38]

Importantly, there tends to be an association of the targeted group with the idea of 'external aggression' or as a threat to the sovereignty of the nation. In the case of India, we see this in the reasonings of the Supreme Court. In Myanmar, the Rohingya are seen as a threat to the territorial integrity of the state, with the assumption that demographic dominance of this group would lead to a partition of Northern Rakhine and its incorporation into Bangladesh. (It is interesting to note that the creation of Bangladesh in 1971 had a deep impact in the domestic immigration and citizenship policies concerning both Assam and Rakhine States.) Similarly, the demographic dominance of ethnic Haitians in the border areas was seen as a threat by Dominican governments, which served to justify violence and discrimination against them. The three cases show in this sense a commonality: the existence of a minority adjacent to the borders of their alleged 'kin-state', who are

---

[38] International Court of Justice, *Application Institution Proceedings and Request for Provisional Measures, Republic of the Gambia vs. Republic of the Union of Myanmar* (11 November 2019), 16, 17, available at http://www.icj-cij.org › 178-20191111-APP-01-00-EN; S. Stecklow, 'Why Facebook is Losing the War on Hate Speech in Myanmar' *Reuters* (15 August 2018), available https://www.reuters.com/investigates/special-report/myanmar-facebook-hate/.

seen as a threat by their host country. The nativist narratives in the three places coincide in re-imagining their internal minorities as dangerous "pacific invaders". In contrast with this nativist vision, both Dominicans of Haitian descent, Assamese Bengali and Rohingya consider themselves full citizens of the countries where they live (or used to live).

From a legal standpoint, the three legal frameworks are quite different: Myanmar is a closed citizenship regime primarily based on *jus sanguinis*[39] (descent from *Taingyintha*) where naturalisation is not possible; both the Dominican Republic and India have eroded existing *jus soli* norms through legal reforms and jurisprudence. In this regard, the similarities between the three depict a trend towards a reliance on *ethnic*, as opposed to *civic*, conceptions of citizenship.

Of note, there is an obvious economic aspect to the xenophobia-induced deprivation of nationality. In Assam, Rakhine and the Dominican Republic, the targeted minorities are poor and often perform the least qualified jobs. In this sense, there is an important element of aporophobia (fear or rejection of the poor) within xenophobia.

Overall, the Rohingya crisis is a cautionary tale as to the extent to which the arbitrary deprivation of nationality and resultant statelessness can lead to forcible displacement and other international crimes. The Dominican Republic, in turn, is a showcase of how both discriminatory practices, legal reforms and jurisprudence can entrench discrimination. In this sense, Assam, with similar trends to both Myanmar and Dominican Republic, represents a statelessness crisis in the making. The three cases are a reminder of the need to promote inclusive citizenship policies and discourses and improve the protection of vulnerable minorities against discrimination and statelessness.

---

[39] The process of citizenship acquisition whereby nationality is determined/acquired by the nationality or ethnicity of one or both parents.

WHY WE CONTINUE TO FIGHT FOR OUR RIGHT TO NATIONALITY IN THE DOMINICAN REPUBLIC AND HOW YOU CAN HELP: *AN ACTIVIST'S PERSPECTIVE*

BY MOVEMENT RECONOCIDO:
ANA MARÍA BELIQUE*,
ALFREDO OGUISTEN*,
ELENA LORAC*
AND PAOLA PELLETIER*

In the Dominican Republic, every time you perform a civil or political act (get a national ID card, get married, register at school or university, get a passport etc.) you need to request a copy of your birth certificate at a local civil registry office. In 2007 the institution in charge of the national civil registry system (Central Electoral Board) passed Resolution No. 12 that stated those who had 'irregularities' in the civil registry would be suspended for investigation. This administrative measure did not indicate what was meant by 'irregularities' nor when the investigations would conclude.

This administrative measure applied in practice affected us, Dominicans of Haitian descent, and not those of other national origin; it suspended or cancelled our birth certificates, national ID cards and passports. We did not know it was happening until we went to the civil registry offices to request a duplicate of our birth certificates

* **Ana María Belique** is a sociologist from Universidad Autonoma de Santo Domingo (UASD). She is also a researcher and co-founder of the Reconocido Movement and the "Black Dolls" Project. She coordinated Reconocido's Lives Stories book titled "It changed our lives" and has worked at the Jesuit Network with Migrants in the Dominican Republic. A member of Latin American network of Afrodescendants and of the national coalition for Women Rights, she has written and spoken about statelessness in various fora.

* **Alfredo Oguisten** is a Law Student at Universidad Autonoma de Santo Domingo (UASD). He is a co-founder of the Reconocido Movement, a human rights defender and an activist. He is an Alumni of ISI's 2019 Summer Course in the Netherlands and has spoken at various national and international conferences.

* **Elena Lorac** is a student social worker at Universidad Autonoma de Santo Domingo (UASD). She is a co-coordinator of the Reconocido Movement and a co-founder of Reconocido's "Black Dolls" Project. She is also a human rights defender and activist. She has experience working with migrants and refugees within NGOs, including with the Haitian and Venezuelan population.

* **Paola Pelletier** is a Litigation Lawyer from PUCMM University and a Law school professor in International Private Law and Human Rights. She is a member of the Reconocido Movement and member of local and regional feminist movements (Foro Feminista and CLADEM). She has Worked for UNHCR (in the Dominican Republic and Senegal) and in NGOs with refugees, stateless individuals and migrants.

and were denied. They said: "you are under investigation", "your parents were illegal when you were born", "you were registered with "ficha"[1], "your parents are Haitians", "your last name is Haitian", "you are Haitian", "you are foreign", "we cannot find the book where you were registered", and so on. We did not understand what was happening.

Then, in 2013, a Constitutional Court Ruling stripped us of our nationality (both those of us registered and unregistered), arguing that our parents had irregular migratory status when our births were registered. The claimant of this case, a Dominican of Haitian decent, Juliana Deguis Pierre, sued when officials in her town refused to issue her ID card because of Resolution No. 12-07. According to Dominican constitutional procedural law, the effect of the ruling of this type of judicial action for fundamental rights (called 'Amparo') only apply to the claimant; however in this case, the Constitutional Court illegally ordered the decision to also apply to all those in "similar situations" who were not part of this judicial case, born between 1929 - 2010. In 2012, it is estimated that approximately 2.5% (250,000) of ten million persons in the Dominican Republic were of Haitian descent, and it is estimated that this ruling affected 210,000 of us.[2]

We are the only population affected by the 2013 Constitutional Court ruling. For us, the solution is the full and collective restoration of our nationality since it was deprived to a huge portion of Dominicans of Haitian Decent. Naturalisation is not the answer: we were born in the country and we have the right to Dominican nationality by *jus soli* as the Constitution stated when we were born. This is our right that has been taken away. This solution and these standards have been established by the Inter-American Commission of Human Rights[3] and the Inter-American Court of Human Rights concerning Dominicans of Haitians descent born in Dominican Republic, who are also stateless.[4]

---

[1] "Ficha" is an informal ID issued in the past by sugar cane industries, mostly owned by the State, to identify Haitian migrant workers, since they do not have identification from Haiti. This was not the official national ID card of the State, neither a residence card. The "ficha" is what our parents held at the time of our registration and its number was registered in our birth certificates. "The ficha" stated in our birth certificate was one indicator used by the State to identify and profile us and suspend the issuance of our duplicate documentation.

[2] ONE (National Office for Statistics of the Dominican Republic). The last official census in Dominican Republic was conducted in 2010 and the population was estimated to be approximately 10 million habitants (ONE-UNFPA-European Union, 'Primera Encuesta Nacional de Inmigrantes de la República Dominicana ENI-2012' (2013), available at http://sicen.one.gob.do/;
http://media.onu.org.do/ONU_DO_web/596/sala_prensa_publicaciones/docs/0321395001368132272.pdf, p. 17). By 2017, 252,349 persons are descendants of Haitian born in Dominican Republic, approximately 2.7% of the population. ('Segunda Encuesta Nacional de Immigrantes ENI-(2017), available at https://dominicanrepublic.unfpa.org/sites/default/files/pub-pdf/ENI-2017%20FinalWeb.pdf, p. 29;75;84).

[3] Inter-American Commission of Human Rights OAS, 'Preliminary Observations from the IACHR's visit to the Dominican Republic' (2013), available at
https://www.oas.org/es/cidh/actividades/visitas/2013RD/Preliminary-Observations-DR-2013.pdf, p. 20; *see also* Inter-American Commission of Human Rights, OAS, 'Situation of Human Rights in the Dominican Republic' (2016), available at https://www.oas.org/en/iachr/reports/pdfs/DominicanRepublic-2015.pdf.

[4] *See* Inter-American Court of Human Rights, *Girls Yean and Bosico (2005) and Expelled Dominicans and Haitians (2014) versus Dominican Republic* concerning Statelessness.

CONTEXT OF DOMINICANS OF HAITIAN DESCENT
BORN IN THE DOMINICAN REPUBLIC

Our parents, grandparents and great grandparents were brought here from Haiti as migrant workers as a result of agreements between Haiti and the Dominican Republic. Others were victims of smuggling and trafficking. They never returned back to Haiti, and a group of us were registered in the civil registry offices at birth while others were never registered. We are Dominicans because at the time of our birth the Dominican Constitution recognised the *jus soli* system.

However, we believe that even before 2007, the State began identifying or 'making a list' of those who were born in the Dominican Republic and were of Haitian origin, listing those who could have their nationality stripped – a vetting process similar to the one undertaken through the National Register of Citizens (NRC) in Assam, India in 2019. When requesting our documents, the State profiled us or our parents from the information contained in our birth certificates (e.g. a name or last name that looked French); our parents not having residency status at the time of our birth registration; the place we were born (we were born in very poor and invisible communities between sugar cane fields called '*bateyes*') and our skin color (visible when we go in person to request our documents).

The Dominican Republic is a mixture of African slaves and Spanish colonials, mostly black and '*mulatos*' (mixture of colonials and Africans brought as slaves).[5] Our independence in 1844 was not from Spain but from Haiti, and throughout the years a narrative of the "other" has been perpetuated: that through Haitian migration, Haiti will invade the Dominican Republic again. This discriminatory narrative has been constructed and fed historically by ex-presidents, ex-dictator Trujillo, ultranationalist groups, the media, literature and the way history is taught at schools. Therefore, statelessness in the Dominican Republic is the result of a historical denial of our black-African identity, post-colonialism and structural racial discrimination.

Nowadays, being Haitian or of Haitian descent in the Dominican Republic means being subject to verbal and physical discrimination and aggression, racism, xenophobia, hate speech and violence, threats of death (including via social media), deportations based on racial profiling and other forms of discrimination. All of these occur with the support of state actors. As a result of this context, many of us deny our own Haitian origin, are scared to speak Créole (the language of our parents) and walk in the streets. Children of Haitian descent, like stateless children in other

---

[5] After almost 40 years there is still no official data concerning ethnic identity. However according LAPOP, a survey about perception of the population in the Dominican Republic, it is interesting that 62.4% of the population considers itself as Indian or "mestizo" (Indians were practically exterminated during colonial times); 14.1% black; 13.6% white; 8.7% mulato. Dominican Republic Vanberbilty University-USAID, 'Latin American Barometer for the Americas (LAPOP): Dominican Republic' (2018-2019), available at
https://www.vanderbilt.edu/lapop/dr/AB2018-
19_Dominican_Republic_Country_Report_V6_Rev_W_01.20.20.pdf, p. 227-228.

countries, are bullied because of their lack of documentation and "weird non-Spanish name or last name", thus they are called "Haitians" in a derogatory manner.

THE "RECONOCIDO MOVEMENT"

> **Reconocido was born as a movement integrated by young leaders Dominicans of Haitian descent to defend our nationality rights against any form of discrimination because of the colour of skin and the origin of our parents. Reconocido was born from the deepest sugar cane fields, from this black land, from the work and strength of our parents and ancestors."**

Elena Lorac,
Reconocido Movement Co-Coordinator

Reconocido ('Recognised') started as a campaign in 2011. We have received support and empowerment from the Jesuit Network with Migrants and Refugees (NGO) since 2007, where cases from all over the country were identified. We are a political movement, comprised mostly of young leaders taking a stand against statelessness and representing hundreds of the affected population. Our objective is to defend our rights and the recognition of our Dominican nationality. We did not know each other before this situation and today we are more than brothers and sisters.

Since 2011 we have been working in communities as paralegals, activists, and providing information to the affected population. We engage in advocacy to key local political actors, journalists and the media, we participate in local and international networks, we are also active in social networks. We organise and participate in public protests, but in the last two years we have not taken part in public protests regarding our right to nationality as we cannot ensure our security due to both the threats from ultranationalist groups and our limited resources.

We are part of the "DominicanosxDerecho" (Dominicans for Rights) Platform, a local civil society statelessness network, where we engage in advocacy. At the beginning of 2014, we and other members of this Platform met the President of the Dominican Republic, Danilo Medina, who promised a solution. We have the support of an International Task Force, "We are Dominicans" (a Diaspora Platform based in New York), as well as other local civil society and key actors. In January 2014 we received protection measures as human rights defenders ordered to the

State by the Inter-American Commission of Human Rights, which are still in force today, but as you have read nothing ensures our security.

Through the "DominicanosxDerecho" Platform, regional and national workshops are organised to inform the population and listen to their concerns. We published a book about our life stories and the impact belonging to Reconocido Movement has had on our lives;[6] we have been screening the documentary "Hasta La Raíz" (Down to Roots)[7] to raise awareness and open reflections about the issue domestically and internationally; we are also developing a pilot project for women in a local community (*batey*) called "*Muñecas Negras*" (Black Dolls) to raise awareness on African-black identity, contributing to women and community empowerment.[8] Moreover, we are reflecting on our African identity through the "Slavery Route" visiting different places in Santo Domingo in memory of African slaves and their resistance to colonialism. Sadly, there is no information provided in their memory by the State in most of the places we have visited, which is also evidence of racism and the denial of our black identity.[9]

WHAT IS HAPPENING NOWADAYS?

The State has always denied that there is statelessness in the Dominican Republic. As a result of international pressure, in May 2014 the State adopted Law No. 169-14 ordering the restoration of nationality of those born between 1929 and 2007 (not until 2010) as a special amnesty. However, the Inter-American Court of Human Rights indicated in 2014 that this Law does not follow international standards since the State continues to consider those born in the country from parents with 'irregular migratory status' before the 2010 Constitution not as Dominican, but as foreigners.[10] Moreover, the aforementioned Resolution No. 12-07, issued by the

---

[6] Media reports concerning the launching of Reconocido's book "Nos cambió la vida" [Our lives were changed] about our life stories and the impact in our lives of becoming part of Reconocido Movement (2018), available at https://teleantillas.com.do/sociales/movimiento-reconocido-puso-circular-hoy-nos-cambio-la-vida/; https://eldigital.com.do/nos-cambio-la-vida/ Accessed 30 January 2020.

[7] Patio Común (Juan Carlos González, Director), Documentary *"Hasta La Raiz"* (Down to Roots) (2017). The documentary explains in 90 minutes the statelessness situation in Dominican Republic through the story of three women of Haitian descent and the activism of Reconocido Movement. Trailer available at https://www.youtube.com/watch?v=EtGFhBMDRxE.

[8] A. Belique, '*Muñecas Negras* Ig: @mujeresnegras', available at https://anabelique.wordpress.com/2019/03/24/munecas-negras-un-sueno-hecho-realidad/ Accessed 30 January 2020.

[9] Acción Afro-Dominicana, Reconocido and others, available at http://accionafrodominicana.blogspot.com/2019/11/palabras-de-apertura-de-la-5ta-jornada.html Accessed 30 January 2020 .

[10] "323. The Court notes that Law No. 169-14, in the same way as judgment TC/0168/13 on which it is based, is founded on considering that those born in Dominican territory, who are the children of aliens in an irregular situation, are aliens. In practice, this understanding, applied to persons who were born before the 2010 constitutional reform, entails a retroactive deprivation of nationality; and, in relation to some presumed victims in

Central Electoral Board and the Constitutional Court ruling of 2013, are still in force.

Both the treatment Dominicans of Haitian descent face and their restrictions in accessing documentation, is completely different from descendants of other national origins born in the Dominican Republic. These people are not discriminated against and they do receive Dominican documentation.[11] Law No. 169-14 and its implementation is also problematic as it contributes to our segregation by dividing us further into groups. After almost six years of this law being in force, approximately 48% of the 61,000 persons who had previously been registered in a civil registry (Group A) have received their documentation back. They now feel like they "exist", "are persons" in the society, and are "recognised" as citizens with access to all rights. However, approximately 52% of Group A have still not yet received their documentation back.[12]

This Law also offered a special regularisation and naturalisation process for those born in the country from parents with "irregular migratory status" and who were never registered in the civil registry (called 'Group B' in the Law). Having to apply for naturalisation means we are considered foreigners in our own country and are only offered a second category of citizenship. The application process was only open for 180 days, a very short deadline for the majority of the population historically affected to get their papers in order. The total number of individuals in Group B is unclear but only 8,755 individuals of this group and only the first generation could apply to this special naturalisation process. There were also legal and material obstacles faced in this application process. The assigned nationality from the Dominican State on the ID residence cards of those who received it read "Haiti" - more evidence of the State not accepting 'statelessness' as a phenomenon. The Law also established that two years after regularisation, the applicants would become Dominican through naturalisation; however, after almost six years of Law's adoption, these applicants still have not been able to acquire Dominican nationality through naturalisation.

There is no legal solution for those who are not included in the civil registry and did not apply to the special naturalisation process, including for those born between 2007 and 2010. Moreover, there is another group of persons born in the country from a mother or parents on 'irregular migratory status' and are registered in a

---

this case, it has already been determined that this is contrary to the Convention", *see also* Inter-American Court of Human Rights, *Expelled Dominicans and Haitians* vs. Dominican Republic (2014), paras. 319-325,

[11] ONE-UNFPA, 'Descendientes de Inmigrantes en la Republica Dominicana. Estudio complementario a la Encuesta ENI-2017' (2018), available at https://dominicanrepublic.unfpa.org/sites/default/files/pub-pdf/ENI-2017_Descendientes%20de%20inmigrantes%20-%202Ed%20-%20Web%20%281%29.pdf, p. 78; 135

[12] UNHCR, 'Dominican Republic Participation (Minutes 2:01:56-2:08:25). General Debate (Cont'd) - 6th Meeting, 70th session of UNHCR Executive Committee' (9 October 2019), available at http://webtv.un.org/watch/general-debate-contd-6th-meeting-70th-session-of-unhcr-executive-committee/6093645658001/?term=.

'Foreign Book' which does not state a nationality; the number of this group is approximately 45,000, and is mostly made up of children.[13]

Since 2016, UNHCR's annual population statistics concerning the number of statelessness people, collated in its 'Global Trends' report does not include the Dominican Republic. This raises concerns because without such reports, the situation remains completely invisible to the world, as if it were resolved. UNHCR's operation in the Dominican Republic does not have their logo outside its office nor on its vehicles, which is evidence of the shrinking space UNHCR has to undertake their work on the ground in the Dominican Republic.

Nevertheless, at the UNHCR High Level Segment on statelessness in October 2019 in Geneva, UNHCR High Commissioner, Filippo Grandi, made the following comments about the situation in the Dominican Republic: concerning "Group B, I understand that some people did not register in time and I would urgently suggest the Dominican Republic to adopt a very pragmatic approach in this respect, so that statelessness issues are progressively but steadily resolved".[14] UNHCR is therefore pointing out to the Dominican Republic that there is statelessness on its territory and the situation is not yet resolved.

There is still disinformation and anxiety felt by the affected population. There is no public information campaign. The State expects us to go to them, but they do not come to us, to our communities. There are material obstacles in accessing documentation, issues with following up on the status of our cases and applications, including travel costs and the distance to civil registry offices and the capital city. People cannot register their children, face obstacles in obtaining ID cards, getting a job and are unable to take national examinations, enter secondary education, or access to tertiary education (university) because birth certificates are required.

In 2020, there will be elections in the Dominican Republic. However, without documentation, our political rights are denied, we are still segregated and not integrated. The most important political parties do not support us, since our inclusion in their speeches would be at a political cost: the loss of votes.

---

[13] ONE-UNFPA, Descendientes de Inmigrantes en la Republica Dominicana. Estudio complementario a la Encuesta ENI-2017 (2018), available at https://dominicanrepublic.unfpa.org/sites/default/files/pub-pdf/ENI-2017_Descendientes_de_inmigrantes_-_web.pdf, p. 18.

[14] UNHCR, 'General Debate (Cont'd) - 6th Meeting, 70th session of UNHCR Executive Committee' (9 October 2019), available at http://webtv.un.org/watch/general-debate-contd-6th-meeting-70th-session-of-unhcr-executive-committee/6093645658001/, Minutes 2:51:37-2:52:28.

WHAT WE ASK OF YOU

We ask the international community to collaborate and support us. Law 169-14, contrary to what the government says, has not resolved the situation. The laws and policies adopted by the State have failed, instead they produce more segregation; for us the State does not show interest in the application of the law nor in restoring our nationality. The first obstacle is the State continuing to deny that there is a stateless population in Dominican Republic.

We request the Dominican Republic to overrule the Constitutional Court Ruling of 2013, recognise the jurisdiction of the Inter-American Court of Human Rights and fulfill its rulings,[15] and adhere to the 22 recommendations from different States in the last UPR session in 2019 concerning the collective restoration of our nationality without administrative procedures.[16]

We also ask the Dominican State to respect the Constitution and international agreements; publicly denounce violence and hate speech, hold perpetrators to account, recognise the existence of the stateless population and work towards implementing a reconciliation process. This is a matter of intercultural education and changing public policies on integration. We have our dialogue channels open, but we need the international community to collaborate and exert pressure on the State to produce positive change.

---

[15] In November 2014, after the Inter-American Court of Human Rights issued the ruling *"Expelled Dominicans and Haitians"*, as reaction, the Constitutional Court of the Dominican Republic issued the Judgment No. 256-14 stating the Inter-American Court of Human Rights does not have jurisdiction over the Dominican Republic, arguing the act of acceptance of the Court´s jurisdiction in 1999 was not ratified by the National Congress. This decision was brought by ultranationalists groups in 2005 challenging the Constitutionality of its jurisdiction, 9 years later, given this political context, the indicated judgement was ruled, and until today remains in force, available at https://www.tribunalconstitucional.gob.do/content/sentencia-tc025614.

[16] Dominican Republic, Responses to Recommendations: UPR, Third Review Session 32 (2019), available at https://www.upr-info.org/sites/default/files/document/dominican_republic/session_32_-_january_2019/2rps_domrep.pdf.

'EASY PRECEDENTS' – FRAUD, DENATIONALISATION AND PERPETUAL SCRUTINY OF THE CITIZENSHIP QUESTION

BY LAURA BINGHAM*

> **On peut être citoyen ou apatride mais il est difficile d'imaginer qu'on est un frontière. "**

André Green[1]

A cursory search of nationality laws globally reveals that there are over 400 provisions that relate to the loss or deprivation of nationality on the grounds that it was acquired through some form of fraud, mistake or misrepresentation.[2] The proposition sounds straightforward: states should have the right to root out fraud to protect the integrity of the institution of citizenship, exposing those masquerading as members for what they are – liars, cheats perhaps even criminals averting justice under an assumed identity and hiding in the midst of an unwitting, welcoming and peace-loving citizenry.

The rationale for such rules becomes more urgent considering the 21st century obsession with borders, particularly in wealthy western states, and the unprecedented powers of scrutiny to police them, anytime, anywhere. If we have the power to identify every citizen who, upon further examination, did not or does not meet the criteria to be a citizen, why shouldn't those powers be used to their fullest extent in order to forge a more perfect and genuine citizen body?

Embedded in this tidy rationale, however, rest important assumptions about those citizenship criteria, their permanence and retroactivity, and the reliability of

---

* **Laura Bingham** is the senior managing legal officer for equality and inclusion in the Open Society Justice Initiative. She leads the programme's work on equality and nondiscrimination, focusing on access to effective remedies for structural discrimination in Europe, and on the right to nationality and access to documentation of identity, comprising litigation, legal empowerment, research and advocacy worldwide. She has taught and published in the fields of international justice, strategic litigation, citizenship, and statelessness and is an adjunct faculty member in New York University's MS program in global affairs.
[1] "One can imagine being a citizen or being a stateless person, but it is difficult to imagine oneself as a borderland." [author's translation].
[2] GlobalCIT, Global Nationality Laws Database (dataset on modes of loss of nationality containing laws of 177 countries, search term: "fraud" (results: 404)), available at http://globalcit.eu/national-citizenship-laws/).

restraint in the exercise of discretion over what the U.S. Supreme Court has termed *"a form of punishment more primitive than torture"*.[3]

Hannah Arendt, stateless herself for decades, called fraud-based denationalisations faced by naturalised citizens in early 20th Century Europe 'easy precedents'.[4] 'Easy' because of the precariousness of naturalised citizenship to begin with and the wide acceptance that loss of nationality *ab initio* is the appropriate remedy in cases of fraudulent acquisition; 'precedents' because of all that followed in their wake, including mass denationalisations and millions of displaced persons without any country, recognition or political agency in society.

In 1939, the American journalist Dorothy Thompson also clairvoyantly wrote:

"If governments get the idea that they can expropriate their citizens and turn them loose on the kindness of the rest of the world, the business will never end. A precedent will be created; a formula will have been found."[5]

As it turns out, within those hundreds of laws that provide for loss of nationality based on fraud, lurk numerous complexities and misconceptions that I will explore through the example of the United States' denaturalisation statutes – 18 U.S.C. s. 1425 (a criminal statute) and 22 U.S.C. s. 1451 (a civil statute).[6]

The first misconception is that the fraud justification is the *true and exclusive* reason why states retain and deploy this fraud-based denationalisation power. The second misconception is that abuse and inappropriate exercise of discretion over this power can be effectively constrained by ordinary due process protections.

A FALSE DICHOTOMY: FRAUD AND 'NATIONAL SECURITY'

As a preliminary matter, it is important to dispel another assumption: that fraud is easily distinguished from other justifications for denationalisation in the first place; and relatedly, the understanding that fraud-based denationalisations are therefore inherently corrective in nature and operate differently from other forms of

---

[3] *Trop v. Dulles*, 356 U.S. 86 (1958).

[4] Hannah Arendt, *The Origins of Totalitarianism*, 277 n.20 (1973) ("The problem of statelessness became prominent after the Great War. Before the war, provisions existed in some countries, notably in the United States, under which naturalisation could be revoked in those cases in which the naturalised person ceased to maintain a genuine attachment to his adopted country. A person so denaturalised became stateless. During the war, the principal European States found it necessary to amend their laws of nationality so as to take power to cancel naturalisation.").

[5] 'Escape in a Frozen World,' Survey Graphic (1939).

[6] Deprivation on account of fraud under these provisions is the sole unilateral denationalisation mechanism available to authorities. *Afroyim* 387 U.S. 253 (1967).

denationalisation, for example those justified as protecting the 'vital interests of the state'.

In reality, justifications and aims of denationalisation combine, overlap, and interact in various ways, leaving considerable uncertainty as to the appropriate means of assessing the lawfulness of the practice or any individual case.

The recent example of Denmark is instructive. On 24 October 2019, Denmark adopted a new law that will allow for administrative deprivation of nationality from suspected 'foreign fighters' who have another citizenship. Historically, however, Denmark advocated for much stricter limits on reopening the question of someone's citizenship, even in cases of fraud. In 1959, during the United Nations Conference on the Elimination or Reduction of Future Statelessness, the Danish representative presided over a session covering what states could or should do about nationality acquired by fraud or misrepresentation. The Danish delegation offered an amendment to what would eventually become Article 8(2)(b) of the 1961 Convention on the Reduction of Statelessness, which allows for denationalisation in cases of fraudulent acquisition even when such action results in statelessness.[7] The Danish representative, Mr. Larsen, stated first,

"It would surely be unjust to deprive a naturalised person of a nationality he had possessed for a number of years merely because there had been some technical irregularity in his application. His delegation therefore proposed that in paragraph 2(b)(i) the words 'provided that deprivation takes place within five years of acquisition of 'the nationality' be inserted after the words 'the Party's nationality.'"[8]

Later, Mr. Larsen further explained the rationale for the proposed amendment:

"There were occasions when Governments wishing to withdraw nationality from persons whom they regarded as politically undesirable, would re-examine applications lodged twenty or thirty years previously. His delegation earnestly wished to see an end put to that practice. In his country, nationality was conferred by legislation and could not be withdrawn or annulled if the application were later found to have been based on false representation."[9]

However, the Danish amendment ultimately failed and there is no temporal limit in the 1961 Convention provision. Due to expediency and exceptionalism, 'fraud' or 'national security' - alone or in combination - can be readily mobilised against 'undesirable' citizens, leaving the citizenship question perpetually open to re-examination. Denmark's shift towards more 'liberal' deprivation powers comes

---

[7] Note that in the U.S. denaturalisation has often resulted in statelessness and there is no known policy within the investigating or prosecuting components of the federal government to identify a risk of statelessness arising from denaturalisation or seek to mitigate such a risk.
[8] A/COKJF.9/C1/SR.15 page 7 (Chairman, Representative of Denmark)
[9] A/CONFo9/C.l/SR.15 page 9.

lockstep with a wider and equally troubling shift in state attitudes away from any serious confrontation with Mr. Larsen's concern for political 'undesirables'. This accountability gap leaves ample room for demagogues and other powerful enemies of democracy and rule of law to manoeuvre.

DENATURALISATION IN THE UNITED STATES: A CASE STUDY

> **The government can always initiate proceedings to revoke a naturalised individual's citizenship if it believes that the naturalisation was illegally procured or procured by concealment of a material fact or by willful misrepresentation... this boundless discretion means that these second-class citizens can never feel entirely secure in their claim to American citizenship... There is also no assurance that the government will always institute these proceedings fairly, as it may harbour any number of ulterior motives."**

U.S. District Judge William B. Shubb (2019)

Immigration control and loss of nationality are deeply intertwined in the United States, including in cases of imputed or presumed non-citizenship of Americans by birth who derive their nationality through the Fourteenth Amendment's Citizenship Clause (providing for universal automatic *jus soli*). Recent examples of U.S. born Americans caught up in immigration raids,[10] deported,[11] denied vital documentary proof of citizenship[12] and deprived of U.S. passports following fraud investigations,[13] share common equally intertwined drivers: nationalism and the criminalisation of the U.S. immigration system.[14] All of the 'errors' listed above disproportionately impact Americans who identify with or are identified with communities that are heavily profiled for immigration enforcement under a growing array of civil and criminal immigration laws.

---

[10] *See, e.g.*, American Civil Liberties Union-Florida, *Citizens on Hold* (March 2019), available at
https://www.aclufl.org/en/publications/citizens-hold-look-ices-flawed-detainer-system-miami-dade-county
[11] *See* Cato Institute, *Immigration Briefing: U.S. Citizens Targeted by ICE* (August 2018), available at
https://www.cato.org/publications/immigration-research-policy-brief/us-citizens-targeted-ice-us-citizens-targeted.
[12] *See Perales v. Texas Dep't of State Health Services* (2015), Case No. 15-cv-00446 (W.D. Texas), more information available at
 https://www.aclutx.org/en/cases/perales-serna-et-al-vs-texas-department-state-health-services-vital-s.
[13] *See* Open Society Justice Initiative, *Unmaking Americans: Insecure Citizenship in the United States* (2019), p. 120-137.
[14] *See* R. E. Rosenbloom, *The Citizenship Line: Rethinking Immigration Exceptionalism* (2013), 54 B.C.L. Rev. 1695, 1993.

Denaturalisation (the denationalisation of naturalised U.S. citizens) falls within this spectrum as well, especially today. Under the same Citizenship Clause of the Fourteenth Amendment, naturalised citizens and born citizens are unqualified, undifferentiated and equal citizens of the country. Yet, since 1906, denaturalisation has been available as an immigration enforcement tool that has, for decades, masqueraded as a measure that *must inherently* be exercised judiciously, reserved for the 'worst of the worst', in order to ensure the 'betterment of the citizenry of the country'.[15] For many years, beginning in the 1970s, denaturalisation operated as an accountability measure that allowed for famous trials of Nazis.[16] Even then, the reassurance that denaturalisations were corrective, administrative, and not a criminal penalty, rang hollow.[17] The Nazi denaturalisations proceeded under the same statutes as widespread political denaturalisations during the first 50 years of their existence, targeting Americans based on their beliefs, actual or imputed, a practice that reached its last peak during the Red Scare.[18]

Since the 1990s, in step with the broadening intersection between the criminal and immigration systems in the United States,[19] successive administrations have, in fact, expanded the use of denaturalisation to an increasing number of case types, including those involving 'national security', sex crimes, and, most recently and most aggressively, individual cases of alleged immigration fraud.

Two heavily-resourced operations, named 'Janus' and 'Second Look' initiated under Presidents Obama and Trump respectively, now use dragnet searches of digitised immigration files to identify cases of potential fraud in the naturalisation process.[20] The methodology is relatively straightforward: there are millions of paper cards bearing fingerprint impressions contained in older files[21] from applicants for immigration status in the 1980s through the early 2000s, which can now be digitised and matched with records in U.S. government databases, including those containing fingerprints of successfully naturalised Americans. These searches may show that the same individual (based on a fingerprint match) had a previous order of removal entered against them but later naturalised under a different name. It is estimated by the administration that there could be at least several thousand Janus/Second Look denaturalisation cases.

---

[15] U.S. Dep't of Justice, Circular Letter Number 107 (1909). *See also* Immigration and Naturalisation Service (INS) Special Agent's Field Manual (1976).

[16] *See* Open Society Justice Initiative, *Unmaking Americans: Insecure Citizenship in the United States* (2019), p.63-65.

[17] *See* Comment, *Denaturalisation of Nazi War Criminals: Is There Sufficient Justice for Those Who Would Not Dispense Justice?* (1981), 40 Maryland L. Rev. 39, p. 88-89.

[18] Open Society Justice Initiative, *Unmaking Americans: Insecure Citizenship in the United States* (2019), p. 62. The Red scare was the fear of the rise of communism in America immediately after World War I and World War II.

[19] *See, e.g.*, Ingrid V. Eagly, Prosecuting Immigration (2010), 104 NW. U. L.REV. 1281.

[20] Trump budget requests of USD 207.6 million (2019 FY) and similar maneuvers for FY 2020. *See* Open Society Justice Initiative, *Unmaking Americans: Insecure Citizenship in the United States* (2019), p. 62.

[21] Known as A-files, or 'alien' files.

Prosecutors have discretion to select which cases to advance within these operations and under the statutes in general, and the Department of Justice has indicated that it will prioritise cases based on the country of origin of the target: with priority given to the cases where the target's country of origin is a 'special interest country' (a fluctuating category of countries 'that are of concern to the national security of the United States').[22] This policy explicitly links fraud-based denaturalisation prosecutions with counterterrorism and other 'national security' issues, just as the 'attachment' cases were linked to anti-Communism. The linkage of 'national security' policy and denaturalisation inevitably means that all of the disparities associated with targeting specific communities based on profiling and stereotypes carry over into the presumably corrective, administrative practice of fraud-based denaturalisation.

The statutory framework for denaturalisations permits the ongoing expansion of case types because of its own breadth. Denaturalisation itself mirrors the lengthy and fact-intensive naturalisation process in that, at any stage and on any substantive fact, a disqualifying mistake or misrepresentation might transpire. The naturalisation form asks for example, under penalty of perjury, whether the applicant **EVER** *committed…a crime or offense for which you were* **NOT** *arrested'* in any jurisdiction.[23] There is no statute of limitations in the civil statute (the criminal statute's is ten years), meaning that proceedings concerning 'new' evidence that an individual misrepresented or omitted information could commence many decades after naturalisation. In 2019, the Open Society Justice Initiative examined 168 cases filed under both statutes in 2017-2018, finding that, on average, cases are instituted more than ten years following naturalisation.[24] As noted above, political denaturalisations during the first half-century of the statutes' operation focused on affirmations that individuals make during the naturalisation process concerning their moral fitness to be citizens and their 'attachment' to the U.S. Constitution.[25] While the enforcement practice has shifted in recent years toward identifying undisclosed criminalised behaviour as a basis for denaturalisation, including immigration crimes like 'illegal entry', the 'attachment' criterion remains available to investigators and prosecutors.[26]

In addition to the statutes' substantive breadth, the procedural mechanics sit uncomfortably between civil and criminal frameworks (the statute of limitations is one example), causing inevitable confusion in case law and consequent gaps in

---

[22] Open Society Justice Initiative, *Unmaking Americans: Insecure Citizenship in the United States* (2019).

[23] Form N-400 (emphasis in original).

[24] Open Society Justice Initiative, *Unmaking Americans: Insecure Citizenship in the United States* (2019) (researchers identified 168 cases after a comprehensive, nationwide search of the unified federal district court case information database, PACER).

[25] *Ibid,* p.62-63.

[26] *Ibid,* p. 100-105 (noting the rapidly expanding powers held by investigating authorities to examine 'non-obvious' relationship patterns, political beliefs, behavior online and offline, and genomic and genealogical profiles).

appropriate protection of the rights of those accused. There is no right to counsel or a trial by jury for defendants in civil cases, for example, and although the government's burden of proof is the civil equivalent of 'beyond a reasonable doubt' (the criminal burden), this is unusual for civil cases and is frequently overlooked or misapplied.[27] The staunch interpretation of the United States Supreme Court holds that denaturalisation is an administrative, not a penal, remedy, and thus consideration of its permanence, harsh individual and family impacts, and even the statelessness it may cause are placed beyond judicial scrutiny.[28]

Threats to rights and liberties in criminal and civil denaturalisation proceedings

Criminal denaturalisation	Civil denaturalisation
Ten-year statute of limitations	No statute of limitations
Pretrial detention	No right to an attorney
Movement restrictions	No right to trial by jury
Forfeiture claims	No right not to testify
Plea agreements with immigration waivers	*In absentia* denaturalisation
Removal by district judge	Settlement agreements with immigration waivers
25 years imprisonment and fine	
Automatic citizenship revocation	

Some American judges tasked with presiding over denaturalisation cases, in the past and today, have recognised the peculiarity of such proceedings, and their consequent due process deficiencies, noting with *unease* that each case creates a precedent with wide repercussions for *all* naturalised Americans, in relation to their rights as equal citizens under the Fourteenth Amendment.[29] These isolated acts of judicial mercy are cold comfort in the face of policies of the Trump administration, which zealously cast off previous self-imposed efforts to contain and guide discretion. The atmosphere of no-holds-barred enforcement begs the question of what interests *should* denaturalisation serve? What are its appropriate aims, are they legitimate, and how should these be balanced, procedurally and substantively, against the

---

[27] *Ibid*, p. 91.
[28] *Ibid*, p. 89 (noting that the government objects to argument by counsel regarding the implications of a guilty verdict).
[29] *See, e.g. Ibid*, p. 70.

uncommon and harsh impacts of the remedy (loss of citizenship, and ultimately deportation)?

The first step toward answering these questions is to recognise that there is a problem with fraud as a purported justification in the first place. At no time in the history of denaturalisation has eliminating 'fraud' been the central guiding aim of enforcement policy; rather, secondary criteria (accountability for war criminals, for example) based on contemporary conceptions of America and Americans guided practice and resources. If this is the case, noting the equality of all Americans under the Fourteenth Amendment, ultimately Congress must confront the heart of the matter, which policymakers face the world over. This is the question that has been identified by Mr. Larsen, Hannah Arendt, Dorothy Thompson and Judges Rutledge and Stubb: can any legal regime effectively constrain governments from abusing provisions for secondary ulterior motives, acting against 'undesirable' citizens, and incidentally making the rest of the citizenry *more* vulnerable, not less? Strict limits on the openness of the citizenship question itself – in terms of time, criteria, and the materiality of evidence – are obvious safeguards. Abandoning the legal fiction that fraud-based measures are non-punitive would likewise bring novel clarity and honesty to laws, policies and practices. In fundamental terms, though, denaturalisation invites inherent inequality into the foundations of equal citizenship. If the chief goal of the entire enterprise is to safeguard the integrity of citizenship as an institution, the value of such a power in the first place must be tabled for a serious and transparent debate.

CITIZENSHIP DEPRIVATION:
A PHILOSOPHER'S PERSPECTIVE

BY CHRISTOPHER BERTRAM[*]

Statelessness sometimes results from a failure of birthright citizenship laws to assign nationality to people, but it also comes about because states strip people of their membership. Such measures of denationalisation, aimed at ethnic minorities and political enemies by totalitarian regimes such as Nazi Germany and Soviet Russia, were common in the interwar period. Partly due to this association, citizenship stripping declined after 1945. In recent years, however, both mass denationalisation and individual stripping of citizenship have seen a revival. An example of mass denationalisation can be found in the Dominican Republic, where, in 2013, citizens of alleged Haitian origin were deprived of their nationality.

Individual citizenship stripping, on the other hand, has occurred primarily in several wealthy democracies, as a component of the "war on terror" after 2001. States including the United Kingdom, Australia and the Netherland have all implemented such measures, often while invoking the claim that "citizenship is a privilege not a right". Often these decisions are made by the executive with little judicial oversight, rather than through legal processes. Since these states are all, in principle, committed to upholding international norms against statelessness, such denationalisations are limited by the requirement that the deprived person not be rendered stateless. For this reason, those at risk of denationalisation are always those whom the depriving state can claim will be left with a residual nationality - rendering dual nationals, naturalised citizens and their children particularly vulnerable.

A constitutive principle of liberal or constitutional democracy, is the idea of equality of status: that we are all bearers of the same basic set of rights, and that we stand equal before the law and in the democratic arena. Such an idea is in profound tension with another feature of the world we live in - its division into different states and nationalities. In such a divided world, there are, inevitably, "people out of place". These people are those living on the territory of a state who lack the citizenship or nationality of that particular state. As a result, they find themselves unequal compared to those they live amongst.

---

[*] **Christopher Bertram** is Professor in Social and Political Philosophy at the University of Bristol and author of *Do States Have the Right to Exclude Immigrants?* (Polity Press, 2018) as well as being chair of trustees for Bristol Refugee Rights. He is currently working on a project on duties to comply with and rights to resist immigration laws.

Liberal internationalist political philosophy, of which John Rawls's *The Law of Peoples* is one example,[1] tries to reduce this tension through the idea that each person belongs, in principle, to a state, and therefore has both access to a social universe of political equals and to a state power through which human and civil rights can be made effective. This idea is a key component of the legitimacy of the international order, and a presupposition of parts of its human rights regime, such as the 1951 Refugee Convention, which conceives of refugeehood as a remedy for an anomalous condition where the normal bond of membership between state and citizen has been broken. Unfortunately, the pretence that everyone has a place is undermined by the fact that some citizenships are more valuable than others, as well as the harsh reality of statelessness that ensures that some people enjoy neither equality among peers, nor secure protection for their rights.

An objection to citizenship deprivation from the perspective of liberal political philosophy is that denationalisation of individuals undermines equality within the class of supposedly equal citizens because of the way the commitment not to render people stateless actually only protects certain citizens and not everyone. The vast majority of citizens of existing constitutional democracies are citizens by birth, and nearly all have no access to another nationality. By contrast, the remaining citizens who are subject to the risk of denationalisation are also likely to be drawn from already disadvantaged racial, ethnic or religious minorities, meaning that this threat correlates to and augments existing patterns of inequality and subordination. The fact that those subject to deprivation of nationality come almost exclusively from minority groups, while those who are immune are drawn from dominant majority populations, also reinforces popular ethnonationalist beliefs about who belongs to the "real" core of the nation, and who are citizens as a matter only of legal formality. This, perhaps, sets the scene for future exclusionary revisions of nationality law.

Denationalisation measures also work to further undermine equality among citizens by exposing some, but not others, to additional punishment for the same offences. This is particularly noteworthy when denationalisation is applied to cases of serious crime rather than to terrorist offences. For terrorist offences, politicians often make the argument that the excluded person has made a choice to place themselves outside the political community by taking up arms against it on behalf of another state-like organisation, such as Islamic State. Such as justification may lack merit even in those cases, but it does not seem to fit the case of criminality at all. One example of this is in the United Kingdom, where several naturalised sex offenders have been stripped of their British nationality, with plans to deport them on release from prison to their country of birth. Naturally, there is little public sympathy for convicted rapists and so the extension of denationalisation to such cases has been largely uncontested. But the worry is that once the precedent of citizenship stripping for one class of serious crime has been set, the practice could then be extended to

---

[1] Harvard University Press 1993.

other categories. Since the "serious crime" category has been used to justify the deportation of long-term resident foreign national offenders for driving offences and common assaults, there has to be a worry about its extensibility to denationalisation.

Many of those subject to denationalisation spent their formative years in, or were born in, the country that proposes to banish them. This raises further difficult questions about membership and citizenship, and how they should be defined. Philosophers such as Joseph Carens have argued that political membership of a state should be closely aligned with social membership.[2] A state where someone has grown up and where they received their education, where their family and friends also live, is a state that bears a high degree of responsibility for how a person has turned out. This responsibility may even be greater when they have grown up angry and alienated in a marginalised community because of the failure of the state to provide resources for integration and social cohesion.

> **Such states, when embarking on the path of denationalisation, rely merely on a person's nominal legal membership of another political community in order to divest themselves of a problem that arose within their own. It undermines international support for a just global order when states are prepared to offload responsibility for their own wayward members onto others, on the basis of legal technicalities.**

A final issue with denationalisation is the stark contrast between theory and practice. Although states may formally recognise that rendering someone stateless is a reason to avoid nationality stripping, in practice they are willing to take action in a way that coheres with their national interest. In the case of the UK, for example, individuals can be deprived of British nationality if they are nationals of another state or, in some cases, if the government believes that they could acquire such a nationality. Often, the other state does not agree with that judgement, and individuals can have difficulty contesting such decisions. This results in stateless persons who lack a state that takes responsibility for their rights and basic interests, even though the excluding state will claim that it has adhered to its duties. The growing practice of citizenship deprivation, then, is a stain against the claim of liberal democratic states to be communities where all enjoy freedom and equality before the law. The practice undermines equality among citizens, damages their commitment to uphold human rights, and unfairly excludes from membership, people who became the people they are within the community that now seeks to banish them. The fact that such banishments can take place through a stroke of a minister's pen ought to

---

[2] J. Carens, *The Ethics of Immigration*, Oxford University Press 2013.

concern anyone worried about the extent of state power and the need to uphold the rule of law.

CITIZENSHIP ERASURE: THE ARBITRARY RETROACTIVE NON-RECOGNITION OF CITIZENSHIP

BY BRONWEN MANBY*

In the vast majority of cases, people deprived of citizenship have not been subject to any formal invocation of deprivation provisions in the citizenship law. Rather, they have simply been denied a document that confirms citizenship. Sometimes, they have never had such a document even though entitled in the law; sometimes officials have destroyed documents they previously held; sometimes a document is cancelled on the grounds that it was obtained by fraud; sometimes, there is just an indefinite delay in renewing a document that has expired, or a failure to take a decision. Thus, the methods most often used to denationalise a person are not to invoke the formal processes of deprivation, but simply to deny that he or she ever had citizenship to start off with and assert that any previous recognition was either in error or obtained by fraud.

Some of the best-known cases of this "citizenship erasure" relate to prominent politicians from the African continent. As far back as 1978, the Botswanan government declared that the leader of the newly founded opposition party, John Modise, previously recognised as a citizen, was not a citizen after all, and deported him to South Africa – which did not recognise him either.[1] A decade and a half later, in 1994, the Zambian government deported to Malawi two leading members of the main opposition party (and former liberation movement), William Steven Banda and John Lyson Chinula, both on the grounds that they were not citizens.[2] They were not accepted as Malawian citizens. Five years after that, the High Court in Zambia declared that the former president, Kenneth Kaunda, was not a citizen of the state he had governed for 27 years.[3] The same year, a tribunal in Côte d'Ivoire annulled the nationality certificate of the former prime minister, Alassane

---

* **Bronwen Manby** is a Senior Policy Fellow at the London School of Economics and an independent consultant in the field of human rights, previously working for Human Rights Watch and the Open Society Foundations. She has written extensively on comparative nationality law, statelessness, and legal identity, especially in Africa, including *Citizenship in Africa: The Law of Belonging* (Hart Publishing, 2018).

[1] African Commission on Human and Peoples' Rights, *John K. Modise v. Botswana* (2000), Communication No. 97/93.

[2] African Commission on Human and Peoples' Rights, *Amnesty International v. Zambia* (2000), Communication No. 212/98.

[3] African Commission on Human and Peoples' Rights, *Legal Resources Foundation v. Zambia* (2001), Communication 211/98.

Ouattara, on grounds that it had been irregularly issued.[4] All these cases reached the African Commission on Human and Peoples' Rights, which ruled every time against the governments concerned. Many others have also been litigated at national level.[5]

These cases, which should perhaps be described as "arbitrary retroactive non-recognition" of citizenship rather than as deprivation (since in no case were formal deprivation procedures mobilised by the governments wishing to silence their critics) are far from confined to these high-profile individuals, though it is these cases that have reached the courts. For those who are not considering running for public office or challenging the government in other ways, it is through the process of applying for or renewing a national identity card or passport, or when they are arrested and deported, that they find that they are in fact not, or no longer, considered to be citizens.

In the most egregious cases of citizenship erasure, citizenship laws are amended or judicially reinterpreted to retroactively remove rights that were previously held by particular segments of the national population. But even in those cases, the key amendments have not been to modify the formal powers to deprive a person of citizenship, but rather to restrict access to citizenship based on birth and residence; to establish discriminatory procedures based on race, religion or ethnicity; to apply rules on dual citizenship strictly even if the person has never held citizenship papers from another country; or to exploit any ambiguity in the rules applied on succession of states.[6] Often, changes in the rules to restrict eligibility for citizenship are then applied retroactively, even if in principle the amendments only apply to those born after the changes.

Myanmar's Citizenship Law of 1982 created a presumption that only members of certain "national groups" are citizens. Although the law still provided for existing citizens to retain their citizenship, the change to the law helped to enable decades-long denationalisation of Rohingya by the imposition of ever-stricter evidential requirements to prove their citizenship. Under the 1982 law's procedures, citizens were required to re-register. Rohingya who submitted their old documents for this purpose had them replaced with new documents which explicitly did not recognise their citizenship.[7] In the Dominican Republic, the notorious 2013 judgment of the

---

[4] African Commission on Human and Peoples' Rights, *Mouvement ivoirien des droits humains (MIDH) v. Côte d'Ivoire* (2008), Communication No.246/02.

[5] B. Manby, *Citizenship in Africa: The Law of Belonging*, (Hart Publishing 2018), chapter 5.5; B. E. Whitaker, 'Citizens and Foreigners: Democratization and the Politics of Exclusion in Africa' (2005), African Studies Review, 8(1), p. 109-126.

[6] B. Manby, 'You can't lose what you haven't got: citizenship acquisition and loss in Africa', in A. Macklin and R. Bauböck (eds.) *The Return of Banishment: Do the New Denationalisation Policies Weaken Citizenship?*, Robert Schuman Centre for Advanced Studies, EUDO Citizenship Observatory, RSCAS 2015/14.

[7] Act No. 4 (1982), article 3. See discussion in N. N. Kyaw 'Unpacking the Presumed Statelessness of Rohingyas' (2017), Journal of Immigrant & Refugee Studies, 15(3), p. 269-286; N. Cheesman, 'Problems with Facts about

Constitutional Tribunal confirmed constitutional amendments that revoked birthright citizenship from anyone born between 1929 and 2007 to a parent deemed "in transit" or "residing illegally", and ordered the government to conduct a retrospective civil registration audit to remove them from the population register.[8] In Mauritania, the government introduced legal reforms in 2010, in advance of the roll out of a new national identity card, that removed all rights based on birth in Mauritania, as well as the possibility of late registration of birth or recognition of nationality based on apparent status as a national.[9] The subsequent discrimination in the issue of new identity cards led to the creation of a protest movement which accused the authorities of "biometric genocide".[10]

In some cases, retroactivity is explicit. In Kenya, legislation adopted in 1985 removed the right to citizenship based on birth in Kenya with retroactive effect, establishing instead a purely descent-based regime (which had already been applied in practice) derived from ancestors who were already two generations born in the country at independence in 1963. The 2010 constitution, adopted after a decades-long struggle to constrain executive powers, placed greater limits on deprivation of citizenship from a naturalised citizen (citizenship by birth was and is not possible to revoke) and provided that every citizen is entitled to "a Kenyan passport and any document of registration or identification issued by the State to citizens". [11] Despite this provision, Kenya's constitutional human rights bodies have repeatedly had to condemn the executive for discrimination and arbitrary decision-making in the issue of documents when it comes to members of certain minority groups: this discrimination has been enabled by the retroactive non-recognition of rights based on birth in Kenya.[12]

It should surely be the case that a change in the rules or retroactive finding that a person previously recognised as a citizen was issued citizenship documents in error is just as subject to the prohibition on arbitrary deprivation of citizenship as any procedure under formal deprivation provisions.[13] The African Court on Human

---

Rohingya Statelessness', e-International Relations (8 December 2015) available at https://www.e-ir.info/2015/12/08/problems-with-facts-about-rohingya-statelessness/.

[8] República Dominicana, Tribunal Constitucional, Sentencia TC/0168/13. See discussion in E. Hayes de Kalaf, *Dismantling Dominicans: Legal Identity, Access to Citizenship and the Contours of Belonging*, (Anthem Press, forthcoming 2020).

[9] Loi. No. 2010-023 du 11 février 2010 abrogeant et remplaçant certaines dispositions de la loi 61-112 du 12 juin 1961 portant Code de la nationalité mauritanienne, especially deletion of article 9 and amendments to articles 13, 19 and 58.

[10] See discussion in B. Manby, *Citizenship in Africa*, chapter 7.6; Z. Ould Ahmed Salem, 'Touche pas à ma nationalité: enrôlement biométrique et controverses sur l'identification en Mauritanie' (2018), Politique africaine, 152(4), p. 77-99.

[11] Constitution of Kenya (1969), as amended to 2008, article 94; Constitution of Kenya (2010), articles 12 & 17.

[12] B. Manby, *Citizenship in Africa*, chapter 7.3; B. Ng'weno and L. Obura Aloo, 'Irony of Citizenship: Descent, National Belonging, and Constitutions in the Postcolonial African State' (2019), Law & Society Review, 53(1), p. 141–172.

[13] UN Human Rights Council, 'Report of the Secretary-General: Human rights and arbitrary deprivation of nationality', A/HRC/13/34 (14 December 2009), para. 23; UNHCR, 'Expert Meeting - Interpreting the 1961

and Peoples' Rights agrees (see *The case of Anudo Ochieng Anudo* below). Yet these executive decisions, often purely administrative in legal character, may be out of reach of any due process protections – whether because excluded in law, or inaccessible in practice.

There is a major push to strengthen population registration systems, through the initiation or strengthening of requirements to hold a national identity card, for birth registration and civil registration in general, and for the use of biometric data in these documents. This push has the potential to reduce statelessness. But it also carries significant risks of arbitrary non-recognition of citizenship in practice. There is a strong possibility – probability in some national contexts – that governments will seek only to police ever more strongly the boundaries of their systems, excluding anyone of "doubtful" nationality, while failing to reform legal provisions and administrative practices that create statelessness by arbitrary exclusion. The avoidance of citizenship erasure by arbitrary retroactive non-recognition through these processes needs international attention.

The case of Anudo Ochieng Anudo[14]

Anudo Ochieng Anudo was born in 1979 in the Butiama district, north-west of Tanzania. In 2012, while he was working in Arusha for a German NGO providing solar power, his passport was retained when he was seeking to register his marriage, on the grounds that there were doubts about his citizenship. In September 2013, he wrote to the Minister of Home Affairs and Immigration protesting the confiscation of his passport. In April 2014, the immigration service opened an investigation. A letter from the minister dated 21 August 2014 informed Anudo that his passport had been cancelled on the grounds that he was not a citizen.

Unaware of the letter, the applicant went to the immigration office on 26 August 2014, hoping to recover his passport. Upon arrival he was arrested, detained and beaten. One week later, he was escorted to the Kenyan border and compelled to sign a notice of deportation and a document attesting that he was a Kenyan citizen. In November however, the Kenyan authorities

---

Statelessness Convention and Avoiding Statelessness resulting from Loss and Deprivation of Nationality' *("Tunis Conclusions")*, (March 2014), especially para. 9.

[14] B. Manby, 'Case Note: Anudo Ochieng Anudo v Tanzania (Judgment) (African Court on Human and Peoples' Rights, App No 012/2015, 22 March 2018)' (June 2019), Statelessness & Citizenship Review, 1(1).

declared that Anudo was an irregular migrant and expelled him back to Tanzania where he was not readmitted.

The applicant's father protested in writing to the Tanzanian Prime Minister, but the Minister of Home Affairs and Immigration confirmed the decision in December. The Tanzanian Citizenship Act 1995 provides that the minister's decision in relation to any application under the Act "shall not be subject to appeal or to review in any court" (Article 23); the Immigration Act, also of 1995, similarly provides that in decisions relating to matters under the act "the Minister's decision shall be final" (Article 10(f)).

Anudo then lived in no man's land between Kenya and Tanzania for the next three years. In May 2015, without the benefit of legal advice, he sent an email directly to the African Court on Human and Peoples' Rights, based in Arusha, to seek its help. The application was registered and, in early 2016, the court itself contacted Asylum Access Tanzania, which agreed to provide legal assistance to the applicant.

In its judgment, delivered in March 2018, the African Court noted that there is no general provision on the right to a nationality in the International Covenant on Civil and Political Rights (ICCPR) nor the African Charter on Human and Peoples' Rights (ACHPR); however, it filled this gap by drawing on the Universal Declaration of Human Rights (UDHR), noting also a reference to the UDHR in the Tanzanian Constitution. Article 15(2) states that "No one shall be arbitrarily deprived of his nationality".

Thus, while the court affirmed that the conferral of nationality is the sovereign right of states, it stated that international law permits loss of nationality only in "very exceptional situations". In addition to affirming a general obligation to avoid the risk of statelessness, the court drew on the UN Secretary-General's 2013 report on human rights and arbitrary deprivation of nationality to state that the conditions to be fulfilled are: (i) a clear legal basis, (ii) a legitimate purpose conforming with international law, (iii) proportionality to the interest protected, and (iv) procedural guarantees allowing the person concerned to defend himself before an independent body.[15]

In considering whether these conditions had been fulfilled, the court held that:

[S]ince the Respondent State is contesting the Applicant's nationality held since his birth on the basis of legal documents established by the Respondent State itself, the burden is on the Respondent State to prove the contrary.[16]

This reversal of the burden of proof is perhaps most important of the African Court's contributions to international law in this field. While welcome, the ruling did not address the situation of those who have never had citizenship documents but have always been treated as citizens – which indeed is the case for most Tanzanians, where a national identity card was only introduced from 2016, and some applications are being indefinitely delayed, without any reason given. The Tanzanian government, moreover, did not implement the African Court's judgment, and Anudo sought refugee status in Uganda.

---

[15] UN Human Rights Council, 'Report of the UN Secretary General: Human rights and arbitrary deprivation of nationality', A/HRC/25/28 (10 December 2013).

[16] African Court on Human and Peoples' Rights, *Anudo Ochieng Anudo v Tanzania* (2018), App. No. 012/2015, para. 80.

QUASI-LOSS OF NATIONALITY: SOME CRITICAL REFLECTIONS

BY RENÉ DE GROOT[*]

INTRODUCTION

In some States, it is possible that a person assumed to be a national is confronted by the authorities and told that (s)he never acquired the nationality of the State involved. Although the authorities argue that the person *never acquired* this nationality in the first place, the individual will still experience this as a *loss* of nationality – especially in cases where they have been treated as a national for many years, before being told that their nationality was not duly acquired. Since this is felt as a loss of nationality, it is labelled in the legal literature as *quasi-loss* of nationality.[1]

In section 2 a case will be described, which illustrates the scope and nature of the *quasi-loss* problem. Section 3 will deal briefly with a special type of *quasi-loss*, cases in which a person who was a national of the State involved is deemed to have lost the nationality due to an act, which is characterised as renunciation, although no formal declaration of renunciation of nationality was lodged to the State authorities. This construction could be labelled as *quasi-renunciation*.

EXAMPLES OF *QUASI-LOSS* OF NATIONALITY

One example of *quasi-loss* of nationality is when a minor child was supposed to be included in the naturalisation of a parent and was being treated as a national until facts come to the attention of the authorities raising doubts on the extension of the naturalisation. A recent decision on 20 August 2019 by the Court of The Hague is a good illustration of this.

---

[*] **René de Groot** is Emeritus Professor of Comparative Law and Private International Law, Maastricht University and Professor of Private Law, University of Aruba (West Indies). He has published extensively on statelessness, nationality and related subjects. .

[1] G. R. de Groot and P. Wautelet, 'Reflections on Quasi-loss of nationality from comparative, international and European perspective', Background paper ILEC-project (project on Involuntary Loss of European Citizenship), (August 2014), CEPS Paper in Liberty and Security in Europe No. 66, available at http://www.ceps.eu/publications/reflections-quasi-loss-nationality-comparative-international-and-european-perspective, p. 28 ; also included as chapter 4 in: S. Carrera Nuñez and G. R. de Groot, *'European citizenship at the Crossroads: The Role of the European Union on Loss and Acquisition of Nationality'* (Oisterwijk: Wolf Legal Publishers 2015), p. 117-157.

In 1990 Nuray[2] was born in Turkey to an unmarried mother, Meryem. The maternal grandparents registered the child as their own and took her to the Netherlands where their residence permit seemed to also include Nuray. In 1995 the grandparents naturalised in the Netherlands. This naturalisation was deemed to extend to all minor children of the naturalised couple with the exception of those children which did not have a valid permanent residence permit in the Netherlands".[3]

In 1992 Meryem married the father of Nuray and moved to the Netherlands. They also acquired Netherlands nationality several years later through naturalisation. In 1995 the original birth certificate of Nuray was amended in Turkey to reflect the true parentage and Meryem was mentioned as her mother.

16 years later in 2011, Nuray, now 21 years old, married in Turkey and wanted to return to the Netherlands. She submitted her marriage certificate, which mentioned Meryem as mother. She also applied to have the modified birth certificate recognised. This however caused the authorities to question whether she was included in the naturalisation procedures of her grandparents or of her mother. Since she is not the child but the grandchild of her grandparents, the authorities concluded that she was not included in their naturalisation. However, she was also not included in the naturalisation of the mother, because the residence permit of the mother did not extent to Nuray. The Court of The Hague sided with the arguments of the State authorities, concluding that she was never a Dutch national, despite the fact that she had been treated as such for at least 15 years.[4] This is one clear example of *quasi-loss* of nationality.

Quasi-loss is also used to describe cases in the Netherlands, where identity fraud is committed during the application for a naturalisation which took place before 1 April 2003.[5] In such cases, the name on the naturalisation certificate is different to the name of the person involved, and authorities use this to nullify the naturalisation. This is also extended to any children who were involved in the naturalisation process. Moreover, children born after the "naturalisation" also never acquired

---

[2] The names Nuray and Meryem are fictitious.

[3] "Het Nederlanderschap wordt onthouden aan de minderjarige kinderen [...] aan wie geen verblijf voor onbepaalde tijd in Nederland [...] is toegestaan." This provision was included in all naturalisation certificates issued from 1993 until 2003.

[4] Rechtbank Den Haag zp Rotterdam, ECLI:NL:RBDHA:2019:8546, in *Jurisprudentie Vreemdelingenrecht* (2019), no. 173, p. 1209-1219. In his case note on this decision, Pieter Boeles argues that the decision of this court could constitute a violation of the law of the European Union, because the person involved also "lost" European citizenship without any proportionality test. This could be a problem in light of the decision of the Court of Justice of the European Union on 12 March 2019 in the case *Tjebbes e.a.* (C-221/17). I completely agree with that view.

[5] This follows from a decision of the Hoge Raad (Supreme Court) of 30 June 2006, *Nederlandse Jurisprudentie* 2007, 551 (with comment of G.R. de Groot). Cases of identity fraud committed during a naturalisation procedure after 1 April 2003 may lead to the application of a withdrawal procedure based on Art. 14 (1) Netherlands Nationality Act (*Rijkswet op het Nederlanderschap*)

Netherlands nationality if they could only acquire it by descent (*jus sanguinis*) of their "naturalised" parent, because the other parent was not a Netherlands national but a foreigner.[6]

In some other countries, *quasi-loss* is used in cases where there has been a successful denial of paternity, if this has retroactive effect.[7] Another example is when someone is considered to be a national because their parent is a national, if it is discovered that the parentage tie is based on an adoption which cannot be recognised.[8] *Quasi-loss* may also be based on the discovery of a wrongful interpretation or application of nationality law rules.[9]

QUASI-RENUNCIATION OF NATIONALITY

In the case of *quasi-renunciation* of nationality, State authorities do not deny that the person involved was a national in the past; rather, they claim that the individual has lost their nationality due to renunciation – in other words, they have themselves chosen to renounce their nationality. The vast majority of States allow a national to renounce their nationality.[10] In most States, renunciation of nationality should occur via lodging a formal declaration to the competent authorities of the State involved, and a very common condition is that this should not cause statelessness. In several States, this type of loss is constructed as a withdrawal of the nationality by the State upon request of the national involved. These two sub-types of renunciation are not problematic because they both can be classified as loss of nationality on request of the person involved.

There is however a third type which is highly problematic. In these cases, States provide that nationality will be lost by behaviour that is characterised as *implicit* renunciation. This includes examples such as burning the national passport in public, using a foreign passport, and behaving as a foreign national.[11] This is an issue as it is often not clear which behaviour constitutes the implicit renunciation of nationality; also, it is difficult to prove whether the behaviour has actually taken place. This causes legal uncertainty, which is highly undesirable in nationality cases, in particular in cases of possible loss of nationality. Legal certainty should be a key feature of nationality law.

---

[6] S. Carrera Nuñez and G. R. de Groot (2015), chapter 4, p. 118-120; 128-130.
[7] This is e.g. the case in Portugal. See S. Carrera Nuñez and G. R. de Groot (2015), p. 120, 121; 124-128.
[8] S. Carrera Nuñez and G. R. de Groot (2015), p. 121, 122.
[9] S. Carrera Nuñez and G. R. de Groot (2015), p. 131-133.
[10] See the Global Database on Modes of Loss of Citizenship, available at globalcit.eu/loss-of-citizenship/ (accessed 14 January 2020), in particular mode L01.
[11] See the Global Database on Modes of Loss of Citizenship, available at globalcit.eu/loss-of-citizenship/ (accessed 14 January 2020), in particular mode L015.

SOME CRITICAL REFLECTIONS

The first difficulty of *quasi-loss* (including cases of *quasi-renunciation* of nationality) is the legal uncertainty caused by this approach, given that legal certainty is especially important in issues related to nationality.[12] Secondly, no rules on temporal limitation of grounds of loss apply.[13] Thirdly, the retroactive nature of this loss is particularly worrisome. Often, as a result, an individual's children and grandchildren may be affected by the loss. If the individuals involved do not possess another nationality, this may result in entrenched, intergenerational statelessness. Fourthly, the quasi-loss approach does not permit any proportionality assessment, which is highly problematic in light of the fact that the deprivation of nationality should never be arbitrary and that decisions on the nationality of children should always pay attention to the best interest of the child.[14] Huge problems arise in particular, if the legal system does not at all protect legitimate expectations in nationality law.[15]

In light of these difficulties, States should treat cases of *quasi-loss* as situations where a person can be *deprived* of his/her nationality, instead of considering the nationality annulled or lost *ex lege*. This should ensure full application of all existing protection measures, including limitation rules and age limits.[16]

---

[12] On the importance of legal certainty in nationality law, see G.R. de Groot, *Nationaliteit en rechtszekerheid*, Rede uitgesproken bij de aanvaarding van het ambt van hoogleraar aan de Universiteit van Aruba op (28 september 2007), Boom Juridische Uitgevers 2008 and G.R. de Groot, Rechts(on)zekerheid in het nationaliteitsrecht, *Asiel- en Migrantenrecht* (2019), p. 419-425.

[13] S. Carrera Nuñez and G. R. de Groot (2015), p. 136-138.

[14] Compare G.R. de Groot in H. Schneider, Willkürlicher Entzug der Staatsangehörigkeit, in: H. Menkhaus and M. Narazaki (ed.), *Japanischer Vorkämpfer für die Rechtsordnung des 21. Jahrhunderts, Festschrift für Koresuke Yamauchi zum 70. Geburtstag*, Schriften zum Internationalen Recht, (Band 220: Berlin: Duncker & Humblot 2017), p.159-172; see also S. Carrera Nuñez and G. R. de Groot (2015), p. 149-151.

[15] S. Carrera Nuñez and G. R. de Groot (2015), p. 138-144; 151.

[16] S. Carrera Nuñez and G. R. de Groot (2015), p. 154.

DEPRIVATION OF CITIZENSHIP THROUGH A POLITICAL LENS: *A POLITICAL SCIENTIST'S PERSPECTIVE*

BY MATTHEW GIBNEY*

Spurred on by new legislation in the UK, I first began researching deprivation of nationality a decade ago. I almost abandoned the topic straight away. For soon after starting my examination, an academic friend cast doubt on my choice of topic. He suggested that the UK's new deprivation powers were of little real significance: they were unlikely to be replicated by other states and would be challenged by the UK judiciary. It's now obvious that he was wrong. Not only have deprivation powers spread across Western states over the last several years, the courts have done little to limit their development and impact.

The rise of deprivation of nationality raises fundamental issues for political scientists because it shapes one of our most important concepts: citizenship. In particular, deprivation challenges the idea that citizenship should be a robust and secure status, even a non-contingent one.

> **Citizenship protects a range of important human goods. It provides the basis for residence within a specific territory, a foothold by which to hold governments to account through voting and running for office, and protection from a range of harmful social and economic forces. To take citizenship away is thus an extreme act of the state.**

Of course, historically, citizenship has rarely been considered an unconditional entitlement. Banishment was practiced quite widely across Europe until the 1800s, and throughout the 20th century most Western states had laws enabling loss of citizenship for treason or its equivalent. The laws on deprivation that have emerged over the last two decades often modify and update old laws rather than create entirely new powers. That said, denationalisation as a practical instrument of the

---

* **Matthew Gibney** is Professor of Politics and Forced Migration at the Refugee Studies Centre, University of Oxford. He has published widely on politics and ethics of expulsion and citizenship. His most recent publication is "Banishment and the pre-History of Legitimate Expulsion Power" in Citizenship Studies, December 2019.

state virtually disappeared in the West after 1945,[1] not least because citizenship stripping was de-legitimised through association with totalitarian regimes. Citizenship became widely understood as an unconditional status and the logic of citizenship in the West was overwhelmingly one of rights rather than obligations.

What happened? How did we move to a situation where the mantra that "citizenship is a privilege not a right" has become ubiquitous? Answering these questions is the stuff of political science. I think a number of different factors have come together over the last few decades to bring us to where we are now. The first and most obvious is the rise of Islamist terrorism, which of course became particularly prominent after September 11, 2001. This kind of terrorism, which has subsequently resulted in attacks across a range of Western countries, was often spearheaded not by foreign armies or powers but by so-called "home grown" militants - people who shared the citizenship of those civilians they wanted to destroy. The fact that these acts were committed by citizens facilitated the characterisation of the terrorists involved not simply as vicious criminals but as betrayers, people disloyal to their societies.

Another key factor was that the perpetrators of terrorist acts were typically naturalised immigrants or the children of such immigrants. Against this background, public hostility to immigration from non-Western countries (typically Muslim-majority countries) could be enlisted to support new denationalisation powers. In many countries, there is a belief that citizens of Muslim background are nationals in law only and are not true members of society. The use of citizenship stripping rather than conventional criminal punishments for terrorists thus seems highly appropriate. There is nothing new about this. Historically, as the experience of Germans during WWI in the US and the Japanese in Canada during WWII show, denationalisation's targets have been a tracer for ethnic, religious and national groups who - citizenship notwithstanding - are already considered foreign in the societies in which they live.

A third factor essential to the prising open of citizenship has been the spread of dual nationality. Over the last several decades, states have increasingly relaxed the expectation that citizens owe them a singular loyalty, creating opportunities for multiple citizenship. One unanticipated result of this change has been that states now find themselves with citizens whom they can deprive of nationality without violating norms on statelessness. Practically, dual nationality also enables countries to deport those who lose their citizenship to a country that is obliged to admit them. Dual nationality has thus provided states with new opportunities to dissolve obligations towards unwanted or undesirable citizens and to set the terms upon

---

[1] See further the essay titled 'Expanding Deprivation of Nationality Powers in the Security Context: Global Trends' at p. 213.

which citizenship will be retained. Ironically, then, the rise of denationalisation simultaneously affirms the strength of norms on statelessness *and* demonstrates just how much states would like to escape them.

If the conjunction of these three factors explains why deprivation of nationality has reappeared in the political repertoire of contemporary states, where are Western countries heading? The answer is not at all clear. On the one hand, some states, notably France and Canada, have witnessed effective political resistance to the extension of denationalisation powers. In Canada, the Liberal Party leader (now Prime Minister), Justin Trudeau, successfully campaigned against new measures under the slogan "A Canadian is a Canadian is a Canadian". In France, attempts to enshrine the deprivation of citizenship into the constitution in 2015 by the President, Francois Hollande, were foiled by critics who saw such powers as gratuitous and at odds with principles of republican equality. On the other hand, UK deprivation powers have been expanded three times since 2002 and the laws have been used to strip citizenship not simply from terrorists, but also individuals involved in organised sexual crimes. In Australia, there are currently attempts to expand further laws passed in 2014 to enable more people to be stripped of citizenship.

It is possible that with the end of the war in Syria and the demise of ISIS, the demand for denationalisation measures might peter out across Western states. After all, there is much doubt about the efficacy of such powers in fighting terrorism and they are hardly uncontroversial. There is a chance, however, that the West is in the midst of a radical revision in the way that citizenship is conceived, one that puts an increasing emphasis on obligations rather than rights. In this context, new targets for citizenship deprivation beyond terrorists may come into view, as has occurred in the UK. A new era of banishment may be only just beginning.

EXPANDING DEPRIVATION OF NATIONALITY POWERS IN THE SECURITY CONTEXT: *GLOBAL TRENDS*

After the atrocities of World War II, which saw millions of people stripped of their nationality before being subjected to grave human rights abuses and forced into seeking refuge elsewhere, deprivation of nationality was increasingly viewed as a repressive and disproportionate practice.[1] The international community placed more emphasis on the protection of human rights and the right of everyone to a nationality, culminating in the prohibition of arbitrary deprivation of nationality in Article 15 of the UDHR in 1948. In the post 9/11 world however, and particularly in the context of the threat of ISIS, a small but growing number of states have revisited and (re)introduced nationality deprivation for national security measures. These measures "have been posited as a tool to counter terrorism",[2] and are justified on the basis that those who join terrorist entities or engage in terrorist activities do not deserve nationality, have turned their back on their state and its values, or that they pose a threat to national security.

The ways in which deprivation of nationality can take place varies between states, but globally, some broad trends can be identified. A 2018 survey of 42 sample countries identified that globally, there is an upward trend of States moving towards adopting deprivation legislation or expanding already existing legislation.[3] Below, are some of the conclusions drawn from this survey as well as our ongoing monitoring of nationality deprivation trends and practices.

GROUNDS FOR DEPRIVATION OF NATIONALITY

States have expanded their nationality deprivation powers by either introducing national security or terrorism as the grounds for revocation of nationality or by

---

[1] See further Matthew Gibney's essay titled 'Deprivation of Citizenship through a Political Lens: a Political Scientist's Perspective' in this report at p. 207.

[2] Institute on Statelessness and Inclusion, Open Society Foundations, Asser Institute and Ashurst, 'Expert Roundtable on Citizenship stripping as a Security Measure' Discussion Paper 1: Global and Regional Trends (June 2018), p. 3.

[3] The research was carried out by Ashurst Law Firm. Ashurst are one of ISI's partners in the development of the Principles on the Deprivation of Nationality as a National Security Measure.

expanding existing powers. States such as Australia, Azerbaijan, Germany, Kazakhstan, Kyrgyzstan, Seychelles, South Africa and Venezuela are all examples of where this has occurred.

German law for example, did not provide for withdrawal of nationality in a national security or counterterrorism context until 2019. The nationality of dual nationals however could be lost "by joining the armed forces or a comparable armed organization of a foreign state".[4] In June 2019, German parliament amended nationality legislation to provide for the automatic loss of citizenship of adults with dual nationality who join foreign terrorist militias.[5] The provision defines a foreign terrorist militia as "a paramilitary organized armed association that aims to violently abolish the structures of a foreign state in violation of international law and replace these structures with a new state or to build state-like structures."[6] The amendment reveals the legislatures' view of those who join foreign terrorist groups as having "turned their back on Germany and its basic values and turned to another foreign power in the form of a terrorist militia."[7] However, the law is not to be applied retroactively.[8] Those who have already joined a terrorist militia will therefore not be affected, but the Interior Ministry "hopes that the law will have a "preventative effect" in the future."[9]

While there are significant concerns over the expansion of deprivation powers and their automatic application, the clarity and non-retroactiveness of the German legislation, does set it apart from some other legislative developments. In other instances, legislative provisions have been drafted very broadly and vaguely which gives the authorities wide discretion over interpretation, undermining the principle of legal certainty.

Turkey

Turkey's nationality deprivation powers have been used as a political tool for internal political repression since the 1980s. After the failed 2017 coup, Turkey issued an executive decree,

---

[4] Section 28 s. 1 of the Nationality Act (Staatsangehörigkeitsgesetz, StAG). Available in English with amendments until 2014 at https://germanlawarchive.iuscomp.org/?p=266.

[5] Article 28(1)2, available in German at https://www.gesetze-im-internet.de/stag/BJNR005830913.html.

[6] 'Germany toughens citizenship laws for terrorists and polygamists' *Deutsche Welle* (28 June 2019), available at https://www.dw.com/en/germany-toughens-citizenship-laws-for-terrorists-and-polygamists/a-49386785 accessed 18 November 2019.

[7] *Id.*

[8] C. Winter, 'Germany approves stripping dual national terrorist fighters of citizenship' *Deutsche Welle* (03 April 2019), available at: https://www.dw.com/en/germany-approves-stripping-dual-national-terrorist-fighters-of-citizenship/a-48177392 accessed 18 November 2019.

[9] C. Winter, 'Germany approves stripping dual national terrorist fighters of citizenship' *Deutsche Welle* (3 April 2019), available at: https://www.dw.com/en/germany-approves-stripping-dual-national-terrorist-fighters-of-citizenship/a-48177392.

establishing nationality deprivation procedures.[10] Those declared under investigation for certain crimes, 'Offences against National Security' and 'Offences against the Constitutional Order and Operation of Constitutional Rules',[11] must surrender themselves and return to for investigation within three months. Those who do not will lose their citizenship, with no right of appeal.[12] The Ministry of Interior proposes the decision to remove nationality is made by the Council of Ministers. No prior judicial approval is needed, and no safeguards against statelessness are included, putting those affected at risk of statelessness.[13]

In 2017, two "return home" notices were issued, one ordering 130 individuals to return to Turkey and surrender themselves for investigation, the second ordering 99. Those named include "US-based Islamic preacher, Fethullah Gülen, who is accused of masterminding the failed July 2016 coup"[14] and "two members of parliament for the Kurdish Peoples' Democratic Party (HDP)."[15]

In Kyrgyzstan for example, following an amendment in 2016, a national may have their nationality withdrawn if they carry out "training abroad aimed at acquiring skills and abilities related to commission of terrorist or extremist crime".[16]

Disloyalty or treason are grounds for deprivation of nationality in many states, and the provisions are often overly broad and vague. An example of this is Article 129(3)(a)(i) of the Constitution of the Republic of Singapore which states that nationality can be deprived of "… any person who is a citizen of Singapore by naturalisation if the Government is satisfied that he has shown himself by act or speech to be disloyal or disaffected towards Singapore".

Furthermore, serving a foreign state body can be a reason for nationality deprivation. According to the Azerbaijani nationality laws, nationality is lost "if a

---

[10] Article 75 of Decree (KHK) 680 (6 January 2017).

[11] Article 302 of Section 14 and Articles 309–315 of Section 15 of the Turkish Penal Code, Law No. 5237 (26 September 2004).

[12] Article 75 of Decree (KHK) 680 (6 January 2017); Institute on Statelessness and Inclusion, 'Policy Brief: Arbitrary deprivation of nationality and denial of consular services to Turkish citizens' (July 2017), available at http://www.institutesi.org/policy-brief-Turkey-arbitrary-deprivation-of-nationality_2017.pdf, p. 3-4.

[13] *Ibid*, p. 5.

[14] *Id.*

[15] 'Turkey seeks to revoke citizenship of another 99 people including a 23-year-old' *Turkey Purge* (10 September 2017), available at https://turkeypurge.com/turkey-seeks-to-revoke-citizenship-of-another-99-people-including-a-23-year-old.

[16] Kyrgyzstan Law on Citizenship (21 May 2007), Article 26(1).

citizen of the Republic of Azerbaijan voluntarily serves in state or municipal bodies, armed forces or other military units of a foreign state".[17]

Lastly, dual citizens of South Africa can be deprived of their nationality if "the Minister is satisfied that it is in the public interest that such citizen shall cease to be a South African citizen",[18] and in the UK, as of 2006, deprivation of nationality is only required to be "conductive to the public good".[19]

As these examples show, the criteria for which nationality can be deprived varies significantly between states. The broad and vague wording of many provisions and the lack of stringent protection against arbitrary deprivation of nationality are of deep concern. Not only is arbitrary deprivation prohibited under international law, but as discussed further below, research has also shown that nationality deprivation is not an effective national security and counterterrorism measure and can in fact be counterproductive.

EXPANSION OF DEPRIVATION POWERS

States have also taken steps to expand upon their already existing deprivation of nationality powers, making it easier to deprive citizens of their nationality, by strengthening executive powers and limiting judicial oversight. Examples include, but are not limited to, no longer requiring a criminal conviction or even judicial approval beforehand or restricting the right of appeal and providing wider discretion to the executive or lowering the threshold of proof.

UK legislation on deprivation of nationality has undergone multiple changes from the turn of the century. In 2002 the Secretary of State was given power to deprive dual nationals of their citizenship if the Secretary was 'satisfied that the person has done anything seriously prejudicial to the vital interests' of the UK.[20] In 2006, the law was amended, lowering the threshold to only require that deprivation of nationality be 'conducive to the public good'.[21] The possibility of depriving a naturalised citizen of their nationality, even in cases where it could lead to statelessness, was introduced in 2014. The amendment requires only that the Home

---

[17] Article 18(2) of the Law of the Azerbaijan Republic on Citizenship of the Azerbaijan Republic, No. 527-IQ (1998) (as amended).
[18] Article S8(2)(b) of the South African Citizenship Act (88 of 1995), commencement date 6 October 1995.
[19] Article 40(2) of the British Nationality Act 1981 (c. 61). See also 'A litigator's perspective of deprivation of nationality' in this report.
[20] Section 4, Article 1(2) of the Nationality, Immigration and Asylum Act 2002 (c. 41), available at https://www.legislation.gov.uk/ukpga/2002/41/contents/enacted.
[21] Section 56, Article 1 of the Immigration, Asylum and Nationality Act 2006 (c. 13), available at https://www.legislation.gov.uk/ukpga/2006/13/contents/enacted.

Secretary have 'reasonable ground that the person is able to become a citizen of another state.'[22]

Shamima Begum's case illustrates how the legislation is being used in practice. Begum left the UK in 2015, when she was 15 years old, to join ISIS in Syria. In February 2019 she was deprived of her citizenship, leaving her stateless, after being found in a "refugee camp in Syria following the collapse of the IS caliphate."[23] The Home Secretary ordered she be stripped of her citizenship for reasons related to national security and counterterrorism, on the grounds that because of her parents Bangladeshi heritage, she could apply for Bangladeshi citizenship. Bangladeshi officials however said that they had "nothing to do with her", she was not a Bangladeshi citizen and that she "could face the death penalty for involvement in terrorism" if she were to go to Bangladesh.[24]

In October 2019, Denmark fast-tracked a Bill amending the nationality laws, which allows the Minister for Immigration and Integration to deprive citizenship of anyone considered to have acted in a manner seriously prejudicial to the vital interests of the country, providing they won't become stateless. The minister may do this without trial, and information included in the assessment undertaken by the Minister of Justice to determine if the individual is a security risk, may be withheld from the parties concerned.[25] This amendment now allows the Executive to deprive individuals of nationality without a court ruling, as was previously required.[26] The Bill was introduced explicitly to try to prevent the return of Danish foreign fighters who fought for ISIS,[27] as concerns rose of imprisoned ISIS fighters escaping the Kurdish-controlled ISIS camps, during the Turkish offensive against Syrian Kurdish forces in October 2019. [28] Danish Prime Minister, Mette Frederiksen, said

---

[22] Section 66, Article 1 of the Immigration Act 2014 (c. 22), available at: https://www.legislation.gov.uk/ukpga/2014/22/contents/enacted.

[23] Institute on Statelessness and Inclusion, November 2019 Bulletin, Citizenship Continued to be Subject of Debate in Dealing with 'Foreign Fighters', available at https://mailchi.mp/786624d82c4a/monthly-bulletin-november-2019.

[24] S. Morrison, 'ISIS bride Shamima Begum set for appeal over removal of British citizenship' *Evening Standard* (22 October 2019), available at https://www.standard.co.uk/news/uk/isis-bride-shamima-begum-set-for-appeal-over-removal-of-british-citizenship-a4267306.html; M. Busby, 'Shamima Begum would face death penalty in Bangladesh, says minister' *The Guardian* (4 May 2019), available at https://www.theguardian.com/uk-news/2019/may/04/shamima-begum-would-face-death-penalty-in-bangladesh-says-minister.

[25] Article 1(1) of the amendment law – Lov om ændring af lov om dansk indfødsret og udlændingeloven, nr. 1057 (24 October 2019) [Danish], available at https://www.retsinformation.dk/Forms/R0710.aspx?id=210778.

[26] Institute on Statelessness and Inclusion, November 2019 Bulletin, Citizenship Continued to be Subject of Debate in Dealing with 'Foreign Fighters', available at https://mailchi.mp/786624d82c4a/monthly-bulletin-november-2019; 'Denmark passes legislation to strip ISIL fighters of citizenship' *Al Jazeera* (24 October 2019), available at https://www.aljazeera.com/news/2019/10/denmark-passes-legislation-strip-isil-fighters-citizenship-191024174102359.html.

[27] 'Denmark passes legislation to strip ISIL fighters of citizenship' *Al Jazeera* (24 October 2019), available at https://www.aljazeera.com/news/2019/10/denmark-passes-legislation-strip-isil-fighters-citizenship-191024174102359.html.

[28] *Id.*

these people had "turned their backs on Denmark and fought with violence against our democracy and freedom. They pose a threat to our security."[29]

Australia

Australia has expanded powers on deprivation of nationality in the context of national security and counter-terrorism over the last 15 years.[30] In 2015, amendments to the Australian Citizenship Act of 2007 introduced Sections 33AA, 35 and 35A. According to Section 33AA, a dual national (who is 14 years or older), "renounces their Australian citizenship" if they engage in terrorism-related conduct inconsistent with their allegiance to Australia, including, but not limited to by providing or receiving training related to terrorist acts. According to Section 35, a dual national of at least 14 years of age, "ceases to be an Australian citizen" if they serve in the armed forces of an enemy country or in a terrorist organisation. Section 35(A) also allows the Minister for Immigration to determine a person ceases to be an Australian if convicted for terrorism-related offences.[31]

This amendment was highly criticised for not requiring a criminal conviction or evidence of guilt, thus contradicting the presumption of innocence and preventing a fair trial.[32] The government introduced the amendment following the Martin Place siege terrorist attack in December 2014[33] as "part of 'a multi-faceted approach" to countering the threats to national security posed by an increasing numbers of foreign fighters, known sympathisers and supporters of extremists and potential terrorists"[34] and as a response to radicalisation fears and the

---

[29] 'id.

[30] Institute on Statelessness and Inclusion, Open Society Foundations, Asser Institute and Ashurst, 'Expert Roundtable on Citizenship stripping as a Security Measure', Discussion Paper 1: Global and Regional Trends (June 2018), p. 23.

[31] Sections 33AA(1)-(2), 35(1)-(3) and 35A of the Australian Citizenship Act 2007 (No. 20, 2007), introduced by Australian Citizenship (Allegiance to Australia) Act 2015 (Cth), No. 166 2015, sch 1, cll 3-5. The Act is available at https://www.legislation.gov.au/Details/C2019C00040.

[32] L. Taylor, 'Proposal to strip citizenship criticised by human rights groups and legal experts' *The Guardian* (3 August 2015), available at https://www.theguardian.com/australia-news/2015/aug/04/proposal-to-strip-citizenship-criticised-by-human-rights-groups-and-legal-experts.

[33] Department of the Prime Minister and Cabinet, 'Review of Australia's Counter-Terrorism Machinery' (January 2015), available at https://www.homeaffairs.gov.au/nat-security/files/review-australia-ct-machinery.pdf, p. iv-v.

[34] Parliament of Australia, Bills Digest no. 15 2015–16, available at https://www.aph.gov.au/Parliamentary_Business/Bills_Legislation/bd/bd1516a/16bd015.

possible threat Australian foreign fighters may pose to domestic security if allowed to return.[35]

WHO CAN BE DEPRIVED OF THEIR NATIONALITY?

Many states are more reluctant to deprive birth-right citizens of their nationality than naturalised citizens, or only allow deprivation of naturalised citizens within a certain number of years after their naturalisation. Legislative changes in recent years have however changed this in many states, by allowing, for example, deprivation of birth-right citizens and not only naturalised citizens i.e. in Israel, the UK and Turkey; allowing for the deprivation of naturalised dual citizens for an increased time period post successful naturalisation or without a time limit i.e. in Belgium and France; or allowing deprivation even if it results in statelessness i.e. in the UK, Italy and Turkey.

Belgian law has provided for deprivation of nationality since 1919.[36] In 2012, the legislation was amended to allow deprivation of nationality of a person found guilty of specific terrorist offenses and sentenced to five years in prison as per the Belgian Criminal Code.[37] The provision only applied to naturalised citizens who had acquired Belgian citizenship less than ten years before the offences were committed.[38]

In 2015, the list of offences which were considered to be acts of terrorism were expanded. The ten-year limit was also removed, so any naturalised dual citizen could be deprived of nationality, no matter how long the person had possessed Belgian citizenship.[39]

---

[35] Parliament of Australia, Bills Digest no. 15 2015–16, available at
https://www.aph.gov.au/Parliamentary_Business/Bills_Legislation/bd/bd1516a/16bd015.

[36] P. Wautelet, 'Deprivation of citizenship for 'jihadists': Analysis of Belgian and French practice and policy in light of the principle of equal treatment' (2016), available at https://ssrn.com/abstract=2713742, p. 1.

[37] Article 23/1, § 1 and Article 23/2, § 1 of The Code on Belgian Nationality of 1 January 1984 (as amended). The offences mentioned in these articles of the Nationality Code refer to articles 101 to 112, 113 to 120bis, 120quater, 120sexies, 120octies, 121 to 123, 123ter, 123quater, second paragraph, 124 to 134, 136bis, 136ter, 136quater, 136quinquies, 136sexies and 136septies, 331bis, 433quinquies to 433octies, 477 to 477sexies and 488bis of the Criminal Code; Articles 77bis, 77ter, 77quater and 77quinquies of the Aliens Act; and Book II, Title Iter, of the Criminal Code.

[38] Institute on Statelessness and Inclusion, Open Society Foundations, Asser Institute and Ashurst, 'Expert Roundtable on Citizenship stripping as a Security Measure' Discussion Paper 1: Global and Regional Trends, (June 2018), p. 9; P. Wautelet, 'Deprivation of citizenship for 'jihadists': Analysis of Belgian and French practice and policy in light of the principle of equal treatment' (2016), available at https://ssrn.com/abstract=2713742, p. 3.

[39] Article 23/2 of the Code on Belgian Nationality, as amended; P. Wautelet, 'Deprivation of citizenship for 'jihadists': Analysis of Belgian and French practice and policy in light of the principle of equal treatment', (2016), available at https://ssrn.com/abstract=2713742, p. 3.

The Netherlands

Multiple amendments have been made to Dutch Nationality Act (NNA) over the last 15 years. The Minister of Security and Justice can deprive nationality of individuals, without prior approval of the judiciary.[40] The NNA allows for citizenship withdrawal from both naturalised citizens and those born Dutch nationals, provided statelessness does not result (with an exception for revocation of nationality obtained by fraud, which can result in statelessness).[41]

The NNA allows for the revocation of nationality for criminal conviction. In 2010, Article 14 was amended imposing "a limit to the acts which could result in revocation of citizenship to those with a sentence of eight years."[42] In 2016, it was amended again allowing for the revocation of citizenship of those convicted of "a serious offence for the preparation or facilitation of a terrorist offence or an offence relating to recruitment for a foreign military service or armed conflict" and "those who join a terrorist organisation abroad."[43]

Under 2017 amendments, neither criminal conviction or reference to a criminal action is needed.[44] The Minister of Justice can deprive Dutch citizenship of "a person 16 years of age or older; (i) who voluntarily enters the armed services of a state involved in combat operations against the Netherlands or against an alliance of which the Netherlands is a member; (ii) or if the actions of an individual demonstrate that (s)he joined an organisation that is on a list of organisations participating in a national or international armed conflict and that poses a threat to national security."[45]

---

[40] Institute on Statelessness and Inclusion, Open Society Foundations, Asser Institute and Ashurst, 'Expert Roundtable on Citizenship stripping as a Security Measure' Discussion Paper 1: Global and Regional Trends, (June 2018), p. 44; NNA Amendment Act Article I B 1(3).

[41] Institute on Statelessness and Inclusion, Open Society Foundations, Asser Institute and Ashurst, 'Expert Roundtable on Citizenship stripping as a Security Measure' Discussion Paper 1: Global and Regional Trends, (June 2018), p. 10.

[42] *Id.*

[43] *Id.*

[44] *Ibid,* p. 14; NNA Article 14(3) or 14(4), NNA Amendment Act Article 1(B)(i); Amnesty International Public Statement, 'Netherlands: Counter-terrorism bills would violate human Rights and undermine rule of law' (2017), available at https://www.amnesty.org/download/Documents/EUR3554322017ENGLISH.pdf.

[45] The Law Library of Congress, 'Netherlands: Three New Laws Adopted to Further Counterterrorism Efforts' (2017), available at https://www.loc.gov/law/foreign-news/article/netherlands-three-new-laws-adopted-to-further-counterterrorism-efforts/.

HOW ARE DEPRIVATION POWERS BEING USED?

Nationality deprivation laws in the context of national security and counterterrorism are not only used for their stated purpose. They are also being used for political repression, to target journalists, human rights defenders, political opponents, religious leaders and minorities.

Examples of this can be seen in a number of countries, including in Azerbaijan, where the government has used its deprivation laws to strip nationality, not just of hundreds of Azerbaijani 'foreign terrorist fighters', but also human rights defenders and opposition party leaders.[46] In Kyrgyzstan, government officials "have called for an independent journalist to be stripped [of] his citizenship after he criticised government social media posts which were inciting hatred against ethnic minorities;"[47] and in Egypt citizenship laws were amended to allow for nationality to be withdrawn from anyone who "joins any group, association, body or organization, gang or entity, of any nature inside or outside the country that aims to harm public order of the state or undermine the social economic or political situation."[48] The amendment was criticized for targeting the Muslim Brotherhood.[49]

The Case of the 'UAE 94'

In the United Arab Emirates, nationality deprivation is being used for political purposes, targeting political opponents and human rights activists. A total of 94 Emirati political and human rights activists, lawyers, academics, students and teachers were charged with founding, organising and administering an organisation aimed at overthrowing the government. The 94 citizens had criticised the government and advocated for democracy and greater rights in the Emirates. 69 of them were convicted and sentenced to 7-15 years in prison, in an unfair mass trial

---

[46] Institute on Statelessness and Inclusion, Open Society Foundations, Asser Institute and Ashurst, 'Expert Roundtable on Citizenship stripping as a Security Measure' Discussion Paper 1: Global and Regional Trends, (June 2018), p. 25; G. Akhundova, 'Deprivation of citizenship marks repressive new low for Azerbaijan' *International Media Support* (11 October 2018), available at https://www.mediasupport.org/blogpost/deprivation-of-citizenship-marks-repressive-new-low-for-azerbaijan/.

[47] Institute on Statelessness and Inclusion, Open Society Foundations, Asser Institute and Ashurst, 'Expert Roundtable on Citizenship stripping as a Security Measure' Discussion Paper 1: Global and Regional Trends, (June 2018), p. 3; 'Bishkek: MPs urge to deprive journalist Ulugbek Babakulov of Kyrgyz citizenship' *Fergana News Agency* (1 June 2017), available at: http://enews.fergananews.com/news.php?id=3361&mode=snews; 'Kyrgyz journalist receives death threats' *Committee to Protect Journalists* (1 June 2017), available at: https://cpj.org/2017/06/kyrgyz-journalist-receives-death-threats.php.

[48] Mada (2017) Amendments to Egypt's nationality law: An obscure state for the 'stateless' [online] available at: https://madamasr.com/en/2017/09/26/feature/politics/amendments-to-egypts-nationality-law-an-obscure-state-for-the-stateless/

[49] Institute on Statelessness and Inclusion, Open Society Foundations, Asser Institute and Ashurst, 'Expert Roundtable on Citizenship stripping as a Security Measure' Discussion Paper 1: Global and Regional Trends, (June 2018), p. 3; 'Amendments to Egypt's nationality law: An obscure state for the 'stateless' *Mada* (2017), available at https://www.madamasr.com/en/2017/09/26/feature/politics/amendments-to-egypts-nationality-law-an-obscure-state-for-the-stateless/.

tainted by due process and human rights violations.[50] In addition to the prison sentence, many of the defendants were stripped of their nationality, rendering them stateless, and some also deported.[51]

Article 8 of the United Arab Emirates Constitution prohibits deprivation of nationality but allows for withdrawal in "exceptional circumstances which shall be defined by law." The exceptional circumstances are defined in the United Arab Emirates Federal Law No. 17 for 1972 Concerning Nationality, which state in Article 15 that any person engaging in military service for a foreign country without permission, works for the interest of an enemy country or adopts voluntarily another nationality, shall lose their United Arab Emirates nationality. Nationality of a naturalised citizen shall, according to Article 16, be withdrawn if: 1) "he commits or attempts to commit an action which is deemed dangerous for the security or safety of the country"; 2) "he has been punished repeatedly for crimes of dishonour". Nationality may also be withdrawn from the person's spouse and underaged children. In practice however nationality deprivation is not in accordance with the Emirati laws, as authorities in the UAE have increasingly been arbitrarily depriving Emirati citizens of their nationality, based on an unpublished presidential decree, as in the 'UAE 94' case, which those who have been arbitrarily deprived of their nationality have been prevented from seeing. The legal grounds which supposedly form the basis for the deprivation are therefore unclear.[52]

Bahrain

Article 17(a) of the Bahraini Constitution states "A person inherently enjoying his Bahraini nationality cannot be stripped of his nationality except in cases of treason, and such other cases as prescribed by law."[53] Acquisition and withdrawal of nationality is governed by the Bahraini Citizenship Act of

---

[50] International Commission of Jurists, 'Mass Convictions Following an Unfair Trial: The UAE 94 Case' (2013), available at https://www.icj.org/wp-content/uploads/2013/10/UAE-report-4-Oct-2013smallpdf.com_.pdf; International Campaign for Freedom in the United Arab Emirates (ICFUAE), 'The UAE 94 Case Fact Sheet', available at http://icfuae.org.uk/research-and-publications-factsheets/fact-sheet-94-uae .

[51] International Commission of Jurists, 'Mass Convictions Following an Unfair Trial: The UAE 94 Case' (2013), available at https://www.icj.org/wp-content/uploads/2013/10/UAE-report-4-Oct-2013smallpdf.com_.pdf, p.13; International Campaign for Freedom in the United Arab Emirates (ICFUAE), 'Revocation of nationalities in the United Arab Emirates' (2017), available at http://icfuae.org.uk/research-and-publications/revocation-nationalities-united-arab-emirates.

[52] Institute on Statelessness and Inclusion, 'Submission to the Human Rights Council at the 29th Session of the Universal Periodic Review: The United Arab Emirates' (January 2018), available at https://files.institutesi.org/UPR29_UAE.pdf, p. 7, para. 22; International Campaign for Freedom in the United Arab Emirates (ICFUAE), 'Revocation of nationalities in the United Arab Emirates' (2017), available at http://icfuae.org.uk/research-and-publications/revocation-nationalities-united-arab-emirates.

[53] Article 17(a) of Bahrain's Constitution of 2002.

1963.[54] In 2013 and 2014, the Act's deprivation of nationality powers were expanded to provide for denaturalisation of Bahrainis convicted of various terrorist offenses, defined broadly under Bahrainis 2006 Anti-Terrorism Law. It also empowers the Minister of Interior, with cabinet approval, to deprive citizenship of a person who "aids or is involved in the service of a hostile state" or who "causes harm to the interests of the Kingdom or acts in a way that contravenes his duty of loyalty to it."[55]

Broad/ambiguous definitions have been used to deprive not only violent extremists of their nationality, but also activists, human rights defenders, political opposition party leaders, religious figures and others. The first mass denationalisation in Bahrain took place in November 2012 as part of a large-scale effort to suppress opposition and contain protests.[56] Many were left stateless. The rate of de-nationalisations since has significantly increased[57] with around 1,000 Bahraini's arbitrarily deprived of their nationality.[58]

CONCLUSIONS

Legislation allowing for deprivation of nationality has been introduced or has been/is being expanded by a growing number of States around the world. How the manner in which deprivation powers are being expanded and used differs from country to country. In some states, deprivation powers are not only being used for their stated national security and counterterrorism purposes, but are also being used to target certain groups, especially political dissidents, journalists, and human rights defenders.

---

[54] Unofficial translation of Bahraini Citizenship Act of 1963 (last amended 1981) available in English at https://www.refworld.org/docid/3fb9f34f4.html.

[55] Institute on Statelessness and Inclusion, Open Society Foundations, Asser Institute and Ashurst, 'Expert Roundtable on Citizenship stripping as a Security Measure' Discussion Paper 1: Global and Regional Trends, (June 2018), p. 26-27.

[56] I. Black, 'Bahrain revokes 31 activists' nationalities' *The Guardian* (7 November 2012), available at https://www.theguardian.com/world/2012/nov/07/bahrain-revokes-activists-nationalities accessed 9 December 2019.

[57] The Institute on Statelessness and Inclusion and Americans for Democracy & Human Rights in Bahrain, 'Joint Submission to the Human Rights Council at the 27ᵗʰ Session of the Universal Periodic Review: The Kingdom of Bahrain', available at https://files.institutesi.org/BahrainUPR2016.pdf, para. 21.

[58] L. Barrington, 'Major opposition figures not among those given back Bahraini citizenship' *Reuters* (29 April 2019), available at https://www.reuters.com/article/us-bahrain-security-idUSKCN1S50PC.

The implications of these trends are a cause for alarm, as they evidence an increasing instrumentalisation of nationality and disregard for everyone's right to a nationality. Further, as research has shown, deprivation of nationality is indeed not an effective national security and counterterrorism measure. Instead of deterring people from engaging in activities that threaten national security, it may have an opposite effect. It can create or increase discrimination among nationals (because in some states only dual nationals can be deprived, and those who possess dual nationality often come from a migration background / belong to a minority group), and "marginalisation and (perceived) discrimination can be one of the many factors that can play a role in people radicalising and joining extremist groups in the first place."[59] Nationality deprivation may also impede prosecution and conviction of suspected terrorists, as the state may lose jurisdiction based on nationality when the person concerned is deprived of their nationality.[60] By depriving the allegedly 'dangerous' individual of their nationality, the state does not eradicate the supposed danger, but rather only transfers the responsibility to another state.[61]

Of serious concern is that these developments make those deprived of their nationality, and sometimes their children or other family members, vulnerable to (the risk of) statelessness. This has wider implications for their enjoyment of other essential human rights, such as their access to education, healthcare and work, their freedom of movement and right to remain in, or re-enter, their home country.

---

[59] 'The Root Causes of Violent Extremism', RAN Issue Paper (4 Jan 2016), available at https://ec.europa.eu/home-affairs/sites/homeaffairs/files/what-we-do/networks/radicalisation_awareness_network/ran-papers/docs/issue_paper_root-causes_jan2016_en.pdf, p. 3; Dr. C. Paulussen, 'Countering Terrorism Through the Stripping of Citizenship: Ineffective and Counterproductive' (International Centre for Counter-Terrorism Publications, 17 October 2018) available at https://icct.nl/publication/countering-terrorism-through-the-stripping-of-citizenship-ineffective-and-counterproductive/.

[60] R. Bauböck, 'Whose Bad Guys Are Terrorists?', in R. Bauböck (ed.), *Debating Transformations of National Citizenship* (Springer 2018), p. 201. (IMISCOE Research Series).

[61] UN Security Council Resolution 1373, S/RES/1373 (2001), from 28 September 2001, para. 2(e), p. 2; 'New blog: The Shamima Begum case: 'Revoking citizenship is ineffective and counterproductive' *Asser Institute* (22 February 2019), available at https://www.asser.nl/about-the-institute/asser-today/new-blog-the-shamima-begum-case-revoking-citizenship-is-ineffective-and-counterproductive/.

DEPRIVATION OF NATIONALITY AS A COUNTER-TERRORISM MEASURE: *A HUMAN RIGHTS AND SECURITY PERSPECTIVE*

BY CHRISTOPHE PAULUSSEN[*]
AND MARTIN SCHEININ[*]

Deprivation of nationality as a counter-terrorism measure is on the rise. To take just one example, in 2017, the British citizenship of 104 individuals was reportedly revoked on the grounds of being "conducive to the public good", a striking increase from the years before (four in 2014, five in 2015 and 14 in 2016).[1]

But just how "conducive to the public good" is depriving a few dozen citizens of their nationality? We will argue that the measure is problematic from both an international law and a security perspective.

An important consideration in the context of international law is to realise that deprivation of nationality impacts the right to have a nationality, a human right linked to the enjoyment of other rights. It constitutes, in the famous words of Hannah Arendt, the right to have rights.[2] Due to this very far-reaching consequence for the enjoyment of other human rights, it has been suggested that any deprivation of citizenship is incompatible with international human rights law.

At a bare minimum, international law imposes an obligation to avoid statelessness, entailing that the nationality of a mono-citizen cannot be revoked, and prohibits any arbitrary deprivation of nationality. Even if deprivation of citizenship were

[*] **Christophe Paulussen** is a senior researcher at the T.M.C. Asser Institute and coordinator of its research strand 'Human Dignity and Human Security in International and European Law'. He also coordinates the inter-faculty research platform 'International Humanitarian and Criminal Law Platform' and is research fellow at the International Centre for Counter-Terrorism in The Hague. Christophe is also editor-in-chief of the journal 'Security and Human Rights' and managing editor of the 'Yearbook of International Humanitarian Law'.

[*] **Martin Scheinin** is Professor of International Law and Human Rights at the European University Institute in Florence, Italy. From 2005–2011 he was the first United Nations Special Rapporteur on the promotion and protection of human rights and fundamental freedoms while countering terrorism. He has also served as a member of the United Nations Human Rights Committee and was President of the International Association of Constitutional Law.

[1] J. Grierson, 'Lib Dems to call for overhaul of revocation of UK citizenship rules', *The Guardian* (15 September 2019), available at https://www.theguardian.com/politics/2019/sep/15/lib-dems-to-call-for-overhaul-of-revocation-of-uk-citizenship-rules-shamima-begum accessed 18 February 2020

[2] H Arendt, *The Origins of Totalitarianism* (New York: Harcourt, Brace and Co. 1951).

permissible under national law, the exercise of such powers must never violate peremptory or non-derogable norms of international law, nor impair the essence of any human right. Where the exercise of functions and powers involves a restriction upon a human right that allows for limitations, any such restriction should utilise the least intrusive means possible and should: (a) be necessary in a democratic society to pursue a defined legitimate aim, as permitted by international law; and (b) be proportionate to the benefit obtained in achieving the legitimate aim in question.[3]

Even if deprivation of nationality might be permissible in national law, one can wonder whether the measure can ever be seen as the least intrusive means available and be necessary and proportionate. After all, in contrast to dual nationals, mono-citizens will not be deprived of their nationality, in order to avoid statelessness. Instead, they will face criminal prosecution, or less far-going administrative measures such as a (temporary) area ban. If mono-citizens can thus be dealt with in a less intrusive way, then why should these same responses not simply apply to citizens with dual nationality? In addition, the measure cannot be discriminatory either.[4] Also here, serious problems arise as the measure (as explained) can and will only be applied to citizens with dual nationality, who are often overrepresented in minority groups. This means these groups are disproportionally targeted by this measure, resulting in the creation of two different classes of citizens. This was also concluded in an *amicus curiae* brief submitted to the Dutch Immigration and Naturalisation Service in 2018 by the UN Special Rapporteur on contemporary forms of racism, racial discrimination, xenophobia and related intolerance, E. Tendayi Achiume.[5]

Finally, the measure clashes with other international law obligations. When used against alleged terrorists who have not been prosecuted, the measure undermines UN Security Council Resolutions such as Resolution 1373, which makes clear that all states must bring terrorists *to justice*. This is also echoed by victims of terrorism, who have indicated they want justice to be done.

---

[3] Report of the Special Rapporteur on the promotion and protection of human rights and fundamental freedoms while countering terrorism, Martin Scheinin, 'Ten areas of best practices in countering terrorism', A/HRC/16/51, (22 December 2010), Practice 2, available at https://www.refworld.org/docid/4e0c2ace15.html.

[4] See OSCE Office for Democratic Institutions and Human Rights (ODIHR), 'Guidelines for Addressing the Threats and Challenges of "Foreign Terrorist Fighters" within a Human Rights Framework', 2018, p. 32, available at: https://www.osce.org/odihr/393503?download=true; UN Counter-Terrorism Implementation Task Force (CTITF), Working Group on Protecting Human Rights while Countering Terrorism, 'Basic Human Rights Reference Guide: Security Infrastructure', Updated 2nd edition, March 2014, para. 5, available at: https://www.un.org/counterterrorism/ctitf/sites/www.un.org.counterterrorism.ctitf/files/StoppingAndSearching_en.pdf and UN General Assembly, 'Report of the Special Rapporteur on contemporary forms of racism, racial discrimination, xenophobia and related intolerance', A/72/287 (4 August 2017), available at: https://undocs.org/pdf?symbol=en/A/72/287

[5] Amicus brief, The UN Special Rapporteur on contemporary forms of racism, racial discrimination, xenophobia and related intolerance (23 October 2018), available at https://www.ohchr.org/Documents/Issues/Racism/SR/Amicus/DutchImmigration_Amicus.pdf.

Bringing terrorists to justice involves terrorism suspects being prosecuted so that a judicial record can be established about what happened to the victims' loved ones. Conversely, deprivation of nationality constitutes an obstacle to accountability and justice, as the connection with the active nationality principle – one of the main possibilities to exercise criminal jurisdiction – is removed.

The above has shown that the measure is not in conformity with international (human rights) law. This already demonstrates that the measure is ineffective from a counter-terrorism perspective. After all, as also stated in the 2006 UN Global Counter-Terrorism Strategy: "States must ensure that any measures taken to combat terrorism comply with their obligations under international law, in particular human rights law, refugee law and international humanitarian law"[6] and "effective counter-terrorism measures and the protection of human rights are not conflicting goals, but complementary and mutually reinforcing".[7]

However, it is not only because of the above-mentioned international law violations that deprivation of citizenship is troublesome from a counter-terrorism or security perspective - the pretext often used by politicians to justify the measure in the first place. Deprivation of nationality constitutes a highly symbolic measure, basically communicating the message that certain behaviour will not be tolerated and that perpetrators have forfeited the bond with their home countries. Depriving someone of his or her nationality may seem like a strong and efficient counter-terrorism measure, but as explained, it does not bring people to justice, and it fails to rehabilitate and reintegrate them; rather, it shoves the problem temporarily away, into the hands of actors that may have fewer or no capabilities to do something about it. Indeed, the measure is characterised by a 'pass the buck mentality', where the potential risk is not addressed, but exported somewhere else, making it the problem of others. Moreover, in the long term, the person deprived of nationality could become a risk for the national security of the depriving country and the security of the people under its jurisdiction, if a person disappears off the radar and manages to get back into the country that turned its back on him or her. In this case, while politicians state that national security will be strengthened because the person will be removed from the territory or will not be allowed to re-enter it, this constitutes a very narrow perspective of the concept of security - both in terms of time and place - and one that is arguably no longer in sync with the realities of our hyper-connected world.

---

[6] United Nations General Assembly (UNGA) Resolution of 8 September 2006, A/RES/60/288, available at: https://documents-dds-ny.un.org/doc/UNDOC/GEN/N05/504/88/PDF/N0550488.pdf?OpenElement
[7] United Nations General Assembly (UNGA) Resolution of 8 September 2006, A/RES/60/288, available at: https://documents-dds-ny.un.org/doc/UNDOC/GEN/N05/504/88/PDF/N0550488.pdf?OpenElement.

Another important aspect to consider is the wider effect of this measure: it not only impacts the person whose nationality has been revoked, but also his/her family (especially children). Moreover, it can have an effect on people further removed from the targeted person, such as friends, neighbours and other members of the minority group the targeted person belongs to. All of these people may feel unjustly singled out by a measure that is not applicable to mono-citizens of the same country, hence also designating them as second-class citizens. As such, citizenship stripping is not only moving the problem around like a hot potato, it may even make the problem worse. If people from certain groups, often minorities, see that only 'their' people are targeted by a specific measure, there is a risk that these people will feel alienated and discriminated against. In this regard, one needs to be mindful that exclusion, marginalisation and (perceived) discrimination are among the drivers of terrorism.

In short, revoking the citizenship of individuals is not "conducive to the public good". To the contrary, it is a measure that is problematic from both an international law and (thus also) a security perspective and may sometimes even turn out to be a condition conducive to terrorism.

CITIZENSHIP STRIPPING AS A SECURITY MEASURE – POLICY ISSUES AND THE "EFFECTIVENESS" QUESTION

INTRODUCTION

This essay presents some main debates and challenges surrounding "effectiveness" of security measures in the counter-terrorism context, consolidating and analysing existing literature on the effectiveness of nationality deprivation as a counter-terrorism measure. At the core of the question lies the issue of necessity and permissibility. Essentially, ineffective measures cannot be legally justified as necessary, thus lacking permissibility. To justify measures as necessary - both their impact on human rights and their status as a security measure - governments must adequately evaluate the effectiveness of counter-terrorism policies.

In the counter-terrorism context, significant restrictions of liberties are often politically justified on the grounds of national security. The argument that the efficacy of counter-terrorism measures underlies the claim of their necessity has notably been articulated by Fiona de Londras.[1] As a matter of good governance, policies that have a strong impact on fundamental rights should be subject to close scrutiny, including assessing their effectiveness. In that sense, measures found to carry high risks of eroding trust and safety in democratic societies in the long term would not be effective and therefore not justified. Furthermore, the notion of necessity is relevant to legal limits on human rights restrictions. Restrictions to human rights that are not necessary, because they are not effective, cannot be legally justified.[2] The link between necessity and effectiveness is expressly acknowledged in multiple international instruments.[3]

---

[1] F. de Londras, 'Evaluation and Effectiveness of Counter-Terrorism' (2016), available at
https://ssrn.com/abstract=2801994, forthcoming in J. P. Burgess, G. Reniers, K. Ponnet, W. Hardyns, and W.
Smit (eds), *Socially Responsible Innovation in Security: Critical Reflections* (2018).
[2] "When a measure restricts human rights, restrictions must be defined as precisely as possible and be necessary
and proportionate to the aim pursued." – Section III (2) on the lawfulness of anti-terrorist measures. Guidelines of
the Council of Europe on Human Rights and the Fight Against Terrorism (2005); "Only in exceptional
circumstances may States restrict certain human rights and freedoms. The justification for any restriction must be
prescribed by law, strictly proportionate with and absolutely necessary for addressing a legitimate need" –
General Principle M on Non-Derogations and Restrictions on Human Rights and Freedoms, 'Principles and
Guidelines on Human and Peoples' Rights while Countering Terrorism in Africa' (2015).
[3] E.g. "Any departures from ordinary principles of criminal law and procedure or derogable international human
rights standards must be strictly necessary to prevent the identified harm and be rationally connected to the
achievement of this goal; they should infringe the rights of those subject to the law as little as possible; and their

The effectiveness and necessity of counter-terrorism measures and considerations regarding long-term impact or unintended consequences of security measures should be integrated at all stages of policy development and implementation. Accounting for effectiveness and reflecting on objectives, risks and assumptions would ensure policies are more soundly justified. Evaluating outcomes and setbacks of existing policies can provide insights and guidance for developing future measures.

THE MEANING OF 'EFFECTIVENESS' AND CONSIDERATIONS ON ITS EVALUATION IN THE CONTEXT OF COUNTER-TERRORISM

The most direct answer to the question of security measure effectiveness is whether the measure achieves its intended objectives.[4] This however raises the question of how to ascertain counter-terrorism measures and policies. The effectiveness question must be seen broadly, accounting for unintended consequences and interplay between different measures.

The effectiveness of counter-terrorism measures can be understood within different scopes and levels:

- specific/general,
- short-term/long-term,
- territorial/global.

Effectiveness first relates to the specific and direct goals of a particular measure, which are usually explicitly stated during legislative debates, and can be inferred from the content of the measure. Entry bans for example, have the direct and specific aim of preventing certain individuals from entering a state's territory. In the counter-terrorism context, these specific goals cannot be seen in isolation, and the general and longer-term goals associated with protection against terrorism, including the overall security from terrorist threats and preservation of democratic principles, must be considered. The narrow motives politically justifying certain measures can therefore not be the benchmark for effectiveness.

Another variable is the geographical scope. While measures are usually justified and deployed in a national context, their effectiveness in the global fight against terrorism should be assessed. For instance, it is difficult to see how sending or keeping abroad individuals who constitute a terrorist threat could be globally effective. Unintended consequences must also be accounted for. A large number of

---

effectiveness should be weighed against the degree of rights infringement that they permit" – Principle 2.3.1 of the Ottawa Principles on Anti-Terrorism and Human Rights (2006).

[4] Interview with two researchers of the Institute of Security and Global Affairs (ISGA), Leiden University. This corresponds to the common definition of effectiveness as 'successful in producing a desired or intended result' (https://en.oxforddictionaries.com/definition/effective).

counter-terrorism measures and policies are justified on the grounds of specific and short-term objectives. However, if a measure meets its direct security goals but simultaneously and unpredictably contributes to further radicalisation, it cannot be considered wholly effective. Better evaluation practices of counter-terrorism policies could avoid counter-productive effects of certain security measures.

Finally, assessing effectiveness measures requires considering the interplay between multiple measures. Counter-terrorism measures do not operate as stand-alone tools and their effect must be appreciated in relation to other measures. For example, citizenship stripping is often applied in conjunction with expulsion or entry denial measures, which has implications on short-term direct effectiveness (for example if the person cannot be expelled due to non-refoulement, or cannot be prosecuted for lack of jurisdictional link), and long-term global effectiveness (for example if a person posing a threat is simply moved abroad). The effectiveness of counter-terrorism measures and policies should be seen as comprising multiple complementary and interrelated layers. It is not limited to achieving intended goals and also relates to broader considerations including comprehensive, long-term and global perspectives.[5]

While countries have been adopting new legislative instruments in the context of counter-terrorism, effectiveness has rarely been assessed. Governments often claim new measures are necessary for national security, but limited efforts are made to prove the efficacy of such measures. More research is needed in this area.[6] Overall, the assessment of effective counter-terrorism measures are elusive. Effectiveness can be affected by external factors, and even the most carefully designed policy cannot foresee every circumstance. Counter-terrorism must be assessed against realistic success rates, in the same way as the fight against regular crime.[7] This perspective also means that the occurrence of terrorist attacks cannot, in and of itself, justify the adoption of stricter policies.

Due to scarce practice, limited indications can be given on methods to evaluate effectiveness. A number of countries have some procedures for parliamentary, judicial, or independent review of counter-terrorism laws, but these include effectiveness discussions. In the current context of intense security-related legislative activity, the necessity argument has been considered by some courts finding certain

---

[5] See also European Parliament, 'The European Union's Policies on Counter-Terrorism: Relevance, Coherence and Effectiveness' (2017), available at:
http://www.europarl.europa.eu/RegData/etudes/STUD/2017/583124/IPOL_STU(2017)583124_EN.pdf, p. 74.

[6] An effort to develop a methodology was made under the EU's 7th Framework Programme for research, technological development and demonstration project SURVEILLE (Surveillance: Ethical Issues, Legal Limitations, and Efficiency). For more information see, https://surveille.eui.eu/.

[7] B. Shuurman and E. Bakker, 'Reintegrating jihadist extremists: evaluating a Dutch initiative, 2013-2014' (2016), 8(1) Behavioral Sciences of Terrorism and Political Aggression, available at
https://www.tandfonline.com/doi/abs/10.1080/19434472.2015.1100648.

new measures unnecessary in view of already existing tools.[8] Generally, existing practice seems to be confined to *ex post* evaluation studies focusing on implementation, and in rare cases includes *ex ante* impact assessments.

Quantitatively, counter-terrorism policies are sometimes evaluated against conviction rates for terrorism-related crimes, however, increases/decreases in the conviction numbers does not fully reflect efficacy and can be influenced by other circumstances e.g. prosecutorial policies. For reintegration measures, recidivism rates are used as part of effectiveness evaluations. The effectiveness of security measures preventatively imposed to reduce terrorist risks (e.g. administrative measures) can hardly be quantitatively evaluated in view of their prospective aim. The effectiveness question seems more suited for a qualitative approach, although devising indicators is challenging.[9] Achieving long-term and overarching policy goals is difficult to measure, but some aspects could be considered in evaluations - for example, assessing the proportionality of measures on a larger scale, thereby impacting the overall enjoyment of human rights, could contribute to assessments of effectiveness.

THE PURPOSE OF DEPRIVATION OF NATIONALITY AS A COUNTER-TERRORISM MEASURE

To understand or evaluate the effectiveness of a particular measure, it is necessary to first identify its intended objectives. Only then can the attainability of such objectives be considered, or more suitable alternatives be identified. An analysis of key 'arguments' given by politicians, practitioners and commentators regarding the purpose of deprivation of nationality as a counter-terrorism measure uncovers four broad justifications or objectives:

The legal consequences of nationality deprivation discourages terrorist activity

During the debate on deprivation of nationality in the House of Lords on 9 October 2002, Lord Filkin stated "Deprivation has, of necessity, to have practical consequences for the person concerned, such that he is made aware of the abhorrence with which his conduct is regarded and is prevented or deterred from

---

8 For instance, the French Constitutional Council considered it was unnecessary to criminalise the consultation of online materials that promote terrorism in view of other existing provisions able to address online radicalisation, and invalidated the provision (Constitutional Council Decision no. 2017-682 QPC (15 December 2017), para 13).

9 "We cannot predict that [measure X] will lead to an 11% reduction in the effective enjoyment of privacy, or 5% reduction in social cohesion." (F. de Londras, 'Evaluation and Effectiveness of Counter-Terrorism' (2016), available at https://ssrn.com/abstract=2801994, forthcoming in J. P. Burgess, G. Reniers, K. Ponnet, W. Hardyns, W. Smit (eds), *Socially Responsible Innovation in Security: Critical Reflections* (2018)).

engaging in similar conduct in the future,"[10] When the UK Nationality, Immigration and Asylum Bill of 2002 was presented, the government argued "deprivation was an important and necessary state power, though one that would be used sparingly".[11] The purpose of the proposed measure was to afford higher levels of protection to the public and deter terrorist activity.

Deprivation of nationality complicates return and keeps threats out of the country

This is a key argument used by the Dutch government in parliamentary debates on the importance of deprivation of nationality as a counter-terrorism measure.[12] The Minister of Justice has the discretionary power to strip Dutch citizenship from alleged foreign terrorist fighters (FTFs). The explanatory memorandum explains that this measure is necessary to prevent terrorist activities in the Netherlands as FTFs are not afraid to use violence in realising their ideologies and, therefore, pose a threat to the Netherlands upon return. To protect national security FTFs should be deprived of citizenship to prevent terrorist attacks. Their denationalisation also results in an exclusion order from Dutch territory, by declaring the individual as an 'undesirable alien'. This complicates the return of FTFs and also allegedly contributes to protecting national security.

The explanatory memorandum made an explicit distinction between the above administrative law measure and existing criminal law; the latter not preventing FTFs from returning to the Netherlands. Deprivation of nationality should not occur once the terrorist has returned and been convicted, rather, they should be excluded from the enjoyment of Dutch nationality and the rights and obligations that come with citizenship, including the right to access Dutch territory due to their immediate threat to national security.

Punitive punishments are not sufficient for terrorist activity

Nationality is often viewed as a status/privilege that people deserve, *not* something everyone has a right to. Those who aim to destroy society are therefore not loyal and forfeit such status. A remarkable case in this context is Bahrain. On 24 July 2014, Bahrain's Official Gazette published amendments to the Citizenship Law of 1963. Article 10 gives the Interior Ministry, with cabinet approval, the power to

---

[10] HL Deb, vol 639 cc263-353 (9 October 2002), available at
https://publications.parliament.uk/pa/ld200102/ldhansrd/vo021009/text/21009-08.htm.
[11] M. Gibney, The Deprivation of Citizenship in the United Kingdom: A Brief History (2014), available at
http://sprc.info/wp-content/uploads/2015/02/Gibney-article.pdf, p. 33.
[12] 'Wijziging van de Rijkswet op het Nederlanderschap in verband met het intrekken van het Nederlanderschap in het belang van de nationale veiligheid. Memorie van Toelichting' [Draft legislative proposal on the amendment of the Netherlands Nationality Act and its explanatory memorandum] (18 December 2014), available at https://www.internetconsultatie.nl/rwn/document/1435 (in Dutch only).

strip the citizenship of a person who "aids or is involved in the service of a hostile state" or who "causes harm to the interests of the Kingdom or acts in a way that contravenes his duty of loyalty to it".[13] The July 2014 amendments to Bahrain's Citizenship Law grants the Interior Ministry additional authority to revoke the citizenship of people who fail in their "duty of loyalty" to the state, as a form of punishment. This provision applies to terrorists but has also been actively used against activists, human rights defenders, journalists and religious scholars.[14]

Terrorism is destructive to fundamental democratic values of society and nationality deprivation protects the integrity of citizenship

This was also made clear by UK Defence Secretary, Gavin Williamson, when speaking about potential return of the 'ISIS Beatles' to the UK. Two British men, Kotey and Elsheik, are alleged members of ISIS and accused of being executioners in Syria and Iraq. They have been deprived of their British nationality and have complained that they are unable to get a fair trial because of their denationalisation. Defence Secretary Williamson said the pair should not return to the UK, because they had "turned their back on British ideas, British values".[15] In a more general context, he publicly stated "jihadis hate everything that Britain stands for, hate our values, hate that Britain is a beacon to the world of democracy and tolerance", harming the integrity of citizenship.[16]

EVALUATING THE EFFECTIVENESS OF NATIONALITY DEPRIVATION AS A COUNTER-TERRORISM MEASURE

Like for other counter-terrorism measures, there is no data available to demonstrate that nationality deprivation 'works'. In order to start to unpack the effectiveness question, we can look at existing literature where the purported objectives of nationality deprivation in the counter-terrorism context are explored and problematised. This next section provides a compilation and analysis of this existing literature. Drawing together the views of commentators in relation to each of these questions helps to situate the discussion on whether or not nationality deprivation is effective and explores the persuasiveness of different arguments.

---

[13] Bahraini Citizenship Act of 1963.

[14] Amnesty International, 'Bahrain: Citizenship of 115 people revoked in 'ludicrous' mass trial' (16 May 2018).

[15] L. Dearden, 'UK Government does not want captured Isis 'Beatles' returned to Britain for trial, says Gavin Williamson' *Independent* (14 February 2018) available at https://www.independent.co.uk/news/uk/home-news/isis-beatles-uk-return-trial-gavin-williamson-defence-secretary-government-alexanda-kotey-el-shafee-a8209741.html.

[16] G. Bowden, ''Brits Fighting For Islamic State Should Be 'Eliminated', Gavin Williamson Says', *Huffington Post* (7 December 2014), available at: https://www.huffingtonpost.co.uk/entry/britons-islamic-state-eliminated-gavin-williamson_uk_5a28f0a6e4b0b185e539540c.

Does deprivation of nationality work as a deterrent for terrorist activity?

In existing literature, scholars challenge the claim that citizenship stripping works as a 'deterrent' for terrorist activity. Firstly, they show that there is no evidence suggesting that denationalisation would deter a terrorist if other counter-terrorism measures fail to do so. The threat of losing citizenship is likely to be insignificant when compared with other penalties for terrorist acts. If threats of self-destruction, criminal prosecution, and capital punishment do not deter a terrorist, possible loss of nationality certainly won't either.[17] Second, they argue that global jihadists do not care about losing citizenship status in a western democracy that they detest.[18] However, in the case above of the UK jihadis (Kotey and Elsheik), the loss of their British nationality did matter as, according to them, it left them unable to get a fair trial in the UK. Finally, commentators also suggest that nationality deprivation is not just an ineffective deterrent but could actually be counterproductive. If deprivation leads to disaffection among target populations and their families/communities, this can result in further radicalisation. Nationality is thus less secure and expanding executive discretion to deprive without insufficient safeguards for review likely increases marginalisation, and thus, radicalisation – exactly what government policy hopes to reduce.[19] It further can potentially alienate communities who might provide useful information.

Does deprivation of nationality reduce the threat of a terrorist attack?

A central focus of academic literature on deprivation of nationality as a counter-terrorism measure is exploring its use for the purpose of reducing or removing the threat of a terrorist attack. Deprivation of nationality is rarely considered the best way to achieve the intended objective of deprivation. There is still a risk that the persons concerned will continue to pose a threat to national security and public safety if they are deprived of their nationality but not deprived of their liberty.[20] Commentators suggest that deprivation of nationality relies on the questionable supposition that it serves to increase security, also known as 'the security fallacy'.

There is a strong consensus in existing literature that the threat of a terrorist attack is not reduced or removed by denationalising people. If a person is rendered stateless as a result of denationalisation, the state cannot deport or otherwise remove the stateless person to another country without violating international law. States would

---

[17] A. Macklin, 'Kick-off Contribution' (2015) in *The Return of Banishment: do the New Denationalisation Policies Weaken Citizenship?* Eds A. Macklin, A and R. Bauböck, available at:
https://cadmus.eui.eu/bitstream/handle/1814/34617/RSCAS_2015_14.pdf?sequence=1.
[18] R. Bauböck, 'Whose Bad Guys are Terrorists? (2018), available at:
https://link.springer.com/chapter/10.1007/978-3-319-92719-0_38.
[19] T. Choudhury, 'The radicalisation of citizenship deprivation' *Critical Social Policy* (2017), available at
https://journals.sagepub.com/doi/abs/10.1177/0261018316684507.
[20] J. Brandvoll, 'Deprivation of nationality: Limitations on rendering persons stateless under international law' in A. Edwards and L. van Waas (Eds) *Nationality and Statelessness under International Law* (2014).

thus be increasing the global incidence of statelessness without achieving tangible security benefits.[21] Meanwhile, Article 12 of the ICCPR protects the right of a person to return to his 'own country' (and not to be exiled from there). In particular, persons who become stateless as a result of being stripped of their only nationality may have a valid claim that the country remains their 'own country' for purposes of ICCPR Article 12. Also, if the individual retains the nationality of another EU Member State, he/she remains entitled to move and reside freely within the entire territory of the EU, including the State of which he/she used to be a citizen.[22]

Even if the person concerned may be removed from national territory, the threat to global security persists.[23] Plotting, financing and orchestrating terrorist atrocities may not be mitigated by denationalisation in the home country or abroad.[24] Deporting terror suspects is not satisfactory, given the result of exporting the threat of terrorism rather than reducing or removing it. If exporting risk were an answer, the motivation that exile equates heightened security through removal of dangerous people knows no limits - it is not obvious why countries would not also be made safer by exiling all citizens who commit violent offences.[25] In reality, persons stripped of nationality continue to pose a threat to global security and may still have the means to plot cross border terrorist attacks.[26] Citizenship does not insulate terror suspects from surveillance or other investigatory activity, so its removal is not required to use such measures.[27]

Citizenship stripping can also actually cause further radicalisation if deprivation leads to being trapped in a conflict zone. While it may work as a temporary security

---

[21] S. Jayaraman, 'International Terrorism and Statelessness: Revoking the Citizenship of ISIL Foreign Fighters' (2016), Chicago Journal of International Law 17(1), available at: https://chicagounbound.uchicago.edu/cjil/vol17/iss1/6/.

[22] Entry in the EU State of which a person used to be a citizen can be restricted if the person's entry is separately denied by the State concerned on the basis of national security grounds that meet EU law requirements.

[23] E. Cloots, 'The Legal Limits of Citizenship Deprivation as a Counterterror Strategy' (2017), European Public Law, volume 21 issue 1.

[24] L. Zedner, 'Citizenship Deprivation, Security and Human Rights' (2016), European Journal of Migration and Law 18(2).

[25] A. Macklin, 'Kick-off Contribution' (2015) in *The Return of Banishment: do the New Denationalisation Policies Weaken Citizenship?* Eds A. Macklin and R. Bauböck, available at https://cadmus.eui.eu/bitstream/handle/1814/34617/RSCAS_2015_14.pdf?sequence=1.

[26] E. F. Cohen, 'When Democracies Denationalize: The Epistemological Case against Revoking Citizenship' (2016), Ethics & International Affairs 30(2); G. R. de Groot, and M. Vink 'Best Practices in Involuntary Loss of Nationality in the EU' (2014), CEPS Papers in Liberty and Security in Europe No. 73, available at https://www.ceps.eu/ceps-publications/best-practices-involuntary-loss-nationality-eu/; A. Macklin, 'Kick-off Contribution' (2015) in *The Return of Banishment: do the New Denationalisation Policies Weaken Citizenship?* Eds A. Macklin and R. Bauböck, available at https://cadmus.eui.eu/bitstream/handle/1814/34617/RSCAS_2015_14.pdf?sequence=1; L. Zedner, 'Citizenship Deprivation, Security and Human Rights' (2016), European Journal of Migration and Law 18(2).

[27] P. Spiro, 'Expatriating terrorists' (2014), Fordham Law Review, Vol. 82(5), available at https://ir.lawnet.fordham.edu/cgi/viewcontent.cgi?article=4981&context=flr .

solution for the depriving state,[28] academics are in widespread agreement that in our shrinking interconnected world, it is naïve to think medieval punishment like nationality deprivation will produce security gains - deprivation of nationality renders people vulnerable and more susceptible to recruitment by terrorist organisations or can force individuals back to terrorist groups and radicalisation, particularly if they are stranded in unstable states or conflict zones.[29]

Does deprivation of nationality help to punish and bring terrorists to justice?

Commentators widely consider that deprivation of nationality is unhelpful in bringing terrorists to justice. It is the state's responsibility to protect national security and bring wrongdoers to justice, but nationality deprivation makes it harder for a state to hold terrorists accountable. Citizenship stripping can be understood as an evasion of the moral and legal responsibility to deal with terrorists.[30]

Deprivation of nationality is often motivated by national security interests, yet, offences against public security are covered by criminal law, often regardless of whether perpetrated by a citizen or not. Providing security and prosecuting/criminally convicting those who jeopardise it is the core function of the state. Simply stripping individuals of citizenship to deport them from the territory or prohibit their return arguably constitutes the failure of the State to prosecute those contravening criminal law.[31]

By limiting the opportunity to re-enter a country through denationalisation, the state is foregoing the opportunity to apprehend the suspect at a point of entry.[32] Deprivation of nationality offers no guarantees that these individuals will make restitution, experience retributive justice or be rehabilitated.[33] Unlike deprivation of nationality, prosecution and detention as punitive measures, bring people to justice but can also result in guidance and rehabilitation. Justice or rehabilitation may not

---

[28] S. Jayaraman, 'International Terrorism and Statelessness: Revoking the Citizenship of ISIL Foreign Fighters' (2016), Chicago Journal of International Law 17(1), available at
https://chicagounbound.uchicago.edu/cjil/vol17/iss1/6/.

[29] S. Jayaraman, 'International Terrorism and Statelessness: Revoking the Citizenship of ISIL Foreign Fighters' (2016), Chicago Journal of International Law 17(1), available at:
https://chicagounbound.uchicago.edu/cjil/vol17/iss1/6/; L. Zedner, 'Citizenship Deprivation, Security and Human Rights' (2016), European Journal of Migration and Law 18(2).

[30] S. Jayaraman 'International Terrorism and Statelessness: Revoking the Citizenship of ISIL Foreign Fighters' (2016), Chicago Journal of International Law 17(1), available at:
https://chicagounbound.uchicago.edu/cjil/vol17/iss1/6/; L. Zedner, 'Citizenship Deprivation, Security and Human Rights' (2016), European Journal of Migration and Law 18(2).

[31] L. Zedner, 'Citizenship Deprivation, Security and Human Rights' (2016), European Journal of Migration and Law 18(2).

[32] S. Jayaraman, 'International Terrorism and Statelessness: Revoking the Citizenship of ISIL Foreign Fighters' (2016), Chicago Journal of International Law 17(1), available at
https://chicagounbound.uchicago.edu/cjil/vol17/iss1/6/.

[33] E. F. Cohen, 'When Democracies Denationalize: The Epistemological Case against Revoking Citizenship' (2016), Ethics & International Affairs 30(2).

be served to someone deprived of nationality and the person may continue to be a threat to national/global security.

A suspected FTF, having learned of his/her denationalisation, might never attempt to return to his home state, making it harder for the 'home' state to capture and hold them accountable. It is more likely that deprivation of nationality will create new hurdles in legal processes if deprivation turns that person into a foreigner or makes them stateless.[34] For example, a person can only be tried under more restrictive circumstances if they do not hold that nationality, so it may be harder to obtain an arrest warrant for a non-national.

Does deprivation of nationality help protect democratic values that terrorism aims to upset?

With every attempted or actual terrorist attack, strict citizenship-stripping laws become harder to resist for national legislatures. Depriving terrorists of citizenship is a policy with significant symbolic appeal and great visibility, while being relatively cheap, unlike, for instance, increasing funding of national security services. Hence, when politicians are called upon to appear 'tough on terror', expanding the scope of application of the existing denationalisation provisions or to diminish the procedural safeguards is alluring.[35] This can put states on a slippery slope in terms of maintaining the value and integrity of citizenship.

States have considered rules of general international law as inadequate in regulating the phenomenon of terrorism, opting for amendments without due consideration of their practical need, their effectiveness and impact on international law as a whole.[36] It is mostly political pressure and not practical necessity that leads to the creation of special counter-terrorism regimes, be it domestically or internationally. Regarding national citizenship-stripping laws, this is graphically exemplified by a statement of former French President, François Hollande, who admitted its symbolic nature… "It is not by denationalisation that one can fight terrorism". It seems that denationalisation laws are not relating to questions of effectiveness, but the appearance of a stronger approach.

Deprivation of nationality turns citizenship into a less secure and more precarious status, hollowing out the core (democratic) values it seeks to protect.[37] By weakening

[34] R. Baubock and V. Paskalev, V, 'Citizenship Deprivation: A Normative Analysis' (2015), available a https://www.ceps.eu/system/files/LSE82_CitizenshipDeprivation.pdf.

[35] E. Cloots, 'The Legal Limits of Citizenship Deprivation as a Counterterror Strategy' (2017), European Public Law, volume 21 issue 1.

[36] D. Burchardt and R. Gulati, *International counter-terrorism regulation and citizenship-stripping laws- reinforcing legal exceptionalism, Journal of Conflict & Security Law* (Oxford University Press 2018).

[37] Choudhury, T (2017) The radicalisation of citizenship deprivation' Critical Social Policy [online] available at: https://journals.sagepub.com/doi/abs/10.1177/0261018316684507

citizenship through deprivation, states damage democratic institutions, systems, processes, principles, and the concept of citizenship, the very aims of groups like ISIS. Democratic values such as equality before the law are eroded through deprivation measures because many states only target specific groups of citizens (i.e. dual nationals and naturalised citizens). Since there is no empirical evidence to show that naturalised citizens pose a greater threat to security than those who are citizens from birth, the provision is also unwarranted and discriminatory.[38] Moreover, to strip a person of citizenship without making them stateless, each of the states involved in a situation of dual citizenship has an incentive to act first making the other state responsible. [39] Plus, to the extent that only dual nationals are subject to security related expatriation, the criterion no longer makes any sense: the other citizenship is random, unrelated to the motivation for expatriation.[40]

Reconstructing citizenries through a security lens on inequitable terms may foster exclusion, expand statelessness, increase distrust of government, hinder political or civic integration of immigrants and refugees, and ultimately weaken citizenship.[41] Even if granting denationalisation powers to officials might be justifiable in principle, denationalisation of 'bad' citizens, like terrorists, is difficult to reconcile with liberalism and evokes memories of tragic incidences. Indeed, there are both past and contemporary examples aplenty to warn of the need to take account of the fact that governments may well extend or abuse such powers over time for political reasons.[42] Conceding even the most limited of powers to the state to revoke citizenship may end, even if it does not begin in, illiberalism.

Commentators fear where we will end up if we try to pierce even a small (liberal sized) hole into citizenship to punish terrorists.[43] Relatedly, laws amended so that "states can treat noncitizens in ways they cannot lawfully treat citizens incentivised states to exploit migration law to pursue counterterrorism objectives post-9/11."[44] If citizenship is relegated to a revocable status, a country's nationals are at risk by the same troubling policy trend.

---

[38] L. Zedner, Citizenship Deprivation, Security and Human Rights' (2016), European Journal of Migration and Law 18(2).

[39] R. Baubock, 'Debating Transformations of National Citizenship' (2018), pp. 204; S. Jayaraman, 'International Terrorism and Statelessness: Revoking the Citizenship of ISIL Foreign Fighters' (2016), Chicago Journal of International Law 17(1), available at https://chicagounbound.uchicago.edu/cjil/vol17/iss1/6/.

[40] P. Spiro, 'Expatriating terrorists' in Fordham Law Review' (2014), Vol. 82(5), available at https://ir.lawnet.fordham.edu/cgi/viewcontent.cgi?article=4981&context=flr.

[41] D. Trimbach and N. Reiz, 'Unmaking Citizens: The Expansion of Citizenship Revocation in Response to Terrorism' (2018), available at https://cmsny.org/publications/unmaking-citizens/.

[42] See for instance, abuse of power in Turkey and Bahrain.

[43] M. Gibney, 'The Deprivation of Citizenship in the United Kingdom: A Brief History' (2014), available at http://sprc.info/wp-content/uploads/2015/02/Gibney-article.pdf, p. 33.

[44] D. Trimbach and N. Reiz, 'Unmaking Citizens: The Expansion of Citizenship Revocation in Response to Terrorism' (2018), available at https://cmsny.org/publications/unmaking-citizens/.

Democratic theory assumes citizens to be subject to developmental processes that can substantially alter a person's character in politically relevant ways. Deprivation of nationality is an irrevocable measure, making academics hesitant about its effectiveness while maintaining the core principles on which our democracy is built. Academics push for only revocable punishments.[45] As Byman and Shapiro state: "Harsh steps are at times necessary, but they must be applied gingerly or else they may backfire." Citizenship revocation is an extremely harsh measure that could be replaced with alternative approaches or policy measures targeting security and terrorist threats, while simultaneously ensuring democratic citizenship for all citizens.[46]

---

[45] E. F. Cohen, 'When Democracies Denationalize: The Epistemological Case against Revoking Citizenship' (2016), Ethics & International Affairs 30(2).

[46] D. Byman and J. Shapiro, (2014) 'Be Afraid. Be a Little Afraid. The Threat of Terrorism from Western Foreign Fighters in Syria and Iraq'.

DEPRIVATION OF NATIONALITY: A HUMAN RIGHTS PERSPECTIVE

BY FATEH AZZAM*

Despite Hannah Arendt's well-known dictum that citizenship is "the right to have rights," the rights of citizens and human rights are not necessarily the same. The former set is guaranteed by national constitutions, basic laws and bills of rights, while the latter is guaranteed by international human rights law, which states voluntarily commit to respecting as a matter of international treaty obligation. While the two sets of rights may differ in texts, they do largely overlap in terms of content. Moreover, they are mutually dependent, and states are obligated to respect, protect and fulfil both sets of rights. Where the texts (and consequently the standards) differ, states must apply the higher standard of protection, whether provided by their domestic laws or by the human rights treaties that they have signed and ratified. Some human rights, including the prohibitions of torture, discrimination and genocide, are peremptory norms of international law and do not require a treaty obligation to be binding.

In state practice, the enjoyment of rights is often contingent upon having a legal personality, which in today's world is primarily conferred through citizenship in a country. Human rights protections do become available for other recognised legal statuses, such as those of asylum seekers, refugees, migrants and stateless persons, but those are considered special regimes that become operable in the absence of state protection and/or citizenship. In the laws of nearly all countries, access to rights for all categories of special status depends on having some form of registration denoting recognition of a legal personality. This establishes one's existence as a matter of law, and it is through this recognition that the enjoyment of many human rights become possible in accordance with the laws of each state.

To actively deprive a person of his or her nationality is therefore tantamount to a 'legal assassination'.

---

* **Fateh Azzam** is a human rights consultant and researcher, Advisory Council member of ISI, and an Executive Committee member of the Boston Consortium for Arab Region Studies. He was founding director of the Asfari Institute for Civil Society and Citizenship at the American University of Beirut and Middle East Regional Representative of the Office of the High Commissioner for Human Rights from 2006-2012.

It deprives an individual of the protection of the state, and resultantly excludes them from accessing any of the rights that are dependent upon citizenship in the country, relegating the individual to other legal regimes for which they may or may not qualify. Deprivation of nationality is perhaps the most comprehensive violation of a multiplicity of civil, political, economic, social and cultural rights.

Despite the overarching human rights principle that everyone has the right to a nationality, international law generally recognises that states have the right to define who belongs and who does not, although human rights law imposes limitations on this right. Denying or depriving a person of his or her existing nationality may not in itself be a violation of international law, unless such denial or deprivation is deemed arbitrary or violates anti-discrimination requirements, or in cases where the withdrawal of citizenship renders the person stateless.

As mentioned above, the enjoyment of human rights is often made contingent upon citizenship, and its withdrawal would have a direct and profoundly negative impact on their enjoyment. Human rights that are affected by lack of citizenship include the right to work and its associated labour protections; the right to join labour unions and professional syndicates and consequently the right to practice many professions; in many countries the right of access to health care and education; the right to adequate housing and property ownership; the right to social security; freedom of expression and assembly; freedom of movement and residence and the right to enter and leave the country, among others. Domestic laws vary widely in the degree to which non-citizens may access those rights and are different dependent on the status of the non-citizen i.e. aliens lawfully within the state territory, asylum seekers, recognised refugees or stateless persons.

However, international human rights law does not ascribe rights to citizens alone. "Citizenship" is not a criterion for any of the rights enumerated in the International Covenant on Economic, Social and Cultural Rights (ICESCR). Moreover, of all the provisions of the International Covenant on Civil and Political Rights (ICCPR), the only reference to "citizens" having a particular right (rather than "everyone" or "every person" or "all") is in Article 25 on the right to participate in the conduct of public affairs, which includes the right to vote and be elected, and "to have access, on general terms of equality, to public service…" This last provision has been interpreted by the ICCPR Committee in its General Comment 25 as to be guaranteeing citizens' rights to equal access to public service positions and employment, rather than receipt of social services.

Where entire groups or communities are deprived of their nationality, there is a risk of running afoul of the racial, religious, gender or other overarching provisions of human rights law relating to non-discrimination. Measures of withdrawal or denial of nationality to entire groups or communities for reasons prohibited by international human rights law are manifestly illegal. A case in point is the refusal to allow women the right to pass nationality to their children and families equally with men, which is a multi-faceted violation of women's rights to equality and non-discrimination, as well as children's right to a nationality. Similarly, there are many countries where religion is a major criterion for citizenship, such as Israel and some of the Moslem Gulf states, which violates non-discrimination provisions.

Revocation of citizenship for reasons of political opinion or activism is also a clear violation of human rights, even though the laws of many countries allow for this measure as a punishment for the crime of terrorism or for serious crimes perceived to threaten national security. In most cases, the power to revoke citizenship is strictly within the purview of the executive authorities and can be taken as an additional administrative measure on top of a conviction and sentencing by a court of law, or in some cases even without any criminal charges or court convictions. Politically-motivated deprivation of nationality as an administrative measure often raises questions of due process and procedural safeguards, whether appeals mechanisms are adequate, and where such appeals may be presented. These issues present serious concerns regarding the separation of powers and the human rights associated with due process and the right to appeal.

State practice and domestic laws vary widely in how they deal with revocation of citizenship, varying even further in their handling of the implications of this measure on the enjoyment of human rights. International law is also somewhat patchy in this arena, although efforts have been recently undertaken by the Human Rights Council to clarify the perspectives.[1] What is very clear in international law is that withdrawal of nationality from any person so as to render him or her stateless is not acceptable, and if expulsion is the next step, the person may not be expelled to another country where he or she may face torture or ill-treatment. Beyond those two, the international community and human rights mechanisms point to the requirement that in undertaking any measure, including withdrawal of nationality, human rights norms and legally binding guarantees must be respected.

---

[1] For further reading, see UN Human Rights Council, 'Human rights and arbitrary deprivation of nationality: report of the Secretary-General', A/HRC/19/43 (2011), available at: https://www.refworld.org/docid/4f181ef92.html; and UN Human Rights Council, 'UN Human Rights Council, 'Human rights and arbitrary deprivation of nationality: report of the Secretary-General', A/HRC/25/28 (2013), available at: https://www.refworld.org/docid/52f8d19a4.html.

INTERNATIONAL LAW STANDARDS PERTAINING TO THE ARBITRARY DEPRIVATION OF NATIONALITY

INTRODUCTION

The human rights impact of deprivation of nationality is immense and can include expulsion from the country of former nationality, refusal of readmission, family separation, loss of employment and societal stigmatisation. Other related consequences may include being sent to a country with which one has no real ties, being sent to a country where one faces a real threat or being left in a limbo in the country of (previous) nationality. Where those concerned do not possess a second nationality, deprivation leaves them stateless, which can have an even greater individual and societal impact. Given the role of nationality as not only an enabling right but also a central element of a person's social identity, the threat of deprivation is a powerful tool in efforts to silence opposition voices or human rights defenders. Moreover, denationalisation also has a permanence to it that sets it apart from many other administrative and even criminal measures.

Drawing from international law norms, soft law instruments, jurisprudence and doctrine, this chapter identifies four core components of the prohibition of arbitrary deprivation of nationality in what is termed the 'arbitrariness test': Legitimate purpose, legal basis, necessary & proportionate, and procedural safeguards. The chapter also looks at the international standards related to the prohibition of discrimination and the avoidance of statelessness, which complement the prohibition of arbitrary deprivation of nationality and collectively strengthen the right to nationality for all.[1]

INTERNATIONAL LAW, JURISRUDENCE AND SOFT LAW

States are free to regulate the acquisition and loss of nationality, within the limits set by international law.[2] In addition to recognising the right to a nationality,[3]

---

[1] This piece is an updated version of a background paper prepared for an expert meeting in June 2018.

[2] Article 1 of the 1930 Hague Convention on Certain Questions Relating to the Conflict of Nationality Laws; Advisory Opinion No. 4, Nationality Decrees in Tunis and Morocco Opinion (1923) PCIJ Series B No. 4; *Yearbook of the International Law Commission* (1999), vol. II (2), p. 24.

[3] See, among others, Article 15(1) of the Universal Declaration of Human Rights; Article 24 of the International Covenant on Civil and Political Rights; Article 5(d)(iii) of the International Convention on the Elimination of All

international law explicitly prohibits the "arbitrary deprivation of nationality". This norm can be found in:

- Article 15(2) of the Universal Declaration of Human Rights (UDHR);
- Article 18(1)(a) of the Convention in the Rights of Persons with Disabilities (CRPD);
- Article 20(3) of the American Convention on Human Rights;
- Article 4(c) of the European Convention on Nationality;
- Article 29(1) of the Arab Charter on Human Rights;
- Article 18 of the ASEAN Human Rights Declaration; and
- Article 24(2) of the Commonwealth of Independent States Convention on Human Rights and Fundamental Freedoms.[4]

In 1996, the UN General Assembly recognised the prohibition of arbitrary deprivation of nationality as a "fundamental principle of international law".[5] Several commentators suggest that the norm has achieved the status of customary international law.[6] Although the right to a nationality is not a non-derogable right - rights that cannot be limited or suspended under any circumstances, including under a declared state of emergency - deprivation of nationality and its consequences can lead to violations of other non-derogable rights under the International Covenant on Civil and Political Rights (ICCPR), including freedom from torture, cruel, inhuman or degrading treatment or punishment and the right to recognition as a person before the law.

From 1997 onwards, resolutions on "Human Rights and the Arbitrary Deprivation of Nationality" have been adopted periodically by the Commission on Human Rights and subsequently the Human Rights Council.[7] These resolutions have formed the basis for a number of studies by the Office of the High Commissioner for Human Rights and the Secretary-General, of which the report published in December 2009 offers the most comprehensive overview of the legal framework

---

Forms of Racial Discrimination; Article 7 of the Convention on the Rights of the Child and Article 9 of the Convention on the Elimination of All Forms of Discrimination Against Women. For a full list of these provisions, see 'the prohibition of arbitrary deprivation of nationality' on p. 266 of this report.

[4] For the full text of all provisions listed, see 'norms relating to statelessness and deprivation of nationality' on p. 263 of this report.

[5] UN General Assembly, Resolution 50/152: Office of the United Nations High Commissioner for Refugees (9 February 1996), para. 16.

[6] In *Anudo v. Tanzania* (2018), the court stated that the UDHR is "recognised as forming part of customary international law" (para 67), referring to Article 15 which states that "no one shall be arbitrarily deprived of his nationality"; The Tunis Conclusions state that "the prohibition of arbitrary deprivation of nationality… [has] crystallized as [a] norm of customary international law" (para. 2). See also UN Human Rights Council, 'Human rights and arbitrary deprivation of nationality: report of the Secretary-General', A/HRC/13/34 (2009), paras 19–22; M. Manly and L. van Waas, 'The Value of the Human Security Framework in Addressing Statelessness', in A. Edwards and C. Ferstman (Eds.), *Human Security and Non-Citizens* (Cambridge University Press, 2010), p. 63.

[7] See, most recently, UN Human Rights Council, 'Human rights and arbitrary deprivation of nationality', A/HRC/RES/32/5 (2016), available at http://www.refworld.org/docid/57e3dc204.html.

applicable to the prohibition of arbitrary deprivation of nationality.[8] Importantly, this report clarifies the meaning of "deprivation" of nationality for the purposes of this norm as applying to any involuntary loss, deprivation or denial of nationality, which includes:

- Arbitrarily precluding a person from obtaining or retaining a nationality, particularly on discriminatory grounds;
- Automatically depriving a person of a nationality by operation of the law; and
- Acts taken by administrative authorities that result in a person being arbitrarily deprived of a nationality.[9]

The reference to "those acts taken by administrative authorities" also brings under scrutiny the denial of national identity documents, refusal to renew documents and confiscation of passports of citizens living abroad by consular authorities.[10]

There have also been a number of international consultation initiatives on deprivation of nationality, aimed at clarifying the content of specific international norms. The most significant of these efforts to date are:

- The *Tunis Conclusions:* a UNHCR-led process that convened global experts regarding the interpretation of the 1961 Convention standards relating to the loss and deprivation of nationality.[11]
- The *ILEC Guidelines:* an initiative focussing on loss and deprivation of nationality in the EU context. The ILEC guidelines discuss general guidelines on loss of nationality (including firm legal basis, discriminatory provisions and prohibition of retroactivity), the principle of proportionality, procedural guidelines, application to specific grounds of loss (for example fraud or loss of family relationship) and treatment of quasi-loss situations.
- The *Principles on Deprivation of Nationality as a National Security Measure,* which have been published in this World's Stateless Report. The Principles set out legal standards that apply to all States that are considering depriving a person of nationality as a national security measure.

The scope and content of the prohibition of arbitrary deprivation of nationality has been further clarified in a number of important rulings by regional adjudication bodies. To date, this body of jurisprudence comprises cases brought before the Inter-American Court on Human Rights (IACtHR), the African Commission on Human and Peoples' Rights (ACHR), the European Court of Human Rights (ECtHR) and

---

[8] UN Human Rights Council, 'Human rights and arbitrary deprivation of nationality: report of the Secretary-General', A/HRC/13/34 (2009), available at http://www.refworld.org/docid/4b83a9cb2.html.

[9] Ibid, para. 23.

[10] See for example, Institute on Statelessness and Inclusion, 'Arbitrary deprivation of nationality and denial of consular services to Turkish citizens – Policy Brief' (July 2017).

[11] UNHCR, 'Expert Meeting Interpreting the 1961 Statelessness Convention and Avoiding Statelessness resulting from Loss and Deprivation of Nationality Summary Conclusions' (2014).

the Court of Justice of the European Union (CJEU).[12] More detailed notes on some of the most important among these cases are presented at the end of this chapter. Significantly, in relation to the prohibition of arbitrariness, the recent *Anudo v. Tanzania* case states as follows:

"International Law does not allow, save under very exceptional situations, the loss of nationality. The said conditions are:

I.   *They must be founded on clear legal basis;*
II. *Must serve a legitimate purpose that conforms with International Law;*
III. *Must be proportionate to the interest protected;*
IV. *Must install procedural guarantees which must be respected, allowing the concerned to defend himself before an independent body".*[13]

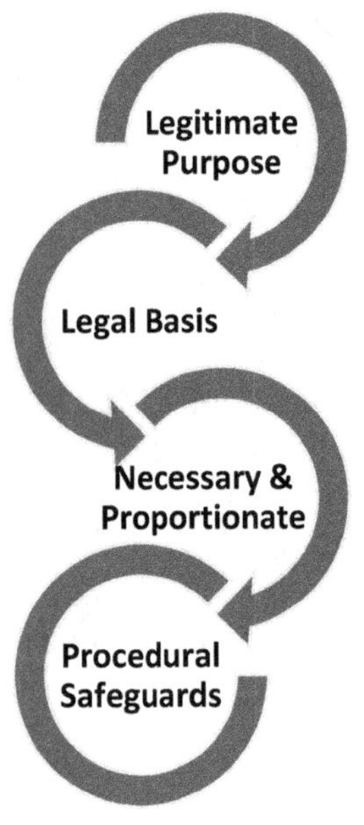

THE 'ARBITRARINESS TEST'

International law stipulates that no one may be arbitrarily deprived of their nationality and obligates the avoidance of statelessness. Below are four core components of the prohibition of arbitrary deprivation of nationality:[14]

1. Legitimate purpose
2. Legal basis
3. Necessary & proportionate
4. Procedural safeguards

This test is cumulative, and its various components are interconnected. If a measure or decision falls short in any of these areas, it must be understood to be arbitrary. Running alongside the test and influencing the assessment of several of its elements is the consideration of whether the deprivation of nationality is discriminatory, and whether it will result in statelessness. Where that is the case, it is more likely that a deprivation will be determined to be arbitrary.

---

[12] Cases include: Inter-American Court of Human Rights, *Case of Expelled Dominican and Haitian persons v. the Dominican Republic* (2014), *Ivcher-Bronstein v. Peru* (2001); African Commission on Human and People's Rights, *Open Society Justice Initiative v. Cote d'Ivoire* (2015), Amnesty International v. Zambia (1999), *Modise v. Botswana* (2000), *Malawi African Association and Others v. Mauritania* (2000), *Anudo v. Tanzania* (2018); European Court of Human Rights, *Ramadan v. Malta* (2016), *K2 v. United Kingdom* (2017); and Court of Justice of the European Union, *Janko Rottmann v Freistaat Bayern* (2010).

[13] African Court on Human and People's Rights, *Anudo v. Tanzania* (2018), para 79.

[14] These are applicable regardless of whether the deprivation decisions results in statelessness. See the 'avoidance of statelessness' section below for more on this.

Legitimate Purpose

Given that deprivation of nationality amounts to an interference of the enjoyment of the right to a nationality, it "must serve a legitimate purpose that is consistent with international law and, in particular, the objectives of international human rights law".[15]

The Human Rights Council has held that there are few circumstances in which the loss of nationality can be seen as serving a legitimate purpose[16] - fraud, for example – but even in these cases, deprivation of nationality must also satisfy other components of the arbitrariness test, such as the principle of proportionality.
What is regarded as a 'legitimate purpose' can be difficult to determine, but the Glion Recommendations on the Use of Rule of Law-Based Administrative Measures in a Counterterrorism Context (GCTF Guidelines) provide that:

"To determine whether the administrative measure is consistent with international human rights law, its purpose should be clearly defined. In addition, a clear rationale on how it will achieve the desired impact should be provided... A clearly defined legitimate aim is also of importance to assess the totality of circumstances warranting the measure, including, where appropriate, respecting the criteria of necessity, adequacy and proportionality of the administrative measure in relation to the effectiveness it aims to achieve."[17]

Article 7 of the European Convention on Nationality seeks to define – in general terms – the grounds for withdrawal of nationality that could constitute a legitimate purpose. Paragraph (d) recognises that a state may strip a person of nationality for "conduct seriously prejudicial to the vital interests of the state party".[18] Beyond this context, however, a State is allowed to deprive nationality on a number of other grounds, including when the individual voluntarily acquires another nationality (if dual nationality is prohibited), when citizenship is obtained fraudulently, or when the individual conducts voluntary service in foreign military force.[19] The 1961 Convention on the Reduction of Statelessness also provides for the possibility of deprivation of nationality on a number of limited grounds, even if this leaves the person concerned stateless, including in relation to conduct which is "seriously prejudicial to the vital interests of the state" (article 8(3bii)).[20]

---

[15] UN Human Rights Council, A/HRC/13/34 (2009), para. 25.

[16] UN Human Rights Council, A/HRC/25/28 (2013), para 4.

[17] GCTF Guidelines (2019), section IV.11.

[18] Note that under article 7(3) of the European Convention on Nationality, nationality cannot be withdrawn on this ground if it would lead to statelessness.

[19] European Convention on Nationality (1997), Article 7(1)(a), (b) and (c).

[20] In fact, the European Convention on Nationality drew its wording from the 1961 Convention on the Reduction of Statelessness on this point. Note that a contracting state to the 1961 Convention can only retain the power to deprive someone of nationality on this ground, with the result of statelessness, if its legislation already provided for this possibility and a declaration was lodged *at the time of accession.*

On the basis of treaty law, it would appear that this ground could be deemed to serve a legitimate purpose. However, the phrasing of this norm is rather broad – what are the 'vital interests' of the state, and what amounts to 'seriously prejudicial conduct'? - and appears to leave significant discretion to states. Drawing from the travaux préparatoires of the 1961 Convention, the Tunis Conclusions explain that "the conduct covered by this exception must threaten the foundations and organisation of the state whose nationality is at issue", whereby the term seriously prejudicial "requires that the individuals concerned have the capacity to negatively impact the state" and vital interests "sets a considerably higher threshold than 'national interests'".[21] The conduct must also be inconsistent with a citizen's duty of loyalty and "therefore applies only to conduct which is seriously prejudicial to the vital interests of that state".[22] The Commentary to the European Convention on Nationality suggests that "such conduct notably includes treason and other activities directed against the vital interests of the State concerned (for example work for a foreign secret service) but would not include criminal offences of a general nature, however serious they might be".[23]

Legal Basis

There must be a firm legal basis for depriving nationality under domestic law.[24] Without this, deprivation of nationality is unlawful, and thereby arbitrary.[25] It is also necessary for the procedure for deprivation of nationality to be in line with domestic law more generally and to be vested with or carried out by the appropriate authority. In the Inter-American Court case of *Ivcher Bronstein v. Peru*, the court found that the nullification of Ivcher's citizenship violated the prohibition of arbitrary deprivation of nationality because "the procedure used to annul the nationality title did not comply with the provisions of domestic legislation [and...] the authorities who annulled Mr Ivcher's nationality title did not have competence, impartiality, or independence".[26]

It is essential that deprivation provisions adhere to the following criteria:
- They should be clear and predictable, in order to guarantee legal certainty;[27]

---

[21] Tunis Conclusions (2013), para. 68.

[22] Ibid.

[23] Explanatory Report to the European Convention on Nationality (1997), available at https://rm.coe.int/16800ccde7, p. 11.

[24] Tunis Conclusions (2013), para. 16. The GCFT Guidelines also provide that "According to international human rights law, any lawful limitation on the exercise of applicable rights should be provided for or prescribed by law" (section IV.10).

[25] UN Human Rights Council, A/HRC/13/34 (2009) para. 25. See also Article 8(4) of the 1961 Convention on the Reduction of Statelessness, which provides that the deprivation of nationality must always be in accordance with the law and allow for the right to a fair hearing; and Article 7 of the European Convention on nationality which prohibits loss of nationality *ex lege* or at the initiative of a State party.

[26] *Ivcher-Bronstein v. Peru* (2001), paras. 95; 115.

[27] UN Human Rights Council, A/HRC/13/34 (2009) para. 25; GCTF Guidelines (2019), section IV.10.

- They should not be enacted or applied with retroactivity – i.e. a person can only be stripped of nationality for a particular act if the law in force at that time allowed this;[28]
- They should not be interpreted extensively or applied by analogy such that they are applied in a context which is not evidently covered by the wording of the provision;[29] rather, they should be implemented on a strict case-by-case basis.[30]

The norms here are clear: that a person may not be deprived of nationality unlawfully (i.e. without any legal basis), in relation to international or domestic law. However, problems arise in part from the use of broad or generic terminology. The GCTF Guidelines stipulate that "the law should avoid broad and vague terminology, or ambiguity in its language or the circumstances under which it can be applied".[31]

Necessary and Proportionate

According to the ILEC Guidelines, a measure must be "necessary, effective, as well as proportional to the goal to be achieved".[32] Therefore, this principle also requires that the 'least intrusive means' be adopted.

In order to assess necessity, "the appropriate authority should justify that the measures taken are necessary to serve the legitimate aim".[33] However, it is difficult to determine what objectives are 'legitimate', especially in the context of citizenship stripping as a security measure. The question comes down to balancing the interests of the state against the interests of the individual, and a value judgement on what exactly constitutes the 'vital interests' of the state. Key to determining the necessity of a decision is assessing whether there are alternatives which are less intrusive, and ensuring that all these alternatives have been exhausted.[34]

Two distinct considerations are important here. Firstly, is deprivation of nationality the least intrusive way in which the State can seek to achieve its goal, or are other measures available that would be less impactful in terms of the rights and freedoms of the person concerned? Considering the permanence of nationality deprivation

---

[28] See Dutch High Court, 201806107/1/V6 and 201806104/1/V6 (17 April 2019).
[29] Tunis Conclusions (2013), paras. 16-17; ILEC Guidelines (2015), section I. See also *Open Society Justice Initiative v. Côte d'Ivoire* (2015), para. 142; *Expelled Dominicans and Haitians v. Dominican Republic* (2014), para. 298.
[30] GCTF Guidelines (2019), section I.1
[31] GCTF Guidelines (2019), section IV.10.
[32] ILEC Guidelines (2015), section I.10.
[33] GCTF Guidelines (2019), section IV.12.
[34] UN Human Rights Council, A/HRC/13/34 (2009), para. 25; UN Human Rights Council, A/HRC/25/28 (2013), para 10; Human Rights Committee, General Comment No 27 on Art 12 ICCPR: "restrictive measures must conform to the principle of proportionality… they must be the least intrusive instruments amongst those, which might achieve the desired result".

and its manifold consequential implications - which has been termed "civil death"[35] - less far-reaching measures such as travel bans must be considered first.[36] The second element of the "least intrusive means" test is whether a connection can actually be drawn between the instrument and the purpose which it seeks to achieve. According to the GCTF Guidelines, "States should consider whether the means used to limit the right are rationally connected to the objective sought".[37] In the case of national security, one could ask: if deprivation of nationality seeks to help protect communities from terrorism and other major national security threats, is this indeed a measure that can contribute to this goal? Relevant here is the effectiveness question, which concerns whether or not the measure achieves its intended objectives.[38]

The principle of proportionality is also an individual assessment,[39] which "requires balancing the impact on the rights of the individual and the interests of the state".[40] Relevant factors which must be considered when conducting the proportionality assessment include:

- The gravity of the act for which deprivation of nationality is sought;[41]
- The strength of the link of the person with the state in question;[42]
- The time that has elapsed since the act was committed;[43]
- The consequences of deprivation of nationality – for the person concerned and for members or their family, in particular whether the deprivation results in statelessness or the loss of the right to reside in the country where the person held nationality.[44]

Given the centrality of the proportionality principle to all decision-making in relation to the deprivation of nationality, it is important to understand whether, how and to what effect States weigh the proportionality of deprivation decisions – either at the point of the decision or if an appeal is brought. To date, this test has been

---

[35] For instance, E.F. Cohen, 'When Democracies Denationalize: The Epistemological Case against Revoking Citizenship' (2016), 30 Ethics & International Affairs.

[36] For instance, A. Macklin and R. Bauböck (eds), 'The Return of Banishment: Do the New Denationalisation Policies Weaken Citizenship?' (2015) EUI Working Paper Series RSCAS 2015/14 Robert Schuman Centre for Advanced Studies EUDO Citizenship Observatory.

[37] GCTF Guidelines (2019), section IV.13.

[38] For more on this, see the piece on 'Citizenship Stripping as a Security Measure - Policy issues and the "Effectiveness" Question' in this report.

[39] Reaffirming the need for individualised and motivated decision-making.

[40] Tunis Conclusions (2013), para. 20.

[41] UN Human Rights Council, A/HRC/25/28 (2013), para. 4.

[42] Tunis Conclusions (2013), para. 21. See for example Human Rights Committee, *Jama Warsame v. Canada* (2011) where Mr Warsame's link to Canada was a crucial factor in the court's decision that his deportation to Somalia from Canada was arbitrary (p18).

[43] Id.

[44] Tunis Conclusions (2013), para 22; ILEC Guidelines (2015), Section II; *Ramadan v. Malta* (2016) and *K2 v. United Kingdom* (2017).

applied in the context of acquisition of nationality by fraud. [45] In *Janko Rottmann v. Freistaat Bayern*, the European Court of Justice (ECJ) ruled that deprivation of nationality upon fraudulent acquisition of nationality could be compatible with EU law (even if it leads to statelessness), but that the national court must ascertain the principle of proportionality when looking at the consequences of this decision, and where appropriate, examine the proportionality of the decision in light of national law.[46] The ECJ ruling made it clear that EU member states have to respect the proportionality principle when determining whether a person's nationality should be revoked, particularly when weighing the consequences of deprivation of nationality for the individual and, if relevant, their family members.[47] Also relevant to proportionality is the ability of the individual to return to one's country. Further, in the case of *Tjebbes and Others v Minister van Buitenlandse Zaken*, the court ruled that the principle of proportionality requires that national law must permit an individual examination of the consequences of loss for the persons concerned from the point of the view of EU law.[48]

Given the increasing use of nationality deprivation as a national security measure, it would be beneficial to consider the specifics and intricacies of the test where deprivation of nationality is a response to a purported terrorist or national security threat. For example, how proportionate would it be to deprive a child of their nationality? (e.g. current Australian deprivation powers apply to anyone over the age of 14).

Procedural Safeguards

Adequate procedural safeguards are also essential to preserving the rule of law, protecting the individual and preventing abuse of the law. States must "observe minimum procedural standards in order to ensure that decisions on nationality matters do not contain any element of arbitrariness" and "violations of the right to a nationality must be open to an effective remedy".[49] Moreover, "the greater the impact of an administrative measure, the more stringent the procedural safeguards should be applied".[50] Given the severe impact of arbitrary deprivation of nationality, extremely strong safeguards are needed.

Article 8(4) of the 1961 Convention provides that States "shall not exercise a power of deprivation [...] except in accordance with law, which shall provide for the person concerned the right to a fair hearing by a court or other independent body". The

---

[45] See *Ramadan v. Malta* (2016), where Ramadan was deprived of Maltese citizenship due to fraudulent acquisition, rendering him stateless.
[46] *Janko Rottman v. Freistaat Bayern* (2010), para 56.
[47] *Janko Rottman v. Freistaat Bayern* (2010), para. 59.
[48] *Tjebbes and Others v Minister van Buitenlandse Zaken* (2019).
[49] UN Human Rights Council, A/HRC/13/34 (2009) paras. 43 and 46.
[50] GCTF Guidelines (2019), section V.

ILEC Guidelines provide further explanation to this provision, noting that such safeguards must apply in all cases of loss and deprivation, including in cases where authorities maintain that a given person never acquired a nationality in the first place.[51]

Various Human Rights Council reports on arbitrary deprivation of nationality detail that, with regards to due process:

- Decisions on deprivation of nationality must be issued in writing, including the reasons for deprivation;[52]
- Decisions must be taken within a reasonable time,[53] with authorities acting "diligently and swiftly";[54]
- Such decisions must be open to effective administrative or judicial review, by a court or other independent body – including meaningful review of relevant substantive issues and the right to be heard;[55]
- An effective remedy must be available in cases of arbitrary deprivation of nationality which allows for restoration of nationality.[56]

---

[51] ILEC Guidelines (2015), section III.

[52] European Convention on Nationality (Article 11); ILEC Guidelines (2015), section III.1; Tunis Conclusions (2013), para. 26; UN Human Rights Council, A/HRC/13/34 (2009) para. 43.

[53] European Convention on Nationality (Article 10); International Covenant on Civil and Political Rights (Art 14(3)(c)).

[54] *Ramadan v. Malta* (2016), para. 88 and *K2 v. United Kingdom* (2017), para. 53.

[55] UN Human Rights Council, A/HRC/25/28 (2013), para. 44; European Convention on Nationality (Article 12); International Covenant on Civil and Political Rights, Art 14(5); In *McGinley and Egan v. The United Kingdom* (1998), the European Court of Human Rights found that where the State, without good cause, prevents appellants from gaining access to documents in its possession that would have assisted in the defence of their case, it would have the effect of denying them a fair hearing under Article 6(1) of the European Convention (paras 86 and 90). Moreover, in *Anudo v. Tanzania* (2018), the court ruled that the court had violated Articles 4 and 7 of the ICCPR given that the applicant was declared an illegal immigrant and denied nationality and the right to be heard by a national court (para 113.) Moreover, fees relating to appeals proceedings must not form an obstacle (Articles 10 and 13 of the European Convention on Nationality; Tunis Conclusions (2013), para. 28; ILEC Guidelines (2015), section III.3).

[56] UN Human Rights Council, A/HRC/13/34 (2009), paras. 43, 44 and 46; UN Human Rights Council, A/HRC/RES/32/5 (2016), para. 15; Secretary General reports A/HRC/31/29, A/HRC/13/34, A/HRC/25/28 and CRC/C/DOM/CO/3-5; Tunis Conclusions (2013), paras. 25 – 29; ILEC Guidelines (2015), section II; GCTF Guidelines (2019), section V. Within the EU context, the Court of Justice of the European Union recently ruled in *Tjebbes and Others v Minister van Buitenlandse Zaken* (2019) that there must be individual assessment of the consequences of that loss from the point of view of EU law, with the option of recovering nationality retroactively if the person has demonstrated a link with the Netherlands (by applying for any document that shows his nationality). This means that automatic loss of nationality does not meet due process standards. See also *Ivcher-Bronstein v. Peru* (2001); *Ramadan v. Malta* (2016) and *K2 v. United Kingdom* (2017); article 8(4) of the 1961 Convention on the Reduction of Statelessness; and articles 11-12 of the European Convention on Nationality. Article 8 of the Universal Declaration of Human Rights also states that "Everyone has the right to an effective remedy by the competent national tribunals for acts violating the fundamental rights granted him by the constitution or by law."

The procedural and substantive suitability of particular bodies or courts has also been raised as a question in some instances – for example, with respect to the Special Immigration Appeals Commission in the United Kingdom.[57]

Individualised decision-making is an important safeguard, whereby the state takes a motivated decision in each case and communicates this with the person concerned.[58] The collective deprivation of nationality would be discriminatory under a number of human rights instruments.[59] However, some of the contemporary practices present a challenge in this respect. So-called "quasi-loss" situations, where individuals who think they have citizenship and who have been treated as if they have citizenship are no longer recognised as nationals or treated as if they never acquired citizenship, present particular difficulties in respect of due process norms.[60] Also problematic are cases of retroactive non-recognition, where a State does not go through the formal processes of deprivation, but rather denies that the person ever had citizenship in the first place, asserting that any previous recognition was in error, or obtained by fraud.[61]

Refusal of re-entry/expulsion

In many cases, decisions to deprive a person of nationality are issued in absentia and often the deprivation of nationality is actually imposed while the person concerned is abroad.[62,63]

This can not only impact the effective communication of the decision, but also the opportunity to appeal, including the right to be heard. [64] The UK practice of deprivation of nationality, for instance, has been described by critics as a two-step process of exile or banishment: nationals are stripped of their citizenship while they are abroad, with a view to preventing their return to the territory of the state, or as a prelude to their deportation.[65] It is not (merely) the removal of citizenship that is

---

[57] See also *Ivcher-Bronstein v. Peru* (2001), where the Court found that the judges to whom Mr. Ivcher could appeal "did not meet the standards of competence, impartiality and independence required by [the right to a fair trial]" (para. 115).

[58] This is also necessary with a view to testing the proportionality of a decision.

[59] If discriminatory on the basis of race, it would breach Article 5(d)(iii) of the Convention on the Elimination of All Forms of Racial Discrimination; if discriminatory on the basis of sex, it would breach Article 1 of the Convention on the Elimination of all Forms of Discrimination Against Women.

[60] See, for instance, the cases *Amnesty International v. Zambia* (1999) and *Modise v. Botswana* (2000). For more on quasi-loss situations, see the piece by Dr. Gerard-René de Groot in Part 2 of this report.

[61] For more on this, see Dr. Bronwen Manby's contribution in Part 2 of this report.

[62] For more on this, see Amanda Weston QC's contribution in Part 2 of this report.

[63] See for example *Modise v. Botswana* (2000), where Mr. Modise was deported 4 times over the course of 17 years.

[64] R. Hofmann, 'Denaturalization and Forced Exile', in W. Rüdiger (Ed.), *The Max Planck Encyclopedia of Public International Law* (2013) Oxford University Press.

[65] A. Macklin and R. Bauböck (eds), 'The Return of Banishment: Do the New Denationalisation Policies Weaken Citizenship?' (2015) EUI Working Paper Series RSCAS 2015/14 Robert Schuman Centre for Advanced Studies EUDO Citizenship Observatory. See for comments on the historic use and justification of 'banishment' M. Gibney, 'Should citizenship be conditional? Denationalisation and liberal principles' (2011) Oxford Refugee Studies Centre Working Paper Series No. 75.

sought, but rather the physical removal or banishment of the individual from the state. [66]In the Netherlands too, a person stripped of nationality under new powers would automatically be declared an "unwanted alien" and be prohibited from re-entering the country.[67]

Such practice implicates other international norms, including the right to enter one's own country, since the test which states must meet with respect to deprivation of nationality relates to the test for deprivation of the right to enter one's own country. There have been concerns that deprivation of nationality is often used for the sole purpose of allowing expulsion or refusing re-entry of a person who has or may have been involved in terrorist activities".[68] As the UN Human Rights Committee has stated, "A State party must not, by stripping a person of nationality or by expelling an individual to a third country, arbitrarily prevent this person from returning to his or her own country".[69] The International Law Commission 'Draft Articles on the Expulsion of Aliens' also states that "A State shall not make its national an alien by deprivation of nationality for the sole purpose of expelling him or her".[70]

In the Human Rights Committee case of *Warsame v. Canada*, it was ruled that the deportation of Mr. Warsame from Canada to Somalia was arbitrary, and that "there are few, if any circumstances in which deprivation of the right to enter one's own country could be reasonable." Therefore, the accused's deportation to Somalia, which impeded his return to his own country, was considered "disproportionate to the legitimate aim of preventing the commission of further crimes and therefore arbitrary."[71] In *K2 v. the United Kingdom*, the European Court of Human Rights found that "an out-of-country appeal" did not necessarily render a decision to deprive someone of citizenship arbitrary, but that an issue "might arise where there exists clear and objective evidence that the person was unable to instruct lawyers or give evidence while outside the jurisdiction". The court stated that K2's inability to re-enter the UK was not because he was not a British citizen, but because he had already left the UK voluntarily when the decision to withdraw his nationality was taken.[72] Moreover, in *Anudo v. Tanzania* (2018), the court declared that Tanzania had violated the Applicant's right not to be expelled arbitrarily, ordering the State to take the necessary steps to restore the applicant's rights and allow him to return to

---

[66] For more on this, see Amanda Weston QC and Matthew Gibney's contributions in Part 2 of this report.

[67] Amnesty International, 'Dangerously Disproportionate. The ever-expanding national security state in Europe' (2017).

[68] Parliamentary Assembly, 'Withdrawing Nationality as a Measure to Combat Terrorism: A Human Rights Compatible Approach?', Resolution 2263 (2019), available at http://assembly.coe.int/nw/xml/XRef/Xref-DocDetails-EN.asp?fileid=25430.

[69] UN Human Rights Committee, General Comment 27, Freedom of movement (Art.12), CCPR/C/21/Rev.1/Add.9 (1999), para. 21.

[70] The International Law Commission, 'Draft Articles on the Expulsion of Aliens' (2014), Article 8.

[71] *Jama Warsame v. Canada* (2011), para 8(6).

[72] *K2 v. United Kingdom* (2017), para. 57.

the national territory.[73] This issue is also raised in the case currently pending before the ECtHR *El Aroud and Soughir v. Belgium.*[74]

How the deprivation occurs

A further procedural consideration relates to the mechanics of the deprivation itself and in particular when it should take effect. There are two main questions to be considered in this respect.

1. Importantly, whether there is a relationship between a decision to deprive a person of nationality and any criminal process that has been undertaken against him/her. This relationship must be carefully scrutinised.

The Tunis Conclusions provide that "where criminal conduct is alleged, it is strongly advisable that deprivation of nationality only occur following a two-step process, logically beginning with a finding of guilt by a criminal court. A decision by the competent authority (preferably a court) on deprivation of nationality would follow."[75] The ILEC Guidelines similarly affirm that "the unacceptable character of undesirable behaviour of the person involved should be proven beyond a reasonable doubt. Such behaviour should constitute a crime and a criminal court should have imposed a sanction".[76] Having said this, the principle of *ne bis in idem* may also come into play, according to which a person should not be punished twice for the same crime.[77] In reality, practice varies and a criminal conviction is not required in all states before deprivation of nationality can proceed.

2. When the decision to deprive a person of nationality can come into effect.

The Tunis Conclusions and ILEC Guidelines also touch on this, asserting that "deprivation decisions are only to enter into effect at the moment all judicial remedies have been exhausted".[78] If, until that time, a person must still be treated as a national, this would have implications not only for accrued rights but also for non-expulsion or the granting of re-entry. Contemporary practice appears, again, to run counter to this notion.

---

[73] *Anudo v. Tanzania* (2018).

[74] *El Aroud and Soughir v Belgium* (pending).

[75] Tunis Conclusions (2013), para. 27; UN High Commissioner for Refugees (UNHCR), 'Expert Meeting - Interpreting the 1961 Statelessness Convention and Avoiding Statelessness resulting from Loss and Deprivation of Nationality ("Tunis Conclusions")' (March 2014), para. 27, available at https://www.refworld.org/docid/533a754b4.html.

[76] ILEC Guidelines (2015), section IV.3c.

[77] J. Brandvoll, 'Deprivation of nationality: Limitations on rendering persons stateless under international law' in A. Edwards and L. van Waas (Eds) *Nationality and Statelessness under International Law* (2014) p. 194-21; A. Macklin 'Citizenship revocation, the privilege to have rights and the production of the Alien' (2014) Queen's Law Journal 40, p.1–54.

[78] Tunis Conclusions (2013), para. 26; ILEC Guidelines (2015), section III.4.

THE PROHIBITION OF DISCRIMINATION

Deprivation of nationality on the basis of discrimination is prohibited under the 1961 Convention. Article 9 forbids Contracting States to deprive any person or group of persons of their nationality on racial, ethnic, religious or political grounds, irrespective of whether or not the deprivation would lead to statelessness.
As set out in the Tunis Conclusions:

"loss or deprivation of nationality may not be based on discrimination on any ground prohibited in international human rights law, either in law or in practice. These include, inter alia, all the grounds established in Article 2 of the ICCPR. Participants noted the jus cogens character of the prohibition of racial discrimination as well as the specific prohibition of racial discrimination in relation to nationality in the CERD and underlined its relevance in many situations of deprivation of nationality. International law prohibits deprivation of nationality on other grounds, including under Article 9 of the 1961 Convention which refers specifically to religious and political as well as ethnic and racial grounds, Article 9 of the CEDAW in relation to discrimination against women and Article 18 of the CRPD which explicitly addresses deprivation on the ground of disability. The resolutions on nationality of the Human Rights Council have also set out a broad range of prohibited grounds for discrimination."[79]

As further set out in the Tunis Conclusions, Article 9 of the 1961 Convention:

"was designed to give effect to Article 15 of the UDHR and is complemented by provisions of conventions such as the CERD, CEDAW and CRPD. The line between deprivation on political grounds and deprivation due to conduct inconsistent with the duty of loyalty to the State will not always be clear. However, a consequence of Article 9 is that a State will need to establish that a deprivation decision is not being made on political or other discriminatory grounds. Furthermore, the deprivation must not be based on conduct which is consistent with an individual's freedom of expression, freedom of assembly or other rights guaranteed under international human rights law."[80]

The 2009 Secretary-General's report on arbitrary deprivation of nationality recalls that "the principle of non-discrimination is a common feature applicable to the context of international human rights instruments", including in respect of "issues related to nationality".[81] Any deprivation of nationality on discriminatory grounds is considered arbitrary for the purposes of international law. This is affirmed across different international conventions, soft law instruments, jurisprudence and enjoys broad consensus in doctrinal writings. The 2016 resolution of the Human Rights Council on this issue provides the following non-exhaustive list of discriminatory grounds in relation to understanding when the deprivation of nationality is

---

[79] Tunis Conclusions (2013), para. 18.
[80] Tunis Conclusions (2013), paras 70-71.
[81] UN Human Rights Council, A/HRC/13/34 (2009), paras. 18 and 26.

arbitrary: "race, colour, sex, language, religion, political or other opinion, national or social origin, property, birth, or other status, including disability".[82]

Even in the absence of explicit treaty norms, "the prohibition of arbitrary deprivation of nationality, which aims at protecting the right to retain a nationality, is implicit in provisions of human rights treaties that proscribe specific forms of discrimination".[83] International jurisprudence confirms this. For instance, in *Open Society Justice Initiative v. Côte d'Ivoire*, the African Commission on Human and Peoples' Rights found a violation of Articles 2 and 3 of the African Charter, which provide for non-discrimination and protect equality before the law.[84] This rule is also recognised in *Girls Yean and Bosico v. Dominican Republic* where the Inter-American Court of Human Rights underlined the prohibition of discrimination regarding access to a nationality;[85] similarly in *Ivcher-Bronstein v. Peru,* where the court recognised "the right to nationality without making a distinction about the way in which it was acquired, either by birth, naturalization or some other means established in the law of the respective State".[86] Further, discriminatory deprivation of nationality may even amount to persecution in the sense of the 1951 Convention relating to the Status of Refugees.[87]

The prohibition of systemic racial discrimination is also a peremptory norm of international law, which all States are obligated to respect, protect and fulfil at all times.[88] States must therefore ensure that their practice of effecting deprivation of citizenship does not further entrench racial discrimination and inequality, including *inter alia* by stigmatising racialised and marginalised groups as threats to national security or by depriving members of racialised and marginalised groups of their nationality at a disproportionate rate.

In order to protect against statelessness, some States differentiate in their law and practice between deprivation of nationality from so-called "mono nationals" (persons with only one citizenship) and individuals with dual or multiple nationalities. This dangerously results in two different tiers of citizenship, whereby for example, someone who has two nationalities, such as of the Netherlands and Morocco, is more vulnerable to having that Dutch nationality withdrawn than someone who only has Dutch nationality. It is important to note that persons with

---

[82] UN Human Rights Council, A/HRC/RES/32/5 (2016), paras. 2 and 4.
[83] UN Human Rights Council, A/HRC/13/34 (2009), para. 26.
[84] *Open Society Justice Initiative v. Côte d'Ivoire* (2015), paras. 151 and 156.
[85] *Girls Yean and Bosico v. Dominican Republic* (2005).
[86] *Ivcher-Bronstein v. Peru* (2014), para. 90.
[87] See for an in depth discussion, E. Fripp, 'Nationality and statelessness in the international law of refugee status' (2016), Hart Publishing; M. Foster and H. Lambert, International Refugee Law and the Protection of Stateless Persons.
[88] See for example, UN General Assembly, 'Fourth report on peremptory norms of general international law (*jus cogens*) by Dire Tladi, Special Rapporteur', A/CN.4/727 (31 January 2019), available at https://undocs.org/en/A/CN.4/727.

dual or multiple nationality are also more likely to have a migratory background and belong to ethnic or religious minority groups within a State. This may also be challenging where a person indeed holds a second nationality, but this is an inherited citizenship from a State with which they have no meaningful ties. Further, under many nationality laws, citizenship acquired by naturalisation or registration is a more precarious status.[89]

The European Convention on Nationality specifies that this inequality between nationals is discriminatory, stating that "Each State Party shall be guided by the principle of non-discrimination between its nationals, whether they are nationals by birth or have acquired its nationality subsequently" (Article 5(2)). The 2009 Secretary-General report also states that "no discrimination with regard to the acquisition of nationality should be admissible under internal law as between legitimate children and children born out of wedlock or of stateless parents, or based on the nationality status of one or both parents".[90]

AVOIDANCE OF STATELESSNESS

According to the UN Secretary General, the avoidance of statelessness exists in close relation to the right to nationality itself: "As a corollary to this right [to a nationality], States must make every effort to avoid statelessness through legislative, administrative and other measures."[91] This position is reflected in the ILEC Guidelines which state that "Loss of nationality due to undesirable behaviour (e.g. acts seriously prejudicial to the vital interests of the State or foreign military service) should never cause statelessness."[92] Recent case law confirms this point. In *Anudo v. Tanzania* (2018), the court found that the State failed to take necessary measures to prevent the Applicant from being in a situation of statelessness, holding that "the power to deprive a person of his or her nationality has to be exercised in accordance with international standards, to avoid the risk of statelessness".[93] This shows that each case must be carefully assessed.

In *Amnesty International v. Zambia,* the African Court found a violation of Article 5 of the African Charter (respect for the inherent dignity of a human being/prohibition of inhuman or degrading punishment and treatment). As held by the Court, "By forcing Banda and Chinula to live as stateless persons under degrading conditions, the government of Zambia has deprived them of their family and is depriving their

---

[89] UN Human Rights Council, A/HRC/25/28 (2013), para. 6.
[90] UN Human Rights Council, A/HRC/13/34 (2009), para. 31
[91] Guidance Note of the Secretary General, The United Nations and Statelessness (2011), available at https://www.un.org/ruleoflaw/blog/document/guidance-note-of-the-secretary-general-the-united-nations-and-statelessness/, p.3. See also, article 8(1) of the 1961 Convention and article 4(b) of the European Convention on Nationality which prohibit deprivation of nationality if it leads to statelessness.
[92] ILEC Guidelines (2015), section IV.3a.
[93] *Anudo v. Tanzania* (2018), para 78.

families of the men's support, and this constitutes a violation of the dignity of a human being, thereby violating Article 5 of the Charter".[94] The reasoning of the Court goes to the heart of why an outcome of statelessness is relevant particularly to the proportionality component of the arbitrariness test (but also to other parts), and stands as a recognition that stripping of citizenship and rendering the person stateless can have a detrimental impact on other non-derogable rights. Therefore, due to the significant impact on the individual (and family), any deprivation of nationality resulting in statelessness must be deemed arbitrary and contrary to international law, with the only possible exception (subject to other considerations) of deprivation in response to fraudulent acquisition of nationality.[95]

However, while avoidance of statelessness is a fundamental principle of international law, there is no evident international norm regarding a right to dual nationality.[96] The 1961 Convention accepts that contracting States may retain the power to deprive people of nationality on this ground even if it leads to statelessness, but only if their law already provided for this at the moment of accession and a declaration was made to that effect. A clear majority of State parties to the 1961 Convention have not invoked this option and do not deprive a person of nationality on this ground if this leads to statelessness. For States that do invoke this option, as with any such exception to the general rule that statelessness is to be avoided, it is essential that the terms be construed narrowly;[97] in other words, the set of exceptional circumstances in which deprivation of nationality may result in statelessness should be extremely restricted,[98] and subject to other safeguards under international law.

Another factor to bear in mind is that the onus of avoiding statelessness impacts the procedural safeguards that a state must have in place. As part of the reasoning of a decision and as an element of an appeal, it must be possible to examine whether a person has been left stateless and thereby whether this has appropriately been taken into account. Guaranteeing due process in this respect will also mean ensuring that the State adheres to the definition of statelessness as set out under international law and that the responsible authorities have the knowledge and capacity to effectively conduct the assessment.[99]

In individual decision-making by states, efforts to ensure the avoidance of statelessness or to give this context due consideration have not always been

---

[94] *Amnesty International v Zambia*, (1999), para 58. Similarly, in *Open Society Justice Initiative v. Côte D'Ivoire* (2015), the court stated that there was a "denial of the right of victims to nationality", and as a consequence "a violation of their right to dignity" (paragraph 142).

[95] See, for instance, the discussion in M. Adjami and J. Harrington, 'The Scope and Content of Article 15 of the Universal Declaration of Human Rights' in Refugee Survey Quarterly (2008), 27 (3), p. 93-109.

[96] Un Human Rights Council, A/HRC/25/28 (2013), para. 6.

[97] UN Human Rights Council, A/HRC/25/28 (2013), para. 12.

[98] Tunis Conclusions (2013), para. 23.

[99] See further on the determination of statelessness, UNHCR, *Handbook on protection of stateless persons* (2014).

satisfactory. In the case of *Pham v. Secretary of State for the Home Department*, the UK courts ruled that a person who was subjected to deprivation of his British citizenship was not rendered stateless, but this conclusion was grounded on an assessment which did not follow relevant international guidance.[100] In the case of *Ramadan v. Malta*, the circumstance of statelessness also appears to have been assessed in an incomplete and potentially appropriate manner. The court used Ramadan's statelessness, for instance, as a reason to justify the position that "it cannot be said that he is under a threat of expulsion as there is no guarantee that the Egyptian authorities would accept him, nor is it likely that he could be removed to another country",[101] such that he cannot claim to be a victim of Article 8 of the European Convention on Human Rights (right to private and family life). However, elsewhere in the same ruling the court seemed unconvinced by the evidence of Ramadan's statelessness, stating that he had not provided the court with any official documents confirming his renunciation, nor had he provided any documents of the possibilities to reacquire his Egyptian nationality.[102] In doing so, the court not only failed to oppose his current status as stateless, but also undermined the legal situation of statelessness which can have negative consequences for Ramadan and his family.[103]

Such cases demonstrate the complexity of the arbitrariness test, raising further questions as to how states can effectively safeguard against the arbitrary deprivation of nationality, where this results in statelessness.

---

[100] See, for instance, the analysis by Open Society Justice Initiative, available at https://www.opensocietyfoundations.org/litigation/pham-previously-b2-v-home-secretary.

[101] *Ramadan v. Malta* (2016), para. 56.

[102] *Ibid*, para. 92.

[103] See also *K2. v. The United Kingdom* (2017), where the court declared a complaint by a suspected terrorist who was stripped of his UK citizenship to be inadmissible.

THE PROHIBITION OF ARBITRARY DEPRIVATION OF NATIONALITY

Universal Declaration of Human Rights

Article 15(2):
No one shall be arbitrarily deprived of his nationality [...]

Convention on the Rights of Persons with Disabilities

Article 18(1)(a):
States Parties shall recognise the rights of persons with disabilities to [...] a nationality, on an equal basis with others, including by ensuring that persons with disabilities: (a) [...] are not deprived of their nationality arbitrarily or on the basis of disability.

American Convention on Human Rights

Article 20(3):
No one shall be arbitrarily deprived of his nationality [...]

European Convention on Nationality

Article 4(c):
No one shall be arbitrarily deprived of his or her nationality.

Arab Charter on Human Rights

Article 29(1):
No one shall be arbitrarily or unlawfully deprived of his nationality.

ASEAN Human Rights Declaration

Article 18:
Every person has the right to a nationality as prescribed by law. No person shall be arbitrarily deprived of such nationality [...]

Commonwealth of Independent States Convention on Human Rights and Fundamental Freedoms

Article 24(2):
No one shall be arbitrarily deprived of his citizenship [...]

NORMS RELATING TO STATELESSNESS AND DEPRIVATION OF NATIONALITY

1961 Convention on the Reduction of Statelessness

Article 6:
If the law of a Contracting State provides for loss of its nationality by a person's spouse or children as a consequence of that person losing or being deprived of that nationality, such loss shall be conditional upon their possession or acquisition of another nationality.

Article 7(4):
A naturalized person may lose his nationality on account of residence abroad for a period, not less than seven consecutive years, specified by the law of the Contracting State concerned if he fails to declare to the appropriate authority his intention to retain his nationality.

Article 8(1):
A Contracting State shall not deprive a person of its nationality if such deprivation would render him stateless [...]

Article 8(3):
[...] A Contracting State may retain the right to deprive a person of his nationality if [...]
(i) [the person] has, in disregard of an express prohibition by the Contracting State rendered or continued to render services to, or received or continued to receive emoluments from, another State, or
(ii) has conducted himself in a manner seriously prejudicial to the vital interests of the State;
(b) The person has taken an oath, or made a formal declaration of allegiance to another State, or given definite evidence of his determination to repudiate his allegiance to the Contracting State.

Article 8(4):
A Contracting State shall not exercise a power of deprivation … except in accordance with law, which shall provide for the person concerned the right to a fair hearing by a court or other independent body.

Article 9:

A Contracting State may not deprive any person or group of persons of their nationality on racial, ethnic, religious or political grounds.

European Convention on Nationality

Article 7(1):

A State Party may not provide in its internal law for the loss of its nationality *ex lege* or at the initiative of the State Party except in the following cases:

a) voluntary acquisition of another nationality;

b) acquisition of the nationality of the State Party by means of fraudulent conduct, false information or concealment of any relevant fact attributable to the applicant;

c) voluntary service in a foreign military force;

d) conduct seriously prejudicial to the vital interests of the State Party;

e) lack of a genuine link between the State Party and a national habitually residing abroad;

f) where it is established during the minority of a child that the preconditions laid down by internal law which led to the *ex lege* acquisition of the nationality of the State Party are no longer fulfilled;

g) adoption of a child if the child acquires or possesses the foreign nationality of one or both of the adopting parents.

Article 10:

Each State Party shall ensure that applications relating to the acquisition, retention, loss, recovery or certification of its nationality be processed within a reasonable time.

Article 11:

Each State Party shall ensure that decisions relating to the acquisition, retention, loss, recovery or certification of its nationality contain reasons in writing.

Article 12:

Each State Party shall ensure that decisions relating to the acquisition, retention, loss, recovery or certification of its nationality be open to an administrative or judicial review in conformity with its internal law.

Article 13(1):
Each State Party shall ensure that the fees for the acquisition, retention, loss, recovery or certification of its nationality be reasonable.

Article 13(2)
Each State Party shall ensure that the fees for an administrative or judicial review be not an obstacle for applicants.

Convention on the Rights of the Child

Article 8(1):
States Parties undertake to respect the right of the child to preserve his or her identity, including nationality […] without unlawful interference.

Article 8(2):
Where a state is illegally deprived of some or all of the elements of his or her identity, States Parties shall provide appropriate assistance and protection, with a view to re-establishing speedily his or her identity.

International Convention for the Protection of All Persons from Enforced Disappearances

Article 25(4):
Given the need to protect the best interests of [children who are or whose parents are subjected to enforced disappearance] and their right to preserve, or to have re-established, their identity, including their nationality […]

The Convention on the Elimination of All Forms of Discrimination Against Women

Article 9(1):
States Parties shall grant women equal rights with men to acquire, change or retain their nationality. They shall ensure in particular that neither the marriage to an alien nor change of nationality by the husband during marriage shall automatically change the nationality of the wife, render her stateless […]

REGIONAL JURISPRUDENCE RELATED TO THE DEPRIVATION OF NATIONALITY

African Court on Human's and People's Rights

Anudo Ochieng Anudo v. United Republic of Tanzania (2018)

Main facts: The case concerns the revocation of Tanzanian nationality (and corresponding passport), and subsequent deportation to Kenya of Mr. Anudo. He was then expelled back to Tanzania by Kenya, who claimed he was in an 'illegal situation', even though he could not enter the country. He then fled to a hiding place between Kenya and Tanzania.

Relevant rulings: The court declared that there had been violations of:
* UDHR Article 15(2): The State arbitrarily deprived the applicant of his Tanzanian nationality (p28)
* Articles 7 and 4 ICCPR: The State violated the right to be heard (p29), given that the applicant was declared an "illegal immigrant" and denied nationality and the right to be heard by a national court (para 113)
* Article 13 ICCPR: the State violated the Applicant's right not to be expelled arbitrarily (p29), since "an alien lawfully in the territory of a State party... may be expelled only in pursuance of a decision reached in accordance with law and shall... be allowed to submit the reasons against his expulsion and to have his case reviewed by ... the competent authority" (para 100)
* The State failed to take necessary measures to prevent the applicant from being in a situation of statelessness (para 102). The court then ordered Tanzania to amend its legislation to provide individuals with judicial remedies in the event of dispute over citizenship (p29), specifically concerning Tanzania's Citizenship Act which contains gaps as it does not allow citizens by birth to exercise judicial remedy where their nationality is challenged as required by international law (p25). The court also ordered the State to take the necessary steps to restore the applicant's rights and allowing him to return to the national territory (p29).

Kennedy Gihana & Others v. Republic of Rwanda (2019)

Main facts: The case concerns the revocation of the passports of several Rwandan citizens. The appellants claimed that they were not informed of, and were unable to appeal, the decision.

Relevant rulings: The court found that the applicants' passports had been arbitrarily revoked, but that this did not constitute arbitrary deprivation of nationality since the applicants were still Rwandan nationals. The court determined that "the revocation of a passport is not tantamount to a revocation of nationality or citizenship" (p5). However, the court did find a violation of Article 12(2) (right to freedom of movement) and Article 13(1) (right to political participation) of the Charter.

African Commission on Human and Peoples' Rights

Amnesty International v. Zambia (1999)

Main facts: The case concerns the deportation of two prominent political figures from Zambia to Malawi, Mr. Chinula and Mr. Banda. In order to affect the deportations, the Zambian authorities asserted that neither man was a citizen, even though Banda had been in possession of a National Registration Card and passport and Chinula's status as a politician had previously been uncontested. There was no formal decision revoking citizenship for either man, they simply came to be treated as non-nationals.

Relevant rulings: The commission mainly focused on the legitimacy of the deportations in this case, however, the commission discussed the complainants' statuses in Zambia, including the question of their citizenship to a limited extent.

- With respect to Mr Banda, the commission determined that it "is not competent to substitute the judgements of the Zambian courts, especially on matters of fact" and that it "must, therefore, accept that Banda was not a Zambian by birth or descent" (at 40). The judge found that "there was no evidence, on a balance of probabilities, to prove that Banda was born in Zambia of Zambian parents" and "possession of a National Registration Card does not confer citizenship" (at 37), ruling thereby that Banda was not a Zambian citizen, although he did not identify the country in which Banda did hold citizenship.
- With respect to Mr Chinula, the commission took a different approach, ruling that "the arbitrary removal of one's citizenship in the case of Chinula cannot be justified" (at 52) and connecting this to article 2 of the Charter (non-discrimination). The Commission does not clarify how it reached the conclusion that Chinula's citizenship was "arbitrarily removed" and as with Banda, the consequential violations found were related to Chinula's deportation and not to the removal of citizenship as such.
- For neither of the complainants does the commission undertake its own independent assessment of their citizenship status (unlike in in the case of *John K. Modise v. Botswana*).

John K. Modise v. Botswana (2000)

Main facts: The case concerns a South African born individual with Botswanian parents, who was a political leader of an opposition party in Botswana. He was arrested and deported to South Africa four times, before finally being readmitted to Botswana. He was granted Botswanian citizenship by naturalisation, which is a second-tier citizenship status. He claims that he is entitled to full Botswanian citizenship by descent.

Relevant rulings: The commission found violations of Article 12(1) (right to freedom of movement and residence), Article 12(2) (right to enter own country), Article 3(2) (right to equal protection before the law) and Article 5 (right to recognition of legal status). This case was tackled in a different manner to *Amnesty International v. Zambia*, where the nationality rules of Zambia are not discussed and the question of citizenship of the complainants is only superficially considered. In this case, however, the commission held that the conferral of citizenship by naturalisation was not sufficient to address the violation of rights, and that Mr. Modise should receive compensation and be recognised as a citizen of Botswana by descent.

Malawi Africa Association and others v. Mauritania (2000)

Main facts: This case focuses on the expulsion of almost 50,000 ethnic black Mauritanians and Beidanes (Moors) to Senegal, who were regarded as a threat to the State. The government claimed that the persons expelled were Senegalese, although many possessed Mauritanian identity cards which were destroyed by the authorities, meaning that they could not return to Mauritania as they could not prove their citizenship.

Relevant rulings: The commission did not comment at length on deprivation of nationality but concluded, without clear reasoning, that evicting Black Mauritanians from their houses and depriving them of their nationality constitutes a violation of Article 12(1) (freedom of movement). It also recommended the government to take diligent measures to replace their national identity documents and to provide necessary reparations. The commission stressed that the expelled people are still citizens of Mauritania and that the government still has responsibility for them.

Open Society Justice Initiative v. Côte d'Ivoire (2015)

Main facts: The case concerns the discriminatory nature of the Ivorian nationality law, which adversely affects the Dioulas (an ethnic group that represents 30% of the population, whose parents migrated to Côte d'Ivoire as laborers). The law considers them as 'foreigners', prohibits them from owning land, voting, or running for public office.

Relevant rulings: The commission called on Cote d'Ivoire to amend its nationality law and to improve access to birth registration. The commission also found major violations of Article 5 (recognition of legal status and right to dignity), Article 2 (non-discrimination) and Article 3 (equal protection before the law).

Court of Justice of the European Union

Janko Rottmann v. Freistaat Bayern (2010)

Main facts: The case concerns a naturalised German citizen, who, as a result, lost his Austrian citizenship by law. German authorities, upon discovering that Rottmann was under criminal investigation in Austria, claimed that he had obtained German nationality in a fraudulent manner, and wished to withdraw Rottmann's naturalised German citizenship with retroactive effect.

Relevant rulings: The court found that deprivation of nationality upon fraudulent acquisition of nationality could be compatible with EU law (even if it leads to statelessness) but the national court must ascertain the principle of proportionality when looking at the consequences of this decision. This involves considering the gravity of the offence, the length of time between the naturalisation and withdrawal decision, the possibility for that person to recover his original nationality, and the consequences for the individual and family members.

Tjebbes and Others v. Minister van Buitenlandse Zaken (2019)

Main facts: A number of Dutch citizens possessing a second nationality of a non-EU country brought proceedings before Netherlands courts following the refusal of the Netherlands to examine applications for renewal of their passports. The Netherlands' decision was based on the nationality law which provides that an adult loses nationality if he also possesses a foreign nationality and has been residing outside the Netherlands and the EU for a period of 10 years. The court also asks whether loss of Netherlands nationality – which entails loss of citizenship of the EU – is compatible with EU law.

Relevant rulings: The court ruled that EU law does not prevent the loss of the nationality of a Member State and, consequently, the loss of citizenship of the EU, where the genuine link between the person concerned and that Member State is durably interrupted. However, the principle of proportionality requires an individual examination of the consequences of that loss for the persons concerned from the point of the view of EU law.
More specifically:

- Relevant national rules must permit individual examination of the consequences of that loss from the point of view of EU law, with the option of recovering nationality retroactively if the person has demonstrated a link with the Netherlands (by applying for any document that shows his nationality).
- The principle of proportionality entails that loss of nationality must be consistent with the Charter of Fundamental Rights of the European Union, specifically the right to respect for family life (Article 7), in conjunction with the best interests of the child (Article 24).

European Court of Human Rights

Ramadan v. Malta (2016)

Main facts: Ramadan is an Egyptian citizen but renounced his Egyptian citizenship after acquiring Maltese citizenship through marriage with a Maltese national. After serious marital problems, the marriage dissolved and Ramadan married a Russian national and applied for an exempt person status. The Maltese government, upon finding out about the divorce, deprived Ramadan of his Maltese citizenship, concluding that it had been obtained in a fraudulent manner. Due to this decision, Ramadan appears to be stateless. He has 3 Maltese children from 2 marriages.

Relevant rulings: The court ruled that the deprivation decision was in accordance with Maltese nationality law and due process guarantees were met. However, Ramadan's statelessness was not taken into consideration, since he did not provide the court with any official documents confirming his renunciation nor demonstrating the possibility to reacquire his Egyptian nationality. The court states that if a person's nationality is renounced, in principle it does not mean that another State has the obligation to regularise a person's stay in the country. However, Judge Albuquerque disagrees with this, arguing that the court undermines the legal situation of statelessness which can have negative consequences for Ramadan and his family. Also, the deprivation decision did not take into account that he has a genuine bond with Malta, which leaves significant shortcomings of the revocation procedure, particularly when assessing fairness and proportionality of the measure taken in this case.

K2 v. The United Kingdom (2017)

Main facts: K2 is a dual citizen (Sudanese since birth and a naturalised British). K2 was deprived of his nationality and barred from re-entering the United Kingdom on account of his terrorism-related activities pursuant to Article 40(2) of the British Nationality Act 1981. K2 claimed that these decisions violated Article 8 ECHR (right to respect for private and family life). He also complained that the decision resulted in being treated different from birth-right British citizens who are considered a threat to national security and who did not hold a second nationality pursuant to Article 8 in conjunction with Article 14 ECHR (prohibition of discrimination). In addition, he complained that his exclusion from the UK had undermined his ability to challenge the deprivation of his citizenship in court.

Relevant rulings: The court held that K2's claim was unfounded.

- Nevertheless, the court recognised that an arbitrary denial or revocation of citizenship might in some circumstances raise an issue under Article 8 ECHR, because of its impact on the private life of the individual. Two things must be assessed: 1) is the revocation arbitrary? 2) What were the consequences for the applicant?
- Unfortunately, the court could not consider K2's complaint about differential treatment pursuant Article 8 and 14 ECHR because he did not raise this complaint in the domestic courts and, therefore, failed to exhaust domestic remedies available to him. Also, the ECHR stated that K2's inability to re-enter the UK was not because he was a British citizen, but because he had already left the UK voluntarily when the decision to withdraw his nationality was taken.

Emin Huseynov v. Azerbaijan (2015)

Main facts: This case concerns the use of deprivation of nationality to silence a human rights activist. Mr. Huseynov was targeted by the authorities and forced into hiding, before being coerced to sign a declaration renouncing his nationality in return for the opportunity to leave the country and seek asylum abroad.

Relevant rulings: The court found that Mr Huseynov had been ill-treated during his arrest and whilst in police detention and that there had been no effective investigation in this respect (Article 3). It further found that he had been unlawfully and arbitrarily deprived of his liberty and that the police intervention had amounted to an unlawful interference with his freedom of assembly (Article 5(1)).

Biao v. Denmark (2016)

Main facts: This case concerns the refusal of Denmark to grant family reunification to a Danish citizen of Tongolese origin and his Ghanaian wife. For Danish nationals to enjoy family reunification in Denmark, there must be no other country with which the family have stronger ties, but the applicant's link to Ghana excluded them from family reunification. This, however, does not apply to those who have held Danish citizenship for more than 28 years, according to a 2003 legislative amendment.

Relevant rulings: The court ruled that Denmark had not violated Article 8 (right to respect for family life) and Article 14 (prohibition of discrimination) taken together. Although Denmark distinguishes between Danish nationals of +28 year and -28 year duration, given that the husband had only been a national for two years, and had ties to his spouse's native Ghana, refusing family reunification was not disproportionate. However, the court did state that "the rule favours Danish nationals of Danish ethnic origin, and places at a disadvantage, or has a disproportionately prejudicial effect on persons who acquired Danish nationality later in life and who were of ethnic origins other than Danish" (para. 138).

Pending case: El Aroud and Soughir v. Belgium

Main facts: This case concerns the decision to revoke the citizenship of the applicants following their conviction of terrorism acts. The applicants contended that they were unable to appeal the decision, and that the decision was arbitrary and not proportional.

Possible rulings:

- Whether deprivation of nationality constitutes a conviction in the sense of Article 2 of Protocol no. 7 ECHR, and whether the applicants' right of appeal was violated.
- Whether deprivation of nationality constitutes a violation of the applicant's right to private life under Article 8, and whether the deprivations were provided by law, had procedural safeguards, and the authorities acted diligently and swiftly.

Pending case: Ghoumid and others v. France

Main facts: These cases concern the decision to revoke the citizenship of the applicants in following their conviction of conspiracy to prepare a terrorist act. The applicants contend that the decision infringed their right to identity.

Possible rulings:

- Whether the revocation of nationality constituted a violation of the right to identity which falls under the scope of Article 8's protection of the right to respect for private life according to ECtHR's case-law.[104]
- Whether deprivation of nationality (as in Article 25 of the French Civil Code) amounts to a 'criminal punishment' under Article 4 of Protocol no. 7 ECHR, and if so, whether the deprivation violates the right not to be punished twice for the same offence (Art. 4 of Proto. 7).

---

[104] A person's nationality is part of their social identity, covered by Article 8 of ECHR, according to ECtHR *Genovese v. Malta*, App. 53124/09 (2011), paras. 30 and 33.

Inter-American Court of Human Rights

Ivcher-Bronstein v. Peru (2001)

Main facts: The case concerns the deprivation of nationality of an individual who acquired Peruvian nationality by naturalisation, subsequently renouncing his original Israeli nationality. After broadcasting critical reports of the authorities from a TV station, the government nullified Ivcher's naturalisation in order to remove him from editorial control, and subsequently disowned him from the TV station.

Relevant rulings: The court found a violation of:

- Article 20(1) (right to a nationality) and Article 20(3) (prohibition of arbitrary deprivation of nationality): "the procedure used to annul the nationality title did not comply with the provisions of domestic legislation" (para 95) and "the authorities who annulled Mr. Ivcher's nationality title did not have competence" (para 96). No considerations were made on the basis of substantive reasons.
- Article 8(1) and (2) (right to a fair trial): "the procedure… did not meet the conditions of due process" (para 110), and "Mr Ivcher was prevented from intervening, fully informed, in all the stages, despite being the person whose rights were being determined" (para 107). In particular, he was not informed of the procedure being undertaken, nor asked to submit information to support his nationality status; and the authority that annulled Ivcher's nationality was not competent, since the judges involved "did not meet the standards of competence, impartiality and independence required by Article 8(1)" (para 115).
- Article 1(1) (obligation to respect rights): "The state violated articles 20, 8, 21, 25 and 13 of the American Convention… and failed to comply with its general obligation to respect the rights and freedoms recognized in it and to ensure their free and full exercise, as stipulated in article 1(1)" (para 169).
- Peru was asked to reinstate Ivcher's nationality, which it did in November 2000, through the annulment of the resolution that had nullified his naturalisation.

Case of the expelled Dominicans and Haitians v. Dominican Republic (2014)

Main facts: The case concerns the arbitrary detention and expulsion of various families from the Dominican Republic to Haiti, which formed part of a collective expulsion directed at Haitians and persons of Haitian descent. Focus in this case revolved around discrimination based on skin colour, immigration detention, the systematic practice of collective expulsions, and statelessness. Since 13 of the victims were children, the principle of "best interests of the child" in the right to nationality has been paid particular attention.

Relevant rulings: The court declared that in relation to judgement TC/0168/13 (the ruling that retroactively withdrew nationality from thousands of Dominicans), the State failed to comply with its obligation to adopt legal provisions in Article 2 (domestic legal effects) of the ACHR regarding Article 3 (right to recognition of juridical personality), Article 18 (right to a name), Article 20 (right to nationality), in relation to Article 1(1) (non-discrimination) and Article 19 (rights of the child).

Girls Yean and Bosico v. Dominican Republic (2005)

Main facts: This case concerns the request of birth certificates from two Dominican mothers of Haitian descent for their daughters. Both mothers had been born in the Dominican Republic and had documents that proved their nationality, but were refused their daughters' birth certificates, although they claimed that their daughters were Dominican citizens due to the principle of *jus soli*.

Relevant rulings: The court found that this was racial discrimination on the part of the State party. The court found violations of Article 17 (rights of the family) in relation to Article 1(1) (non-discrimination); Article 20 (right to a nationality), in relation to Article 1(1) and Article 19 (rights of the child), and Article 3 (right to juridical personality), in relation to Article 1(1) and Article 19 (rights of the child).

DEPRIVATION OF CITIZENSHIP IN THE UK: *A LITIGATOR'S PERSPECTIVE*

BY AMANDA WESTON[*]

Recent press coverage of the horrifying circumstances in which Shamima Begum has seen her three children die in infancy in the face of the United Kingdom's decision to block the 19 year old's return to the country of her birth, her family, her language and her home, has thrown a public spotlight on the government's broad and practically unfettered powers to deprive a person of their British citizenship with immediate effect.[1] This short piece reflects on the escalation of citizenship deprivation powers in the UK, and the due process lacunae which undermine the effectiveness of appeal rights and contribute to a global trend which sees citizenship status devalued and under threat.

In 2002, when the law was amended to permit the removal of citizenship from Britons who had acquired it from birth, the test for deprivation of citizenship reflected the "conduct seriously prejudicial to the vital interests of the state" threshold in article 8(3) of the 1961 Convention on the Reduction of Statelessness. Since then, Parliament has lowered the threshold for deprivation to the same as for the deportation of foreign nationals, that is, "conducive to the public good".[2] When, following his criminal convictions under anti-terror legislation, Abu Hamza[3] was deprived of his British citizenship in 2003, his right of appeal was suspensive - that meant that he remained British until his appeal was determined. However, since the repeal in 2004 of the suspensive provision, the impact on access to due process for those deprived has been profound. That is because in almost all cases those deprived have been outside the UK at the time including where the Secretary of State has deliberately delayed the making of the decision to coincide with absence from the

---

[*] **Amanda Weston** was called to the Bar of England & Wales in 1995. A Queen's Counsel, over the past 12 years, she has advised and represented in SIAC and the higher courts, litigants who have been subject to deprivation of citizenship on national security grounds. Amanda is a public law specialist and a member of the 'A' Panel of Counsel who act for the Equality & Human Rights Commission. She also teaches, trains and writes on civil liberties and access to justice.

[1] 'Shamima Begum begins appeal against loss of UK citizenship' *The Guardian* (22 October 2019), available at https://www.theguardian.com/uk-news/2019/oct/22/shamima-begum-begins-appeal-against-loss-of-uk-citizenship.

[2] By an amendment introduced by section 56 of the Immigration, Asylum and Nationality Act (2006). At the time, this massive conceptual shift - effectively equating British citizens who may hold another nationality with foreign nationals - attracted heavyweight criticism: see e.g. N. Blake Q.C. 'Why is there no song and dance about this Act?' *The Times* (25 April 2006).

[3] Also known as Mustafa Kamel Mustafa.

UK in order to prevent that person from returning.[4] This is described as an immediate 'security gain' or 'operational benefit'. There is also a significant further aspect to deprivations of those 'in absentia'. Article 1 of the European Convention on Human Rights imposes a duty upon contracting states to secure Convention rights and freedoms to those 'within its jurisdiction'. Thus, the UK is able to circumvent human rights arguments which would have been justiciable had the deprived person appealed from within the UK.[5]

An interesting question is whether the UK Parliament ever grappled with the consequences of removing the suspensive appeal right. At the time of the repeal, Lord Rooker, speaking at a late stage during the passage of the legislation in the House of Lords indicated that the draft repeal had been an accident, but was a good idea because: "we believe that it would make considerable sense to be able to run the appeals—the deprivation appeal on citizenship and the deportation and or certification appeal—together".[6] In fact, such concurrent proceedings have hardly ever been pursued. Deprivation is almost exclusively used against British people when they are outside the UK. As a consequence, the legislation is silent as to the content of procedural rights for British people deprived 'in absentia' and the circumstances in which that power may be exercised.[7] Somewhat of a legislative lacuna, for such a 'radical'[8] act against a Briton - the removal of the 'right to have rights'. By contrast, in the Immigration Acts Parliament clearly set out the circumstances in which immigration powers may be used against people both in and outside the UK, with express provision for foreign nationals to appeal removal decisions from within the UK and the prohibition on their removal pending the appeal.

Compounding the practical problem of exercising appeal rights from abroad has been the 'secret evidence' procedure which, Parliament has provided, the courts must adopt in scrutinising the legal justification on national security grounds for such extreme measures. The Special Immigration Appeals Commission (SIAC) is empowered - indeed required - to derogate from the fundamental common law principle that both parties should be on an equal footing and that a party should know the case against her. The current system of 'Special Advocates' (SAs) permitted to see the secret or sensitive material which justifies deprivation has serious limitations in securing an effective remedy because SAs are expressly denied the

---

[4] Special Immigration Appeals Commission (SIAC) has held this deliberate manipulation of process to be lawful in UK SIAC, *L1 v. Secretary Of State For The Home Department* (2014), UKSIAC SC_100_2010.

[5] The UK Supreme Court is yet to consider whether the sovereign exercise by a signatory state of its cower to deprive its own citizen of that citizenship falls within the exceptions to the 'territoriality' principle.

[6] Hansard Lords, Recommitment, Asylum & Immigration (Treatment of Claimants etc) Bill (15 June 2004).

[7] Lord Justice Rix described the consequence that foreign nationals have greater procedural protections than British citizens as 'counter-intuitive': England and Wales Court of Appeal, *G1 v. Secretary of State for the Home Department* (2012), EWCA Civ 867.

[8] Lord Mance's description of deprivation powers at §98 in UK Supreme Court, *Pham v. Secretary of State for the Home Department* (2015), UKSC 19.

ability to seek instructions from the deprived person on the material disclosed to them.[9] This means that in order to succeed in an appeal - to hit the target - a deprived person must try and define - often across many years past - what it is that is held against them, who may bear a grudge or provided untrue or inaccurate information on them, what they may have said in a phone call which may have been misconstrued, mistranslated or misunderstood. The concept of an 'extremist mindset' is indefinably vague. To defeat it, an appellant must be able to show the court that they are an open book. In this jurisdiction, what is not said is often so much more significant than what is.

Some judicial anxiety has been expressed on the cumulative impact that being required to conduct the appeal from outside the UK has on the effectiveness of an appeal in SIAC: "…an appellant who has to pursue an appeal while he is out of the country faces considerable disadvantages, particularly in the context of an appeal to SIAC…The handicaps under which appellants labour in SIAC are well established. Parliament has authorised a procedure which deprives appellants in SIAC of a fundamental right - to see the whole of the case against them - to which they would otherwise be entitled as a matter of fairness under the common law…In this procedural context the Court should be vigilant to ensure that appellants in SIAC are not further disadvantaged…"[10]

However, such vigilance has been hard to discern. SIAC treats issues of access to justice arising for Britons deprived 'in absentia' not as issues of principle but as part of the overall question of whether the deprivation is lawful having regard to unchallenged closed material.[11] Let me spell it out because even now after acting in a number of cases it is somewhat difficult to believe - a person who is deprived of her citizenship outside the UK and who asserts that she is unable effectively to participate in the proceedings owing to the risks to her, should she seek to do so, will have the justification for the precipitate and summary deprivation of her citizenship adjudged by material and allegations which she is unable to challenge. The hopes and wishes expressed during the early judicial scrutiny of the effectiveness of SIAC procedures, that all parties involved would be astute to assist the fairness and balance of the process does not appear to have borne fruit. Fairness in UK common law is a 'flexible concept'. Developing arguments for more effective procedural safeguards in deprivation cases harness upon the absence of adequate protection against arbitrariness both procedural and substantive. The larger questions as to the wisdom of and consequences for international co-operation of abandoning former citizens and their children in post-conflict states are beyond the scope of this piece.

---

[9] See the evidence of Special Advocates to the Joint Human Rights Committee, available at
https://publications.parliament.uk/pa/jt200910/jtselect/jtrights/64/6402.htm
[10] Lord Justice Sullivan, Royal Courts of Justice, *E1 (OS Russia) v. Secretary of State for the Home Department* (2012), EWCA Civ 357.
[11] This approach was indorsed by the Court of Appeal in *R (W2 & IA) v. Secretary of State for the Home Department* (2017), EWCA Civ 2146.

PRINCIPLES

ON DEPRIVATION OF NATIONALITY
AS A NATIONAL SECURITY MEASURE

INTRODUCTION

**❝ Everyone has the right to a nationality.
No one shall be arbitrarily deprived of his nationality...❞**

*Article 15 (1) & (2) of
the Universal Declaration of Human Rights*

The Principles on Deprivation of Nationality as a National Security Measure were developed over a 30-month research and consultation period, with input from more than 60 leading experts in the fields of human rights, nationality and statelessness, counter-terrorism, refugee protection, child rights, migration and other related areas.[1] The Principles restate or reflect international law and legal standards under the UN Charter, treaty law, customary international law, general principles of law, judicial decisions and legal scholarship, regional and national law and practice. They articulate the international law obligations of States and apply to all situations in which States take or consider taking steps to deprive a person of nationality as a national security measure.

The Principles were developed in response to a 21st Century trend of a small, but growing number of States resorting to deprivation of nationality as a counterterrorism and national security measure. While some States have amended their laws to expand existing powers or introduce new powers to enable deprivation of nationality, others have relied on existing powers, which have been construed expansively to apply to situations not previously envisaged. There has also been an increase in deprivation of nationality for other stated purposes (such as fraud), which serve as proxies to the purpose of safeguarding national security; as well proxy measures, which do not amount to deprivation of nationality but are likely to have a similarly adverse impact on individual human rights (such as the revocation of passports, refusal to repatriate and the imposition of travel and entry bans).

---

[1] The Principles were drafted by the Institute on Statelessness and Inclusion in collaboration with the Open Society Justice Initiative and with support from the Asser Institute and Ashurst LLP. Over a 30 month period, extensive research was conducted into global trends, the effectiveness of citizenship deprivation and international standards related to deprivation, three expert meetings were convened (London – 2017, and The Hague – 2018 & 2019) and multiple drafts were developed by the team, under the guidance of an expert Drafting Committee and subject to the review of a wider group of experts. The Principles were finalised in February 2020 and remain open for institutional and individual endorsement until June 2021. For more information, visit www.institutesi.org.

The deprivation of nationality as a national security measure disproportionately targets those of minority and migrant heritage and is likely to be discriminatory on various grounds including race, ethnicity, religion, political or other opinion and national origin. Such measures are also likely to be arbitrary and can cause statelessness. There is no evidence to support the use of such measures as being an effective means of protecting national security, and there is growing concern that such actions may actually be counterproductive. There are also significant concerns related to the permanent nature of the measure of deprivation of nationality, its disproportionate impact on individuals, families and communities, and the detrimental impact on other fundamental human rights.

States have a duty to cooperate with each other and to act responsibly and in accordance with international law, to maintain international peace and security and to promote and encourage respect for human rights and fundamental freedoms. The practice of deprivation of nationality, in particular when coupled with the refusal to repatriate and the imposition of entry bans, runs counter to these obligations and can result in the 'exporting' of a challenge for other States to deal with.

The Principles present a wide range of well-established and developing international law standards, which States are obliged to uphold, when considering the introduction of new powers or the implementation of existing powers to deprive the nationality of their citizens. The Principles serve to provide a clear and authoritative overview of existing international law obligations; they do not establish any new standards. However, by collating the numerous international law standards at play, the Principles articulate the extremely high threshold to be met, for a State to deprive nationality while satisfying its international obligations. An analysis of current State practice shows that this threshold is not being respected by any State which has taken the measure of depriving nationality of its citizens to safeguard national security.

The **Basic Rule** articulated in Principle 4, synthesises all relevant international standards, to conclude that "States shall not deprive persons of nationality for the purpose of safeguarding national security". It asserts that any exercise of an exception to this rule, must be "interpreted and applied narrowly", and is further limited by other well-established standards of international law. Namely:

- The avoidance of statelessness;
- The prohibition of discrimination;
- The prohibition of arbitrary deprivation of nationality;
- The right to a fair trial, remedy and reparation; and
- Other obligations and standards set forth in international human rights law, international humanitarian law and international refugee law.

Subsequent Principles provide further elaborations on each of these limitations, which are to be individually and collectively applied and respected. This means for example, that it is not lawful for a State to abide by its obligation to avoid statelessness, by resorting to discrimination between single and dual nationals.

At a time when the institution of citizenship is increasingly under threat, the Principles serve to remind us of the longstanding and strong international law framework which obligates States to respect, protect, promote and fulfil everyone's right to a nationality; and which recognises the importance of doing so, in order to also protect other fundamental human rights. It is no coincidence that these international standards were developed in response to our shared world history in which the State's power to deprive citizens of their nationality has been a precursor to committing the gravest crimes and unimaginable atrocities.

The drafters and endorsers of the Principles hope that they will be a useful tool in the hands of the legal community and other stakeholders, to promote and protect our fundamental human rights, security and the rule of law.

PREAMBLE

Affirming that States are obligated under the Charter of the United Nations to take joint and separate action to maintain international peace and security and to achieve universal respect for, and observance of, human rights and fundamental freedoms for all without distinction;

Recalling basic principles of international law, as set out in the UN Charter, general principles of law, treaties, customary international law, judicial decisions and legal scholarship, regional legal frameworks and other sources;

Recognising that States have an international legal obligation to protect all persons in their territory or subject to their jurisdiction and a right to take effective and lawful steps to protect national security;

Upholding the principle of non-regression and encouraging the progressive development and codification of international law;

Reaffirming that States and the international community as a whole must ensure that any measures taken to protect security and counter terrorism comply with all their obligations under international law, in particular international human rights law, international refugee law and international humanitarian law;

Underscoring that respect for human rights, fundamental freedoms and principles of non-discrimination, equality and the rule of law are complementary and mutually reinforcing with effective security measures, and are an essential part of a successful security and counter-terrorism effort;

Remembering our shared world history in which the State's power to deprive citizens of their nationality has been a precursor to committing the gravest crimes and unimaginable atrocities which deeply shocked the conscience of humanity;

Noting that a small but growing number of States have resorted to deprivation of nationality as a counter-terrorism and national security measure, with some States amending their laws to expand existing powers or introduce new powers to enable deprivation of nationality, and other States relying on existing powers, which are being construed expansively to apply to situations not previously envisaged;

Recognising that States have increasingly used deprivation of nationality to safeguard national security, despite the lack of any evidence of its effectiveness and in the face of evidence that such practices are likely to be counterproductive.

Recalling Article 15 of the Universal Declaration of Human Rights, according to which everyone has the right to a nationality and no one shall be arbitrarily deprived of his or her nationality, and asserting that States should ensure that they exercise their discretionary powers concerning nationality issues in a manner that is consistent with their international obligations in the field of human rights;

Concerned at the permanent nature of the measure of deprivation of nationality, and its potential for being unnecessary, without legitimate purpose, disproportionate, discriminatory, arbitrary and unlawful, while at the same time being ineffective and subject to abuse;

Equally concerned that the deprivation of nationality can entail or facilitate other violations of international law, affecting both the person deprived and connected persons including children, impairing access to a wide range of civil, cultural, economic, political and social rights, including through: denial of the right to enter and remain in one's own country; discrimination; *refoulement*; torture, cruel, inhuman or degrading treatment or punishment; deprivation of liberty and security of the person; denial of access to education, healthcare and housing; denial of legal personhood; denial of private and family life; denial of access to justice; and denial of the right to an effective remedy;

Affirming that the prohibition of racial discrimination is a peremptory norm of international law, and noting that prevailing national laws and practices of deprivation of nationality are likely to disproportionately target members of minority or marginalised communities;

Recognising that international law prohibits the expulsion of nationals, as a measure which undermines international cooperation and the national sovereignty of other States, and emphasising that it is not a legitimate purpose to deprive nationality in order to effect expulsion;

Recognising that under relevant UN Security Council, Human Rights Council and General Assembly Resolutions, States are required and called upon to address threats to international peace and security, in a manner consistent with international human rights law, international humanitarian law and international refugee law, and through a comprehensive approach that addresses underlying factors which can be conducive to terrorism, including by promoting political and religious tolerance, good governance, economic development, and social cohesion and full national inclusion;

These **Principles** restate international law, reflect existing standards and draw on practices that guide and limit State power to deprive persons of their nationality as a purported counter-terrorism and national security measure.

PRINCIPLES ON DEPRIVATION OF NATIONALITY AS A NATIONAL SECURITY MEASURE

---

1. SCOPE OF APPLICATION, SOURCES & INTERPRETATION

1.1. Scope of application

1.1.1. These Principles apply to all situations in which States take or consider taking steps to deprive a person of nationality as a national security measure.

1.1.2. Any existing or proposed national legal provisions which provide for the deprivation of nationality for the purpose of safeguarding national security should fully comply with international law standards as set out in these Principles.

1.1.3. The Principles are also relevant in the interpretation and application of international law to other situations of deprivation of nationality.

1.1.4. The Principles are also relevant to other practices, including measures to revoke passports, expel or prohibit entry of nationals as a national security measure.

1.2. Sources of law

The Principles restate or reflect international law and legal standards under the UN Charter, treaty law, customary international law, general principles of law, judicial decisions and legal scholarship, regional and national law and practice.

1.3. Interpretation

1.3.1. In all circumstances, the Principles should be interpreted in accordance with international human rights law and standards, applying the most favourable provision of protection.

1.3.2. The Principles set out minimum standards. Nothing in these Principles shall be invoked as a reason to apply a lower level of protection against deprivation of nationality than that currently provided in national laws.

1.3.3. Where permitted, any exceptions stated in the Principles should be interpreted in the narrowest possible manner.

2.   DEFINITIONS

For the purpose of the Principles, the following definitions are applied:

2.1.   Nationality

2.1.1. *Nationality* refers to a legal status of an individual in relation to a State and embodies the legal bond between the individual and State for the purposes of international law.

2.1.2. It is for each State to determine who is considered a national according to its law, in compliance with international law standards.

2.1.3. For the scope of application and interpretation of the Principles, the terms *nationality* and *citizenship* are synonymous.

2.2.   Deprivation of nationality

2.2.1. *Deprivation of nationality* refers to any loss, withdrawal or denial of nationality that was not voluntarily requested by the individual. This includes where a State precludes a person or group from obtaining or retaining a nationality, where nationality is automatically lost by operation of the law, and where acts taken by administrative authorities result in a person being deprived of a nationality.

2.2.2. *Deprivation of nationality* also covers situations where there is no formal act by a State but where the practice of its competent authorities clearly shows that they have ceased to consider a person as a national, including where authorities persistently refuse to issue or renew documents, or in cases of confiscation of identity documents and/or expulsion from the territory coupled with a statement by authorities that a person is not considered a national.

2.3.   Statelessness

2.3.1. The term *stateless person* means a person who is not considered as a national by any State under the operation of its law.

2.3.2. Establishing whether a person is considered as a national under the operation of a State's law requires a careful analysis of how the competent authority of a State applies its nationality laws in an individual's case in practice; it is a mixed question of law and fact.

3. THE RIGHT TO A NATIONALITY

3.1. Every person has the right to a nationality.

3.2. No one shall be arbitrarily deprived of their nationality nor denied the right to change their nationality.

4. BASIC RULE

4.1. States shall not deprive persons of nationality for the purpose of safeguarding national security.

4.2. Where a State, in exception to this basic rule, provides for the deprivation of nationality for the purpose of safeguarding national security, the exercise of this exception should be interpreted and applied narrowly, only in situations in which it has been determined by a lawful conviction that meets international fair trial standards, that the person has conducted themselves in a manner seriously prejudicial to the vital interests of the state.

4.3. The exercise of this narrow exception to deprive a person of nationality is further limited by other standards of international law. Such limitations include:

4.3.1. The avoidance of statelessness;
4.3.2. The prohibition of discrimination;
4.3.3. The prohibition of arbitrary deprivation of nationality;
4.3.4. The right to a fair trial, remedy and reparation; and
4.3.5. Other obligations and standards set forth in international human rights law, international humanitarian law and international refugee law.

4.4. This basic rule also applies to the deprivation of nationality for other purposes, which serve as proxies to the purpose of safeguarding national security, as well proxy measures, which do not amount to deprivation of nationality but are likely to have a similarly adverse impact on individual rights.

5. THE AVOIDANCE OF STATELESSNESS

5.1.   States must not render any person stateless through deprivation of nationality.

5.2.   An assessment of whether deprivation of nationality will render a person stateless, is neither a historic nor a predictive exercise. The question to be answered is whether, at the point of deprivation, the individual is considered by the competent authority of any other State, as a national under the operation of its law.

6. THE PROHIBITION OF DISCRIMINATION

6.1.   A State must not deprive any person or group of persons of their nationality as a result of direct or indirect discrimination in law or practice, on any ground prohibited under international law, including race, colour, sex, language, religion, political or other opinion, national or social origin, ethnicity, property, birth or inheritance, disability, sexual orientation or gender identity, or other real or perceived status, characteristic or affiliation.

6.2.   Each State is bound by the principle of non-discrimination between its nationals, regardless of whether they acquired nationality at birth or subsequently, and whether they have one or multiple nationalities.

7. THE PROHIBITION OF ARBITRARY DEPRIVATION OF NATIONALITY

7.1.   Arbitrary deprivation of nationality

The deprivation of nationality of citizens on national security grounds is presumptively arbitrary. This presumption may only be overridden in circumstances where such deprivation is, at a minimum:

7.1.1.   Carried out in pursuance of a legitimate purpose;
7.1.2.   Provided for by law;
7.1.3.   Necessary;
7.1.4.   Proportionate; and
7.1.5.   In accordance with procedural safeguards.

7.2. Legitimate purpose

7.2.1. The following, among others, do not constitute legitimate purposes for deprivation of nationality:

> 7.2.1.1. Administering sanction or punishment;
> 7.2.1.2. Facilitating expulsion or preventing entry; or
> 7.2.1.3. Exporting the function and responsibility of administering justice to another State.

7.2.2. Regardless of the stated purpose, any punitive impact incurred by deprivation of nationality is likely to render this measure incompatible with international law.

7.3. Legality

There must be a clear and clearly articulated legal basis for any deprivation of nationality. This requires *inter alia* that:

7.3.1. The powers and criteria for deprivation of nationality are provided in law, publicly accessible, clear, precise, comprehensive and predictable in order to guarantee legal certainty;

7.3.2. The power to deprive nationality must not be enacted or applied with retroactive effect; and

7.3.3. Deprivation of nationality must only be considered lawful if it is carried out by an appropriate and legally vested competent authority whose deprivation powers are clearly established by law.

7.4. Necessity

The deprivation of nationality as a national security measure must be strictly necessary for achieving a legitimate purpose, which is clearly articulated.

7.5. Proportionality

The decision to deprive someone of their nationality must respect the principle of proportionality. This requires that in any case of deprivation:

7.5.1. The immediate and long-term impact of deprivation of nationality on the rights of the individual, their family, and on society is proportionate to the legitimate purpose being pursued;

7.5.2. The deprivation of nationality is the least intrusive means of achieving the stated legitimate purpose; and

7.5.3. The deprivation of nationality is an effective means of achieving the stated legitimate purpose.

7.6. Procedural Safeguards

Any administrative, executive or judicial process to deprive nationality must be in accordance with procedural safeguards under international law, including:

7.6.1. Deprivation of nationality for the purpose of national security must never be automatic by operation of the law.

7.6.2. The individual concerned must be notified of the intent to deprive nationality prior to the actual decision to do so, to ensure that the person concerned is able to provide facts, arguments and evidence in defence of their case, which are to be taken into account by the relevant authority.

7.6.3. Decisions on deprivation of nationality must be individual, as opposed to collective.

7.6.4. With regard to the principle of the avoidance of statelessness, the burden of proof in determining that the person concerned holds another nationality must lie with the competent authorities of the depriving state.

7.6.5. Individuals must be notified in writing of the decision to deprive nationality and of the reasons underlying the decision. This must be done so in a prompt manner and in a language that they understand.

7.6.6. Decisions on the deprivation of nationality must be open to effective judicial review and appeal to a court, in compliance with the right to a fair trial.

7.6.7. No person whose nationality has been withdrawn shall be deprived of the right to enter and remain in that country in order to participate in person in legal proceedings related to that decision.

8. THE RIGHTS TO A FAIR TRIAL, EFFECTIVE REMEDY AND REPARATION

8.1. Everyone has the right to a fair trial or hearing. In any proceedings concerning the deprivation of nationality, the right to equal access to a competent, independent and impartial judicial body established by law and to equal treatment before the law must be respected, protected and fulfilled.

8.2. Everyone has the right to an effective remedy and reparation. States must provide those who claim to be victims of a violation with equal and effective access to justice and effective remedies and reparation, which include the following forms: restitution, compensation, rehabilitation, satisfaction and guarantees of non-repetition.

9. FURTHER HUMAN RIGHTS, HUMANITARIAN AND REFUGEE LAW OBLIGATIONS AND STANDARDS

Deprivation of nationality is also limited by other obligations and standards set forth in international human rights law, international humanitarian law and international refugee law.

9.1. The right to enter and remain in one's own country

9.1.1. All persons have the right to enter, remain in and return to their own country.

9.1.2. States are prohibited from expelling their own nationals.

9.1.3. In no situation, including where a person has been deprived of their nationality, may a person be arbitrarily expelled from their own country or denied the right to return to and remain in their own country.

9.1.4. The scope of the term "own country" is broader than the term "country of nationality". It includes a country of former nationality that has arbitrarily deprived the individual of its nationality, regardless of the purpose of the measure and whether or not this deprivation causes statelessness.

9.2. The prohibition of *refoulement*

9.2.1. In line with principles of international refugee law, States must not expel or return (*refouler*) any person, including one whom they have stripped of nationality, to a situation in which they face a threat to life or freedom or risk facing persecution, including on the grounds of race, religion, nationality, membership of a particular social group or political opinion.

9.2.2. In line with the principles of international human rights law, States must not expel or return (*refouler*) any person, including one whom they have stripped of nationality, to a situation in which they face a real risk of serious human rights violations, including torture or cruel, inhuman or degrading treatment or punishment, enforced disappearances, capital punishment, flagrant denial of justice and the right to liberty, or arbitrary deprivation of life.

9.3. Prohibition against torture and cruel, inhuman or degrading treatment or punishment

9.3.1. No one shall be subjected to torture or to cruel, inhuman or degrading treatment or punishment.

9.3.2. Deprivation of nationality is likely to constitute cruel, inhuman or degrading treatment or punishment, particularly where it results in statelessness.

9.3.3. Attempted expulsion consequent to deprivation of nationality is likely to meet the threshold of cruel, inhuman or degrading treatment or punishment when this leads to:

9.3.3.1. arbitrary detention;
9.3.3.2. a violation of the principle of *non-refoulement*; or
9.3.3.3. the forcible separation of families.

9.4. Liberty and security of person

9.4.1. Everyone has the right to liberty and security of the person and no one shall be subject to arbitrary arrest or detention.

9.4.2. The arbitrary detention of persons who have been deprived of their nationality is prohibited.

9.5. Legal personhood

9.5.1. Everyone has the right to recognition everywhere as a person before the law. All persons are equal before the law.

9.5.2. It is not permissible for States to deny any person's legal personhood or their equality before the law through the deprivation of nationality and denial of the right to enter and remain in their own country.

9.6. Right to private and family life

9.6.1. Everyone has the right to private and family life.

9.6.2. This includes the right to live together as a family and not be separated as a result of a family member being deprived of their nationality and subject to detention or expulsion in violation of international law.

9.7.   The rights of the child

9.7.1.   Every child has the right to a nationality. States must protect the child's right to acquire and preserve their nationality and to re-establish their nationality when arbitrarily deprived of it.

9.7.2.   States are required to treat all persons under the age of 18 in accordance with their rights as children.

9.7.3.   States must protect the rights of the child and the best interests of the child must be a primary consideration in all proceedings affecting the nationality of children, their parents and other family members.

9.7.4.   It can never be in the best interest of a child to be made stateless or be deprived of nationality.

9.7.5.   States must take all appropriate measures to ensure that the child is protected against all forms of discrimination or punishment on the basis of the status, activities, expressed opinions, or beliefs of the child's parents, legal guardians, or family members.

9.8.   Derivative deprivation of nationality

The derivative deprivation of nationality is prohibited.

10.   DEPRIVATION BY PROXY AND PROXY MEASURES

10.1.   States must not use powers to deprive nationality for other stated purposes, including fraud, with the ulterior purpose of depriving nationality as a national security measure.

10.2.   States must not subject persons to proxy measures, which do not amount to deprivation of nationality, but which have a similar impact and implications on human rights, without subjecting such decisions to the same tests and standards set out in these Principles. Such measures may include the withdrawal or refusal to renew passports or other travel documents and the imposition of travel or entry bans.

10.3.   The measures referred to in section 10.2 may in some circumstances, be considered to constitute deprivation of nationality, particularly when imposed on persons when they are abroad.

11.   *INTERNATIONAL COOPERATION*

11.1.   States have a duty to cooperate and to act responsibly and in accordance with international law to maintain international peace and security and to promote and encourage respect for human rights and fundamental freedoms.

11.2.   States must not undermine the principle of reciprocity or commitments to international cooperation, by stripping a person of nationality, expelling a person to a third country or subjecting a person to removal proceedings, thereby exporting the stated security risk to a third country and failing to take responsibility for their own nationals.

11.3.   States are obligated to take responsibility for their own citizens and to investigate and prosecute crimes and threats to national security through their national criminal justice frameworks in accordance with international standards.